A HISTORY OF ENGLISH ROMANTICISM IN THE EIGHTEENTH CENTURY

A HISTORY OF ENGLISH ROMANTICISM IN THE EIGHTEENTH CENTURY

BY

HENRY A. BEERS

Author of "A Suburban Pastoral," "The Ways of Yale," etc.

" Was unsterblich im Gesang soll leben
Muss im Leben untergehen."—SCHILLER

GORDIAN PRESS, INC.
NEW YORK
1966

Originally Published 1898
Published by Gordian Press, Inc. 1966 with
permission of Holt, Rinehart and Winston, Inc.

Library of Congress Catalog Card No. 66-29574

Printed in U.S.A. by
EDWARDS BROTHERS, INC.
Ann Arbor, Michigan

PREFACE.

Historians of French and German literature are
accustomed to set off a period, or a division of their
subject, and entitle it "Romanticism" or "the
Romantic School." Writers of English literary
history, while recognizing the importance of England's share in this great movement in European
letters, have not generally accorded it a place by itself
in the arrangement of their subject-matter, but have
treated it cursively, as a tendency present in the work
of individual authors; and have maintained a simple
chronological division of eras into the "Georgian,"
the "Victorian," etc. The reason of this is perhaps
to be found in the fact that, although Romanticism began earlier in England than on the Continent and lent
quite as much as it borrowed in the international
exchange of literary commodities, the native movement was more gradual and scattered. It never
reached so compact a shape, or came so definitely to
a head, as in Germany and France. There never was
precisely a "romantic school" or an all-pervading
romantic fashion in England.

There is, therefore, nothing in English corresponding to Heine's fascinating sketch "Die Romantische
Schule," or to Théophile Gautier's almost equally
fascinating and far more sympathetic "Histoire du

Romantisme." If we can imagine a composite personality of Byron and De Quincey, putting on record his
half affectionate and half satirical reminiscences of
the contemporary literary movement, we might have
something nearly equivalent. For Byron, like Heine,
was a repentant romanticist, with "radical notions
under his cap," and a critical theory at odds with his
practice; while De Quincey was an early disciple of
Wordsworth and Coleridge,—as Gautier was of Victor
Hugo,—and at the same time a clever and slightly mischievous sketcher of personal traits.

The present volume consists, in substance, of a
series of lectures given in elective courses in Yale
College. In revising it for publication I have striven
to rid it of the air of the lecture room, but a few
repetitions and didacticisms of manner may have in-
advertently been left in. Some of the methods and
results of these studies have already been given to
the public in "The Beginnings of the English
Romantic Movement," by my present associate and
former scholar, Professor William Lyon Phelps.
Professor Phelps' little book (originally a doctorate
thesis) follows, in the main, the selection and arrangement of topics in my lectures. *En revanche* I have
had the advantage of availing myself of his independent researches on points which I have touched
but slightly; and particularly of his very full treatment of the Spenserian imitations.

I had at first intended to entitle the book "Chapters
toward a History of English Romanticism, etc."; for,
though fairly complete in treatment, it makes no claim
to being exhaustive. By no means every eighteenth-
century writer whose work exhibits romantic motives

is here passed in review. That very singular genius William Blake, *e. g.*, in whom the influence of "Ossian," among other things, is so strongly apparent, I leave untouched; because his writings—partly by reason of their strange manner of publication—were without effect upon their generation and do not form a link in the chain of literary tendency.

If this volume should be favorably received, I hope before very long to publish a companion study of English romanticism in the nineteenth century.

H. A. B.

October, 1898.

CONTENTS.

A HISTORY OF ENGLISH ROMANTICISM.

CHAPTER I.

The Subject Defined.

To attempt at the outset a rigid definition of the word *romanticism* would be to anticipate the substance of this volume. To furnish an answer to the question—What is, or was, romanticism? or, at least, What is, or was, English romanticism?—is one of my main purposes herein, and the reader will be invited to examine a good many literary documents, and to do a certain amount of thinking, before he can form for himself any full and clear notion of the thing. Even then he will hardly find himself prepared to give a dictionary definition of romanticism. There are words which connote so much, which take up into themselves so much of the history of the human mind, that any compendious explanation of their meaning—any definition which is not, at the same time, a rather extended description—must serve little other end than to supply a convenient mark of identification. How can we define in a sentence words like renaissance, philistine, sentimentalism, transcendental, Bohemia, preraphaelite, impressionist, realistic? *Definitio est negatio.* It may be possible to hit upon a form of words which will mark romanticism off from everything else—tell in a clause what it is *not;* but to add a positive content to the definition—to tell what romanticism *is*, will require a very different and more gradual process.*

Nevertheless a rough, working definition may be useful to start with. Romanticism, then, in the sense in which I shall commonly employ the word, means the reproduction in modern art or literature of the life and thought of the Middle Ages. Some other elements will have to be added to this definition, and some modifications of it will suggest themselves from time to time. It is provisional, tentative, elastic, but will serve our turn till we are ready to substitute a better. It is the definition which Heine gives in his brilliant little book on the Romantic School in Germany.† " All the poetry of the Middle Ages," he adds, " has a certain definite character, through which it differs from the poetry of the Greeks and Romans. In reference to this difference, the former is called Romantic, the latter Classic. These names, however, are mis-

---

* Les définitions ne se posent pas *a priori*, si ce n'est peutêtre en mathématiques. En histoire, c'est de l'étude patiente de la réalité qu'elles se dégagent insensiblement. Si M. Deschanel ne nous a pas donné du *romantisme* la définition que nous réclamions tout à l'heure, c'est, à vrai dire, que son enseignement a pour objet de préparer cette définition même. Nous la trouverons où elle doit être, à la fin du cours et non pas à début.—*F. Brunetière:* " *Classiques et Romantiques, Études Critiques,*" Tome III. p. 296.

† Was war aber die romantische Schule in Deutschland? Sie war nichts anders als die Wiedererweckung der Poesie des Mittelalters, wie sie sich in dessen Liedern, Bild- und Bauwerken, in Kunst und Leben, manifestiert hatte.—*Die romantische Schule (Cotta edition),* p. 158.

leading, and have hitherto caused the most vexatious confusion." *

Some of the sources of this confusion will be considered presently. Meanwhile the passage recalls the fact that *romantic*, when used as a term in literary nomenclature, is not an independent, but a referential word. It implies its opposite, the classic; and the ingenuity of critics has been taxed to its uttermost to explain and develop the numerous points of contrast. To form a thorough conception of the romantic, therefore, we must also form some conception of the classic. Now there is an obvious unlikeness between the thought and art of the nations of pagan antiquity and the thought and art of the peoples of Christian, feudal Europe. Everyone will agree to call the Parthenon, the "Diana" of the Louvre, the "Œdipus" of Sophocles, the orations of Demosthenes classical; and to call the cathedral of Chartres, the walls of Nuremberg—*die Perle des Mittelalters*—the "Legenda Aurea" of Jacobus de Voragine, the "Tristan und Isolde" of Gottfried of Strasburg, and the illuminations in a Catholic missal of the thirteenth century romantic.

The same unlikeness is found between modern works conceived in the spirit, or executed in direct imitation, of ancient and mediæval art respectively. It is easy to decide that Flaxman's outline drawings in illustration of Homer are classic; that Alfieri's tragedies, Goethe's "Iphigenie auf Tauris" Landor's "Hellenics," Gibson's statues, David's paintings, and the church of the Madeleine in Paris are classical, at least in intention and in the models which they follow; while Victor Hugo's "Notre Dame de Paris," Scott's

* "The Romantic School" (Fleishman's translation), p. 13.

"Ivanhoe," Fouqué's "Der Zauberring," and Rossetti's painting, "The Girlhood of Mary," are no less certainly romantic in their inspiration.

But critics have given a wider extension than this to the terms classic and romantic. They have discerned, or imagined, certain qualities, attitudes of mind, ways of thinking and feeling, traits of style which distinguish classic from romantic art; and they have applied the words accordingly to work which is not necessarily either antique or mediæval in subject. Thus it is assumed, for example, that the productions of Greek and Roman genius were characterized by clearness, simplicity, restraint, unity of design, subordination of the part to the whole; and therefore modern works which make this impression of noble plainness and severity, of harmony in construction, economy of means and clear, definite outline, are often spoken of as classical, quite irrespective of the historical period which they have to do with. In this sense, it is usual to say that Wordsworth's "Michael" is classical, or that Goethe's "Hermann und Dorothea" is classical; though Wordsworth may be celebrating the virtues of a Westmoreland shepherd, and Goethe telling the story of two rustic lovers on the German border at the time of the Napoleonic wars.

On the other hand, it is asserted that the work of mediæval poets and artists is marked by an excess of sentiment, by over-lavish decoration, a strong sense of color and a feeble sense of form, an attention to detail, at the cost of the main impression, and a consequent tendency to run into the exaggerated, the fantastic, and the grotesque. It is not uncommon,

therefore, to find poets like Byron and Shelley classified as romanticists, by virtue of their possession of
these, or similar, characteristics, although no one
could be more remote from mediæval habits of thought
than the author of "Don Juan" or the author of
"The Revolt of Islam."

But the extension of these opposing terms to the
work of writers who have so little in common with
either the antique or the mediæval as Wordsworth, on
the one hand, and Byron, on the other, does not stop
here.　It is one of the embarrassments of the literary
historian that nearly every word which he uses has
two meanings, a critical and a popular meaning.　In
common speech, classic has come to signify almost
anything that is good.　If we look in our dictionaries
we find it defined somewhat in this way:　"Conform-
ing to the best authority in literature and art; pure;
chaste; refined; originally and chiefly used of the best
Greek and Roman writers, but also applied to the
best modern authors, or their works."　"Classic, *n.*
A work of acknowledged excellence and authority."
In this sense of the word, "Robinson Crusoe" is a
classic; the "Pilgrim's Progress" is a classic; every
piece of literature which is customarily recommended
as a safe pattern for young writers to form their style
upon is a classic.*

Contrariwise the word *romantic,* as popularly employed, expresses a shade of disapprobation.　The

* Un classique est tout artiste à l'école de qui nous pouvons nous
mettre sans craindre que ses leçons ou ses exemples nous fourvoient.
Ou encore, c'est celui qui possède . . . des qualités dont l'imitation,
si elle ne peut pas faire de bien, ne peut pas non plus faire de mal.
—*F. Brunetière,* "*Études Critiques,*" Tome III. p. 300.

dictionaries make it a synonym for *sentimental, fanciful, wild, extravagant, chimerical,* all evident derivatives
from their more critical definition, "pertaining or
appropriate to the style of the Christian and popular
literature of the Middle Ages, as opposed to the classical antique." The etymology of *romance* is familiar.
The various dialects which sprang from the corrup-
tion of the Latin were called by the common name of
romans. The name was then applied to any piece of
literature composed in this vernacular instead of in the
ancient classical Latin. And as the favorite kind of
writing in Provençal, Old French, and Spanish was the
tale of chivalrous adventure, that was called *par excellence,* a *roman, romans,* or *romance.* The adjective *romantic* is much later, implying, as it does, a certain
degree of critical attention to the species of fiction
which it describes in order to a generalizing of its
peculiarities. It first came into general use in the
latter half of the seventeenth century and the early
years of the eighteenth; and naturally, in a period
which considered itself classical, was marked from
birth with that shade of disapproval which has been
noticed in popular usage.

The feature that struck the critics most in the
romances of the Middle Ages, and in that very different
variety of romance which was cultivated during the seventeenth century—the prolix, sentimental fictions of
La Calprenède, Scudéri, Gomberville, and d'Urfé—was
the fantastic improbability of their adventures. Hence
the common acceptation of the word *romantic* in such
phrases as "a romantic notion," "a romantic elope-
ment," "an act of romantic generosity." The application of the adjective to scenery was somewhat

later;* and the abstract *romanticism* was, of course, very much later; as the literary movement, or the revolution in taste, which it entitles, was not enough developed to call for a name until the opening of the nineteenth century. Indeed it was never so compact, conscious, and definite a movement in England as in Germany and France; and its baptism doubtless came from abroad, from the polemical literature which attended the career of the German *romanticismus* and the French *romantisme*.

While accepting provisionally Heine's definition, it will be useful to examine some of the wider meanings that have been attached to the words *classic* and *romantic*, and some of the analyses that have been attempted of the qualities that make one work of art classical and another romantic. Walter Pater took them to indicate opposite tendencies or elements which are present in varying proportions in all good art. It is the essential function of classical art and literature, he thought, to take care of the qualities of measure, purity, temperance. "What is classical comes to us out of the cool and quiet of other times, as a measure of what a long experience has shown us will, at least, never displease us. And in the classical literature of Greece and Rome, as in the classics of the last century, the essentially classical element is that quality of order in beauty which they possess, indeed, in a pre-eminent degree."† "The charm, then, of what is

---

* Mr. Perry thinks that one of the first instances of the use of the word *romantic* is by the diarist Evelyn in 1654 : "There is also, on the side of this horrid alp, a very romantic seat."—*English Literature in the Eighteenth Century, by Thomas Sergeant Perry*, p. 148, *note*.

† "Romanticism," *Macmillan's Magazine*, Vol. XXXV.

classical in art or literature is that of the well-known
tale, to which we can nevertheless listen over and
over again, because it is told so well.   To the
absolute beauty of its form is added the accidental,
tranquil charm of familiarity."

On the other hand, he defines the romantic character in art as consisting in "the addition of strangeness
to beauty"—a definition which recalls Bacon's saying,
"There is no excellent beauty that hath not some
strangeness in the proportion."   "The desire of
beauty," continues Pater, "being a fixed element in
every artistic organization, it is the addition of curiosity to this desire of beauty that constitutes the
romantic temper."   This critic, then, would not confine the terms *classic* and *classicism* to the literature of
Greece and Rome and to modern works conceived in
the same spirit, although he acknowledges that there
are certain ages of the world in which the classical tradition predominates, *i. e.*, in which the respect for
authority, the love of order and decorum, the disposition to follow rules and models, the acceptance of
academic and conventional standards overbalance the
desire for strangeness and novelty.   Such epochs are,
e. g., the Augustan age of Rome, the *Siècle de Louis
XIV.* in France, the times of Pope and Johnson in
England—indeed, the whole of the eighteenth century
in all parts of Europe.

Neither would he limit the word *romantic* to work
conceived in the spirit of the Middle Ages.   "The
essential elements," he says, "of the romantic spirit
are curiosity and the love of beauty; and it is as the
accidental effect of these qualities only, that it seeks
the Middle Age; because in the overcharged atmos-

phere of the Middle Age there are unworked sources of
romantic effect, of a strange beauty to be won by
strong imagination out of things unlikely or remote."
"The sense in which Scott is to be called a romantic
writer is chiefly that, in opposition to the literary tradition of the last century, he loved strange adventure
and sought it in the Middle Age."

Here again the essayist is careful to explain that
there are certain epochs which are predominantly
romantic. "Outbreaks of this spirit come naturally
with particular periods: times when . . . men come
to art and poetry with a deep thirst for intellectual
excitement, after a long *ennui.*" He instances, as
periods naturally romantic, the time of the early Provençal troubadour poetry: the years following the
Bourbon Restoration in France (say, 1815–30); and
"the later Middle Age; so that the mediæval
poetry, centering in Dante, is often opposed to
Greek or Roman poetry, as romantic to classical
poetry."

In Pater's use of the terms, then, classic and romantic do not describe particular literatures, or particular periods in literary history, so much as certain
counterbalancing qualities and tendencies which run
through the literatures of all times and countries.
There were romantic writings among the Greeks and
Romans; there were classical writings in the Middle
Ages; nay, there are classical and romantic traits in
the same author. If there is any poet who may safely
be described as a classic, it is Sophocles; and yet Pater
declares that the "Philoctetes" of Sophocles, if
issued to-day, would be called romantic. And he points
out—what indeed has been often pointed out— that the

" Odyssey "* is more romantic than the " Iliad :" is, in
fact, rather a romance than a hero-epic.   The adventures of the wandering Ulysses, the visit to the land
of the lotus-eaters, the encounter with the Læstrygonians, the experiences in the cave of Polyphemus, if
allowance be made for the difference in sentiments and
manners, remind the reader constantly of the mediæval
romans d'aventure.   Pater quotes De Stendhal's saying that all good art was romantic in its day.
" Romanticism," says De Stendhal, " is the art of presenting to the nations the literary works which, in the
actual state of their habits and beliefs, are capable of
giving them the greatest possible pleasure: classicism,
on the contrary, presents them with what gave the
greatest possible pleasure to their great grand-
fathers "—a definition which is epigrammatic, if not
convincing.†   De Stendhal (Henri Beyle) was a
pioneer and a special pleader in the cause of French
romanticism, and, in his use of the terms, romanticism

* The Odyssey has been explained throughout in an allegorical
sense.   The episode of Circe, at least, lends itself obviously to such
interpretation.   Circe's cup has become a metaphor for sensual
intoxication, transforming men into beasts ; Milton, in " Comus,"
regards himself as Homer's continuator, enforcing a lesson of
temperance in Puritan times hardly more consciously than the old
Ionian Greek in times which have no other record than his poem.

†" Racine et Shakespeare, Études en Romantisme " (1823), p. 32, ed.
of Michel Lévy Frères, 1854.   Such would also seem to be the view
maintained by M. Émile Deschanel, whose book " Le Romantisme des
Classiques " (Paris, 1883) is reviewed by M. Brunetière in an article
already several times quoted.   " Tous les classiques," according to M.
Deschanel—at least, so says his reviewer—" ont jadis commencé par
être des romantiques."   And again : " Un *romantique* serait tout
simplement un classique en route pour parvenir ; et, réciproquement,
un classique ne serait de plus qu'un romantique arrivé."

stands for progress, liberty, originality, and the spirit
of the future; classicism, for conservatism, authority,
imitation, the spirit of the past. According to him,
every good piece of romantic art is a classic in the
making. Decried by the classicists of to-day, for its
failure to observe traditions, it will be used by the
classicists of the future as a pattern to which new
artists must conform.

It may be worth while to round out the conception of the term by considering a few other definitions of *romantic* which have been proposed. Dr.
F. H. Hedge, in an article in the *Atlantic Monthly**
for March, 1886, inquired, "What do we mean by
romantic?" Goethe, he says, characterized the difference between classic and romantic "as equivalent to
[that between] healthy and morbid. Schiller proposed
'naïve and sentimental.'† The greater part [of the
German critics] regarded it as identical with the difference between ancient and modern, which was partly
true, but explained nothing. None of the definitions
given could be accepted as quite satisfactory."‡

Dr. Hedge himself finds the origin of romantic feeling in wonder and the sense of mystery. "The
essence of romance," he writes, "is mystery"; and
he enforces the point by noting the application of the
word to scenery. "The woody dell, the leafy glen,
the forest path which leads, one knows not whither,
are romantic: the public highway is not." "The

* " Classic and Romantic," Vol. LVII.

† See Schiller's " Ueber naive und sentimentalische Dichtung."

‡ Le mot de romantisme, après cinquante ans et plus de discussions
passionnées, ne laisse pas d'être encore aujourd'hui bien vague et bien
flottant.—*Brunetière, ibid.*

winding secret brook . . . is romantic, as compared
with the broad river." "Moonlight is romantic, as
contrasted with daylight." Dr. Hedge attributes this
fondness for the mysterious to "the influence of the
Christian religion, which deepened immensely the
mystery of life, suggesting something beyond and
behind the world of sense."

This charm of wonder or mystery is perhaps only
another name for that "strangeness added to beauty"
which Pater takes to be the distinguishing feature of
romantic art.   Later in the same article, Dr. Hedge
asserts that "the essence of romanticism is aspiration."   Much might be said in defense of this position.
It has often been pointed out, *e. g.*, that a Gothic
cathedral expresses aspiration, and a Greek temple
satisfied completeness.   Indeed if we agree that, in a
general way, the classic is equivalent to the antique,
and the romantic to the mediæval, it will be strange if
we do not discover many differences between the two
that can hardly be covered by any single phrase.   Dr.
Hedge himself enumerates several qualities of romantic art which it would be difficult to bring under his
essential and defining category of wonder or aspiration.   Thus he announces that "the peculiarity of the
classic style is reserve, self-suppression of the writer";
while "the romantic is self-reflecting."   "Clear,
unimpassioned, impartial presentation of the subject . . . is the prominent feature of the classic
style.   The modern writer gives you not so much the
things themselves as his impression of them."   Here
then is the familiar critical distinction between the
objective and subjective methods—Schiller's *naiv und
sentimentalisch*—applied as a criterion of classic and

romantic style. This contrast the essayist develops at some length, dwelling upon "the cold reserve and colorless simplicity of the classic style, where the medium is lost in the object"; and "on the other hand, the inwardness, the sentimental intensity, the subjective coloring of the romantic style."

A further distinguishing mark of the romantic spirit, mentioned by Dr. Hedge in common with many other critics, is the indefiniteness or incompleteness of its creations. This is a consequence, of course, of its sense of mystery and aspiration. Schopenhauer said that music was the characteristic modern art, because of its subjective, indefinite character. Pursuing this line of thought, Dr. Hedge affirms that "romantic relates to classic somewhat as music relates to plastic art. . . It [music] presents no finished ideal, but suggests ideals beyond the capacity of canvas or stone. Plastic art acts on the intellect, music on the feelings; the one affects us by what it presents, the other by what it suggests. This, it seems to me, is essentially the difference between classic and romantic poetry"; and he names Homer and Milton as examples of the former, and Scott and Shelley of the latter school.

Here then we have a third criterion proposed for determining the essential *differentia* of romantic art. First it was mystery, then aspiration; now it is the appeal to the emotions by the method of suggestion. And yet there is, perhaps, no inconsistency on the critic's part in this continual shifting of his ground. He is apparently presenting different facets of the same truth; he means one thing by this mystery, aspiration, indefiniteness, incompleteness, emotional suggestive-

ness: that quality or effect which we all feel to be
present in romantic and absent from classic work, but
which we find it hard to describe by any single term.
It is open to any analyst of our critical vocabulary to
draw out the fullest meanings that he can, from
such pairs of related words as classic and romantic,
fancy and imagination, wit and humor, reason and
understanding, passion and sentiment. Let us, for
instance, develop briefly this proposition that the ideal
of classic art is completeness * and the ideal of romantic art indefiniteness, or suggestiveness.

A. W. Schlegel † had already made use of two of the
arts of design, to illustrate the distinction between
classic and romantic, just as Dr. Hedge uses plastic
art and music. I refer to Schlegel's famous saying
that the genius of the antique drama was statuesque,
and that of the romantic drama picturesque. A Greek
temple, statue, or poem has no imperfection and offers
no further promise, indicates nothing beyond what it
expresses. It fills the sense, it leaves nothing to the
imagination. It stands correct, symmetric, sharp in
outline, in the clear light of day. There is nothing
more to be done to it; there is no concealment about it.
But in romantic art there is seldom this completeness.
The workman lingers, he would fain add another
touch, his ideal eludes him. Is a Gothic cathedral
ever really finished? Is " Faust " finished? Is
" Hamlet " explained? The modern spirit is mystical;
its architecture, painting, poetry employ shadow to

* Ce qui constitue proprement un classique, c'est l'équilibre en lui
de toutes les facultés qui concourent à la perfection de l'œuvre d'art.
—*Brunetière, ibid.*

† " Vorlesungen über dramatische Kunst und Litteratur."

produce their highest effects: shadow and color rather than contour. On the Greek heroic stage there were a few figures, two or three at most, grouped like statuary and thrown out in bold relief at the apex of the scene: in Greek architecture a few clean, simple lines: in Greek poetry clear conceptions easily express-ible in language and mostly describable in sensuous images.

The modern theater is crowded with figures and colors, and the distance recedes in the middle of the scene. This love of perspective is repeated in cathedral aisles,* the love of color in cathedral win-dows, and obscurity hovers in the shadows of the vault. In our poetry, in our religion these twilight thoughts prevail. We seek no completeness here. What is beyond, what is inexpressible attracts us. Hence the greater spirituality of romantic literature, its deeper emotion, its more passionate tenderness. But hence likewise its sentimentality, its melancholy and, in particular, the morbid fascination which the thought of death has had for the Gothic mind. The classic nations concentrated their attention on life and light, and spent few thoughts upon darkness and the tomb. Death was to them neither sacred nor beauti-ful. Their decent rites of sepulture or cremation seem designed to hide its deformities rather than to prolong its reminders. The presence of the corpse was pollution. No Greek could have conceived such a book as the "Hydriotaphia" or the "Anatomy of Melancholy."

* Far to the west the long, long vale withdrawn,
  Where twilight loves to linger for a while.
                                        —*Beattie's " Minstrel."*

It is observable that Dr. Hedge is at one with Pater, in desiring some more philosophical statement of the difference between classic and romantic than the common one which makes it simply the difference between the antique and the mediæval. He says: "It must not be supposed that ancient and classic, on one side, and modern and romantic, on the other, are inseparably one; so that nothing approaching to romantic shall be found in any Greek or Roman author, nor any classic page in the literature of modern Europe. . . The literary line of demarcation is not identical with the chronological one." And just as Pater says that the Odyssey is more romantic than the Iliad, so Dr. Hedge says that "the story of Cupid and Psyche,* in the 'Golden Ass' of Apuleius, is as much a romance as any composition of the seventeenth or eighteenth century." Mediævalism he regards as merely an accident of romance: Scott, as most romantic in his themes, but Byron, in his mood.

So, too, Mr. Sidney Colvin † denies that "a predilection for classic subjects . . . can make a writer that which we understand by the word classical as distinguished from that which we understand by the word romantic. The distinction lies deeper, and is a dis-

---

* The modernness of this "latest born of the myths" resides partly in its spiritual, almost Christian conception of love, partly in its allegorical theme, the soul's attainment of immortality through love. The Catholic idea of penance is suggested, too, in Psyche's "wandering labors long." This apologue has been a favorite with platonizing poets, like Spenser and Milton. See "The Faërie Queene," book iii. canto vi. stanza 1., and "Comus," lines 1002-11

† "Selections from Walter Savage Landor," Preface, p. vii.

tinction much less of subject than of treatment. . .
In classical writing every idea is called up to the mind
as nakedly as possible, and at the same time as distinctly; it is exhibited in white light, and left to produce its effect by its own unaided power.* In romantic
writing, on the other hand, all objects are exhibited, as it were, through a colored and iridescent
atmosphere. Round about every central idea the romantic writer summons up a cloud of accessory and
subordinate ideas for the sake of enhancing its effect,
if at the risk of confusing its outlines. The temper,
again, of the romantic writer is one of excitement,
while the temper of the classical writer is one of self-
possession. . . On the one hand there is calm, on the
other hand enthusiasm. The virtues of the one style
are strength of grasp, with clearness and justice of
presentment; the virtues of the other style are glow of
spirit, with magic and richness of suggestion." Mr.
Colvin then goes on to enforce and illustrate this contrast between the "accurate and firm definition of
things" in classical writers and the "thrilling vagueness
and uncertainty," the tremulous, coruscating, vibrating
or colored light—the " halo "—with which the romantic writer invests his theme. " The romantic manner, . . with its thrilling uncertainties and its rich
suggestions, may be more attractive than the classic
manner, with its composed and measured preciseness
of statement. . . But on the other hand the romantic manner lends itself, as the true classical does not,
to inferior work. Second-rate conceptions excitedly
and approximately put into words derive from it an

* See also Walter Bagehot's essay on " Pure, Ornate, and Grotesque
Art," " Literary Studies, Works " (Hartford, 1889), Vol I. p. 200.

illusive attraction which may make them for a time, and with all but the coolest judges, pass as first-rate. Whereas about true classical writing there can be no illusion.   It presents to us conceptions calmly realized in words that exactly define them, conceptions depending for their attraction, not on their halo, but on themselves."

As examples of these contrasting styles, Mr. Colvin puts side by side passages from "The Ancient Mariner" and Keats' "Ode to a Nightingale," with passages, treating similar themes, from Landor's "Gebir" and "Imaginary Conversations."   The contrast might be even more clearly established by a study of such a piece as Keats' "Ode on a Grecian Urn," where the romantic form is applied to classical content; or by a comparison of Tennyson's "Ulysses" and "The Lotus Eaters," in which Homeric subjects are treated respectively in the classic and the romantic manner.

Alfred de Musset, himself in early life a prominent figure among the French romanticists, wrote some capital satire upon the baffling and contradictory definitions of the word *romantisme* that were current in the third and fourth decades of this century.*   Two worthy provincials write from the little town of La Ferté-sous-Jouarre to the editor of the "Revue des Deux Mondes," appealing to him to tell them what romanticism means.   For two years Dupuis and his friend Cotonet had supposed that the term applied only to the theater, and signified the disregard of the unities. "Shakspere, for example, makes people travel from

* Lettres de Dupuis et Cotonet (1836), "Œuvres Complètes" (Charpentier edition, 1881), Tome IX. p. 194.

Rome to London, and from Athens to Alexandria in a quarter of an hour. His heroes live ten or twenty years between two acts. His heroines, angels of virtue during a whole scene, have only to pass into the *coulisses*, to reappear as wives, adulteresses, widows, and grandmothers. There, we said to ourselves, is the romantic. Contrariwise, Sophocles makes Œdipus sit on a rock, even at the cost of great personal inconvenience, from the very beginning of his tragedy. All the characters come there to find him, one after the other. Perhaps he stands up occasionally, though I doubt it; unless, it may be, out of respect for Theseus, who, during the entire play, obligingly walks on the highway, coming in or going out continually. . . There, we said to ourselves, is the classic."

But about 1828, continues the letter, "we learned that there were romantic poetry and classical poetry, romantic novels and classical novels, romantic odes and classical odes; nay, a single line, my dear sir, a sole and solitary line of verse might be romantic or classic, according as the humor took it. When we received this intelligence, we could not close our eyes all night. Two years of peaceful conviction had vanished like a dream. All our ideas were turned topsy-turvy; for if the rules of Aristotle were no longer the line of demarcation which separated the literary camps, where was one to find himself, and what was he to depend upon? How was one to know, in reading a book, which school it belonged to? . . Luckily in the same year there appeared a famous preface, which we devoured straightway.* . . This said very distinctly

* Preface to Victor Hugo's "Cromwell," dated October, 1827. The play was printed, but not acted, in 1828.

that romanticism was nothing else than the alliance of
the playful and the serious, of the grotesque and the
terrible, of the jocose and the horrible, or in other
words, if you prefer, of comedy and tragedy."

This definition the anxious inquirers accepted for
the space of a year, until it was borne in upon them
that Aristophanes—not to speak of other ancients—
had mixed tragedy and comedy in his dramas.   Once
again the friends were plunged in darkness, and their
perplexity was deepened when they were taking a
walk one evening and overheard a remark made by
the niece of the *sous-préfet*.   This young lady had
fallen in love with English ways, as was—somewhat
strangely—evidenced by her wearing a green veil,
orange-colored gloves, and silver-rimmed spectacles.
As she passed the promenaders, she turned to look at
a water-mill near the ford, where there were bags of
grain, geese, and an ox in harness, and she exclaimed
to her governess, "*Voilà un site romantique.*"

This mysterious sentence roused the flagging curiosity of MM. Dupuis and Cotonet, and they renewed
their investigations.   A passage in a newspaper led
them to believe for a time that romanticism was the
imitation of the Germans, with, perhaps, the addition
of the English and Spanish.   Then they were tempted
to fancy that it might be merely a matter of literary
form, possibly this *vers brisé* (run-over lines, *enjam-
bement*) that they are making so much noise about.
"From 1830 to 1831 we were persuaded that romanticism was the historic style (*genre historique*) or, if you
please, this mania which has lately seized our authors
for calling the characters of their novels and melodramas Charlemagne, Francis I., or Henry IV., in-

stead of Amadis, Oronte, or Saint-Albin. . . From 1831 to the year following we thought it was the *genre intime*, about which there was much talk. But with all the pains that we took we never could discover what the *genre intime* was. The 'intimate' novels are just like the others. They are in two volumes octavo, with a great deal of margin. . . They have yellow covers and they cost fifteen francs." From 1832 to 1833 they conjectured that romanticism might be a system of philosophy and political economy. From 1833 to 1834 they believed that it consisted in not shaving one's self, and in wearing a waistcoat with wide facings very much starched.

At last they bethink themselves of a certain lawyer's clerk, who had first imported these literary disputes into the village, in 1824. To him they expose their difficulties and ask for an answer to the question, What is romanticism? After a long conversation, they receive this final definition. "Romanticism, my dear sir! No, of a surety, it is neither the disregard of the unities, nor the alliance of the comic and tragic, nor anything in the world expressible by words. In vain you grasp the butterfly's wing; the dust which gives it its color is left upon your fingers. Romanticism is the star that weeps, it is the wind that wails, it is the night that shudders, the bird that flies and the flower that breathes perfume: it is the sudden gush, the ecstasy grown faint, the cistern beneath the palms, rosy hope with her thousand loves, the angel and the pearl, the white robe of the willows. It is the infinite and the starry," etc., etc.

Then M. Ducoudray, a magistrate of the department, gives his theory of romanticism, which he considers to be an effect of the religious and political reaction under the restored Bourbon monarchy of Louis XVIII. and Charles X. "The mania for ballads, arriving from Germany, met the legitimist poetry one fine day at Ladvocat's bookshop; and the two of them, pickax in hand, went at nightfall to a churchyard, to dig up the Middle Ages." The taste for mediævalism, M. Ducoudray adds, has survived the revolution of 1830, and romanticism has even entered into the service of liberty and progress, where it is a manifest anachronism, "employing the style of Ronsard to celebrate railroads, and imitating Dante when it chants the praises of Washington and Lafayette." Dupuis was tempted to embrace M. Ducoudray's explanation, but Cotonet was not satisfied. He shut himself in, for four months, at the end of which he announced his discovery that the true and only difference between the classic and the romantic is that the latter uses a good many adjectives. He illustrates his principle by giving passages from "Paul and Virginia" and the "Portuguese Letters," written in the romantic style.

Thus Musset pricks a critical bubble with the point of his satire; and yet the bubble declines to vanish. There must really be some more substantial difference than this between classic and romantic, for the terms persist and are found useful. It may be true that the romantic temper, being subjective and excited, tends to an excess in adjectives; the adjective being that part of speech which attributes qualities, and is therefore most freely used by emotional persons. Still it would be possible to cut out all the adjectives, not strictly necessary, from one of Tieck's *Märchen* without in the slightest degree disturbing its romantic character.

It remains to add that romanticism is a word which faces in two directions. It is now opposed to realism, as it was once opposed to classicism. As, in one way, its freedom and lawlessness, its love of novelty, experiment, "strangeness added to beauty," contrast with the classical respect for rules, models, formulæ, precedents, conventions; so, in another way, its discontent with things as they are, its idealism, aspiration, mysticism contrast with the realist's conscientious adherence to fact. "Ivanhoe" is one kind of romance; "The Marble Faun" is another.*

* In modern times romanticism, typifying a permanent tendency of the human mind, has been placed in opposition to what is called realism. . . [But] there is, as it appears to us, but one fundamental note which all romanticism . . . has in common, and that is a deep disgust with the world as it is and a desire to depict in literature something that is claimed to be nobler and better.— *Essays on German Literature, by H. H. Boyesen*, pp. 358 and 356.

CHAPTER II.

The Augustans.

THE Romantic Movement in England was a part of the general European reaction against the spirit of the eighteenth century. This began somewhat earlier in England than in Germany, and very much earlier than in France, where literary conservatism went strangely hand in hand with political radicalism. In England the reaction was at first gradual, timid, and unconscious. It did not reach importance until the seventh decade of the century, and culminated only in the early years of the nineteenth century. The mediæval revival was only an incident—though a leading incident—of this movement; but it is the side of it with which the present work will mainly deal. Thus I shall have a great deal to say about Scott; very little about Byron, intensely romantic as he was in many meanings of the word. This will not preclude me from glancing occasionally at other elements besides mediævalism which enter into the concept of the term "romantic."

Reverting then to our tentative definition—Heine's definition—of romanticism, as the reproduction in modern art and literature of the life of the Middle Ages, it should be explained that the expression, "Middle Ages," is to be taken here in a liberal sense. Contributions to romantic literature such as Macpherson's "Ossian," Collins' "Ode on the Superstitions of the Scottish Highlands," and Gray's translations from the Welsh and the Norse, relate to periods which ante-date that era of Christian chivalry and feudalism, extending roughly from the eleventh century to the fifteenth, to which the term, "Middle Ages," more strictly applies. The same thing is true of the ground-work, at least, of ancient hero-epics like "Beowulf" and the "Nibelungen Lied," of the Icelandic "Sagas," and of similar products of old heathen Europe which have come down in the shape of mythologies, popular superstitions, usages, rites, songs, and traditions. These began to fall under the notice of scholars about the middle of the last century and made a deep impression upon contemporary letters.

Again, the influence of the Middle Age proper prolonged itself beyond the exact close of the mediæval period, which it is customary to date from the fall of Constantinople in 1453. The great romantic poets of Italy, Boiardo, Ariosto, Tasso, wrote in the full flush of the pagan revival and made free use of the Greek and Roman mythologies and the fables of Homer, Vergil, and Ovid; and yet their work is hardly to be described as classical. Nor is the work of their English disciples, Spenser and Sidney; while the entire Spanish and English drama of the sixteenth and seventeenth centuries (down to 1640, and with an occasional exception, like Ben Jonson) is romantic. Calderon is romantic; Shakspere and Fletcher are romantic. If we agree to regard mediæval literature, then, as comprising all the early literature of Europe which drew its inspiration from other than Greek-Latin sources, we shall do no great violence to the

usual critical employment of the word. I say *early*
literature, in order to exclude such writings as are
wholly modern, like " Robinson Crusoe," or " Gulliver's
Travels," or Fielding's novels, which are neither classic
nor romantic, but are the original creation of our own
time.   With works like these, though they are perhaps the most characteristic output of the eighteenth
century, our inquiries are not concerned.

It hardly needs to be said that the reproduction, or
imitation, of mediæval life by the eighteenth- and
nineteenth-century romanticists, contains a large admixture of modern thought and feeling.   The brilliant
pictures of feudal society in the romances of Scott
and Fouqué give no faithful image of that society,
even when they are carefully correct in all ascertain-
able historical details.* They give rather the impression left upon an alien mind by the quaint,
picturesque features of a way of life which seemed
neither quaint nor picturesque to the men who lived
it, but only to the man who turns to it for relief from
the prosaic, or at least familiar, conditions of the

---

*As another notable weakness of the age is its habit of looking
back, in a romantic and passionate idleness, to the past ages—not
understanding them all the while . . . so Scott gives up nearly
the half of his intellectual power to a fond yet purposeless dreaming
over the past ; and spends half his literary labors in endeavors to
revive it, not in reality, but on the stage of fiction : endeavors
which were the best of the kind that modernism made, but still successful only so far as Scott put under the old armor the everlasting
human nature which he knew ; and totally unsuccessful so far as concerned the painting of the armor itself, which he knew *not*. . . .
His romance and antiquarianism, his knighthood and monkery, are
all false, and he knows them to be false.—*Ruskin, " Modern Painters,"* Vol. III. p. 279 (First American Edition, 1860).

modern world. The offspring of the modern imagination, acting upon mediæval material, may be a perfectly legitimate, though not an original, form of art.
It may even have a novel charm of its own, unlike
either parent, but like Euphorion, child of Faust by
Helen of Troy, a blend of Hellas and the Middle Age.
Scott's verse tales are better poetry than the English
metrical romances of the thirteenth and fourteenth
centuries. Tennyson has given a more perfect shape
to the Arthurian legends than Sir Thomas Malory,
their compiler, or Walter Map and Chrestien de Troyes,
their possible inventors. But, of course, to study the
Middle Age, as it really was, one must go not to Tennyson and Scott, but to the "Chanson de Roland,"
and the "Divine Comedy," and the "Romaunt of the
Rose," and the chronicles of Villehardouin, Joinville,
and Froissart.

And the farther such study is carried, the more
evident it becomes that "mediæval" and "romantic"
are not synonymous. The Middle Age was not, at all
points, romantic: it is the modern romanticist who
makes, or finds, it so. He sees its strange, vivid
peculiarities under the glamour of distance.
Chaucer's temper, for instance, was by no means romantic. That "good sense" which Dryden mentions
as his prominent trait; that "low tone" which Lowell
praises in him, and which keeps him close to the common ground of experience, pervade his greatest work,
the "Canterbury Tales," with an insistent realism. It
is true that Chaucer shared the beliefs and influences
of his time and was a follower of its literary fashions.
In his version of the "Romaunt of the Rose," his
imitations of Machault, and his early work in general,

he used the mediæval machinery of allegory and dreams. In "Troilus and Cresseide" and the tale of "Palamon and Arcite," he carries romantic love and knightly honor to a higher pitch than his model, Boccaccio. But the shrewdly practical Pandarus of the former poem—a character almost wholly of Chaucer's creation—is the very embodiment of the anti-romantic attitude, and a remarkable anticipation of Sancho Panza; while the "Rime of Sir Thopas" is a distinct burlesque of the fantastic chivalry romances.* Chaucer's pages are picturesque with tournament, hunting parties, baronial feasts, miracles of saints, feats of magic; but they are solid, as well, with the everyday life of fourteenth-century England. They have the *naïveté* and garrulity which are marks of mediæval work, but not the quaintness and grotesquerie which are held to be marks of romantic work. Not archaic speech, but a certain mental twist constitutes quaintness. Herbert and Fuller are quaint; Blake is grotesque; Donne and Charles Lamb are willfully quaint, subtle, and paradoxical. But Chaucer is always straight-grained, broad, and natural.

Even Dante, the poet of the Catholic Middle Age; Dante, the mystic, the idealist, with his intense spirituality and his passion for symbolism, has been sometimes called classic, by virtue of the powerful construction of his great poem, and his scholastic rigidity of method.

The relation between modern romanticizing litera-

---

* See also the sly hit at popular fiction in the *Nonnë Prestës Tale:*
"This story is also trewe, I undertake,
As is the book of Launcelot de Lake,
That women hold in ful gret reverence."

ture and the real literature of the Middle Ages, is
something like that between the literature of the
renaissance and the ancient literatures of Greece and
Rome. But there is this difference, that, while the
renaissance writers fell short of their pattern, the
modern schools of romance have outgone their masters—not perhaps in the intellectual—but certainly
in the artistic value of their product. Mediæval
literature, wonderful and stimulating as a whole and
beautiful here and there in details of execution, affords
few models of technical perfection. The civilization
which it reflected, though higher in its possibilities
than the classic civilizations, had not yet arrived at an
equal grade of development, was inferior in intelligence and the matured results of long culture. The
epithets of Gothic ignorance, rudeness, and barbarism,
which the eighteenth-century critics applied so freely
to all the issue of the so-called dark ages, were not
entirely without justification. Dante is almost the
only strictly mediæval poet in whose work the form
seems adequate to the content; for Boccaccio and
Petrarca stand already on the sill of the renaissance.

In the arts of design the case was partly reversed. If
the artists of the renaissance did not equal the Greeks
in sculpture and architecture, they probably excelled
them in painting. On the other hand, the restorers
of Gothic have never quite learned the secret of the
mediæval builders. However, if the analogy is not
pushed too far, the romantic revival may be regarded
as a faint counterpart of the renaissance. Just as, in
the fifteenth century, the fragments of a half-forgotten
civilization were pieced together; Greek manuscripts
sought out, cleaned, edited, and printed: statues, coins,

vases dug up and ranged in museums: débris cleared
away from temples, amphitheaters, basilicas; till
gradually the complete image of the antique world
grew forth in august beauty, kindling an excitement
of mind to which there are few parallels in history;
so, in the eighteenth century, the despised ages of
monkery, feudalism, and superstition began to reassert
their claims upon the imagination.   Ruined castles
and abbeys, coats of mail, illuminated missals, manuscript romances, black-letter ballads, old tapestries,
and wood carvings acquired a new value.   Antiquaries
and virtuosos first, and then poets and romancers,
reconstructed in turn an image of mediæval society.

True, the later movement was much the weaker of
the two.   No such fissure yawned between modern
times and the Middle Ages as had been opened between
the ancient world and the Middle Ages by the ruin of
the Roman state and by the barbarian migrations.
Nor had ten centuries of rubbish accumulated over the
remains of mediæval culture.   In 1700 the Middle Ages
were not yet so very remote.   The nations and languages of Europe continued in nearly the same limits
which had bounded them two centuries before.   The
progress in the sciences and mechanic arts, the discovery and colonizing of America, the invention of
printing and gunpowder, and the Protestant refor-
mation had indeed drawn deep lines between modern
and mediæval life.   Christianity, however, formed a
connecting link, though, in Protestant countries, the
continuity between the earlier and later forms of the
religion had been interrupted.   One has but to compare the list of the pilgrims whom Chaucer met at the
Tabard, with the company that Captain Sentry or

Peregrine Pickle would be likely to encounter at
a suburban inn, to see how the face of English
society had changed between 1400 and 1700. What
has become of the knight, the prioress, the sumner,
the monk, pardoner, squire, alchemist, friar; and
where can they or their equivalents be found in all
England?

The limitations of my subject will oblige me to
treat the English romantic movement as a chapter in
literary history, even at the risk of seeming to adopt a
narrow method. Yet it would be unphilosophical to
consider it as a merely æsthetic affair, and to lose
sight altogether of its deeper springs in the religious
and ethical currents of the time. For it was, in part,
a return of warmth and color into English letters;
and that was only a symptom of the return of warmth
and color—that is, of emotion and imagination—into
English life and thought: into the Church, into politics, into philosophy. Romanticism, which sought to
evoke from the past a beauty that it found wanting in
the present, was but one phase of that revolt against
the coldness and spiritual deadness of the first half
of the eighteenth century which had other sides in the
idealism of Berkeley, in the Methodist and Evangel-
ical revival led by Wesley and Whitefield, and in the
sentimentalism which manifested itself in the writings
of Richardson and Sterne. Corresponding to these on
the Continent were German pietism, the transcendental philosophy of Kant and his continuators, and the
emotional excesses of works like Rousseau's " Nou-
velle Héloise " and Goethe's " Sorrows of Werther."

Romanticism was something more, then, than a
new literary mode; a taste cultivated by dilettante

virtuosos, like Horace Walpole, college recluses like
Gray, and antiquarian scholars like Joseph and
Thomas Warton. It was the effort of the poetic imagination to create for itself a richer environment;
but it was also, in its deeper significance, a reaching
out of the human spirit after a more ideal type of
religion and ethics than it could find in the official
churchmanship and the formal morality of the time.
Mr. Leslie Stephen * points out the connection
between the three currents of tendency known as
sentimentalism, romanticism, and naturalism. He
explains, to be sure, that the first English sentimentalists, such as Richardson and Sterne, were anything
but romantic. "A more modern sentimentalist would
probably express his feelings † by describing some past
state of society. He would paint some ideal society
in mediæval times and revive the holy monk and the
humble nun for our edification." He attributes the
subsequent interest in the Middle Ages to the progress
made in historical inquiries during the last half of the
eighteenth century, and to the consequent growth
of antiquarianism. "Men like Malone and Stevens
were beginning those painful researches which have
accumulated a whole literature upon the scanty
records of our early dramatists. Gray, the most
learned of poets, had vaguely designed a history of
English poetry, and the design was executed with
great industry by Thomas Warton. His brother
Joseph ventured to uphold the then paradoxical thesis

* "History of English Thought in the Eighteenth Century," Vol.
II. chap. xii. section vii.

† Sentimentalism approaches its subject through the feelings;
romanticism through the imagination.

that Spenser was as great a man as Pope. Everywhere a new interest was awakening in the minuter details of the past." At first, Mr. Stephen says, the result of these inquiries was "an unreasonable contempt for the past. The modern philosopher, who could spin all knowledge out of his own brain; the skeptic, who had exploded the ancient dogmas; or the free-thinker of any shade, who rejoiced in the destruction of ecclesiastical tyranny, gloried in his conscious superiority to his forefathers. Whatever was old was absurd; and Gothic—an epithet applied to all mediæval art, philosophy, or social order—became a simple term of contempt." But "an antiquarian is naturally a conservative, and men soon began to love the times whose peculiarities they were so diligently studying. Men of imaginative minds promptly made the discovery that a new source of pleasure might be derived from these dry records. . . The 'return to nature' expresses a sentiment which underlies . . . both the sentimental and romantic movements. . . To return to nature is, in one sense, to find a new expression for emotions which have been repressed by existing conventions; or, in another, to return to some simpler social order which had not yet suffered from those conventions. The artificiality attributed to the eighteenth century seems to mean that men were content to regulate their thoughts and lives by rules not traceable to first principles, but dependent upon a set of special and exceptional conditions. . . To get out of the ruts, or cast off the obsolete shackles, two methods might be adopted. The intellectual horizon might be widened by including a greater number of ages and countries; or men might try to fall back upon the thoughts and emotions common to all races, and so cast off the superficial incrustation. The first method, that of the romanticists, aims at increasing our knowledge: the second, that of the naturalistic school, at basing our philosophy on deeper principles." *

The classic, or pseudo-classic, period of English literature lasted from the middle of the seventeenth till the end of the eighteenth century. Inasmuch as the romantic revival was a protest against this reigning mode, it becomes necessary to inquire a little more closely what we mean when we say that the time of Queen Anne and the first two Georges was our Augustan or classical age. In what sense was it classical? And was it any more classical than the time of Milton, for example, or the time of Landor? If the "Dunciad," and the "Essay on Man," are

---

* Ruskin, too, indicates the common element in romanticism and naturalism—a desire to escape from the Augustan formalism. I condense the passage slightly : " To powder the hair, to patch the cheek, to hoop the body, to buckle the foot, were all part and parcel of the same system which reduced streets to brick walls and pictures to brown stains. Reaction from this state was inevitable, and accordingly men steal out to the fields and mountains; and, finding among these color and liberty and variety and power, rejoice in all the wildest shattering of the mountain side, as an opposition to Gower Street. It is not, however, only to existing inanimate nature that our want of beauty in person and dress has driven us. The imagination of it, as it was seen in our ancestors, haunts us continually. We look fondly back to the manners of the age of chivalry. The furniture and personages of our romance are sought in the centuries which we profess to have surpassed in everything. . . This romantic love of beauty, forced to seek in history and in external nature the satisfaction it cannot find in ordinary life."— *Modern Painters*, Vol. III. p. 260.

classical, what is Keats' "Hyperion"? And with
what propriety can we bring under a common rubric
things so far asunder as Prior's "Carmen Seculare"
and Tennyson's "Ulysses," or as Gay's "Trivia"
and Swinburne's "Atalanta in Calydon"? Evidently
the Queen Anne writers took hold of the antique
by a different side from our nineteenth-century poets.
Their classicism was of a special type. It was, as has
been often pointed out, more Latin than Greek, and
more French than Latin.* It was, as has likewise
been said, "a classicism in red heels and a periwig."
Victor Hugo speaks of "cette poésie fardée,
mouchetée, poudrée, du dix-huitième siècle, cette
littérature à paniers, à pompons et à falbalas." † The
costumes of Watteau contrast with the simple folds

---

* Although devout in their admiration for antiquity, the writers
of the seventeenth century have by no means always clearly grasped
the object of their cult. Though they may understand Latin tradition, they have certainly never entered into the freer, more original
spirit of Greek art. They have but an incomplete, superficial conception of Hellenism. . . Boileau celebrates but does not understand Pindar. . . The seventeenth century comprehended Homer
no better than Pindar. What we miss in them is exactly what we
like best in his epopee—the vast living picture of a semi-barbarous
civilization. . . No society could be less fitted than that of the
seventeenth century to feel and understand the spirit of primitive
antiquity. In order to appreciate Homer, it was thought necessary
to civilize the barbarian, make him a scrupulous writer, and convince
him that the word "ass" is a "very noble" expression in Greek.—
*Pellissier: "The Literary Movement in France" (Brinton's trans-
lation,* 1897), pp. 8–10. So Addison apologizes for Homer's failure
to observe those qualities of nicety, correctness, and what the French
call *bienséance* (decorum,) the necessity of which had only been found
out in later times. See *The Spectator,* No. 160.

† Preface to "Cromwell."

of Greek drapery very much as the "Rape of the
Lock," contrasts with the Iliad, or one of Pope's
pastorals with an idyl of Theocritus.   The times were
artificial in poetry as in dress—

> " Tea-cup times of hood and hoop,
> And when the patch was worn."

Gentlemen wore powdered wigs instead of their own
hair, and the powder and the wig both got into their
writing. *Perruque* was the nickname applied to the
classicists by the French romanticists of Hugo's
generation, who wore their hair long and flowing—
cheveux mérovingiennes—and affected an *outré* freedom
in the cut and color of their clothes.   Similarly the
Byronic collar became, all over Europe, the symbol
of daring independence in matters of taste and
opinion.   Its careless roll, which left the throat
exposed, seemed to assist the liberty of nature
against cramping conventions.

The leading Queen Anne writers are so well known
that a somewhat general description of the literary
situation in England at the time of Pope's death
(1744) will serve as an answer to the question, how
was the eighteenth century classical.   It was remarked by Thomas Warton * that, at the first revival
of letters in the sixteenth century, our authors were
more struck by the marvelous fables and inventions
of ancient poets than by the justness of their conceptions and the purity of their style.   In other words,
the men of the renaissance apprehended the ancient
literatures as poets: the men of the *éclaircissement*

* " History of English Poetry," section lxi. Vol. III. p. 398 (edition
of 1840).

apprehended them as critics. In Elizabeth's day the new learning stimulated English genius to creative activity. In royal progresses, court masques, Lord Mayors' shows, and public pageants of all kinds, mythology ran mad. "Every procession was a pantheon." But the poets were not careful to keep the two worlds of pagan antiquity and mediæval Christianity distinct. The art of the renaissance was the flower of a double root, and the artists used their complex stuff naïvely. The "Faërie Queene" is the typical work of the English renaissance; there hamadryads, satyrs, and river gods mingle unblushingly with knights, dragons, sorcerers, hermits, and personified vices and virtues. The "machinery" of Homer and Vergil—the "machinery" of the "Seven Champions of Christendom" and the "Roman de la Rose"! This was not shocking to Spenser's contemporaries, but it seemed quite shocking to classical critics a century later. Even Milton, the greatest scholar among English poets, but whose imagination was a strong agent, holding strange elements in solution, incurred their censure for bringing Saint Peter and the sea-nymphs into dangerous juxtaposition in "Lycidas."

But by the middle of the seventeenth century the renaissance schools of poetry had become effete in all European countries. They had run into extravagances of style, into a vicious manner known in Spain as Gongorism, in Italy as Marinism, and in England best exhibited in the verse of Donne and Cowley and the rest of the group whom Dr. Johnson called the metaphysical poets, and whose Gothicism of taste Addison ridiculed in his *Spectator* papers

on true and false wit. It was France that led the
reform against this fashion. Malherbe and Boileau
insisted upon the need of discarding tawdry ornaments of style and cultivating simplicity, clearness,
propriety, decorum, moderation; above all, good sense.
The new Academy, founded to guard the purity of
the French language, lent its weight to the precepts
of the critics, who applied the rules of Aristotle, as
commented by Longinus and Horace, to modern conditions. The appearance of a number of admirable
writers—Corneille, Molière, Racine, Bossuet, La
Fontaine, La Bruyère—simultaneously with this critical movement, gave an authority to the new French
literature which enabled it to impose its principles
upon England and Germany for over a century. For
the creative literature of France conformed its practice, in the main, to the theory of French criticism;
though not, in the case of Corneille, without some
protest; and not, in the case of Regnier, without open
defiance. This authority was re-enforced by the political glories and social *éclat* of the *siècle de Louis
Quatorze.*

It happened that at this time the Stuart court was
in exile, and in the train of Henrietta Maria at Paris,
or scattered elsewhere through France, were many
royalist men of letters, Etherege, Waller, Cowley, and
others, who brought back with them to England in
1660 an acquaintance with this new French literature
and a belief in its æsthetic code. That French influence would have spread into England without the
aid of these political accidents is doubtless true, as it
is also true that a reform of English versification and
poetic style would have worked itself out upon native

lines independent of foreign example, and even had
there been no such thing as French literature.   Mr.
Gosse has pointed out couplets of Waller, written as
early as 1623, which have the formal precision of
Pope's; and the famous passage about the Thames in
Denham's "Cooper's Hill" (1642) anticipates the
best performance of Augustan verse:

> " O could I flow like thee, and make thy stream
>   My great example, as it is my theme!
>   Though deep, yet clear, though gentle, yet not dull,
>   Strong without rage, without o'erflowing full."

However, as to the general fact of the powerful impact of French upon English literary fashions, in the
latter half of the seventeenth century, there can be
no dispute.*

This change of style was symptomatic of a corresponding change in the national temper.   It was the
mission of the eighteenth century to assert the universality of law and, at the same time, the sufficiency of
the reason to discover the laws which govern in every
province: a service which we now, perhaps, undervalue in our impatience with the formalism which
was its outward sign.   Hence its dislike of irregularity in art and irrationality in religion.   England,
in particular, was tired of unchartered freedom, of
spiritual as well as of literary anarchy.   The religious
tension of the Commonwealth period had relaxed—
men cannot be always at the heroic pitch—and theo-
logical disputes had issued in indifference and a skep-

* See, for a fuller discussion of this subject, " From Shakspere to
Pope : An Inquiry into the Causes and Phenomena of the Rise of
Classical Poetry in England," by Edmund Gosse, 1885.

ticism which took the form of deism, or "natural religion." But the deists were felt to be a nuisance. They were unsettling opinions and disturbing that decent conformity with generally received beliefs which it is the part of a good citizen to maintain. Addison instructs his readers that, in the absence of certainty, it is the part of a prudent man to choose the safe side and make friends with God. The free-thinking Chesterfield * tells his son that the profession of atheism is ill-bred. De Foe, Swift, Richardson, Fielding, Johnson all attack infidelity. "Conform! conform!" said in effect the most authoritative writers of the century. "Be sensible: go to church: pay your rates: don't be a vulgar deist—a fellow like Toland who is poor and has no social position. But, on the other hand, you need not be a fanatic or superstitious, or an enthusiast. Above all, *pas de zèle!*"

"Theology," says Leslie Stephen, "was, for the most part, almost as deistical as the deists. A hatred for enthusiasm was as strongly impressed upon the whole character of contemporary thought as a hatred of skepticism. . . A good common-sense religion should be taken for granted and no questions asked. . . With Shakspere, or Sir Thomas Browne, or Jeremy Taylor, or Milton, man is contemplated in his relations to the universe; he is in presence of eternity and infinity; life is a brief drama; heaven and hell are behind the veil of phenomena; at every step

---

* The cold-hearted, polished Chesterfield is a very representative figure. Johnson, who was really devout, angrily affirmed that his celebrated letters taught "the morality of a whore with the manners of a dancing-master."

our friends vanish into the abyss of ever present mystery. To all such thoughts the writers of the eighteenth century seemed to close their eyes as resolutely as possible. . . The absence of any deeper speculative ground makes the immediate practical questions of life all the more interesting. We know not what we are, nor whither we are going, nor whence we come; but we can, by the help of common sense, discover a sufficient share of moral maxims for our guidance in life. . . Knowledge of human nature, as it actually presented itself in the shifting scene before them, and a vivid appreciation of the importance of the moral law, are the staple of the best literature of the time." *

The God of the deists was, in truth, hardly more impersonal than the abstraction worshiped by the orthodox—the " Great Being " of Addison's essays, the "Great First Cause " of Pope's " Universal Prayer," invoked indifferently as " Jehovah, Jove, or Lord." Dryden and Pope were professed Catholics, but there is nothing to distinguish their so-called sacred poetry from that of their Protestant contemporaries. Contrast the mere polemics of " The Hind and the Panther " with really Catholic poems like Southwell's " Burning Babe " and Crashaw's " Flaming Heart," or even with Newman's " Dream of Gerontius." In his " Essay on Man," Pope versified, without well understanding, the optimistic deism of Leibnitz, as expounded by Shaftesbury and Bolingbroke. The Anglican Church itself was in a strange condition, when

---

* " History of English Thought in the Eighteenth Century," Vol. II. chap. xii. section iv. See also " Selections from Newman," by Lewis E. Gates, Introduction, pp. xlvii–xlviii. (1895).

Jonathan Swift, a dean and would-be bishop, came to its defense with his "Tale of a Tub" and his ironical "Argument against the Abolition of Christianity." Among the Queen Anne wits Addison was the man of most genuine religious feeling. He is always reverent, and "the feeling infinite" stirs faintly in one or two of his hymns. But, in general, his religion is of the rationalizing type, a religion of common sense, a belief resting upon logical deductions, a system of ethics in which the supernatural is reduced to the lowest terms, and from which the glooms and fervors of a deep spiritual experience are almost entirely absent. This "parson in a tie-wig" is constantly preaching against zeal, enthusiasm, superstition, mysticism, and recommending a moderate, cheerful, and reasonable religion.* It is instructive to contrast his amused contempt for popular beliefs in ghosts, witches, dreams, prognostications, and the like, with the reawakened interest in folk lore evidenced by such a book as Scott's "Demonology and Witchcraft."

Queen Anne literature was classical, then, in its lack of those elements of mystery and aspiration which we have found described as of the essence of romanticism. It was emphatically a literature of this world. It ignored all vague emotion, the phenomena of subconsciousness, "the electric chain wherewith we are darkly bound," the shadow that rounds man's little life, and fixed its attention only upon what it could thoroughly comprehend.† Thereby it escaped obscu-

---

* See especially *Spectator*, Nos. 185, 186, 201, 381, and 494.

† The classical Landor's impatience of mysticism explains his dislike of Plato, the mystic among Greeks. Diogenes says to Plato: "I meddle not at present with infinity or eternity: when I can

rity. The writings of the Augustans in both verse
and prose are distinguished by a perfect clearness,
but it is a clearness without subtlety or depth. They
never try to express a thought, or to utter a feeling,
that is not easily intelligible. The mysticism of
Wordsworth, the incoherence of Shelley, the darkness
of Browning—to take only modern instances—proceed, however, not from inferior art, but from the
greater difficulty of finding expression for a very different order of ideas.

Again the literature of the Restoration and Queen
Anne periods—which may be regarded as one, for
present purposes—was classical, or at least unroman-
tic, in its self-restraint, its objectivity, and its lack of
curiosity; or, as a hostile criticism would put it, in its
coldness of feeling, the tameness of its imagination,
and its narrow and imperfect sense of beauty. It was
a literature not simply of this world, but of *the* world,
of the *beau monde*, high life, fashion, society, the court
and the town, the salons, clubs, coffee-houses, assem-
blies, ombre-parties. It was social, urban, gregarious,
intensely though not broadly human. It cared little for
the country or outward nature, and nothing for the life
of remote times and places. Its interest was centered
upon civilization and upon that peculiarly artificial
type of civilization which it found prevailing. It was
as indifferent to Venice, Switzerland, the Alhambra,
the Nile, the American forests, and the islands of the
South Sea as it was to the Middle Ages and the manners of Scotch Highlanders. The sensitiveness to the

comprehend them, I will talk about them," "Imaginary Conversations," 2d series, Conversation XV. Landor's contempt for German literature is significant.

picturesque, the liking for local color and for **whatever** is striking, characteristic, and peculiarly national in foreign ways is a romantic note. The eighteenth century disliked "strangeness added to beauty"; it disapproved of anything original, exotic, tropical, bizarre for the same reason that it disapproved of mountains and Gothic architecture.

Professor Gates says that the work of English literature during the first quarter of the present century was "the rediscovery and vindication of the concrete. The special task of the eighteenth century had been to order, and to systematize, and to name; its favorite methods had been analysis and generalization. It asked for no new experience. . . The abstract, the typical, the general—these were everywhere exalted at the expense of the image, the specific experience, the vital fact." * Classical tragedy, *e. g.*, undertook to present only the universal, abstract, permanent truths of human character and passion.† The impres-

* "Selections from Newman," Introduction, pp. xlvii–xlviii.

† Racine observes that good sense and reason are the same in all ages. What is the result of this generalization? Heroes can be transported from epoch to epoch, from country to country, without causing surprise. Their Achilles is no more a Greek than is Porus an Indian; Andromache feels and talks like a seventeenth-century princess: Phædra experiences the remorse of a Christian.—*Pellissier*, "*Literary Movement in France*," p. 18.

In substituting men of concrete, individual lives for the ideal figures of tragic art, romanticism was forced to determine their physiognomy by a host of local, casual details. In the name of universal truth the classicists rejected the coloring of time and place; and this is precisely what the romanticists seek under the name of particular reality.—*Ibid.* p. 220. Similarly Montezuma's Mexicans in Dryden's "Indian Emperor" have no more national individuality than the Spanish Moors in his "Conquest of Granada." The only attempt at

sion of the mysterious East upon modern travelers and poets like Byron, Southey, De Quincey, Moore, Hugo,* Ruckert, and Gérard de Nerval, has no counterpart in the eighteenth century. The Oriental allegory or moral apologue, as practiced by Addison in such papers as " The Vision of Mirza," and by Johnson in " Rasselas," is rather faintly colored and gets what color it has from the Old Testament. It is significant that the romantic Collins endeavored to give a novel turn to the decayed pastoral by writing a number of " Oriental Eclogues," in which dervishes and camel-drivers took the place of shepherds, but the experiment was not a lucky one. Milton had more of the East in his imagination than any of his successors. His " vulture on Imaus bred, whose snowy ridge the roving Tartar bounds "; his " plain of Sericana where Chineses drive their cany wagons light "; his " utmost Indian isle Taprobane," are touches of the picturesque which anticipate a more modern mood than Addison's.

" The difference," says Matthew Arnold, "between genuine poetry and the poetry of Dryden, Pope, and all their school is briefly this: their poetry is conceived and composed in their wits, genuine poetry is conceived and composed in the soul." The representative minds of the eighteenth century were such as Voltaire, the master of persiflage, destroying superstition with

---

local color in " Aurungzebe "—an heroic play founded on the history of a contemporary East Indian potentate who died seven years after the author—is the introduction of the *suttee*, and one or two mentions of elephants.

* See " Les Orientales " (Hugo) and Nerval's " Les Nuits du Rhamadan " and " La Légende du Calife Hakem."

his *sourire hideux;* Gibbon, " the lord of irony," " sapping a solemn creed with solemn sneer "; and Hume, with his thorough-going philosophic skepticism, his dry Toryism, and cool contempt for " zeal " of any kind. The characteristic products of the era were satire, burlesque, and travesty: " Hudibras," " Absalom and Achitophel," " The Way of the World," " Gulliver's Travels " and " The Rape of the Lock." There is a whole literature of mockery: parodies like Prior's " Ballad on the Taking of Namur" and " The Country Mouse and the City Mouse "; Buckingham's " Rehearsal " and Swift's " Meditation on a Broomstick "; mock-heroics, like the " Dunciad " and " MacFlecknoe " and Garth's " Dispensary," and John Phillips' " Splendid Shilling " and Addison's " Machinæ Gesticulantes "; Prior's " Alma," a burlesque of philosophy; Gay's " Trivia " and " The Shepherd's Week," and " The Beggars' Opera "—a " Newgate pastoral " ; " Town Eclogues " by Swift and Lady Montague and others. Literature was a polished mirror in which the gay world saw its own grinning face. It threw back a most brilliant picture of the surface of society, showed manners but not the elementary passions of human nature. As a whole, it leaves an impression of hardness, shallowness, and levity. The polite cynicism of Congreve, the ferocious cynicism of Swift, the malice of Pope, the pleasantry of Addison, the easy worldliness of Prior and Gay are seldom relieved by any touch of the ideal. The prose of the time was excellent, but the poetry was merely rhymed prose. The recent Queen Anne revival in architecture, dress, and bric-à-brac, the recrudescence of society verse in Dobson and others, is perhaps

symptomatic of the fact that the present generation
has entered upon a prosaic reaction against romantic
excesses and we are finding our picturesque in that era
of artifice which seemed so unpicturesque to our forerunners. The sedan chair, the blue china, the fan,
farthingale, and powdered head dress have now got the
"rime of age" and are seen in fascinating perspective,
even as the mailed courser, the buff jerkin, the cowl,
and the cloth-yard shaft were seen by the men of
Scott's generation.

Once more, the eighteenth century was classical in
its respect for authority. It desired to put itself
under discipline, to follow the rules, to discover a
formula of correctness in all the arts, to set up a
tribunal of taste and establish canons of composition,
to maintain standards, copy models and patterns,
comply with conventions, and chastise lawlessness.
In a word, its spirit was academic. Horace was its
favorite master—not Horace of the Odes, but Horace
of the Satires and Epistles, and especially Horace as
interpreted by Boileau.* The "Ars Poetica" had
been englished by the Earl of Roscommon, and
imitated by Boileau in his "L'Art Poétique," which
became the parent of a numerous progeny in England;
among others an "Essay on Satire" and an "Essay
on Poetry," by the Earl of Mulgrave;† an "Essay on

---

* The rules a nation, born to serve, obeys;
    And Boileau still in right of Horace sways.
                —*Pope, "Essay on Criticism."*

† These critical verse essays seem to have been particularly affected
by this order of the peerage ; for, somewhat later, we have one,
"On Unnatural Flights in Poetry," by the Earl of Lansdowne—
"Granville the polite."

Translated Verse" by the Earl of Roscommon, who, says Addison, "makes even rules a noble poetry ";* and Pope's well-known " Essay on Criticism."

The doctrine of Pope's essay is, in brief, follow Nature, and in order that you may follow Nature, observe the rules, which are only " Nature metho-dized," and also imitate the ancients.

> " Learn hence for ancient rules a just esteem ;
>   To copy nature is to copy them."

Thus Vergil when he started to compose the Æneid may have seemed above the critic's law, but when he came to study Homer, he found that Nature and Homer were the same.   Accordingly,

> " he checks the bold design,
> And rules as strict his labor'd work confine."

Not to stimulate, but to check, to confine, to regulate, is the unfailing precept of this whole critical school. Literature, in the state in which they found it, appeared to them to need the curb more than the spur.

Addison's scholarship was almost exclusively Latin, though it was Vergilian rather than Horatian. Macaulay † says of Addison's " Remarks on Italy ": "To the best of our remembrance, Addison does not mention Dante, Petrarch, Boccaccio, Boiardo, Berni, Lorenzo de' Medici, or Machiavelli.   He coldly tells us that at Ferrara he saw the tomb of Ariosto, and that at Venice he heard the gondoliers sing verses of Tasso. But for Tasso and Ariosto he cared far less than for Valerius Flaccus and Sidonius Apollinaris.   The gentle

---

* " Epistle to Sacheverel."   † " Essay on Addison."

flow of the Ticino brings a line of Silius to his mind.
The sulphurous stream of Albula suggests to him
several passages of Martial. But he has not a word
to say of the illustrious dead of Santa Croce; he
crosses the wood of Ravenna * without recollecting
the specter huntsman, and wanders up and down
Rimini without one thought of Francesca. At Paris
he had eagerly sought an introduction to Boileau;
but he seems not to have been at all aware that at
Florence he was in the vicinity of a poet with whom
Boileau could not sustain a comparison: of the
greatest lyric poet of modern times [!] Vincenzio
Filicaja. . . The truth is that Addison knew little
and cared less about the literature of modern Italy.
His favorite models were Latin. His favorite critics
were French. Half the Tuscan poetry that he had
read seemed to him monstrous and the other half
tawdry." †

There was no academy in England, but there was
a critical tradition that was almost as influential.
French critics gave the law: Boileau, Dacier, LeBossu,
Rapin, Bouhours; English critics promulgated it: Dennis, Langbaine, Rymer, Gildon, and others now little

---

* Sweet hour of twilight !—in the solitude
    Of the pine forest, and the silent shore
Which bounds Ravenna's immemorial wood,
    Rooted where once the Adrian wave flowed o'er,
To where the last Cæsarian fortress stood,
    Evergreen forest ! which Boccaccio's lore
And Dryden's lay made haunted ground to me,
    How have I loved the twilight hour and thee !
                      —*Don Juan.*

† I must entirely agree with Monsieur Boileau, that one verse of
Vergil is worth all the *clinquant* or tinsel of Tasso.—*Spectator*, No. 5.

read. Three writers of high authority in three successive generations—Dryden, Addison, and Johnson—
consolidated a body of literary opinion which may be
described, in the main, as classical, and as consenting,
though with minor variations. Thus it was agreed on
all hands that it was a writer's duty to be "correct."
It was well indeed to be "bold," but bold with discretion. Dryden thought Shakspere a greater poet than
Jonson, but an inferior artist. He was to be admired,
but not approved. Homer, again, it was generally
conceded, was not so correct as Vergil, though he had
more "fire." Chesterfield preferred Vergil to Homer,
and both of them to Tasso. But of all epics the one
he read with most pleasure was the "Henriade." As
for "Paradise Lost," he could not read it through.
William Walsh, "the muses' judge and friend," advised
the youthful Pope that "there was one way still left
open for him, by which he might excel any of his predecessors, which was by correctness; that though
indeed we had several great poets, we as yet could
boast of none that were perfectly correct; and that
therefore he advised him to make this quality his particular study." "The best of the moderns in all
languages," he wrote to Pope, "are those that have
the nearest copied the ancients." Pope was thankful
for the counsel and mentions its giver in the "Essay
on Criticism" as one who had

> " taught his muse to sing,
> Prescribed her heights and pruned her tender wing."

But what was correct? In the drama, *e. g.*, the ob-
servance of the unities was almost universally recommended, but by no means universally practiced.

Johnson, himself a sturdy disciple of Dryden and Pope, exposed the fallacy of that stage illusion, on the supposed necessity of which the unities of time and place were defended. Yet Johnson, in his own tragedy "Irene," conformed to the rules of Aristotle. He pronounced "Cato" "unquestionably the noblest production of Addison's genius," but acknowledged that its success had "introduced, or confirmed among us, the use of dialogue too declamatory, of unaffecting elegance and chill philosophy." On the other hand Addison had small regard for poetic justice, which Johnson thought ought to be observed. Addison praised old English ballads, which Johnson thought mean and foolish; and he guardedly commends * "the fairy way of writing," a romantic foppery that Johnson despised.†

Critical opinion was pronounced in favor of separating tragedy and comedy, and Addison wrote one sentence which condemns half the plays of Shakspere and Fletcher: "The tragi-comedy, which is the product of the English theater, is one of the most monstrous inventions that ever entered into a poet's thought." ‡ Dryden made some experiments in tragi-comedy, but, in general, classical comedy was pure comedy—the prose comedy of manners—and classical tragedy admitted no comic intermixture. Whether tragedy should be in rhyme, after the French manner, or in blank verse, after the precedent of the old English stage, was a moot point. Dryden at first argued for rhyme and used it in his "heroic plays"; and it is significant that he defended its use on the ground that

---

* *Spectator*, No. 419.
† See his "Life of Collins."   ‡ *Spectator*, No. 40.

it would act as a check upon the poet's fancy. **But** afterward he grew "weary of his much-loved mistress, rhyme," and went back to blank verse in his later plays.

As to poetry other than dramatic, the Restoration critics were at one in judging blank verse too "low" for a poem of heroic dimensions; and though Addison gave it the preference in epic poetry, Johnson was its persistent foe, and regarded it as little short of immoral. But for that matter, Gray could endure no blank verse outside of Milton. This is curious, that rhyme, a mediæval invention, should have been associated in the last century with the classical school of poetry; while blank verse, the nearest English equivalent of the language of Attic tragedy, was a shibboleth of romanticizing poets, like Thomson and Akenside. The reason was twofold: rhyme came stamped with the authority of the French tragic alexandrine; and, secondly, it meant constraint where blank verse meant freedom, "ancient liberty, recovered to heroic poem from the troublesome and modern bondage of rhyming." * Pope, among his many thousand rhymed couplets, has left no blank verse except the few lines contributed to Thomson's "Seasons." Even the heroic couplet as written by earlier poets was felt to have been too loose in structure. "The excellence and dignity of it," says Dryden, "were never fully known till Mr. Waller taught it; he first made writing easily an art; first showed us how to conclude the sense most commonly in distichs, which, in the verse of those before him, runs on for so many

* "The Verse": Preface to "Paradise Lost."

lines together, that the reader is out of breath to overtake it." * All through the classical period the tradition is constant that Waller was the first modern English poet, the first correct versifier. Pope is praised by Johnson because he employed but sparingly the triplets and alexandrines by which Dryden sought to vary the monotony of the couplet; and he is censured by Cowper because, by force of his example, he "made poetry a mere mechanic art." Henceforth the distich was treated as a unit: the first line was balanced against the second, and frequently the first half of the line against the second half.

> " To err is human, to forgive divine."
> " And so obliging, that he ne'er obliged."
> " Charms strike the eye, but merit wins the soul," etc., etc.

This type of verse, which Pope brought to perfection, and to which he gave all the energy and variety of which it was capable, so prevailed in our poetry for a century or more that one almost loses sight of the fact that any other form was employed. The sonnet, for instance, disappeared entirely, until revived by Gray, Stillingfleet, Edwards, and Thomas Warton, about the middle of the eighteenth century.† When the poets wished to be daring and irregular, they were apt to give vent in that species of pseudo-Pindaric ode which Cowley had introduced—a literary disease which,

---

* Dedicatory epistle to " The Rival Ladies."

† Mr. Gosse says that a sonnet by Pope's friend Walsh is the only one " written in English between Milton's in 1658, and Warton's about 1750," Ward's " English Poets," Vol. III. p. 7. The statement would have been more precise if he had said published instead of *written*.

Dr. Johnson complained, infected the British muse
with the notion that " he who could do nothing else
could write like Pindar."

Sir Charles Eastlake in his " History of the Gothic
Revival " testifies to this formal spirit from the point
of view of another art than literature. " The age in
which Batty Langley lived was an age in which it was
customary to refer all matters of taste to rule and
method. There was one standard of excellence in
poetry—a standard that had its origin in the smooth
distichs of heroic verse which Pope was the first to
perfect, and which hundreds of later rhymers who
lacked his nobler powers soon learned to imitate. In
pictorial art, it was the grand school which exercised
despotic sway over the efforts of genius and limited the
painter's inventions to the field of Pagan mythology.
In architecture, Vitruvius was the great authority.
The graceful majesty of the Parthenon—the noble proportions of the temple of Theseus—the chaste enrich-
ment which adorns the Choragic monument of Lysic-
rates, were ascribed less to the fertile imagination and
refined perceptions of the ancient Greek, than to the
dry and formal precepts which were invented centuries
after their erection. Little was said of the magnificent
sculpture which filled the metopes of the temple of
Minerva; but the exact height and breadth of the trig-
lyphs between them were considered of the greatest
importance. The exquisite drapery of caryatids and
canephoræ, no English artist, a hundred years ago,
thought fit to imitate; but the cornices which they
supported were measured inch by inch with the utmost
nicety. Ingenious devices were invented for enabling
the artificer to reproduce, by a series of complicated

curves, the profile of a Doric capital, which probably owed its form to the steady hand and uncontrolled taste of the designer. To put faith in many of the theories propounded by architectural authorities in the last century, would be to believe that some of the grandest monuments which the world has ever seen raised, ōwe their chief beauty to an accurate knowledge of arithmetic. The diameter of the column was divided into modules: the modules were divided into minutes; the minutes into fractions of themselves. A certain height was allotted to the shaft, another to the entablature. . . Sometimes the learned discussed how far apart the columns of a portico might be." *

This kind of mensuration reminds one of the disputes between French critics as to whether the unity of time meant thirty hours, or twenty-four, or twelve, or the actual time that it took to act the play; or of the geometric method of the "Saturday papers" in the *Spectator*. Addison tries "Paradise Lost" by Aristotle's rules for the composition of an epic. Is it the narrative of a single great action? Does it begin *in medias res*, as is proper, or *ab ovo Ledæ*, as Horace has said that an epic ought not? Does it bring in the introductory matter by way of episode, after the approved recipe of Homer and Vergil? Has it allegorical characters, contrary to the practice of the ancients? Does the poet intrude personally into his poem, thus mixing the lyric and epic styles? etc. Not a word as to Milton's puritanism, or his *Weltanschauung*, or the relation of his work to its environment. Nothing of that historical and sympathetic method—that

* " History of the Gothic Revival," pp. 49–50 (edition of 1872).

endeavor to put the reader at the poet's point of view—by which modern critics, from Lessing to Sainte-Beuve, have revolutionized their art.   Addison looks at " Paradise Lost " as something quite distinct from Milton : as a manufactured article to be tested by comparing it with standard fabrics by recognized makers, like the authors of the Iliad and Æneid.

When the Queen Anne poetry took a serious turn, the generalizing spirit of the age led it almost always into the paths of ethical and didactic verse. " It stooped to truth and moralized its song," finding its favorite occupation in the sententious expression of platitudes—the epigram in satire, the maxim in serious work.   It became a poetry of aphorisms, instructing us with Pope that

> " Virtue alone is happiness below; "

or, with Young, that

> " Procrastination is the thief of time; "

or, with Johnson, that

> " Slow rises worth by poverty depressed."

When it attempted to deal concretely with the passions, it found itself impotent.   Pope's " Epistle of Eloisa to Abelard " rings hollow: it is rhetoric, not poetry. The closing lines of " The Dunciad "—so strangely overpraised by Thackeray—with their metallic clank and grandiose verbiage, are not truly imaginative. The poet is simply working himself up to a climax of the false sublime, as an orator deliberately attaches a sounding peroration to his speech.   Pope is always " heard," never " overheard."

The poverty of the classical period in lyrical verse is particularly significant, because the song is the most primitive and spontaneous kind of poetry, and the most direct utterance of personal feeling. Whatever else the poets of Pope's time could do, they could not sing. They are the despair of the anthologists.* Here and there among the brilliant reasoners, *raconteurs*, and satirists in verse, occurs a clever epigrammatist like Prior, or a ballad writer like Henry Carey, whose " Sally in Our Alley " shows the singing, and not talking, voice, but hardly the lyric cry. Gay's "Blackeyed Susan " has genuine quality, though its *rococo* graces are more than half artificial. Sweet William is very much such an opera sailor-man as Bumkinet or Grubbinol is a shepherd, and his wooing is beribboned with conceits like these :

> " If to fair India's coast we sail,
>   Thy eyes are seen in diamonds bright,
>   Thy breath is Afric's spicy gale,
>   Thy skin is ivory so white.
>   Thus every beauteous prospect that I view,
>   Wakes in my soul some charm of lovely Sue."

It was the same with the poetry of outward nature as with the poetry of human passion.† In Addison's "Letter from Italy," in Pope's "Pastorals," and

* Palgrave says that the poetry of passion was deformed, after 1660, by " levity and an artificial tone "; and that it lay " almost dormant for the hundred years between the days of Wither and Suckling and the days of Burns and Cowper," " Golden Treasury " (Sever and Francis edition, 1866), pp. 379–80.

† Excepting the "Nocturnal Reverie " of Lady Winchelsea, and a passage or two in the " Windsor Forest " of Pope, the poetry of the period intervening between the publication of the " Paradise Lost "

"Windsor Forest," the imagery, when not actually false, is vague and conventional, and the language abounds in classical insipidities, epithets that describe nothing, and generalities at second hand from older poets, who may once, perhaps, have written with their "eyes upon the object." Blushing Flora paints the enameled ground; cheerful murmurs fluctuate on the gale; Eridanus through flowery meadows strays; gay gilded * scenes and shining prospects rise; while everywhere are balmy zephyrs, sylvan shades, winding vales, vocal shores, silver floods, crystal springs, feathered quires, and Phœbus and Philomel and Ceres' gifts assist the purple year. It was after this fashion that Pope rendered the famous moonlight passage in his translation of the Iliad:

> " Then shine the vales, the rocks in prospect rise,
> A flood of glory bursts from all the skies," etc.

"Strange to think of an enthusiast," says Wordsworth, "reciting these verses under the cope of a moonlight sky, without having his raptures in the least disturbed by a suspicion of their absurdity." The poetic diction against which Wordsworth protested was an outward sign of the classical preference for the general over the concrete. The vocabulary was Latinized because, in English, the *mot propre* is com-

---

and the " Seasons " [1667–1726] does not contain a single new image of external nature.— *Wordsworth, Appendix to Lyrical Ballads,* (1815).

* *Gild* is a perfect earmark of eighteenth-century descriptive verse : the shore is gilded and so are groves, clouds, etc. Contentment gilds the scene, and the stars gild the gloomy night (Parnell) or the glowing pole (Pope).

monly a Saxon word, while its Latin synonym has a
convenient indefiniteness that keeps the subject at
arm's length. Of a similar tendency was the favorite
rhetorical figure of personification, which gave a false
air of life to abstractions by the easy process of spelling them with a capital letter. Thus:

> " From bard to bard the frigid caution crept,
>   Till Declamation roared whilst Passion slept;
>   Yet still did Virtue deign the stage to tread,
>   Philosophy remained though Nature fled, . . .
>   Exulting Folly hailed the joyful day,
>   And Pantomime and Song confirmed her sway." *

Everything was personified: Britannia, Justice, Liberty, Science, Melancholy, Night. Even vaccination
for the smallpox was invoked as a goddess,

> " Inoculation, heavenly maid, descend ! " †

But circumlocution or periphrasis was the capital
means by which the Augustan poet avoided precision and attained nobility of style. It enabled him
to speak of a woman as a " nymph," or a "fair"; of
sheep as " the fleecy care"; of fishes as " the scaly
tribe "; and of a picket fence as a " spiculated paling."
Lowell says of Pope's followers: " As the master had
made it an axiom to avoid what was mean or low, so
the disciples endeavored to escape from what was
common. This they contrived by the ready expedient
of the periphrasis. They called everything something
else. A boot with them was

> " ' The shining leather that encased the limb.'

* Johnson, " Prologue at the Opening of Drury Lane," 1747.
† See Coleridge, " Biographia Literaria," chap. xviii

Coffee became

" ' The fragrant juice of Mocha's berry brown.' "*

" For the direct appeal to Nature, and the naming of specific objects," says Mr. Gosse,† "they substituted generalities and second-hand allusions. They no longer mentioned the gillyflower and the daffodil, but permitted themselves a general reference to Flora's vernal wreath. It was vulgar to say that the moon was rising; the gentlemanly expression was, ' Cynthia is lifting her silver horn!' Women became nymphs in this new phraseology, fruits became ' the treasures of Pomona,' a horse became ' the impatient courser.' The result of coining these conventional counters for groups of ideas was that the personal, the exact, was lost in literature. Apples were the treasures of Pomona, but so were cherries, too, and if one wished to allude to peaches, they also were the treasures of Pomona. This decline from particular to general language was regarded as a great gain in elegance. It was supposed that to use one of these genteel counters, which passed for coin of poetic language, brought the speaker closer to the grace of Latinity. It was thought that the old direct manner of speaking was crude and futile; that a romantic poet who wished to allude to caterpillars could do so without any exercise of his ingenuity by simply introducing the word ' caterpillars,' whereas the classical poet had to prove that he was a scholar and a gentleman by inventing some circumlocution, such as ' the crawling scourge

* Essay on Pope, in " My Study Windows."
† " From Shakespere to Pope," pp. 9–11.

that smites the leafy plain.' . . In the generation
that succeeded Pope really clever writers spoke of a
'gelid cistern,' when they meant a cold bath, and 'the
loud hunter-crew' when they meant a pack of fox-
hounds."

It would be a mistake to suppose that the men of
Pope's generation, including Pope himself, were altogether wanting in romantic feeling. There is a
marked romantic accent in the Countess of Winchelsea's ode "To the Nightingale"; in her "Nocturnal
Reverie"; in Parnell's "Night Piece on Death," and
in the work of several Scotch poets, like Allan Ramsay and Hamilton of Bangour, whose ballad, "The
Braes of Yarrow," is certainly a strange poem to come
out of the heart of the eighteenth century. But these
are eddies and back currents in the stream of literary
tendency. We are always in danger of forgetting that
the literature of an age does not express its entire,
but only its prevailing, spirit. There is commonly
a latent, silent body of thought and feeling underneath
which remains inarticulate, or nearly so. It is this
prevailing spirit and fashion which I have endeavored
to describe in the present chapter. If the picture
seems to lack relief, or to be in any way exaggerated,
the reader should consult the chapters on "Classicism" and "The Pseudo-Classicists" in M. Pellissier's
"Literary Movement in France," already several times
referred to. They describe a literary situation which
had a very exact counterpart in England.

CHAPTER III.

The Spenserians.

DISSATISFACTION with a prevalent mood or fashion in literature is apt to express itself either in a fresh and independent criticism of life, or in a reversion to older types. But, as original creative genius is not always forthcoming, a literary revolution commonly begins with imitation. It seeks inspiration in the past, and substitutes a new set of models as different as possible from those which it finds currently followed. In every country of Europe the classical tradition had hidden whatever was most national, most individual, in its earlier culture, under a smooth, uniform veneer. To break away from modern convention, England and Germany, and afterward France, went back to ancient springs of national life; not always, at first, wisely, but in obedience to a true instinct.

How far did any knowledge or love of the old romantic literature of England survive among the contemporaries of Dryden and Pope? It is not hard to furnish an answer to this question. The prefaces of Dryden, the critical treatises of Dennis, Winstanley, Oldmixon, Rymer, Langbaine, Gildon, Shaftesbury, and many others, together with hundreds of passages in prologues and epilogues to plays; in periodical essays like the *Tatler* and *Spectator;* in verse essays

like Roscommon's, Mulgrave's, and Pope's; in prefaces
to various editions of Shakspere and Spenser; in
letters, memoirs, etc., supply a mass of testimony to
the fact that neglect and contempt had, with a few
exceptions, overtaken all English writers who wrote
before the middle of the seventeenth century. The
exceptions, of course, were those supreme masters
whose genius prevailed against every change of taste:
Shakspere and Milton, and, in a less degree, Chaucer
and Spenser. Of authors strictly mediæval, Chaucer
still had readers, and there were reprints of his works
in 1687, 1721 and 1737,* although no critical edition
appeared until Tyrwhitt's in 1775–78. It is probable,
however, that the general reader, if he read Chaucer
at all, read him in such modernized versions as Dryden's "Fables" and Pope's "January and May."
Dryden's preface has some admirable criticism of
Chaucer, although it is evident, from what he says
about the old poet's versification, that the secret of
Middle English scansion and pronunciation had
already been lost. Prior and Pope, who seem to have
been attracted chiefly to the looser among the
"Canterbury Tales," made each a not very successful experiment at burlesque imitation of Chaucerian
language.

Outside of Chaucer, and except among antiquarians
and professional scholars, there was no remembrance
of the whole *corpus poetarum* of the English Middle
Age: none of the metrical romances, rhymed chronicles, saints' legends, miracle plays, minstrel ballads,
verse homilies, manuals of devotion, animal fables,

* A small portion of the "Canterbury Tales." Edited by Morell.

courtly or popular allegories and love songs of the thirteenth, fourteenth, and fifteenth centuries. Nor was there any knowledge or care about the master-pieces of mediæval literature in other languages than English; about such representative works as the " Nibelungenlied," the " Chanson de Roland," the " Roman de la Rose," the " Parzival " of Wolfram von Eschenbach, the " Tristan " of Gottfried of Stras-burg, the " Arme Heinrich " of Hartmann von Aue, the chronicles of Villehardouin, Joinville, and Frois-sart, the " Morte Artus," the " Dies Iræ," the lyrics of the troubadour Bernart de Ventadour, and of the minnesinger Walther von der Vogelweide, the Span-ish Romancero, the poems of the Elder Edda, the romances of "Amis et Amile " and " Aucassin et Nicolete," the writings of Villon, the " De Imitatione Christi " ascribed to Thomas à Kempis. Dante was a great name and fame, but he was virtually un-read.

There is nothing strange about this; many of these things were still in manuscript and in unknown tongues, Old Norse, Old French, Middle High Ger-man, Middle English, Mediæval Latin. It would be hazardous to assert that the general reader, or even the educated reader, of to-day has much more acquaintance with them at first hand than his ancestor of the eighteenth century; or much more acquaintance than he has with Æschylus, Thucydides, and Lu-cretius, at first hand. But it may be confidently asserted that he knows much more *about* them; that he thinks them worth knowing about; and that through modern, popular versions of them—through poems, historical romances, literary histories, essays,

and what not—he has in his mind's eye a picture of
the Middle Age, perhaps as definite and fascinating as
the picture of classical antiquity. That he has so is
owing to the romantic movement. For the significant
circumstance about the attitude of the last century
toward the whole mediæval period was, not its ignorance, but its incuriosity. It did not want to hear
anything about it.* Now and then, hints Pope, an

* The sixteenth [*sic. Quære,* seventeenth?] century had an in-
stinctive repugnance for the crude literature of the Middle Ages, the
product of so strange and incoherent a civilization. Here classicism
finds nothing but grossness and barbarism, never suspecting that it
might contain germs, which, with time and genius, might develop
into a poetical growth, doubtless less pure, but certainly more complex in its harmonies, and of a more expressive form of beauty. The
history of our ancient poetry, traced in a few lines by Boileau,
clearly shows to what degree he either ignored or misrepresented it.
The singular, confused architecture of Gothic cathedrals gave those
who saw beauty in symmetry of line and purity of form but further
evidence of the clumsiness and perverted taste of our ancestors. All
remembrance of the great poetic works of the Middle Ages is completely effaced. No one supposes in those barbarous times the existence of ages classical also in their way; no one imagines either their
heroic songs or romances of adventure, either the rich bounty of
lyrical styles or the naïve, touching crudity of the Christian drama.
The seventeenth century turned disdainfully away from the monuments of national genius discovered by it; finding them sometimes
shocking in their rudeness, sometimes puerile in their refinements.
These unfortunate exhumations, indeed, only serve to strengthen its
cult for a simple, correct beauty, the models of which are found in
Greece and Rome. Why dream of penetrating the darkness of our
origin? Contemporary society is far too self-satisfied to seek dis-
traction in the study of a past which it does not comprehend. The
subjects and heroes of domestic history are also prohibited. Corneille
is Latin, Racine is Greek; the very name of Childebrande suffices to
cover an epopee with ridicule.—*Pellissier,* pp. 7–8.

antiquarian pedant, a university don, might affect an admiration for some obsolete author:

> " Chaucer's worst ribaldry is learned by rote,
> And beastly Skelton heads of houses quote:
> One likes no language but the ' Faery Queen ';
> A Scot will fight for " ' Christ's Kirk o' the Green.' " *

But, furthermore, the great body of Elizabethan and Stuart literature was already obsolescent. Dramatists of the rank of Marlowe and Webster, poets like George Herbert and Robert Herrick—favorites with our own generation—prose authors like Sir Thomas Browne—from whom Coleridge and Emerson drew inspiration—had fallen into "the portion of weeds and outworn faces." Even writers of such recent, almost contemporary, repute as Donne, whom Carew had styled

> " —a king who ruled, as he thought fit,
> The universal monarchy of wit " :

or as Cowley, whom Dryden called the darling of his youth, and who was esteemed in his own lifetime a better poet than Milton; even Donne and Cowley had no longer a following. Pope "versified" some of Donne's rugged satires, and Johnson quoted passages from him as examples of the bad taste of the metaphysical poets. This in the "Life of Cowley," with which Johnson began his "Lives of the Poets," as though Cowley was the first of the moderns. But,

> " Who now reads Cowley ? "

asks Pope in 1737.* The year of the Restoration (1660) draws a sharp line of demarcation between the

---

* " Epistle to Augustus."

old and the new. In 1675, the year after Milton's death, his nephew, Edward Philips, published "Theatrum Poetarum," a sort of biographical dictionary of ancient and modern authors. In the preface, he says: "As for the antiquated and fallen into obscurity from their former credit and reputation, they are, for the most part, those that have written beyond the verge of the present age; for let us look back as far as about thirty or forty years, and we shall find a profound silence of the poets beyond that time, except of some few dramatics."

This testimony is the more convincing, since Philips was something of a *laudator temporis acti*. He praises several old English poets and sneers at several new ones, such as Cleaveland and Davenant, who were high in favor with the royal party. He complains that nothing now "relishes so well as what is written in the smooth style of our present language, taken to be of late so much refined"; that "we should be so compliant with the French custom, as to follow set fashions"; that the imitation of Corneille has corrupted the English stage; and that Dryden, "complying with the modefied and gallantish humour of the time," has, in his heroic plays, "indulged a little too much to the French way of continual rime." One passage, at least, in Philips' preface has been thought to be an echo of Milton's own judgment on the pretensions of the new school of poetry. "Wit, ingenuity, and learning in verse; even elegancy itself, though that comes nearest, are one thing. True native poetry is another; in which there is a certain air and spirit which perhaps the most learned and judicious in other arts do not perfectly apprehend,

much less is it attainable by any study or industry.
Nay, though all the laws of heroic poem, all the laws
of tragedy were exactly observed, yet still this *tour
entrejeant*—this poetic energy, if I may so call it,
would be required to give life to all the rest; which
shines through the roughest, most unpolished, and
antiquated language, and may haply be wanting in
the most polite and reformed.   Let us observe
Spenser, with all his rusty, obsolete words, with all
his rough-hewn clouterly verses; yet take him
throughout, and we shall find in him a graceful and
poetic majesty.   In like manner, Shakspere in spite
of all his unfiled expressions, his rambling and
indigested fancies—the laughter of the critical—yet
must be confessed a poet above many that go beyond
him in literature * some degrees."

The laughter of the critical!   Let us pause upon the
phrase, for it is a key to the whole attitude of the
Augustan mind toward "our old tragick poet."
Shakspere was already a national possession.   Indeed
it is only after the Restoration that we find any clear
recognition of him, as one of the greatest—as perhaps
himself the very greatest—of the dramatists of all
time.   For it is only after the Restoration that criticism begins.   "Dryden," says Dr. Johnson, "may be
properly considered as the father of English criticism,
as the writer who first taught us to determine, upon
principles, the merit of composition. . . Dryden's
'Essay of Dramatic Poesy' [1667] was the first
regular and valuable treatise on the art of writing." †
The old theater was dead and Shakspere now emerged

---

* *I. e.*, learning.   † " Life of Dryden."

from amid its ruins, as the one unquestioned legacy
of the Elizabethan age to the world's literature. He
was not only the favorite of the people, but in a
critical time, and a time whose canons of dramatic
art were opposed to his practice, he united the suf-
frages of all the authoritative leaders of literary
opinion. Pope's lines are conclusive as to the veneration in which Shakspere's memory was held a century
after his death.

> " On Avon's banks, where flowers eternal blow,
>   If I but ask, if any weed can grow ;
>   One tragic sentence if I dare deride
>   Which Betterton's grave action dignified. . .
>   How will our fathers rise up in a rage,
>   And swear, all shame is lost in George's age. " *

The Shaksperian tradition is unbroken in the history of English literature and of the English theater.
His plays, in one form or another, have always kept
the stage even in the most degenerate condition of
public taste.† Few handsomer tributes have been

* " Epistle to Augustus."

† The tradition as to Chaucer, Spenser, and Milton is almost
equally continuous. A course of what Lowell calls "penitential
reading," in Restoration criticism, will convince anyone that these
four names already stood out distinctly, as those of the four greatest
English poets. See especially Winstanley, " Lives of the English
Poets," 1687 ; Langbaine, " An Account of the English Dramatic
Poets," 1691 ; Dennis, " Essay on the Genius and Writings of
Shakspere," 1712 ; Gildon, " The Complete Art of Poetry," 1718.
The fact mentioned by Macaulay, that Sir Wm. Temple's " Essay
on Ancient and Modern Learning" names none of the four, is without importance. Temple refers by name to only three English
" wits," Sidney, Bacon, and Selden. This very superficial performance of Temple's was a contribution to the futile controversy over the

paid to Shakspere's genius than were paid in prose and verse, by the critics of our classical age, from Dryden to Johnson. "To begin then with Shakspere," says the former, in his "Essay of Dramatic Poesy," "he was the man who, of all modern and perhaps ancient poets, had the largest and most comprehensive soul." And, in the prologue to his adaptation of "The Tempest," he acknowledges that

> "Shakspere's magic could not copied be :
> Within that circle none durst walk but he."

"The poet of whose works I have undertaken the revision," writes Dr. Johnson, "may now begin to assume the dignity of an ancient, and claim the privilege of established fame and prescriptive veneration." *

> " Each change of many-colored life he drew,
> Exhausted worlds, and then imagined new." †

Yet Dryden made many petulant, and Johnson many fatuous mistakes about Shakspere; while such minor criticasters as Thomas Rymer ‡ and Mrs. Charlotte Lenox § uttered inanities of blasphemy about the finest touches in " Macbeth " and " Othello." For if we look closer, we notice that everyone who bore

relative merits of the ancients and moderns, which is now only of interest as having given occasion to Bentley to display his great scholarship in his " Dissertation on the Epistles of Phalaris," (1698), and to Swift to show his powers of irony in " The Battle of the Books " (1704).

* Preface to the '' Plays of Shakspere,'' 1765.

† Prologue, spoken by Garrick at the opening of Drury Lane Theater, 1747.

‡'' The Tragedies of the Last Age Considered and Examined,'' 1678

§ " Shakspere Illustrated," 1753.

witness to Shakspere's greatness qualified his praise
by an emphatic disapproval of his methods.   He was a
prodigious genius, but a most defective artist.   He was
the supremest of dramatic poets, but he did not know
his business.   It did not apparently occur to anyone
—except, in some degree, to Johnson—that there was
an absurdity in this contradiction; and that the real
fault was not in Shakspere, but in the standards by
which he was tried.   Here are the tests which technical criticism has always been seeking to impose, and
they are not confined to the classical period only.
They are used by Sidney, who took the measure of the
English buskin before Shakspere had begun to write;
by Jonson, who measured socks with him in his own
day; by Matthew Arnold, who wanted an English Academy, but in whom the academic vaccine, after so long a
transmission, worked but mildly.   Shakspere violated
the unities; his plays were neither right comedies nor
right tragedies; he had small Latin and less Greek;
he wanted art and sometimes sense, committing anach-
ronisms and Bohemian shipwrecks; wrote hastily,
did not blot enough, and failed of the grand style.   He
was "untaught, unpractised in a barbarous age"; a
wild, irregular child of nature, ignorant of the rules,
unacquainted with ancient models, succeeding—when
he did succeed—by happy accident and the sheer force
of genius; his plays were "roughdrawn," his plots
lame, his speeches bombastic; he was guilty on every
page of "some solecism or some notorious flaw in
sense." *

Langbaine, to be sure, defends him against Dryden's

* See Dryden's " Grounds of Criticism in Tragedy " and " Defence
of the Epilogue to the Conquest of Granada."

censure. But Dennis regrets his ignorance of poetic art and the disadvantages under which he lay from not being conversant with the ancients.   If he had known his Sallust, he would have drawn a juster picture of Cæsar; and if he had read Horace "Ad Pisones," he would have made a better Achilles.   He complains that he makes the good and the bad perish promiscuously; and that in "Coriolanus"—a play which Dennis "improved" for the new stage—he represents Menenius as a buffoon and introduces the rabble in a most undignified fashion.*   Gildon, again, says that Shakspere must have read Sidney's "Defence of Poesy" and therefore, ought to have known the rules and that his neglect of them was owing to laziness. "Money seems to have been his aim more than reputation, and therefore he was always in a hurry . . . and he thought it time thrown away, to study regularity and order, when any confused stuff that came into his head would do his business and fill his house." †

It would be easy, but it would be tedious, to multiply proofs of this patronizing attitude toward Shakspere.   Perhaps Pope voices the general sentiment of his school, as fairly as anyone, in the last words of his preface.‡   "I will conclude by saying of Shakspere that, with all his faults and with all the irregularity of his *drama*, one may

* "Essay on the Genius and Writings of Shakspere," 1712.

† "The Art of Poetry," pp. 63 and 99. *Cf*. Pope, "Epistle to Augustus":

> "Shakspere (whom you and every play-house bill
> Style the divine, the matchless, what you will)
> For gain, not glory, winged his roving flight,
> And grew immortal in his own despite."

‡ Pope's "Shakspere," 1725.

look upon his works, in comparison of those that
are more finished and regular, as upon an ancient,
majestic piece of Gothic architecture compared with a
neat, modern building. The latter is more elegant
and glaring, but the former is more strong and
solemn. . . It has much the greater variety, and
much the nobler apartments, though we are often conducted to them by dark, odd and uncouth passages.
Nor does the whole fail to strike us with greater reverence, though many of the parts are childish, ill-
placed and unequal to its grandeur." This view of
Shakspere continued to be the rule until Coleridge and
Schlegel taught the new century that this child of
fancy was, in reality, a profound and subtle artist, but
that the principles of his art—as is always the case with
creative genius working freely and instinctively—were
learned by practice, in the concrete, instead of being
consciously thrown out by the workman himself into
an abstract *theoria;* so that they have to be discovered by a reverent study of his work and lie deeper
than the rules of French criticism. Schlegel, whose
lectures on dramatic art were translated into English
in 1815, speaks with indignation of the current
English misunderstanding of Shakspere. "That
foreigners, and Frenchmen in particular, who frequently speak in the strangest language about antiquity and the Middle Age, as if cannibalism had been
first put an end to in Europe by Louis XIV., should
entertain this opinion of Shakspere might be pardon-
able. But that Englishmen should adopt such a ca-
lumniation . . . is to me incomprehensible."*

* For a fuller discussion of this subject, consult " A History of
Opinion on the Writings of Shakspere," in the supplemental volume

The beginnings of the romantic movement in England were uncertain.   There was a vague dissent
from current literary estimates, a vague discontent
with reigning literary modes, especially with the
merely intellectual poetry then in vogue, which did

of Knight's Pictorial Edition.   Editions of Shakspere issued within
the century following the Restoration were the third Folio, 1664 ; the
fourth Folio, 1685; Rowe's (the first critical edition, with a Life, etc.)
1709 (second edition, 1714) ; Pope's, 1725 (second edition, 1728);
Theobald's, 1733 ; Hanmer's 1744 ; Warburton-Pope's, 1747 ; and
Johnson's, 1765.   Meanwhile, though Shakspere's plays continued to
be acted, it was mostly in doctored versions.   Tate changed " Lear"
to a comedy.   Davenant and Dryden made over " The Tempest " into
" The Enchanted Island," turning blank verse into rhyme and introducing new characters, while Shadwell altered it into an opera.
Dryden rewrote " Troilus and Cressida "; Davenant, " Macbeth."
Davenant patched together a thing which he called " The
Law against Lovers," from " Measure for Measure " and " Much
Ado about Nothing."   Dennis remodeled the " Merry Wives
of Windsor " as " The Comical Gallant " ; Tate, " Richard II."
as " The Sicilian Usurper"; and Otway, " Romeo and Juliet,"
as " Caius Marius."   Lord Lansdowne converted " The Merchant
of Venice " into " The Jew of Venice, " wherein Shylock
was played as a comic character down to the time of Mack-
lin and Kean.   Durfey tinkered " Cymbeline."   Cibber meta-
morphosed " King John " into " Papal Tyranny," and his version
was acted till Macready's time.   Cibber's stage version of " Richard III." is played still.   Cumberland " engrafted " new features
upon " Timon of Athens " for Garrick's theater, about 1775.   In his
life of Mrs. Siddons, Campbell says that " Coriolanus " " was never
acted genuinely from the year 1660 till the year 1820 " (Phillimore's
" Life of Lyttelton," Vol. I. p. 315).   He mentions a revision by
Tate, another by Dennis (" The Invader of his Country "), and a third
brought out by the elder Sheridan in 1764, at Covent Garden, and put
together from Shakspere's tragedy and an independent play of the
same name by Thomson.   " Then in 1789 came the Kemble edition
in which . . .   much of Thomson's absurdity is still preserved."

not feed the soul. But there was, at first, no conscious, concerted effort toward something better;
still less was there any sudden outburst of creative
activity. The new group of poets, partly contemporaries of Pope, partly successors to him—Thomson,
Shenstone, Dyer, Akenside, Gray, Collins, and the
Warton brothers—found their point of departure
in the loving study and revival of old authors.
From what has been said of the survival of Shakspere's influence it might be expected that his would
have been the name paramount among the pioneers of
English romanticism. There are several reasons why
this was not the case.

In the first place, the genius of the new poets was
lyrical or descriptive, rather than dramatic. The
divorce between literature and the stage had not yet,
indeed, become total; and, in obedience to the expectation that every man of letters should try his
hand at play-writing, Thomson, at least, as well as his
friend and disciple Mallet, composed a number of
dramas. But these were little better than failures
even at the time; and while "The Seasons" has
outlived all changes of taste, and "The Castle of
Indolence" has never wanted admirers, tragedies like
"Agamemnon" and "Sophonisba" have been long
forgotten. An imitation of Shakspere to any effective purpose must obviously have taken the shape of
a play; and neither Gray nor Collins nor Akenside,
nor any of the group, was capable of a play. Inspiration of a kind, these early romanticists did draw from
Shakspere. Verbal reminiscences of him abound in
Gray. Collins was a diligent student of his works.
His "Dirge in Cymbeline" is an exquisite variation

on a Shaksperian theme.   In the delirium of his last
sickness, he told Warton that he had found in an
Italian novel the long-sought original of the plot of
"The Tempest."   It is noteworthy, by the way, that
the romanticists were attracted to the poetic, as
distinguished from the dramatic, aspect of Shakspere's genius; to those of his plays in which fairy lore
and supernatural machinery occur, such as "The
Tempest" and "A Midsummer Night's Dream."

Again, the stage has a history of its own, and, in
so far as it was now making progress of any kind, it
was not in the direction of a more poetic or romantic
drama, but rather toward prose tragedy and the sentimental comedy of domestic life, what the French call
la tragédie bourgeoise and *la comédie larmoyante.*   In
truth the theater was now dying; and, though, in the
comedies of Goldsmith and Sheridan, it sent up one
bright, expiring gleam, the really dramatic talent of
the century had already sought other channels in the
novels of Richardson, Fielding, and Smollett.

After all, a good enough reason why the romantic
movement did not begin with imitation of Shakspere
is the fact that Shakspere is inimitable.   He has no
one manner that can be caught, but a hundred
manners; is not the poet of romance, but of human-
ity; nor mediæval, but perpetually modern and con-
temporaneous in his universality.   The very familiarity of his plays, and their continuous performance,
although in mangled forms, was a reason why they
could take little part in a literary revival; for what
has never been forgotten cannot be revived.   To
Germany and France, at a later date, Shakspere
came with the shock of a discovery and begot Schiller

and Victor Hugo. In the England of the eighteenth century he begot only Ireland's forgeries.

The name inscribed in large letters on the standard of the new school was not Shakspere but Spenser. If there is any poet who is *par excellence* the poet of romance, whose art is the antithesis of Pope's, it is the poet of the "Faërie Queene." To ears that had heard from childhood the tinkle of the couplet, with its monotonously recurring rhyme, its inevitable cæsura, its narrow imprisonment of the sense, it must have been a relief to turn to the amplitude of Spenser's stanza, "the full strong sail of his great verse." To a generation surfeited with Pope's rhetorical devices —antithesis, climax, anticlimax—and fatigued with the unrelaxing brilliancy and compression of his language; the escape from epigram and point (snap after snap, like a pack of fire-crackers), from a style which has made his every other line a proverb or current quotation— the escape from all this into Spenser's serene, leisurely manner, copious Homeric similes, and lingering detail must have seemed most restful. To go from Pope to Spenser was to exchange platitudes, packed away with great verbal cunning in neat formulas readily portable by the memory, for a wealth of concrete images: to exchange saws like,

" A little learning is a dangerous thing,"

for a succession of richly colored pictures by the greatest painter among English poets. It was to exchange the most prosaic of our poets—a poet about whom question has arisen whether he is a poet at all —for the most purely poetic of our poets, "the poet's poet." And finally, it was to exchange the world of everyday manners and artificial society for an imaginary kingdom of enchantment, "out of space, out of time."

English poetry has oscillated between the poles of Spenser and Pope. The poets who have been accepted by the race as most truly national, poets like Shakspere, Milton, and Byron, have stood midway. Neither Spenser nor Pope satisfies long. We weary, in time, of the absence of passion and intensity in Spenser, his lack of dramatic power, the want of actuality in his picture of life, the want of brief energy and nerve in his style; just as we weary of Pope's inadequate sense of beauty. But at a time when English poetry had abandoned its true function— the refreshment and elevation of the soul through the imagination—Spenser's poetry, the poetry of ideal beauty, formed the most natural corrective. Whatever its deficiencies, it was not, at any rate, "conceived and composed in his wits."

Spenser had not fared so well as Shakspere under the change which came over public taste after the Restoration. The age of Elizabeth had no literary reviews or book notices, and its critical remains are of the scantiest. But the complimentary verses by many hands published with the "Faërie Queene" and the numerous references to Spenser in the whole poetic literature of the time, leave no doubt as to the fact that his contemporaries accorded him the foremost place among English poets. The tradition of his supremacy lasted certainly to the middle of the seventeenth century, if not beyond. His influence is visible not only in the work of professed disciples like Giles and Phineas Fletcher, the pastoral poet William

Browne, and Henry More, the Cambridge Platonist, but in the verse of Jonson, Fletcher, Milton, and many others. Milton confessed to Dryden that Spenser was his "poetical father." Dryden himself and Cowley, whose practice is so remote from Spenser's, acknowledged their debt to him. The passage from Cowley's essay "On Myself" is familiar: "I remember when I began to read, and to take some pleasure in it, there was wont to lie in my mother's parlour (I know not by what accident, for she herself never read any book but of devotion—but there was wont to lie) Spenser's works. This I happened to fall upon, and was infinitely delighted with the stories of the knights and giants and monsters and brave houses which I found everywhere there (though my understanding had little to do with all this), and, by degrees, with the tinkling of the rime and dance of the numbers; so that I think I had read him all over before I was twelve years old, and was thus made a poet as irremediably as a child is made an eunuch." It is a commonplace that Spenser has made more poets than any other one writer. Even Pope, whose empire he came back from Fairyland to overthrow, assured Spence that he had read the "Faërie Queene" with delight when he was a boy, and re-read it with equal pleasure in his last years. Indeed, it is too readily assumed that writers are insensible to the beauties of an opposite school. Pope was quite incapable of making romantic poetry, but not, therefore, incapable of appreciating it. He took a great liking to Allan Ramsay's "Gentle Shepherd"; he admired "The Seasons," and did Thomson the honor to insert a few lines of his own in "Summer." Among his youthful parodies of old English poets is one piece entitled "The Alley," a not over clever burlesque of the famous description of the Bower of Bliss.*

As for Dryden, his reverence for Spenser is qualified by the same sort of critical disapprobation which we noticed in his eulogies of Shakspere. He says that the "Faërie Queene" has no uniformity: the language is not so obsolete as is commonly supposed, and is intelligible after some practice; but the choice of stanza is unfortunate, though in spite of it, Spenser's verse is more melodious than any other English poet's except Mr. Waller's.† Ambrose Philips — Namby Pamby Philips—whom Thackeray calls "a dreary idyllic cockney," appealed to "The Shepherd's Calendar" as his model, in the introduction to his insipid "Pastorals," 1709. Steele, in No. 540 of the *Spectator* (November 19, 1712), printed some mildly commendatory remarks about Spenser. Altogether it is clear that Spenser's greatness was accepted, rather upon trust, throughout the classical period, but that this belief was coupled with a general indifference to his writings. Addison's lines in his "Epistle to Sacheverel; An Account of the Greatest English Poets," 1694, probably represent accurately enough the opinion of the majority of readers:

> " Old Spenser next, warmed with poetic rage,
>   In ancient tales amused a barbarous age;
>   An age that, yet uncultivate and rude,
>   Where'er the poet's fancy led, pursued,
>   Through pathless fields and unfrequented floods,
>   To dens of dragons and enchanted woods.

* " Faërie Queene," II. xii. 71.
† " Essay on Satire." Philips says a good word for the Spenserian stanza: " How much more stately and majestic in epic poems, espe-

> But now the mystic tale, that pleased of yore,
> Can charm an understanding age no more.
> The long-spun allegories fulsome grow,
> While the dull moral lies too plain below.
> We view well pleased at distance all the sights
> Of arms and palfreys, battles, fields and fights,
> And damsels in distress and courteous knights,
> But when we look too near, the shades decay
> And all the pleasing landscape fades away."

Addison acknowledged to Spence that, when he wrote this passage, he had never read Spenser! As late as 1754 Thomas Warton speaks of him as " this admired but neglected poet," * and Mr. Kitchin asserts that "between 1650 and 1750 there are but few notices of him, and very few editions of his works." † There was a reprint of Spenser's works—being the third folio of the " Faërie Queene "—in 1679, but no critical edition till 1715. Meanwhile the title of a book issued in 1687 shows that Spenser did not escape that process of "improvement" which we have seen applied to Shakspere: " Spenser Redivivus; containing the First Book of the ' Faëry Queene.' His Essential Design Preserved, but his Obsolete Language and Manner of Verse totally laid aside. Delivered in Heroic Numbers by a Person of Quality." The preface praises Spenser, but declares that "his style seems no less unintelligible at this day than the obso-

---

cially of heroic argument, Spenser's stanza . . . is above the way either of couplet or alternation of four verses only, I am persuaded, were it revived, would soon be acknowledged."— *Theatrum Poetatarum*, Preface, pp. 3–4.

* " Observations on the Faëry Queene," Vol. II. p. 317.

† " The Faëry Queene," Book I., Oxford, 1869. Introduction, p. xx.

letest of our English or Saxon dialect." One instance
of this deliverance into heroic numbers must suffice:

> " By this the northern wagoner had set
> His sevenfold team behind the steadfast star
> That was in ocean waves yet never wet,
> But firm is fixed, and sendeth light from far
> To all that in the wide deep wandering are."
>
> *—Spenser.*

In 1715 John Hughes published his edition of
Spenser's works in six volumes. This was the first
attempt at a critical text of the poet, and was accompanied with a biography, a glossary, an essay on allegorical poetry, and some remarks on the "Faërie
Queene." It is curious to find in the engravings, from
designs by Du Guernier, which illustrate Hughes'
volumes, that Spenser's knights wore the helmets and
body armor of the Roman legionaries, over which is
occasionally thrown something that looks very much
like a toga. The lists in which they run a tilt have the
façade of a Greek temple for a background. The
house of Busyrane is Louis Quatorze architecture, and
Amoret is chained to a renaissance column with
Corinthian capital and classical draperies. Hughes'
glossary of obsolete terms includes words which are in
daily use by modern writers: aghast, baleful, behest,
bootless, carol, craven, dreary, forlorn, foray, guer-
don, plight, welkin, yore. If words like these, and
like many which Warton annotates in his "Observations," really needed explanation, it is a striking

---

* "Canto " ii. stanza i.
  " Now had Bootes' team far passed behind
    The northern star, when hours of night declined."
  —Person of Quality

proof, not only of the degree in which our older poets had been forgotten, but also of the poverty to which the vocabulary of English poetry had been reduced by 1700.

In his prefatory remarks to the "Faërie Queene," the editor expresses the customary regrets that the poet should have chosen so defective a stanza, "so romantick a story," and a model, or framework for the whole, which appears so monstrous when "examined by the rules of epick poetry"; makes the hackneyed comparison between Spenser's work and Gothic architecture, and apologizes for his author, on the ground that, at the time when he wrote, "the remains of the old Gothick chivalry were not quite abolished." "He did not much revive the curiosity of the public," says Johnson, in his life of Hughes; "for near thirty years elapsed before his edition was reprinted." Editions of the "Faërie Queene" came thick and fast about the middle of the century. One (by Birch) was issued in 1751, and three in 1758; including the important edition by Upton, who, of all Spenser's commentators, has entered most elaborately into the interpretation of the allegory.

In the interval had appeared, in gradually increasing numbers, that series of Spenserian imitations which forms an interesting department of eighteenth-century verse. The series was begun by a most unlikely person, Matthew Prior, whose "Ode to the Queen," 1706, was in a ten-lined modification of Spenser's stanza and employed a few archaisms like *weet* and *ween*, but was very unspenserian in manner. As early as the second decade of the century, the horns of Elfland may be heard faintly blowing in the poems of the Rev. Samuel Croxall, the translator of Æsop's "Fables." Mr. Gosse * quotes Croxall's own description of his poetry, as designed " to set off the dry and insipid stuff " of the age with " a whole piece of rich and glowing scarlet." His two pieces " The Vision," 1715, and " The Fair Circassian," 1720, though written in the couplet, exhibit a rosiness of color and a luxuriance of imagery manifestly learned from Spenser. In 1713 he had published, under the pseudonym of Nestor Ironside, "An Original Canto of Spenser," and in 1714 " Another Original Canto," both, of course, in the stanza of the " Faërie Queene." The example thus set was followed before the end of the century by scores of poets, including many well-known names, like Akenside, Thomson, Shenstone, and Thomas Warton, as well as many second-rate and third-rate versifiers. †

* " Eighteenth Century Literature," p. 139.

† For a full discussion of this subject the reader should consult Phelps' " Beginnings of the English Romantic Movement," chap. iv., " The Spenserian Revival." A partial list of Spenserian imitations is given in Todd's edition of Spenser, Vol. I. But the list in Prof. Phelps' Appendix, if not exhaustive, is certainly the most complete yet published and may be here reproduced. 1706 : Prior : " Ode to the Queen." 1713–21 : Prior (?) : " Colin's Mistakes." 1713 : Croxall : " An Original Canto of Spenser." 1714 : Croxall : " Another Original Canto." 1730 (*circa*) : Whitehead : " Vision of Solomon," " Ode to the Honorable Charles Townsend," " Ode to the Same." 1736 : Thompson : " Epithalamium." 1736 Cambridge : " Marriage of Frederick." 1736–37 : Boyse : " The Olive," " Psalm XLII." 1737 : Akenside : " The Virtuoso." 1739: West : " Abuse of Traveling." 1739 : Anon.: " A New Canto of Spenser's Fairy Queen." 1740 : Boyse : " Ode to the Marquis of Tavistock." 1741 (*circa*) : Boyse : " Vision of Patience." 1742 : Shenstone : " The Schoolmistress." 1742–50 : Cambridge : " Archimage." 1742 : Dodsley : " Pain and Patience." 1743 :

It is noteworthy that many, if not most, of the imitations were at first undertaken in a spirit of burlesque; as is plain not only from the poems themselves, but from the correspondence of Shenstone and others.* The antiquated speech of an old author is in itself a challenge to the parodist: *teste* our modern ballad imitations. There is something ludicrous about the very look of antique spelling, and in the sound of words like *eftsoones* and *perdy;* while the sign, *Ye Olde Booke Store,* in Old English text over a bookseller's door, strikes the public invariably as a most merry conceited jest; especially if the first letter be pronounced as a *y,*

Anon.: "Albion's Triumph." 1744 (*circa*) : Dodsley : "Death of Mr. Pope." 1744 : Akenside : "Ode to Curio." 1746 : Blacklock: "Hymn to Divine Love," "Philantheus." 1747 : Mason : Stanzas in "Musæus." 1747 : Ridley : "Psyche." 1747 : Lowth : "Choice of Hercules." 1747 : Upton : "A New Canto of Spenser's Fairy Queen." 1747 : Bedingfield : "Education of Achilles." 1747 : Pitt : "The Jordan." 1748 : T. Warton, Sr. : "Philander." 1748 : Thomson : "The Castle of Indolence." 1749 : Potter : "A Farewell Hymn to the Country." 1750 : T. Warton : "Morning." 1751 : West : "Education." 1751 : T. Warton : "Elegy on the Death of Prince Frederick." 1751 : Mendez : "The Seasons." 1751 : Lloyd : "Progress of Envy." 1751 : Akenside : "Ode." 1751 : Smith : "Thales." 1753 : T. Warton : "A Pastoral in the Manner of Spenser." 1754 : Denton : "Immortality." 1755 : Arnold : "The Mirror." 1748–58 : Mendez : "Squire of Dames." 1756 : Smart : "Hymn to the Supreme Being." 1757 : Thompson : "The Nativity," "Hymn to May." 1758 : Akenside : "To Country Gentlemen of England." 1759: Wilkie : "A Dream." 1759 : Poem in "Ralph's Miscellany." 1762 : Denton : "House of Superstition." 1767 : Mickle : "The Concubine." 1768 : Downman : "Land of the Muses." 1771–74 : Beattie : "The Ministrel." 1775 : Anon.: "Land of Liberty." 1775 : Mickle : Stanzas from "Introduction to the Lusiad."

* See Phelps, pp. 66–68.

instead of, what it really is, a mere abbreviation of *th*.
But in order that this may be so, the language
travestied should not be too old.   There would be
nothing amusing, for example, in a burlesque imitation
of Beowulf, because the Anglo-Saxon of the original
is utterly strange to the modern reader.   It is conceiv-
able that quick-witted Athenians of the time of Aristophanes might find something quaint in Homer's Ionic
dialect, akin to that quaintness which we find in
Chaucer; but a Grecian of to-day would need to be very
Attic indeed, to detect any provocation to mirth in
the use of the genitive in-*οιο*, in place of the genitive
in-*ον*.   Again, as one becomes familiar with an old
author, he ceases to be conscious of his archaism:
the final *e* in Chaucer no longer strikes him as funny,
nor even the circumstance that he speaks of little
birds as *smalë fowlës*.   And so it happened, that poets
in the eighteenth century who began with burlesque
imitation of the " Faërie Queene " soon fell in love with
its serious beauties.

The only poems in this series that have gained permanent footing in the literature are Shenstone's
"Schoolmistress " and Thomson's "Castle of Indolence."   But a brief review of several other members
of the group will be advisable.   Two of them were
written at Oxford in honor of the marriage of Frederick, Prince of Wales in 1736 : one by Richard Owen
Cambridge; * the other by William Thompson, then
bachelor of arts and afterward fellow of Queen's College.   Prince Fred, it will be remembered, was a

---

* See the sumptuous edition of Cambridge's " Works," issued by
his son in 1803.

somewhat flamboyant figure in the literary and personal gossip of his day. He quarreled with his father, George II., who "hated boetry and bainting," and who was ironically fed with soft dedication by Pope in his "Epistle to Augustus"; also with his father's prime minister, Sir Robert Walpole, "Bob, the poet's foe." He left the court in dudgeon and set up an opposition court of his own where he rallied about him men of letters, who had fallen into a neglect that contrasted strangely with their former importance in the reign of Queen Anne. Frederick's chief ally in this policy was his secretary, George Lord Lyttelton, the elegant if somewhat amateurish author of "Dialogues of the Dead" and other works; the friend of Fielding, the neighbor of Shenstone at Hagley, and the patron of Thomson, for whom he obtained the sinecure post of Surveyor of the Leeward Islands.

Cambridge's spousal verses were in a ten-lined stanza. His "Archimage," written in the strict Spenserian stanza, illustrates the frequent employment of this form in occasional pieces of a humorous intention. It describes a domestic boating party on the Thames, one of the oarsmen being a family servant and barber-surgeon, who used to dress the chaplain's hair:

> "Als would the blood of ancient beadsman spill,
> Whose hairy scalps he hangëd in a row
> Around his cave, sad sight to Christian eyes, I trow."

Thompson's experiments, on the contrary, were quite serious. He had genuine poetic feeling, but little talent. In trying to reproduce Spenser's richness of imagery and the soft modulation of his verse, he succeeds only in becoming tediously ornate. His stanzas are nerveless, though not unmusical. His college exercise, "The Nativity," 1736, is a Christmas vision which comes to the shepherd boy Thomalin, as he is piping on the banks of Isis. It employs the pastoral machinery, includes a masque of virtues,—Faith, Hope, Mercy, etc.,—and closes with a compliment to Pope's "Messiah." The preface to his "Hymn to May," has some bearing upon our inquiries: "As Spenser is the most descriptive and florid of all our English writers, I attempted to imitate his manner in the following vernal poem. I have been very sparing of the antiquated words which are too frequent in most of the imitations of this author. . . His lines are most musically sweet, and his descriptions most delicately abundant, even to a wantonness of painting, but still it is the music and painting of nature. We find no ambitious ornaments or epigrammatical turns in his writings, but a beautiful simplicity which pleases far above the glitter of pointed wit." The "Hymn to May" is in the seven-lined stanza of Phineas Fletcher's "Purple Island"; a poem, says Thompson, "scarce heard of in this age, yet the best in the allegorical way (next to 'The Fairy Queen') in the English language."

William Wilkie, a Scotch minister and professor, of eccentric habits and untidy appearance, published, in 1759, "A Dream: in the Manner of Spenser," which may be mentioned here not for its own sake, but for the evidence that it affords of a growing impatience of classical restraints. The piece was a pendant to Wilkie's epic, the "Epigoniad." Walking by the Tweed, the poet falls asleep and has a vision of Homer, who reproaches him with the bareness of style in his

"Epigoniad." The dreamer puts the blame upon the critics,

> " Who tie the muses to such rigid laws
>   That all their songs are frivolous and poor."

Shakspere, indeed,

> " Broke all the cobweb limits fixed by fools " ;

but the only reward of his boldness

> " Is that our dull, degenerate age of lead
>   Says that he wrote by chance, and that he scarce could read."

One of the earlier Spenserians was Gilbert West, the translator of Pindar, who published, in 1739, "On the Abuse of Travelling: A Canto in Imitation of Spenser."* Another imitation, "Education," appeared in 1751. West was a very tame poet, and the only quality of Spenser's which he succeeded in catching was his prolixity. He used the allegorical machinery of the "Faërie Queene" for moral and mildly satirical ends. Thus, in "The Abuse of Travelling,"

---

* " Mr. Walpole and I have frequently wondered you should never mention a certain imitation of Spenser, published last year by a namesake of yours, with which we are all enraptured and enmarveiled."— *Letter from Gray to Richard West*, Florence, July 16, 1740. There was no relationship between Gilbert West and Gray's Eton friend, though it seems that the former was also an Etonian, and was afterwards at Oxford, " whence he was seduced to a more airy mode of life," says Dr. Johnson, " by a commission in a troop of horse, procured him by his uncle." Cambridge, however, was an acquaintance of Gray, Walpole, and Richard West, at Eton. Gray's solitary sonnet was composed upon the death of Richard West in 1742 ; and it is worth noting that in the introduction to Cambridge's works are a number of sonnets by his friend Thomas Edwards, himself a Spenser lover, whose " sugared sonnets among his private friends " begin about 1750 and reach the number of fifty.

the Red Cross Knight is induced by Archimago to em-
bark in a painted boat steered by Curiosity, which
wafts him over to a foreign shore where he is entertained by a bevy of light damsels whose leader "hight
Politessa," and whose blandishments the knight resists.
Thence he is conducted to a stately castle (the court
of Louis XV. whose minister—perhaps Cardinal
Fleury?—is "an old and runkled mage "); and finally
to Rome, where a lady yclept Vertù holds court in the
ruins of the Colosseum, among mimes, fiddlers, pipers,
eunuchs, painters, and *ciceroni.*

Similarly the canto on "Education" narrates how
a fairy knight, while conducting his young son to the
house of Paidia, encounters the giant Custom and
worsts him in single combat. There is some humor
in the description of the stream of science into which
the crowd of infant learners are unwillingly plunged,
and upon whose margin stands

> "A *birchen* grove that, waving from the shore,
> Aye cast upon the tide its falling bud
> And with its bitter juice empoisoned all the flood."

The piece is a tedious arraignment of the pedantic
methods of instruction in English schools and colleges.
A passage satirizing the artificial style of gardening
will be cited later. West had a country-house at
Wickham, in Kent, where, says Johnson,* "he was
very often visited by Lyttelton and Pitt; who, when
they were weary of faction and debates, used at
Wickham to find books and quiet, a decent table and
literary conversation. There is at Wickham a walk
made by Pitt." Like many contemporary poets, West
interested himself in landscape gardening, and some

* " Life of West."

of his shorter pieces belong to that literature of inscriptions to which Lyttelton, Akenside, Shenstone, Mason, and others contributed so profusely. It may be said for his Spenserian imitations that their archaisms are unusually correct *—if that be any praise—a feature which perhaps recommended them to Gray, whose scholarship in this, as in all points, was nicely accurate. The obligation to be properly "obsolete" in vocabulary was one that rested heavily on the consciences of most of these Spenserian imitators. "The Squire of Dames," for instance, by the wealthy Jew, Moses Mendez, fairly bristles with seld-seen costly words, like *benty*, *frannion*, etc., which it would have puzzled Spenser himself to explain.

One of the pleasantest outcomes of this literary fashion was William Shenstone's "Schoolmistress," published in an unfinished shape in 1737 and, as finally completed, in 1742. This is an affectionate half-humorous description of the little dame-school of Shenstone's—and of everybody's—native village, and has the true idyllic touch. Goldsmith evidently had it in memory when he drew the picture of the school in his "Deserted Village." † The application to so

* Lloyd, in " The Progress of Envy," defines *wimpled* as " hung down " ; and Akenside, in " The Virtuoso," employs the ending *en* for the singular verb !

† *Cf.* " And as they looked, they found their horror grew."
    —*Shenstone.*
  " And still they gazed, and still the wonder grew."
    —*Goldsmith.*
    " The noises intermixed, which thence resound,
    Do learning's little tenement betray."
    —*Shenstone.*
  " There in his noisy mansion, skilled to rule," etc.
    —*Goldsmith*

humble a theme of Spenser's stately verse and **grave**, ancient words gives a very quaint effect. The humor of "The Schoolmistress" is genuine, not dependent on the mere burlesque, as in Pope's and Cambridge's experiments; and it is warmed with a certain tenderness, as in the incident of the hen with her brood of chickens, entering the open door of the schoolhouse in search of crumbs, and of the grief of the little sister who witnesses her brother's flogging, and of the tremors of the urchins who have been playing in the dame's absence:

> " Forewarned, if little bird their pranks behold,
>   'Twill whisper in her ear and all the scene unfold."

But the only one among the professed scholars of Spenser who caught the glow and splendor of the master was James Thomson. It is the privilege of genius to be original even in its imitations. Thomson took shape and hue from Spenser, but added something of his own, and the result has a value quite independent of its success as a reproduction. "The Castle of Indolence," 1748,* is a fine poem; at least the first part of it is, for the second book is tiresomely allegorical, and somewhat involved in plot. There is a magic art in the description of the " land of drowsyhead," with its "listless climate" always "atween June and May,"† its "stockdove's plaint amid the forest deep," its hillside woods of solemn pines, its gay castles in the summer clouds, and its murmur of

* The poem was projected, and perhaps partly written, fourteen or fifteen years earlier.

† *Cf.* Tennyson's "land in which it seemed always afternoon."— *The Lotus Eaters.*

the distant main. The nucleus of Thomson's conception is to be found in Spenser's House of Morpheus ("Faërie Queene," book i. canto i. 41), and his Country of Idlesse is itself an anticipation of Tennyson's Lotus Land, but verse like this was something new in the poetry of the eighteenth century:

> " Was nought around but images of rest:
> Sleep-soothing groves and quiet lawns between ;
> And flowery beds that slumbrous influence kest,
> From poppies breathed; and beds of pleasant green,
> Where never yet was creeping creature seen.
> Meantime unnumbered glittering streamlets played
> And hurlëd everywhere their waters sheen ;
> That, as they bickered through the sunny glade,
> Though restless still themselves, a lulling murmur made."

"The Castle of Indolence" had the romantic iridescence, the "atmosphere" which is lacking to the sharp contours of Augustan verse. That is to say, it produces an effect which cannot be wholly accounted for by what the poet says; an effect which is wrought by subtle sensations awakened by the sound and indefinite associations evoked by the words. The secret of this art the poet himself cannot communicate. But poetry of this kind cannot be translated into prose—as Pope's can—any more than music can be translated into speech, without losing its essential character. Like Spenser, Thomson was an exquisite colorist and his art was largely pictorial. But he has touches of an imagination which is rarer, if not higher in kind, than anything in Spenser. The fairyland of Spenser is an unreal, but hardly an unearthly region. He seldom startles by glimpses behind the curtain which hangs between nature and the supernatural, as in Milton's

> " Airy tongues that syllable men's names
> On sands and shores and desert wildernesses."

There is something of this power in one stanza, at least, of "The Castle of Indolence:"

> " As when a shepherd of the Hebrid Isles,
> Placed far amid the melancholy main
> (Whether it be lone fancy him beguiles,
> Or that aërial beings sometimes deign
> To stand embodied to our senses plain),
> Sees on the naked hill or valley low,
> The whilst in ocean Phœbus dips his wain,
> A vast assembly moving to and fro,
> Then all at once in air dissolves the wondrous show."

It may be guessed that Johnson and Boswell, in their tour to the Hebrides or Western Islands, saw nothing of the "spectral puppet play" hinted at in this passage—the most imaginative in any of Spenser's school till we get to Keats'

> ".Magic casements opening on the foam
> Of perilous seas in fairy lands forlorn."

William Julius Mickle, the translator of the "Lusiad," was a more considerable poet than any of the Spenserian imitators thus far reviewed, with the exception of Thomson and the possible exception of Shenstone. He wrote at least two poems that are likely to be remembered. One of these was the ballad of "Cumnor Hall" which suggested Scott's "Kenilworth," and came near giving its name to the novel

The other was the dialect song of "The Mariner's Wife," which Burns admired so greatly:

> " Sae true his heart, sae smooth his speech,
>   His breath like caller air.
>   His very foot has music in't,
>   As he comes up the stair.
>   For there's nae luck about the house,
>   There is nae luck at a',
>   There's little pleasure in the house
>   When our gudeman's awa'." *

Mickle, like Thomson, was a Scotchman who came to London to push his literary fortunes. He received some encouragement from Lyttelton, but was disappointed in his hopes of any substantial aid from that British Mæcenas. His biographer informs us that "about his thirteenth year, on Spenser's 'Faërie Queene' falling accidentally in his way, he was immediately struck with the picturesque descriptions of that much admired ancient bard and powerfully incited to imitate his style and manner." † In 1767 Mickle published "The Concubine," a Spenserian poem in two cantos. In the preface to his second edition, 1778, in which the title was changed to "Syr Martyn," he said that: "The fullness and wantonness of description, the quaint simplicity, and, above all, the ludicrous, of which the antique phraseology and manner of Spenser are so happily and peculiarly susceptible, inclined him to esteem it not solely as the

---

* Mickle's authorship of this song has been disputed in favor of one Jean Adams, a poor Scotch school-mistress, whose poems were printed at Glasgow in 1734.

† Rev. John Sim's "Life of Mickle" in "Mickle's Poetical Works," 1806, p. xi.

best, but the only mode of composition adapted to his subject."

"Syr Martyn" is a narrative poem not devoid of animation, especially where the author forgets his Spenser. But in the second canto he feels compelled to introduce an absurd allegory, in which the nymph Dissipation and her henchman Self-Imposition conduct the hero to the cave of Discontent. This is how Mickle writes when he is thinking of the "Faërie Queene":

> " Eke should he, freed from foul enchanter's spell,
> Escape his false Duessa's magic charms,
> And folly quaid, yclept an hydra fell,
> Receive a beauteous lady to his arms ;
> While bards and minstrels chaunt the soft alarms
> Of gentle love, unlike his former thrall :
> Eke should I sing, in courtly cunning terms,
> The gallant feast, served up by seneschal,
> To knights and ladies gent in painted bower or hall."

And this is how he writes when he drops his pattern:

> " Awake, ye west winds, through the lonely dale,
> And, Fancy, to thy faërie bower betake !
> Even now, with balmy freshness, breathes the gale,
> Dimpling with downy wing the stilly lake ;
> Through the pale willows faltering whispers wake,
> And evening comes with locks bedropt with dew ;
> On Desmond's moldering turrets slowly shake
> The trembling rye-grass and the harebell blue,
> And ever and anon fair Mulla's plaints renew."

A reader would be guilty of no very bad guess who should assign this stanza—which Scott greatly admired—to one of the Spenserian passages that prelude the " Lady of the Lake."

But it is needless to extend this catalogue any

farther. By the middle of the century Spenserism had
become so much the fashion as to provoke a rebuke
from Dr. Johnson, who prowled up and down before
the temple of the British Muses like a sort of classical
watch-dog. "The imitation of Spenser," said the
Rambler of May 14, 1751, "by the influence of some
men of learning and genius, seems likely to gain
upon the age. . . To imitate the fictions and sentiments of Spenser can incur no reproach, for allegory
is perhaps one of the most pleasing vehicles of instruction. But I am very far from extending the same
respect to his diction or his stanza. His style was, in
his own time, allowed to be vicious; so darkened with
old words and peculiarities of phrase, and so remote
from common use, that Jonson boldly pronounces
him *to have written no language.* His stanza is at once
difficult and unpleasing: tiresome to the ear by its
uniformity, and to the attention by its length. . .
Life is surely given us for other purposes than to
gather what our ancestors have wisely thrown away
and to learn what is of no value but because it has been
forgotten." * In his "Life of West," Johnson says of

* *Cf.* Joseph Warton's " Essay on Pope," Vol. II. p. 35. " It has
been fashionable of late to imitate Spenser ; but the likeness of most
of these copies hath consisted rather in using a few of his ancient
expressions than in catching his real manner. Some, however, have
been executed with happiness, and with attention to that simplicity,
that tenderness of sentiment and those little touches of nature that
constitute Spenser's character. I have a peculiar pleasure in mentioning two of them, ' The Schoolmistress ' by Mr. Shenstone, and
' The Education of Achilles ' by Mr. Bedingfield. And also Dr.
Beattie's charming ' Minstrel.' To these must be added that
exquisite piece of wild and romantic imagery, Thomson's ' Castle of
Indolence.' "

West's imitations of Spenser, " Such compositions are not to be reckoned among the great achievements of intellect, because their effect is local and temporary: they appeal not to reason or passion, but to memory, and presuppose an accidental or artificial state of mind.   An imitation of Spenser is nothing to a reader, however acute, by whom Spenser has never been perused."

The critic is partly right.   The nice points of a parody are lost upon a reader unacquainted with the thing parodied.   And as for serious imitations, the more cleverly a copyist follows his copy, the less value his work will have.   The eighteenth-century Spenserians, like West, Cambridge, and Lloyd, who stuck most closely to their pattern, oblivion has covered. Their real service was done in reviving a taste for a better kind of poetry than the kind in vogue, and particularly in restoring to English verse a stanza form, which became so noble an instrument in the hands of later poets, who used it with as much freedom and vigor as if they had never seen the " Faërie Queene." One is seldom reminded of Spenser while reading " Childe Harold " * or " Adonais " or " The Eve of Saint Agnes "; but in reading West or Cambridge, or even in reading Shenstone and Thomson, one is reminded of him at every turn.   Yet if it was necessary to imitate anyone, it might be answered to Dr.

---

* Byron, to be sure, began his first canto with conscious Spenserism.   He called his poem a " romaunt," and his valet, poor Fletcher, a " stanch yeomán," and peppered his stanzas thinly with *sooths* and *wights* and *whiloms*, but he gave over this affectation in the later cantos and made no further excursions into the Middle Ages.

Johnson that it was better to imitate Spenser than Pope. In the imitation of Spenser lay, at least, a future, a development; while the imitation of Pope was conducting steadily toward Darwin's "Botanic Garden."

It remains to notice one more document in the history of this Spenserian revival, Thomas Warton's "Observations on the Faërie Queen," 1754. Warton wrote with a genuine delight in his subject. His tastes were frankly romantic. But the apologetic air which antiquarian scholars assumed, when venturing to recommend their favorite studies to the attention of a classically minded public, is not absent from Warton's commentary. He writes as if he felt the pressure of an unsympathetic atmosphere all about him. "We who live in the days of writing by rule are apt to try every composition by those laws which we have been taught to think the sole criterion of excellence. Critical taste is universally diffused, and we require the same order and design which every modern performance is expected to have, in poems where they never were regarded or intended. . . If there be any poem whose graces please because they are situated beyond the reach of art *. . . it is this. In reading Spenser, if the critic is not satisfied, yet the reader is transported." "In analyzing the plan and conduct of this poem, I have so far tried it by epic rules, as to demonstrate the inconveniences and incongruities which the poet might have avoided, had he been more studious of design and uniformity. It is true that his romantic materials claim great liberties; but no

---

* Pope's, "Snatch a grace beyond the reach of art."
                                    —*Essay on Criticism.*

materials exclude order and perspicacity." Warton
assures the reader that Spenser's language is not "so
difficult and obsolete as it is generally supposed to
be;" and defends him against Hume's censure,* that
"Homer copied true natural manners . . . but the
pencil of the English poet was employed in drawing the affectations and conceits and fopperies of
chivalry."

Yet he began his commentary with the stock
denunciations of "Gothic ignorance and barbarity."
"At the renaissance it might have been expected that,
instead of the romantic manner of poetical composition . . . a new and more legitimate taste of writing
would have succeeded. . . But it was a long time
before such a change was effected. We find Ariosto,
many years after the revival of letters, rejecting truth
for magic, and preferring the ridiculous and incoherent
excursions of Boiardo to the propriety and uniformity
of the Grecian and Roman models. Nor did the
restoration of ancient learning produce any effectual
or immediate improvement in the state of criticism.
Beni, one of the most celebrated critics of the sixteenth
century, was still so infatuated with a fondness for the
old Provençal vein, that he ventured to write a regular
dissertation, in which he compares Ariosto with
Homer." Warton says again, of Ariosto and the
Italian renaissance poets whom Spenser followed, "I
have found no fault in general with their use of magical
machinery; notwithstanding I have so far conformed
to the reigning maxims of modern criticism as to
recommend classical propriety." Notwithstanding
this prudent determination to conform, the author

* "History of England," Vol. II. p. 739.

takes heart in his second volume to speak out as follows about the pseudo-classic poetry of his own age:
"A poetry succeeded in which imagination gave way
to correctness, sublimity of description to delicacy
of sentiment, and majestic imagery to conceit and
epigram. Poets began now to be more attentive to
words than to things and objects. The nicer beauties
of happy expression were preferred to the daring
strokes of great conception. Satire, that bane of the
sublime, was imported from France. The muses were
debauched at court; and polite life and familiar manners became their only themes."

By the time these words were written Spenser had
done his work. Color, music, fragrance were stealing
back again into English song, and " golden-tongued
romance with serene lute " stood at the door of the
new age, waiting for it to open.

CHAPTER IV.

The Landscape Poets.

THERE is nothing necessarily romantic in literature
that concerns itself with rural life or natural scenery.
Yet we may accept, with some qualification, the truth
of Professor McClintock's statement, that the "beginning and presence of a creative, romantic movement is
almost always shown by the love, study, and interpretation of physical nature."* Why this should be true,
at all events of the romantic movement that began in
the eighteenth century, is obvious enough. Ruskin and
Leslie Stephen have already been quoted, as witnesses
to the fact that naturalism and romanticism had a
common root: the desire, namely, to escape into the
fresh air and into freer conditions, from a literature
which dealt, in a strictly regulated way, with the indoor life of a highly artificial society. The pastoral
had ceased to furnish any relief. Professing to chant
the praises of innocence and simplicity, it had become
itself utterly unreal and conventional, in the hands of
cockneys like Philips and Pope. When the romantic
spirit took possession of the poetry of nature, it manifested itself in a passion for wildness, grandeur, solitude. Of this there was as yet comparatively little
even in the verse of Thomson, Shenstone, Akenside,
and Dyer.

* W. D. McClintock, "The Romantic and Classical in English
Literature," *Chautauquan*, Vol. XIV. p. 187.

Still the work of these pioneers in the "return to nature" represents the transition, and must be taken into account in any complete history of the romantic movement. The first two, as we have seen, were among the earliest Spenserians: Dyer was a landscape painter, as well as a poet; and Shenstone was one of the best of landscape gardeners. But it is the beginnings that are important. It will be needless to pursue the history of nature poetry into its later developments; needless to review the writings of Cowper and Crabbe, for example,—neither of whom was romantic in any sense,—or even of Wordsworth, the spirit of whose art, as a whole, was far from romantic.

Before taking up the writers above named, one by one, it will be well to notice the general change in the forms of verse, which was an outward sign of the revolution in poetic feeling. The imitation of Spenser was only one instance of a readiness to lay aside the heroic couplet in favor of other kinds which it had displaced, and in the interests of greater variety. "During the twenty-five years," says Mr. Gosse, "from the publication of Thomson's 'Spring' ['Winter'] in 1726, to that of Gray's 'Elegy' in 1751, the nine or ten leading poems or collections of verse which appeared were all of a new type; somber, as a rule, certainly stately, romantic in tone to the extreme, prepared to return, ignorantly indeed, but with respect, to what was 'Gothic' in manners, architecture, and language; all showing a more or less vague aspiration towards the study of nature, and not one composed in the heroic couplet hitherto so vigorously imposed on serious verse. 'The Seasons,' 'Night

Thoughts' and 'The Grave' are written in blank
verse: 'The Castle of Indolence' and 'The Schoolmistress' in Spenserian stanza; 'The Spleen' and
'Grongar Hill' in octosyllabics, while the early odes
of Gray and those of Collins are composed in a great
variety of simple but novel lyric measures." *

The only important writer who had employed blank
verse in undramatic poetry between the publication
of "Paradise Regained" in 1672, and Thomson's
"Winter" in 1726, was John Philips. In the brief
prefatory note to "Paradise Lost," the poet of
"L'Allegro" and "Il Penseroso," forgetting or dis-
daining the graces of his youthful muse, had spoken
of rhyme as "the invention of a barbarous age," as "a
thing trivial and of no true musical delight." Milton's
example, of course, could not fail to give dignity and
authority to the majestic rhythm that he had used;
and Philips' mock-heroic "The Splendid Shilling"
(1701), his occasional piece, "Blenheim" (1705), and
his Georgic "Cyder" (1706), were all in avowed imitation of Milton. But the well-nigh solitary character of
Philips' experiments was recognized by Thomson, in
his allusion to the last-named poem:

> "Philips, Pomona's bard, the second thou
> Who nobly durst, in rime-unfettered verse,
> With British freedom sing the British song." †

In speaking of Philips' imitations of Milton, Johnson said that if the latter "had written after the
improvements made by Dryden, it is reasonable to

---

* "Eighteenth Century Literature," p. 207.
† "Autumn," lines 645–47.

believe he would have admitted a more pleasing modulation of numbers into his work." * Johnson hated Adam Smith, but when Boswell mentioned that Smith, in his rhetorical lectures at Glasgow University, had given the preference to rhyme over blank verse, the doctor exclaimed, "Sir, I was once in company with Smith and we did not take to each other; but had I known that he loved rhyme as much as you tell me he does, I should have hugged him."

In 1725 James Thomson, a young Scotchman, came to London to push his literary fortunes. His countryman, David Malloch,—or Mallet, as he called himself in England,—at that time private tutor in the family of the Duke of Montrose, procured Thomson introductions into titled society, and helped him to bring out "Winter," the first installment of "The Seasons," which was published in 1726. Thomson's friend and biographer (1762), the Rev. Patrick Murdoch, says that the poem was "no sooner read than universally admired; those only excepted who had not been used to feel, or to look for anything in poetry beyond a *point* of satirical or epigrammatic wit, a smart antithesis richly trimmed with rhyme." This is a palpable hit at the Popean school; and indeed there could be no stronger contrast than between Thomson and Pope, not alone in subject and feeling, but in diction and verse. Thomson's style is florid and luxuriant, his numbers flowing and diffuse, while Pope had wonted the English ear to the extreme of compression in both language and meter. Pope is among the most quotable of poets, while Thomson's long poem, in spite of

* " Life of Philips."

its enduring popularity, has contributed but a single phrase to the stock of current quotation:

> " To teach the young idea how to shoot."

"Winter" was followed by "Summer" in 1727, "Spring" in 1728, and the completed "Seasons" in 1730. Thomson made many changes and additions in subsequent editions. The original "Seasons" contained only 3902 lines (exclusive of the "Hymn"), while the author's final revision of 1746 gave 5413. One proof that "The Seasons" was the work of a fresh and independent genius is afforded by the many imitations to which it soon gave birth. In Germany, a passage from Brockes' translation (1745) was set to music by Haydn. J. P. Uz (1742) and Wieland each producd a "Frühling," in Thomson's manner; but the most distinguished of his German disciples was Ewald Christian von Kleist, whose "Frühling" (1749) was a description of a country walk in spring, in 460 hexameter lines, accompanied, as in Thomson's "Hymn," with a kind of "Gloria in excelsis," to the creator of nature. "The Seasons" was translated into French by Madame Bontemps in 1759, and called forth, among other imitations, "Les Saisons" of Saint Lambert, 1769 (revised and extended in 1771.) In England, Thomson's influence naturally manifested itself less in direct imitations of the scheme of his poem than in the contagion of his manner, which pervades the work of many succeeding poets, such as Akenside, Armstrong, Dyer, Somerville and Mallet. "There was hardly one verse writer of any eminence," says Gosse, * "from 1725–50, who was not in some

* "Eighteenth Century Literature," p. 221.

manner guided or biased by Thomson, whose genius is to this day fertile in English literature."

We have grown so accustomed to a more intimate treatment and a more spiritual interpretation of nature, that we are perhaps too apt to undervalue Thomson's simple descriptive or pictorial method. Compared with Wordsworth's mysticism, with Shelley's passionate pantheism, with Byron's romantic gloom in presence of the mountains and the sea, with Keats' joyous re-creation of mythology, with Thoreau's Indianlike approach to the innermost arcana—with a dozen other moods familiar to the modern mind—it seems to us unimaginative. Thomson has been likened, as a colorist, to Rubens; and possibly the glow, the breadth, and the vital energy of his best passages, as of Rubens' great canvases, leave our finer perceptions untouched, and we ask for something more esoteric, more intense. Still there are permanent and solid qualities in Thomson's landscape art, which can give delight even now to an unspoiled taste. To a reader of his own generation, "The Seasons" must have come as the revelation of a fresh world of beauty. Such passages as those which describe the first spring showers, the thunderstorm in summer, the trout-fishing, the sheep-washing, and the terrors of the winter night, were not only strange to the public of that day, but were new in English poetry.

That the poet was something of a naturalist, who wrote lovingly and with his "eye upon the object," is evident from a hundred touches, like "auriculas with shining meal";

"The yellow wall-flower stained with iron brown ; "

or,

> " The bittern knows his time, with bill engulfed,
>   To shake the sounding marsh." *

Thomson's scenery was genuine. His images of
external nature are never false and seldom vague,
like Pope's. In a letter to Lyttelton,† he speaks of
"the Muses of the great simple country, not the
little fine-lady Muses of Richmond Hill." His
delineations, if less sharp and finished in detail than
Cowper's, have greater breadth. Coleridge's comparison of the two poets is well known: "The love
of nature seems to have led Thomson to a cheerful
religion, and a gloomy religion to have led Cowper to
a love of nature. . . In chastity of diction and the
harmony of blank verse, Cowper leaves Thomson
immeasurably below him; yet I still feel the latter to
have been the born poet."

The geologist Hugh Miller, who visited Lyttelton's
country seat at Hagley in 1845, describes the famous
landscape which Thomson had painted in "Spring":

> " Meantime you gain the height from whose fair brow
>   The bursting prospect spreads immense around,
>   And, snatched o'er hill and dale and wood and lawn,
>   And verdant field and darkening heath between,
>   And villages embosomed soft in trees,
>   And spiry towns, by surging columns marked
>   Of household smoke, your eye extensive roams. . .
>   To where the broken landscape, by degrees
>   Ascending, roughens into rigid hills,
>   O'er which the Cambrian mountains, like far clouds,
>   That skirt the blue horizon, dusky rise."

* *Cf.* Chaucer: " And as a bitoure bumbleth in the mire."
                                                — *Wyf of Bathes Tale.*
† Phillimore's " Life of Lyttelton," Vol. I. p. 286.

"The entire prospect," says Miller,*—"one of the finest in England, and eminently characteristic of what is best in English scenery—enabled me to understand what I had used to deem a peculiarity—in some measure a defect—in the landscapes of the poet Thomson. It must have often struck the Scotch reader that, in dealing with very extended prospects, he rather enumerates than describes. His pictures are often mere catalogues, in which single words stand for classes of objects, and in which the entire poetry seems to consist in an overmastering sense of vast extent, occupied by amazing multiplicity. . . Now the prospect from the hill at Hagley furnished me with the true explanation of this enumerative style. Measured along the horizon, it must, on the lowest estimate, be at least fifty miles in longitudinal extent; measured laterally, from the spectator forwards, at least twenty. . . The real area must rather exceed than fall short of a thousand square miles: the fields into which it is laid out are small, scarcely averaging a square furlong in superficies. . . With these there are commixed innumerable cottages, manor-houses, villages, towns. Here the surface is dimpled by unreckoned hollows; there fretted by uncounted mounds; all is amazing, overpowering multiplicity—a multiplicity which neither the pen nor the pencil can adequately express; and so description, in even the hands of a master, sinks into mere enumeration. The picture becomes a catalogue."

Wordsworth † pronounced "The Seasons" "a work of inspiration," and said that much of it was "written

* "First Impressions of England," p. 135.
† Appendix to Preface to the Second Edition of "Lyrical Ballads."

from himself, and nobly from himself," but complained
that the style was vicious. Thomson's diction is, in
truth, not always worthy of his poetic feeling and
panoramic power over landscape. It is academic and
often tumid and wordy, abounding in latinisms like
effusive, precipitant, irriguous, horrific, turgent, amusive.
The lover who hides by the stream where his mistress
is bathing—that celebrated " serio-comic bathing "—
is described as "the latent Damon"; and when the
poet advises against the use of worms for trout bait,
he puts it thus:

> " But let not on your hook the tortured worm
> Convulsive writhe in agonizing folds," etc.

The poets had now begun to withdraw from town
and go out into the country, but in their retirement to
the sylvan shades they were accompanied sometimes,
indeed, by Milton's "mountain nymph, sweet Liberty,"
but quite as frequently by Shenstone's nymph, "coy
Elegance," who kept reminding them of Vergil.

Thomson's blank verse, although, as Coleridge says,
inferior to Cowper's, is often richly musical and with
an energy unborrowed of Milton—as Cowper's is too
apt to be, at least in his translation of Homer.* Mr.

---

* There are, of course, Miltonic reminiscences in " The Seasons."
The moon's " spotted disk " (" Autumn," 1091) is Milton's " spotty
globe." The apostrophe to light (" Spring " 90–96) borrows its
" efflux divine" from Milton's " bright effluence of bright essence
increate" (" Paradise Lost," III. 1–12.) And *cf.* " Autumn,'
783–84:

> " —from Imaus stretcht
> Athwart the roving Tartar's sullen bounds,"

with P. L., III. 431–32; and " Winter," 1005–08.

> "—moors
> Beneath the shelter of an icy isle,
> While night o'erwhelms the sea."

with P. L., I. 207–208.

Saintsbury * detects a mannerism in the verse of
"The Seasons," which he illustrates by citing three
lines with which the poet "caps the climax of three
several descriptive passages, all within the compass of
half a dozen pages," viz. :

> " And Egypt joys beneath the spreading wave."
> " And Mecca saddens at the long delay."
> " And Thule bellows through her utmost isles."

It would be easy to add many other instances of
this type of climacteric line, *e. g.* ("Summer," 859),

> " And Ocean trembles for his green domain."

For the blank verse of " The Seasons " is a blank verse
which has been passed through the strainer of the
heroic couplet.   Though Thomson, in the flow and
continuity of his measure, offers, as has been said, the
greatest contrast to Pope's system of versification;
yet wherever he seeks to be nervous, his modulation
reminds one more of Pope's antithetical trick than of
Shakspere's or Milton's freer structure.   For instance
("Spring," 1015):

> " Fills every sense and pants in every vein."

or (*Ibid.* 1104):

> " Flames through the nerves and boils along the veins."

To relieve the monotony of a descriptive poem, the
author introduced moralizing digressions: advice to
the husbandman and the shepherd after the manner of
the "Georgics"; compliments to his patrons, like
Lyttelton, Bubb Dodington, and the Countess of

* " Ward's English Poets," Vol. III. p. 171.

Hertford; and sentimental narrative episodes, such as
the stories of Damon and Musidora,* and Celadon
and Amelia in "Summer," and of Lavinia and Palemon†
in "Autumn"; while ever and anon his eye extensive
roamed over the phenomena of nature in foreign
climes, the arctic night, the tropic summer, etc.
Wordsworth asserts that these sentimental passages
"are the parts of the work which were probably most
efficient in first recommending the author to general
notice." ‡ They strike us now as insipid enough.
But many coming attitudes cast their shadows before
across the page of "The Seasons." Thomson's denunciation of the slave trade, and of cruelty to animals,
especially the caging of birds and the coursing of
hares; his preference of country to town; his rhapso-
dies on domestic love and the innocence of the Golden
Age; his contrast between the misery of the poor and
the heartless luxury of the rich; all these features of
the poem foretoken the sentimentalism of Sterne and
Goldsmith, and the humanitarianism of Cowper and
Burns. They anticipate, in particular, that half affected itch of simplicity which titillated the sensibili-
ties of a corrupt and artificial society in the writings
of Rousseau and the idyllic pictures of Bernardin de
St. Pierre's "Paul and Virginia." Thomson went so

---

* There were originally *three* damsels in the bathing scene!

† It was to this episode that Pope supplied the lines (207-14)

"Thoughtless of beauty, she was beauty's self," etc.,
which form his solitary essay in blank verse. Thomson told Collins that he took the first hint of "The Seasons" from the names
of the divisions—Spring, Summer, Autumn, Winter—in Pope's
"Pastorals."

‡ Appendix to Preface to Second Edition of "Lyrical Ballads."

far in this vein as to decry the use of animal food in a
passage which recalls Goldsmith's stanza : *

> " No flocks that range the valley free
>   To slaughter I condemn:
> Taught by the power that pities me,
>   I learn to pity them."

This sort of thing was in the air. Pope was not a
sentimental person, yet even Pope had written

> " The lamb thy riot dooms to bleed to-day,
>   Had he thy reason, would he skip and play ?
> Pleased to the last, he crops the flowery food.
> And licks the hand just raised to shed his blood." †

It does not appear that Thomson was personally
averse to a leg of mutton. His denunciations of
luxury, and his praise of early rising ‡ and cold bathing § sound rather hollow from the lips of a bard—
" more fat than bard beseems "—who used to lie abed
till noon, and who, as Savage told Johnson, " was perhaps never in cold water in his life." Johnson reports,
not without some spice of malice, that the Countess of
Hertford, " whose practice it was to invite every summer some poet into the country, to hear her verses and
assist her studies," extended this courtesy to Thomson,
" who took more delight in carousing with Lord Hertford and his friends than assisting her ladyship's

---

* " The Hermit."
† " Essay on Man," Epistle I.
‡ " Falsely luxurious, will not man awake ? " etc.
> —*Summer*, 67.
§ " Nor, when cold winter keens the brightening flood,
>   Would I, weak shivering, linger on the brink."
> —*Ibid.* 1259–60.

poetical operations, and therefore never received another summons." *

The romantic note is not absent from "The Seasons," but it is not prominent. Thomson's theme was the changes of the year as they affect the English landscape, a soft, cultivated landscape of lawns, gardens, fields, orchards, sheep-walks, and forest preserves. Only now and then that attraction toward the savage, the awful, the mysterious, the primitive, which marks the romantic mood in naturalistic poetry, shows itself in touches like these:

> " High from the summit of a craggy cliff,
> Hung o'er the deep, such as amazing frowns
> On utmost Kilda's shore, whose lonely race
> Resigns the setting sun to Indian worlds." †

> " Or where the Northern Ocean, in vast whirls,
> Boils round the naked, melancholy isles
> Of farthest Thule, and the Atlantic surge
> Pours in among the stormy Hebrides." ‡

Compare also the description of the thunderstorm in the mountains ("Summer," 1156–68), closing with the lines:

> " Far seen the heights of heathy Cheviot blaze,
> And Thule bellows through her utmost isles."

The Western Islands appear to have had a peculiar fascination for Thomson. The passages above quoted, and the stanza from "The Castle of Indolence," cited on page 94, gave Collins the clew for his "Ode on the Superstitions of the Scottish Highlands," which contained, says Lowell, the whole romantic school

---

* " Life of Thomson."   † " Spring." 755–58.
‡ " Autumn," 862–65.

in the germ. Thomson had perhaps found the
embryon atom in Milton's " stormy Hebrides," in
" Lycidas," whose echo is prolonged in Wordsworth's " Solitary Reaper "—

> " Breaking the silence of the seas
> Among the farthest Hebrides."

Even Pope—he had a soul—was not unsensitive to
this, as witness his

> " Loud as the wolves, on Orcas' stormy steep,
> Howl to the roarings of the Northern deep." *

The melancholy which Victor Hugo pronounces a distinguishing badge of romantic art, and which we shall
see gaining more and more upon English poetry as
the century advanced, is also discernible in " The
Seasons " in a passage like the following :

> " O bear me then to vast embowering shades,
> To twilight groves and visionary vales,
> To weeping grottos and prophetic glooms ;
> Where angel-forms athwart the solemn dusk
> Tremendous sweep, or seem to sweep along ;
> And voices more than human, through the void,
> Deep-sounding, seize the enthusiastic ear ; " †

or this, which recalls " Il Penseroso" :

> " Now all amid the rigors of the year,
> In the wild depth of winter, while without
> The ceaseless winds blow ice, be my retreat

* " Epistle to Augustus."
† " Autumn," 1030–37. *Cf.* Cowper's

> "O for a lodge in some vast wilderness,
> Some boundless contiguity of shade ! "

> Between the groaning forest and the shore,
> Beat by the boundless multitude of waves,
> A rural, sheltered, solitary scene ;
> Where ruddy fire and beaming tapers join
> To cheer the gloom.   There studious let me sit
> And hold high converse with the mighty dead." *

The revival again, of the preternatural and of popular
superstitions as literary material, after a rationalizing
and skeptical age, is signalized by such a passage as
this:

> " Onward they pass, o'er many a panting height,
>   And valley sunk and unfrequented, where
>   At fall of eve the fairy people throng,
>   In various game and revelry to pass
>   The summer night, as village stories tell.
>   But far around they wander from the grave
>   Of him whom his ungentle fortune urged
>   Against his own sad breast to lift the hand
>   Of impious violence.   The lonely tower
>   Is also shunned, whose mournful chambers hold,
>   So night-struck fancy dreams, the yelling ghost."

It may not be uninstructive to note the occurrence of
the word *romantic* at several points in the poem:

> " glimmering shades and sympathetic glooms,
> Where the dim umbrage o'er the falling stream
> Romantic hangs.†

This is from a passage in which romantic love once
more comes back into poetry, after its long eclipse;
and in which the lover is depicted as wandering abroad
at "pensive dusk," or by moonlight, through groves

---

* "Winter," 424–32.   † " Spring," 1026–28.

and along brooksides.* The word is applied likewise
to clouds, "rolled into romantic shapes, the dream of
waking fancy"; and to the scenery of Scotland—
"Caledonia in romantic view." In a subtler way, the
feeling of such lines as these is romantic:

> " Breathe your still song into the reaper's heart,
> As home he goes beneath the joyous moon ; "

or these, of the comparative lightness of the summer
night:

> " A faint, erroneous ray,
> Glanced from the imperfect surfaces of things,
> Flings half an image on the straining eye."

In a letter to Stonehewer (June 29, 1760), Gray comments thus upon a passage from Ossian:

> " ' Ghosts ride on the tempest to-night:
> Sweet is their voice between the gusts of wind:
> *Their songs are of other worlds.'*

Did you never observe (*while rocking winds are piping
loud*) that pause, as the gust is re-collecting itself, and
rising upon the ear in a shrill and plaintive note, like
the soul of an Æolian harp? I do assure you, there
is nothing in the world so like the voice of a spirit.
Thomson had an ear sometimes: he was not deaf to
this, and has described it gloriously, but given it
another, different turn, and of more horror. I cannot

---

* Shakspere's " broom groves whose shade the dismist bachelor
loves ; "

Fletcher's

> " Fountain heads and pathless groves,
> Places which pale passion loves,"

and his

> " Moonlight walks when all the fowls
> Are safely housed, save bats and owls."

repeat the lines: it is in his 'Winter.'" The lines
that Gray had in mind were probably these (191–94):

> " Then, too, they say, through all the burdened air,
>   Long groans are heard, shrill sounds and distant sighs
>   That, uttered by the demon of the night,
>   Warn the devoted wretch of woe and death."

Thomson appears to have been a sweet-tempered,
indolent man, constant in friendship and much loved
by his friends. He had a little house and grounds
in Kew Lane where he used to compose poetry on
autumn nights and loved to listen to the nightingales
in Richmond Garden; and where, sang Collins, in his
ode on the poet's death (1748),

> " Remembrance oft shall haunt the shore,
>   When Thames in summer wreaths is drest,
>   And oft suspend the dashing oar
>   To bid his gentle spirit rest."

Collins had been attracted to Richmond by Thomson's
residence there, and forsook the neighborhood after
his friend's death.

Joseph Warton, in his "Essay on Pope" (1756),
testified that "The Seasons" had been "very instru-
mental in diffusing a taste for the beauties of nature
and landscape." One evidence of this diffused taste
was the rise of the new or natural school of landscape
gardening. This was a purely English art, and Gray,
writing in 1763,* says "It is not forty years since the
art was born among us; and it is sure that there was
nothing in Europe like it": he adds that "our skill in
gardening and laying out grounds" is "the only

* Letter to Howe, September 10.

taste we can call our own, the only proof of our
original talent in matter of pleasure." "Neither
Italy nor France have ever had the least notion of it,
nor yet do at all comprehend it, when they see it."*
Gray's "not forty years" carries us back with sufficient precision to the date of "The Seasons" (1726–
30), and it is not perhaps giving undue credit to
Thomson, to acknowledge him as, in a great measure,
the father of the national school of landscape gardening. That this has always been recognized upon the
Continent as an art of English invention, is evidenced
by the names *Englische Garten, jardin Anglais,* still
given in Germany and France to pleasure grounds
laid out in the natural taste.† Schopenhauer gives
the philosophy of the opposing styles as follows:
"The great distinction between the English and the
old French garden rests, in the last analysis, upon
this, viz., that the former are laid out in the object-

---

* Letter to Howe, November, 1763.

† Alicia Amherst ("History of Gardening in England," 1896, p.
283) mentions a French and an Italian work, entitled respectively
"Plan de Jardins dans le gout Anglais," Copenhagen, 1798; and
"Del Arte dei Giardini Inglesi," Milan, 1801. "This passion for
the imitation of nature," says the same authority, "was part of the
general reaction which was taking place, not only in gardening but
in the world of literature and of fashion. The extremely artificial
French taste had long taken the lead in civilized Europe, and now
there was an attempt to shake off the shackles of its exaggerated
formalism. The poets of the age were also pioneers of this school of
nature. Dyer, in his poem of 'Grongar Hill,' and Thomson, in his
'Seasons,' called up pictures which the gardeners and architects of
the day strove to imitate." See in this work, for good examples
of the formal garden, the plan of Belton House, Lincoln, p. 245; of
Brome Hall, Suffolk ; of the orangery and canal at Euston, p. 201 ;
and the scroll work patterns of turf and parterres on ʃ p. 217-18.

ive, the latter in the subjective sense, that is to say,
in the former the will of Nature, as it manifests
(*objektivirt*) itself in tree, mountain, and water, is
brought to the purest possible expression of its ideas,
i. e., of its own being.   In the French gardens, on the
other hand, there is reflected only the will of the
owner who has subdued Nature, so that, instead of
her own ideas, she wears as tokens of her slavery,
the forms which he has forced upon her—clipped
hedges, trees cut into all manner of shapes, straight
alleys, arched walks, etc."

It would be unfair to hold the false taste of Pope's
generation responsible for that formal style of gardening which prevailed when "The Seasons" was written.
The old-fashioned Italian or French or Dutch garden—
as it was variously called—antedated the Augustan era,
which simply inherited it from the seventeenth century.   In Bacon's essay on gardens, as well as in the
essays on the same subject by Cowley and Sir William
Temple, the ideal pleasure ground is very much like that
which Le Nôtre realized so brilliantly at Versailles.*
Addison, in fact, in the *Spectator* (No. 414) and Pope
himself in the *Guardian* (No. 173) ridiculed the
excesses of the reigning mode, and Pope attacked
them again in his description of Timon's Villa in the
"Epistle to the Earl of Burlington" (1731), which was
thought to be meant for Canons, the seat of the Duke
of Chandos.

---

*In Temple's gardens at Moor Park, Hertfordshire, *e. g.*, there
were terraces covered with lead.   Charles II. imported some of Le
Nôtre's pupils and assistants, who laid out the grounds at Hampton
Court in the French taste.   The maze at Hampton Court still existed
in Walpole's time (1770).

His gardens next your admiration call,
On every side you look, behold the wall !
No pleasing intricacies intervene,
No artful wildness to perplex the scene ;
Grove nods at grove, each alley has a brother,
And half the platform just reflects the other.
The suffering eye inverted nature sees,
Trees cut to statues, statues thick as trees ;
With here a fountain, never to be played ;
And there a summer house, that knows no shade ;
Here Amphitrite sails through myrtle bowers ;
There gladiators fight, or die in flowers ;
Unwatered see the drooping sea-horse mourn,
And swallows roost in Nilus' dusty urn."

Still the criticism is not merely fanciful which discovers an analogy between the French garden, with
its trim regularity and artificial smoothness, and the
couplets which Pope wrote: just such an analogy as
exists between the whole classical school of poetry and
the Italian architecture copied from Palladio and introduced in England by Inigo Jones and Christopher
Wren. Grounds were laid out in rectangular plots,
bordered by straight alleys, sometimes paved with
vari-colored sand, and edged with formal hedges of
box and holly. The turf was inlaid with parterres cut
in geometric shapes and set, at even distances, with
yew trees clipped into cubes, cones, pyramids, spheres,
sometimes into figures of giants, birds, animals, and
ships—called "topiary work" (*opus topiarium*). Terraces, fountains, bowling-greens (Fr. *boulingrin*)
statues, arcades, quincunxes, espaliers, and artificial
mazes or labyrinths loaded the scene. The whole was
inclosed by a wall, which shut the garden off from the
surrounding country.

"When a Frenchman reads of the Garden of Eden,' says Horace Walpole, in his essay "On Modern Gardening" (written in 1770, published in 1785), "I do not doubt but he concludes it was something approaching to that of Versailles, with clipped hedges, *berceaux* and trellis work. . . The measured walk, the quincunx and the *étoile* imposed their unsatisfying sameness on every royal and noblé garden. . . Many French groves seem green chests set upon poles. . . In the garden of Marshal de Biron at Paris, consisting of fourteen acres, every walk is buttoned on each side by lines of flower-pots, which succeed in their seasons. When I saw it, there were nine thousand pots of asters, or *la reine Marguerite*. . . At Lady Orford's, at Piddletown, in Dorsetshire, there was, when my brother married, a double enclosure of thirteen gardens, each I suppose not much above a hundred yards square, with an enfilade of correspondent gates; and before you arrived at these, you passed a narrow gut between two stone terraces that rose above your head, and which were crowned by a line of pyramidaˡ yews. A bowling green was all the lawn admitted in those times: a circular lake the extent of magnificence."*

Walpole names Theobalds and Nonsuch as famous examples of the old formal style of garden; Stourhead, Hagley, and Stowe—the country seat of Lyttelton's brother-in-law, Lord Cobham—of the new. He says that mottoes and coats of arms were sometimes cut in yew, box, and holly. He refers with respect to a recent work by the Rev. Thomas Whately, or

---

* It is worth noticing that **Batty Langley, the** abortive restorer of Gothic, also recommended the natural style of landscape gardening as early as 1728 in his " New Principles of Gardening."

Wheatley, "Observations on Modern Gardening," 1770; and to a poem, then and still in manuscript, but passages of which are given by Amherst,* entitled "The Rise and Progress of the Present Taste in Planting Parks, Pleasure Grounds, Gardens, etc. In a poetic epistle to Lord Viscount Irwin," 1767.

Gray's friend and editor, the Rev. William Mason, in his poem "The English Garden," 1757, speaks of the French garden as already a thing of the past.

> " O how unlike the scene my fancy forms,
> Did Folly, heretofore, with Wealth conspire
> To plant that formal, dull disjointed scene
> Which once was called a garden ! Britain still
> Bears on her breast full many a hideous wound
> Given by the cruel pair, when, borrowing aid
> From geometric skill, they vainly strove
> By line, by plummet and unfeeling shears
> To form with verdure what the builder formed
> With stone. . .
>   Hence the sidelong walls
> Of shaven yew ; the holly's prickly arms
> Trimmed into high arcades ; the tonsile box,
> Wove in mosaic mode of many a curl
> Around the figured carpet of the lawn. . .
> The terrace mound uplifted ; the long line
> Deep delved of flat canal." †

But now, continues the poet, Taste "exalts her voice " and

>   " At the awful sound
> The terrace sinks spontaneous ; on the green,
> Broidered with crispëd knots, the tonsile yews
> Wither and fall ; the fountain dares no more
> To fling its wasted crystal through the sky,
> But pours salubrious o'er the parchëd lawn."

* " History of Gardening in England."
† I. 384—404.

The new school had the intolerance of reformers.
The ruthless Capability Brown and his myrmidons
laid waste many a prim but lovely old garden, with
its avenues, terraces, and sun dials, the loss of which
is deeply deplored, now that the Queen Anne revival
has taught us to relish the *rococo* beauties which
Brown's imitation landscapes displaced.

We may pause for a little upon this "English
Garden" of Mason's, as an example of that brood of
didactic blank-verse poems, begotten of Philips'
"Cyder" and Thomson's "Seasons," which includes
Mallet's "Excursion" (1728), Somerville's "Chase"
(1734), Akenside's "Pleasures of Imagination" (1742-
44), Armstrong's "Art of Preserving Health" (1744),
Dyer's "Fleece" (1757) and Grainger's "Sugar
Cane" (1764). Mason's blank verse, like Mallet's, is
closely imitative of Thomson's, and the influence of
Thomson's inflated diction is here seen at its worst.
The whole poem is an object lesson on the absurdity of
didactic poetry. Especially harrowing are the author's
struggles to be poetic while describing the various kinds
of fences designed to keep sheep out of his inclosures.

> " Ingrateful sure,
> When such the theme, becomes the poet's task :
> Yet must he try by modulation meet
> Of varied cadence and selected phrase
> Exact yet free, without inflation bold,
> To dignify that theme."

Accordingly he dignifies his theme by speaking of a
net as the "sportsman's hempen toils," and of a gun as
the

> " —fell tube
> Whose iron entrails hide the sulphurous blast
> Satanic engine ! "

When he names an ice-house, it is under a form of conundrum:

> " —the structure rude where Winter pounds,
> In conic pit his congelations hoar,
> That Summer may his tepid beverage cool
> With the chill luxury."

This species of verbiage is the earmark of all eighteenth-century poetry and poets; not only of those who used the classic couplet, but equally of the romanticizing group who adopted blank verse. The best of them are not free from it, not even Gray, not even Collins; and it pervades Wordsworth's earliest verses, his " Descriptive Sketches " and " Evening Walk " published in 1793. But perhaps the very worst instance of it is in Dr. Armstrong's " Economy of Love," where the ludicrous contrast between the impropriety of the subject and the solemn pomp of the diction amounts almost to *bouffe.*

In emulation of " The Seasons " Mason introduced a sentimental love story—Alcander and Nerina—into his third book. He informs his readers (book II. 34–78) that, in the reaction against straight alleys, many gardeners had gone to an extreme in the use of zigzag meanders; and he recommends them to follow the natural curves of the footpaths which the milkmaid wears across the pastures "from stile to stile," or which

> —" the scudding hare
> Draws to her dew-sprent seat o'er thymy heaths."

The prose commentary on Mason's poem, by W. Burgh,* asserts that the formal style of garden had

* " The Works of William Mason," in 4 vols., London, 1811.

begun to give way about the commencement of the
eighteenth century, though the new fashion had but
very lately attained to its perfection.   Mason mentions
Pope as a champion of the true taste,* but the descriptions of his famous villa at Twickenham, with its
grotto, thickets, and artificial mounds, hardly suggest
to the modern reader a very successful attempt to
reproduce nature.   To be sure, Pope had only five

---

* See Pope's paper in the *Guardian* (173) for some rather elaborate
foolery about topiary work.   " All art," he maintains, " consists in
the imitation and study of nature."   " We seem to make it our
study to recede from nature, not only in the various tonsure of greens
into the most regular and formal shapes, but," etc., etc.   Addison,
too, *Spectator* 414, June 25, 1712, upholds " the rough, careless
strokes of nature " against " the nice touches and embellishments of
art," and complains that " our British gardeners, instead of humor-
ing nature, love to deviate from it as much as possible.   Our trees
rise in cones, globes and pyramids.   We see the marks of the scissors
upon every plant and bush.   I do not know whether I am singular in
my opinion, but for my own part, I would rather look upon a tree in
all its luxuriancy and diffusion of boughs and branches, than when
it is thus cut and trimmed into a mathematical figure."   See also
Spectator, 477, for a pretty scheme of a garden laid out with
" the beautiful wildness of nature."   Gilbert West's Spenserian
poem " Education," 1751 (see *ante,* p. 90), contains an attack, in six
stanzas, upon the geometric garden, from which I give a single
stanza.

> " Alse other wonders of the sportive shears,
>   Fair nature mis-adorning, there were found :
>   Globes, spiral columns, pyramids and piers,
>   With sprouting urns and budding statues crowned ;
>   And horizontal dials on the ground,
>   In living box by cunning artists traced ;
>   And gallies trim, on no long voyage bound,
>   But by their roots there ever anchored fast,
>   All were their bellying sails out-spread to every blast."

acres to experiment with, and that parklike scenery which distinguishes the English landscape garden requires a good deal of room. The art is the natural growth of a country where primogeniture has kept large estates in the hands of the nobility and landed gentry, and in which a passion for sport has kept the nobility and gentry in the country a great share of the year. Even Shenstone—whose place is commended by Mason—Shenstone at the Leasowes, with his three hundred acres, felt his little pleasance rather awkwardly dwarfed by the neighborhood of Lyttelton's big park at Hagley.

The general principle of the new or English school was to imitate nature; to let trees keep their own shapes, to substitute winding walks for straight alleys, and natural waterfalls or rapids for *jets d'eau* in marble basins. The plan upon which Shenstone worked is explained in his "Unconnected Thoughts on Gardening"* (1764), a few sentences from which will indicate the direction of the reform: "Landscape should contain variety enough to form a picture upon canvas; and this is no bad test, as I think the landscape painter is the gardener's best designer. The eye requires a sort of balance here; but not so as to encroach upon probable nature. A wood or hill may balance a house or obelisk; for exactness would be displeasing. . . It is not easy to account for the fondness of former times for straight-lined avenues to their houses; straight-lined walks through their woods; and, in short, every kind of straight line, where the foot has to travel over what the eye has done before. . . To

* "Essays on Men and Manners," Shenstone's Works, Vol II. Dodsley's edition.

stand still and survey such avenues may afford some
slender satisfaction, through the change derived from
perspective; but to move on continually and find no
change of scene in the least attendant on our change
of place, must give actual pain to a person of taste. . .
I conceived some idea of the sensation he must feel
from walking but a few minutes, immured between
Lord D——'s high shorn yew hedges, which run exactly
parallel at the distance of about ten feet, and are
contrived perfectly to exclude all kind of objects
whatsoever. . . The side trees in vistas should be so
circumstanced as to afford a probability that they grew
by nature. . . The shape of ground, the disposition of
trees and the figure of water must be sacred to nature;
and no forms must be allowed that make a discovery
of art. . . The taste of the citizen and of the mere
peasant are in all respects the same: the former gilds
his balls, paints his stonework and statues white, plants
his trees in lines or circles, cuts his yew-trees four-
square or conic, or gives them what he can of the
resemblance of birds or bears or men: squirts up his
rivulets in *jets d'eau;* in short, admires no part of
nature but her ductility; exhibits everything that is
glaring, that implies expense, or that effects a surprise
because it is unnatural.   The peasant is his admirer. . .
Water should ever appear as an irregular lake or winding stream. . . Hedges, appearing as such, are universally bad.   They discover art in nature's province."

There is surely a correspondence between this new
taste for picturesque gardening which preferred freedom, variety, irregularity, and naturalness to rule,
monotony, uniformity, and artifice, and that new taste
in literature which discarded the couplet for blank

verse, or for various stanza forms, which left the world of society for the solitudes of nature, and ultimately went, in search of fresh stimulus, to the remains of the Gothic ages and the rude fragments of Norse and Celtic antiquity.

Both Walpole and Mason speak of William Kent, the architect and landscape painter, as influential in introducing a purer taste in the gardener's art. Kent was a friend of Pope and a *protégé* of Lord Burlington to whom Pope inscribed his "Epistle on the Use of Riches," already quoted (see *ante* p. 121), and who gave Kent a home at his country house. Kent is said to have acknowledged that he caught his taste in gardening from the descriptive passages in Spenser, whose poems he illustrated. Walpole and Mason also unite in contrasting with the artificial gardening of Milton's time the picture of Eden in "Paradise Lost:"

> "—where not nice art in curious knots,
> But nature boon poured forth on hill and dale
> Flowers worthy of Paradise; while all around
> Umbrageous grots, and caves of cool recess,
> And murmuring waters, down the slope dispersed,
> Or held by fringèd banks in crystal lakes.
> Compose a rural seat of various hue."

But it is worth noting that in "L'Allegro" "retired leisure," takes his pleasure in "*trim* gardens," while in Collins,

> "Ease and health retire
> To breezy lawn or forest deep."

Walpole says that Kent's "ruling principle was that nature abhors a straight line." Kent "leaped the fence and saw that all nature was a garden. He felt

the delicious contrast of hill and valley, changing
imperceptibly into each other . . . and remarked
how loose groves crowned an easy eminence with
happy ornament. . . The great principles on which
he worked were perspective and light and shade. . .
But of all the beauties he added to the face of this
beautiful country, none surpassed his management of
water. Adieu to canals, circular basins, and cascades
tumbling down marble steps. . . The gentle stream
was taught to serpentine seemingly at its pleasure." *
The treatment of the garden as a part of the landscape
in general was commonly accomplished by the removal
of walls, hedges, and other inclosures, and the substitution of the ha-ha or sunken fence. It is odd that
Walpole, though he speaks of Capability Brown,
makes no mention of the Leasowes, whose proprietor,
William Shenstone, the author of "The Schoolmistress," is one of the most interesting of amateur
gardeners. "England," says Hugh Miller, "has produced many greater poets than Shenstone, but she
never produced a greater landscape gardener."

At Oxford, Shenstone had signalized his natural
tastes by wearing his own hair instead of the wig then
(1732) universally the fashion.† On coming of age,
he inherited a Shropshire farm, called the Leasowes,
in the parish of Hales Owen and an annuity of some
three hundred pounds. He was of an indolent, retir-
ing, and somewhat melancholy temperament; and,
instead of pursuing a professional career, he settled
down upon his property and, about the year 1745,

---

* "On Modern Gardening," Works of the Earl of Orford,
London, 1798, Vol. II.

† Graves, "Recollections of Shenstone," 1788.

began to turn it into a *ferme ornée.* There he wooed the rustic muse in elegy, ode, and pastoral ballad, sounding upon the vocal reed the beauties of simplicity and the vanity of ambition, and mingling with these strains complaints of Delia's cruelty and of the shortness of his own purse, which hampered him seriously in his gardening designs. Mr. Saintsbury has described Shenstone as a master of " the artificial-natural style in poetry." * His pastoral insipidities about pipes and crooks and kids, Damon and Delia, Strephon and Chloe, excited the scorn of Dr. Johnson, who was also at no pains to conceal his contempt for the poet's horticultural pursuits. " Whether to plant a walk in undulating curves and to place a bench at every turn where there is an object to catch the view; to make water run where it will be heard, and to stagnate where it will be seen; to leave intervals where the eye will be pleased, and to thicken the plantation where there is something to be hidden, demands any great powers of mind, I will not enquire." The doctor reports that Lyttelton was jealous of the fame which the Leasowes soon acquired, and that when visitors to Hagley asked to see Shenstone's place, their host would adroitly conduct them to inconvenient points of view—introducing them, *e. g.*, at the wrong end of a walk, so as to detect a deception in perspective, "injuries of which Shenstone would heavily complain." † Graves, however, denies that any rivalry was in question between the great domain of Hagley and the poet's little estate. " The truth of the case," he writes, " was that the Lyttelton family went so fre·

* " Ward's English Poets," Vol. III. 271.
† " Life of Shenstone."

quently with their company to the Leasowes, that they
were unwilling to break in upon Mr. Shenstone's retirement on every occasion, and therefore often went to
the principal points of view, without waiting for anyone to conduct them regularly through the whole
walks. Of this Mr. Shenstone would sometimes
peevishly complain."

Shenstone describes in his "Thoughts on Gardening," several artifices that he put in practice for
increasing the apparent distance of objects, or for
lengthening the perspective of an avenue by widening
it in the foreground and planting it there with dark-
foliaged trees, like yews and firs, "then with trees
more and more fady, till they end in the almond-
willow or silver osier." To have Lord Lyttleton bring
in a party at the small, or willow end of such a walk,
and thereby spoil the whole trick, must indeed have
been provoking. Johnson asserts that Shenstone's
house was ruinous and that "nothing raised his indignation more than to ask if there were any fishes in his
water." "In time," continues the doctor, "his expenses brought clamors about him that overpowered
the lamb's bleat and the linnet's song; and his groves
were haunted by beings very different from fawns and
fairies;" to wit, bailiffs; but Graves denies this.

The fame of the Leasowes attracted visitors from
all parts of the country—literary men like Spence,
Home, and Dodsley: picturesque tourists, who came
out of curiosity; and titled persons, who came, or
sent their gardeners, to obtain hints for laying out
their own grounds. Lyttelton brought William Pitt,
who was so much interested that he offered to contribute two hundred pounds toward improvements,

an offer that Shenstone, however, declined. Pitt had himself some skill in landscape gardening, which he exercised at Enfield Chase and afterward at Hayes.* Thomson, who was Lyttelton's guest at Hagley every summer during the last three or four years of his life, was naturally familiar with the Leasowes. There are many references to the "sweet descriptive bard," in Shenstone's poems † and a seat was inscribed to his memory in a part of the grounds known as Vergil's Grove. "This seat," says Dodsley, "is placed upon a steep bank on the edge of the valley, from which the eye is here drawn down into the flat below by the light that glimmers in front and by the sound of various cascades, by which the winding stream is agreeably broken. Opposite to this seat the ground rises again in an easy concave to a kind of dripping fountain, where a small rill trickles down a rude niche of rock work through fern, liverwort, and aquatic weeds. . . The whole scene is opaque and gloomy." ‡

English landscape gardening is a noble art. Its

---

*See *ante*, p. 90, for his visits to Gilbert West at Wickham.

† See especially " A Pastoral Ode," and " Verses Written toward the Close of the Year 1748."

‡ " A Description of the Leasowes by R. Dodsley," Shenstone's Works, Vol. II. pp. 287–320 (3d ed.) This description is accompanied with a map. For other descriptions consult Graves' " Recollections," Hugh Miller's " First Impressions of England," and Wm. Howitt's " Homes of the Poets " (1846), Vol. I. pp. 258–63. The last gives an engraving of the house and grounds. Miller, who was at Hagley—" The British Tempe "—and the Leasowes just a century after Shenstone began to embellish his paternal acres, says that the Leasowes was the poet's most elaborate poem, "the singularly ingenious composition, inscribed on an English hillside, which employed for twenty long years the taste and genius of Shenstone."

principles are sound and of perpetual application.
Yet we have advanced so much farther in the passion
for nature than the men of Shenstone's day that we
are apt to be impatient of the degree of artifice present
in even the most skillful counterfeit of the natural
landscape.   The poet no longer writes odes on "Rural
Elegance," nor sings

> " The transport, most allied to song,
>   In some fair valley's peaceful bound
>   To catch soft hints from Nature's tongue,
>   And bid Arcadia bloom around ;
>   Whether we fringe the sloping hill,
>   Or smooth below the verdant mead ;
>   Whether we break the falling rill,
>   Or through meandering mazes lead,
>   Or in the horrid brambles' room
>   Bid careless groups of roses bloom ;
>   Or let some sheltered lake serene
>   Reflect flowers, woods and spires, and brighten all the
>   scene."

If we cannot have the mountains, the primeval forest, or the shore of the wild sea, we can at least have
Thomson's " great simple country," subdued to man's
use but not to his pleasure.   The modern mood pre-
fers a lane to a winding avenue, and an old orchard or
stony pasture to a lawn decorated with coppices.   "I
do confess," says Howitt, "that in the 'Leasowes' I
have always found so much ado about nothing; such a
parade of miniature cascades, lakes, streams conveyed
hither and thither; surprises in the disposition of
woods and the turn of walks . . . that I have heartily
wished myself out upon a good rough heath."

For the "artificial-natural" was a trait of Shen-

stone's gardening no less than of his poetry. He
closed every vista and emphasized every opening in
his shubberies and every spot that commanded a pros-
spect with some object which was as an exclamation
point on the beauty of the scene: a rustic bench, a
root-house, a Gothic alcove, a grotto, a hermitage, a
memorial urn or obelisk dedicated to Lyttelton, Thomson, Somerville,* Dodsley, or some other friend. He
supplied these with inscriptions expressive of the sentiments appropriate to the spot, passages from Vergil,
or English or Latin verses of his own composition.
Walpole says that Kent went so far in his imitation
of natural scenery as to plant *dead* trees in Kensing-
ton Garden. Walpole himself seems to approve of
such devices as artificial ruins, "a feigned steeple of a
distant church or an unreal bridge to disguise the termination of water." Shenstone was not above these
little effects: he constructed a " ruinated priory " and
a temple of Pan out of rough, unhewn stone; he put up
a statue of a piping faun, and another of the Venus dei
Medici beside a vase of gold fishes.

Some of Shenstone's inscriptions have escaped the
tooth of time. The motto, for instance, cut upon the
urn consecrated to the memory of his cousin, Miss
Dolman, was prefixed by Byron to his "Elegy upon
Thyrza ": "Heu quanto minus est cum reliquis versari
quam tui meminisse!" The habit of inscription prevailed down to the time of Wordsworth, who composed
a number for the grounds of Sir George Beaumont at

---

* See " Lady Luxborough's Letters to Shenstone," 1775, for a long
correspondence about an urn which *she* was erecting to Somerville's
memory. She was a sister of Bolingbroke, had a seat at Barrels, and
exchanged visits with Shenstone.

Coleorton.   One of Akenside's best pieces is his
"Inscription for a Grotto," which is not unworthy
of Landor.   Matthew Green, the author of "The
Spleen," wrote a poem of some 250 lines upon Queen
Caroline's celebrated grotto in Richmond Garden.
" A grotto," says Johnson, apropos of that still more
celebrated one at Pope's Twickenham villa, " is not
often the wish or pleasure of an Englishman, who has
more frequent need to solicit than exclude the
sun "; but the increasing prominence of the mossy
cave and hermit's cell, both in descriptive verse and in
gardening, was symptomatic.   It was a note of the
coming romanticism, and of that pensive, elegiac strain
which we shall encounter in the work of Gray, Collins,
and the Wartons.   It marked the withdrawal of the
muse from the world's high places into the cool
sequestered vale of life.   All through the literature of
the mid-century, the high-strung ear may catch the drip-
drip of spring water down the rocky walls of the grot.

At Hagley, halfway up the hillside, Miller saw
a semi-octagonal temple dedicated to the genius of
Thomson.   It stood in a grassy hollow which commanded a vast, open prospect and was a favorite resting place of the poet of "The Seasons."   In a shady,
secluded ravine he found a white pedestal, topped by
an urn which Lyttelton had inscribed to the memory
of Shenstone.   This contrast of situation seemed to
the tourist emblematic.   Shenstone, he says, was an
egotist, and his recess, true to his character, excludes
the distant landscape.   Gray, who pronounced "The
Schoolmistress" a masterpiece in its kind, made a
rather slighting mention of its author.*   " I have read

* " Letter to Nichols," June 24, 1769.

an 8vo volume of Shenstone's letters; poor man! he was always wishing for money, for fame and other distinctions; and his whole philosophy consisted in living, against his will, in retirement and in a place which his taste had adorned, but which he only enjoyed when people of note came to see and commend it." Gray unquestionably profited by a reading of Shenstone's "Elegies," which antedate his own "Elegy Written in a Country Churchyard" (1751). He adopted Shenstone's stanza, which Shenstone had borrowed from the love elegies of a now forgotten poet, James Hammond, equerry to Prince Frederick and a friend of Cobham, Lyttelton, and Chesterfield. "Why Hammond or other writers," says Johnson, "have thought the quatrain of ten syllables elegiac, it is difficult to tell. The character of the elegy is gentleness and tenuity, but this stanza has been pronounced by Dryden . . . to be the most magnificent of all the measures which our language affords." *

* Dryden's "Annus Mirabilis," Davenant's "Gondibert," and Sir John Davies' "Nosce Teipsum" were written in this stanza, but the universal currency of Gray's poem associated it for many years almost exclusively with elegiac poetry. Shenstone's collected poems were not published till 1764, though some of them had been printed in Dodsley's "Miscellanies." Only a few of his elegies are dated in the collected editions (Elegy VIII, 1745 ; XIX, 1743 ; XXI, 1746), but Graves says that they were all written before Gray's. The following lines will recall to every reader corresponding passages in Gray's "Churchyard" :

> "O foolish muses, that with zeal aspire
>   To deck the cold insensate shrine with bays !

> "When the free spirit quits her humble frame
>   To tread the skies, with radiant garlands crowned ;

Next after " The Schoolmistress," the most engaging of Shenstone's poems is his " Pastoral Ballad,"
written in 1743 in four parts and in a tripping ana-
pestic measure.   Familiar to most readers is the
stanza beginning:

> " I have found out a gift for my fair,
>   I have found where the wood-pigeons breed."

Dr. Johnson acknowledged the prettiness of the
conceit:

> " So sweetly she bade me adieu,
>   I thought that she bade me return;"

and he used to quote and commend the well-known
lines " Written at an Inn at Henley:

> " Whoe'er has travell'd life's dull round,
>   Where'er his stages may have been,
> May sigh to think he still has found
>   The warmest welcome at an inn."

As to Shenstone's blank verse—of which there is not
much—the doctor says: " His blank verses, those

> Say, will she hear the distant voice of Fame,
> Or hearing, fancy sweetness in the sound ?"
>   —*Elegy* II.

> " I saw his bier ignobly cross the plain."
>   —*Elegy* III.

> " No wild ambition fired their spotless breast."
>   —*Elegy* XV.

> " Through the dim veil of evening's dusky shade
>   Near some lone fane or yew's funereal green," etc.
>   —*Elegy* IV.

> " The glimmering twilight and the doubtful dawn
>   Shall see your step to these sad scenes return,
>   Constant as crystal dews impearl the lawn," etc.
>   —*Ibid.*

that can read them may probably find to be like the blank verses of his neighbors." Shenstone encouraged Percy to publish his " Reliques." The plans for the grounds at Abbotsford were somewhat influenced by Dodsley's description of the Leasowes, which Scott studied with great interest.

In 1744 Mark Akenside, a north country man and educated partly in Scotland, published his " Pleasures of Imagination," afterwards rewritten as " The Pleasures of the Imagination " and spoiled in the process. The title and something of the course of thought in the poem were taken from Addison's series of papers on the subject (*Spectator*, Nos. 411–421). Akenside was a man of learning and a physician of distinction. His poem, printed when he was only twenty-three, enjoyed a popularity now rather hard to account for. Gray complained of its obscurity and said it was issued nine years too early, but admitted that now and then it rose " even to the best, particularly in description." Akenside was harsh, formal, and dogmatic, as a man. Smollett caricatured him in " Peregrine Pickle." Johnson hated his Whig principles and represents him, when settled at Northampton, as " having deafened the place with clamors for liberty." * He furthermore disliked the class of poetry to which Akenside's work belonged, and he told Boswell that he couldn't read it. Still he speaks of him with a certain cautious respect, which seems rather a concession to contemporary opinion than an appreciation of the critic's own. He even acknowledges that Akenside has " fewer artifices of disgust than most of his brethren of the blank song." Lowell says that the very title of Akenside's poem pointed " away from the level

* " Life of Akenside."

highway of commonplace to mountain paths and less domestic prospects. The poem was stiff and unwilling, but in its loins lay the seed of nobler births. Without it, the 'Lines Written at Tintern Abbey' might never have been."

One cannot read "The Pleasures of Imagination" without becoming sensible that the writer was possessed of poetic feeling, and feeling of a kind that we generally agree to call romantic. His doctrine at least, if not his practice, was in harmony with the fresh impulse which was coming into English poetry. Thus he celebrates heaven-born genius and the inspiration of nature, and decries "the critic-verse" and the effort to scale Parnassus "by dull obedience." He invokes the peculiar muse of the new school:

> " Indulgent *Fancy*, from the fruitful banks
> Of Avon, whence thy rosy fingers cull
> Fresh flowers and dews to sprinkle on the turf
> Where Shakspere lies."

But Akenside is too abstract. In place of images, he presents the reader with dissertations. A poem which takes imagination as its subject rather than its method will inevitably remain, not poetry but a lecture on poetry—a theory of beauty, not an example of it. Akenside might have chosen for his motto Milton's lines:

> " How charming is divine philosophy !
> Not harsh and crabbëd, as dull fools suppose,
> But musical as is Apollo's lute."

Yet he might have remembered, too, what Milton said about the duty of poetry to be simple, sensuous, and passionate. Akenside's is nothing of these; it is, on the contrary obscure, metaphysical, and, as a consequence, frigid. Following Addison, he names greatness and novelty, *i. e.*, the sublime and the wonderful, as, equally with beauty, the chief sources of imaginative pleasure, and the whole poem is a plea for what we are now accustomed to call the ideal. In the first book there is a passage which is fine in spirit and—though in a less degree—in expression:

> " Who that from Alpine heights his laboring eye
> Shoots round the wide horizon, to survey
> Nilus or Ganges rolling his bright wave
> Through mountains, plains, through empires black with shade.
> And continents of sand, will turn his gaze
> To mark the windings of a scanty rill
> That murmurs at his feet? The high-born soul
> Disdains to rest her heaven-aspiring wing
> Beneath its native quarry. Tired of earth
> And this diurnal scene, she springs aloft
> Through fields of air ; pursues the flying storm ;
> Rides on the vollied lightning through the heavens ;
> Or, yoked with whirlwinds and the northern blast,
> Sweeps the long tract of day."

The hint for this passage was furnished by a paragraph in Addison's second paper (*Spectator*, 412) and the emotion is the same to which Goethe gives utterance in the well-known lines of "Faust":

> " Doch jedem ist es eingeboren
> Dass sein Gefühl hinauf und vorwärts dringt," etc.

But how greatly superior in sharpness of detail, richness of invention, energy of movement is the German to the English poet!

Akenside ranks among the earlier Spenserians by virtue of his "Virtuoso" (1737) and of several odes

composed in a ten-lined variation on Spenser's stanza.
A collection of his "Odes" appeared in 1745—the
year before Collins' and Joseph Warton's—and a
second in 1760. They are of little value, but show
here and there traces of Milton's minor poetry and
that elegiac sentiment, common to the lyrical verse of
the time, noticeable particularly in a passage on the
nightingale in Ode XV. book i., "To the Evening Star."
"The Pleasures of Imagination" was the parent of a
numerous offspring of similarly entitled pieces, among
which are Joseph Warton's "Pleasures of Melancholy," Campbell's "Pleasures of Hope," and Rogers'
"Pleasures of Memory."

In the same year with Thomson's "Winter" (1726)
there were published in two poetical miscellanies a pair
of little descriptive pieces, "Grongar Hill" and
"The Country Walk," written by John Dyer, a young
Welshman, in the octosyllabic couplet of Milton's
"L'Allegro" and "Il Pensoroso." ("Grongar Hill,"
as first printed was a sort of irregular ode with alternate rhyming; but it was much improved in later editions, and rewritten throughout in couplets.)

Dyer was a landscape painter who had been educated
at Westminster school, studied under Richardson at
London, and spent some time wandering about the
mountains of Wales in the practice of his art.
"Grongar Hill" is, in fact, a pictorial poem, a sketch
of the landscape seen from the top of his favorite
summit in South Wales. It is a slight piece of work,
careless and even slovenly in execution, but with an
ease and lightness of touch that contrast pleasantly
with Thomson's and Akenside's ponderosity. When
Dyer wrote blank verse he slipped into the Thom-

sonian diction, "cumbent sheep" and "purple groves pomaceous." But in "Grongar Hill"—although he does call the sun Phœbus—the shorter measure seems to bring shorter words, and he has lines of Wordsworthian simplicity—

> " The woody valleys warm and low,
> The windy summit, wild and high:"

or the closing passage, which Wordsworth alludes to in his sonnet on Dyer—"Long as the thrush shall pipe on Grongar Hill":

> " Grass and flowers Quiet treads
> On the meads and mountain heads. . .
> And often, by the murmuring rill,
> Hears the thrush while all is still,
> Within the groves of Grongar Hill."

Wordsworth was attracted by Dyer's love of "mountain turf" and "spacious airy downs" and "naked Snowdon's wide, aërial waste." The "power of hills" was on him. Like Wordsworth, too, he moralized his song. In "Grongar Hill," the ruined tower suggests the transience of human life: the rivers running down to the sea are likened to man's career from birth to death; and Campbell's couplet,

> " 'Tis distance lends enchantment to the view
> And robes the mountain in its azure hue," *

is thought to owe something to Dyer's

> " As yon summits soft and fair,
> Clad in colors of the air,
> Which to those who journey near
> Barren, brown and rough appear,
> Still we tread the same coarse way,
> The present's still a cloudy day."

> * " Pleasures of Hope."

Dyer went to Rome to pursue his art studies and, on his return in 1740, published his " Ruins of Rome " in blank verse.　He was not very successful as a painter, and finally took orders, married, and settled down as a country parson.　In 1757 he published his most ambitious work, " The Fleece," a poem in blank verse and in four books, descriptive of English wool-growing.　" The subject of 'The Fleece,' sir," pronounced Johnson, "cannot be made poetical.　How can a man write poetically of serges and druggets?"　Didactic poetry, in truth, leads too often to ludicrous descents. Such precepts as " beware the rot," " enclose, enclose, ye swains," and

> " —the utility of salt
> Teach thy slow swains " ;

with prescriptions for the scab, and advice as to divers kinds of wool combs, are fatal.　A poem of this class has to be *made* poetical, by dragging in episodes and digressions which do not inhere in the subject itself but are artificially associated with it.　Of such a nature is the loving mention—quoted in Wordsworth's sonnet—of the poet's native Carmarthenshire

> "—that soft tract
> Of Cambria, deep embayed, Dimetian land,
> By green hills fenced, by Ocean's murmur lulled."

Lowell admired the line about the Siberian exiles, met

> " On the dark level of adversity."

Miltonic reminiscences are frequent in Dyer.　Sabrina is borrowed from "Comus"; "bosky bourn" and "soothest shepherd" from the same; "the light fantastic toe" from "L'Allegro"; "level brine" and "nor taint-worm shall infect the yeaning herds," from "Lycidas"; "audience pure be thy delight, though few," from "Paradise Lost."

"Mr. Dyer," wrote Gray to Horace Walpole in 1751, "has more of poetry in his imagination than almost any of our number; but rough and injudicious." Akenside, who helped Dyer polish the manuscript of "The Fleece," said that "he would regulate his opinion of the reigning taste by the fate of Dyer's 'Fleece'; for if that were ill received, he should not think it any longer reasonable to expect fame from excellence." The romantic element in Dyer's imagination appears principally in his love of the mountains and of ancient ruins. Johnson cites with approval a sentence in "The Ruins of Rome":

> "At dead of night,
> The hermit oft, midst his orisons, hears
> Aghast the voice of Time disparting towers." *

These were classic ruins. Perhaps the doctor's sympathy would not have been so quickly extended to the picture of the moldering Gothic tower in "Grongar Hill," or of "solitary Stonehenge gray with moss," in "The Fleece."

* *Cf.* Wordsworth's
> "Some casual shout that broke the silent air,
> Or the unimaginable touch of time."
> —*Mutability : Ecclesiastical Sonnets*, **XXXIV.**

CHAPTER V.

The Miltonic Group.

THAT the influence of Milton, in the romantic revival of the eighteenth century, should have been hardly second in importance to Spenser's is a confirmation of our remark that Augustan literature was "classical" in a way of its own. It is another example of that curiously topsy-turvy condition of things in which rhyme was a mark of the classic, and blank verse of the romantic. For Milton is the most truly classical of English poets; and yet, from the angle of observation at which the eighteenth century viewed him, he appeared a romantic. It was upon his romantic side, at all events, that the new school of poets apprehended and appropriated him.

This side was present in Milton in a fuller measure than his completed works would show. It is well known that he, at one time, had projected an Arthuriad, a design which, if carried out, might have anticipated Tennyson and so deprived us of "The Idyls of the King." "I betook me," he writes, "among those lofty fables and romances which recount in solemn cantos the deeds of knighthood."* And in the "Epitaphium Damonis" he thus apprises the reader of his purpose:

> Ipse ego Pardanias Rutupina per æquora puppes,
> Dicam, et Pandrasidos regnum vetus Inogeniæ,

* "An Apology for Smectymnuus."

Brennumque Arviragumque duces, priscumque Belinum,
Et tandem Armoricos Britonum sub lege colonos ;
Tum gravidam Arturo fatali fraude Iörgernen ;
Mendaces vultus, assumptaque Gorlöis arma,
Merlini dolus."*

The "matter of Britain" never quite lost the fascination which it had exercised over his youthful
imagination, as appears from passages in "Paradise
Lost"† and even in "Paradise Regained."‡ But
with his increasing austerity, both religious and
literary, Milton gravitated finally to Hebraic themes
and Hellenic art forms. He wrote Homeric epics and
Æschylean tragedies, instead of masques and sonnets,
of rhymed pieces on the Italian model, like "L'Allegro"
and "Il Penseroso," and of stanzaic poems, like the
"Nativity Ode," touched with Elizabethan conceits.
He relied more and more upon sheer construction and
weight of thought and less upon decorative richness of
detail. His diction became naked and severe, and he
employed rhyme but sparingly, even in the choral

---

* Lines 162–168. See also " Mansus," 80–84.
      † " What resounds
    In fable or romance of Uther's son,
    Begirt with British and Armoric knights ;
    And all who since, baptized or infidel,
    Jousted in Aspramont, or Montalban,
    Damasco, or Marocco, or Trebisond,
    Or whom Biserta sent from Afric shore
    When Charlemain with all his peerage fell
    By Fontarabbia."
                              —*Book I.* 579–587.
    ‡ " Faery damsels met in forest wide
        By knights of Logres, or of Lyones,
        Lancelot, or Pelleas, or Pellenore."
                              —*Book II.* 359–361.

parts of "Samson Agonistes." In short, like Goethe, he grew classical as he grew old. It has been mentioned that "Paradise Lost" did much to keep alive the tradition of English blank verse through a period remarkable for its bigoted devotion to rhyme, and especially to the heroic couplet. Yet it was, after all, Milton's early poetry, in which rhyme is used—though used so differently from the way in which Pope used it—that counted for most in the history of the romantic movement. Professor Masson contradicts the common assertion, that "Paradise Lost" was first written into popularity by Addison's Saturday papers. While that series was running, Tonson brought out (1711–13) an edition of Milton's poetical works which was "the ninth of 'Paradise Lost,' the eighth of 'Paradise Regained,' the seventh of 'Samson Agonistes' and the sixth of the minor poems." The previous issues of the minor poems had been in 1645, 1673, 1695, 1705, and 1707. Six editions in sixty-eight years is certainly no very great showing. After 1713 editions of Milton multiplied rapidly; by 1763 "Paradise Lost" was in its forty-sixth, and the minor poems in their thirtieth.*

Addison selected an occasional passage from Milton's juvenile poems, in the *Spectator;* but from all obtainable evidence, it seems not doubtful that they had been comparatively neglected, and that, although reissued from time to time in complete editions of Milton's poetry, they were regarded merely as pendents to "Paradise Lost" and floated by its reputation. "Whatever causes," says Dryden, "Milton alleges for the abolishing of rime . . . his own par-

* "Masson's Life of Milton," Vol. VI. p. 789.

ticular reason is plainly this, that rime was not his talent: he had neither the ease of doing it, nor the graces of it: which is manifest in his 'Juvenilia' or verses written in his youth; where his rime is always constrained and forced and comes hardly from him."

Joseph Warton, writing in 1756,* after quoting copiously from the "Nativity Ode," which, he says, is "not sufficiently read nor admired," continues as follows: "I have dwelt chiefly on this ode as much less celebrated than 'L'Allegro' and 'Il Penseroso,' † which are now universally known; but which, by a strange fatality, lay in a sort of obscurity, the private enjoyment of a few curious readers, till they were set to admirable music by Mr. Handel. And indeed this volume of Milton's miscellaneous poems

* "Essay on Pope," Vol. I. pp. 36–38 (5th edition). In the dedication to Young, Warton says: "The Epistles [Pope's] on the Characters of Men and Women, and your sprightly Satires, my good friend, are more frequently perused and quoted than 'L'Allegro' and 'Il Penseroso' of Milton."

† The Rev. Francis Peck, in his "New Memoirs of the Life and Poetical Works of Mr. John Milton," in 1740, says that these two poems are justly admired by foreigners as well as Englishmen, and have therefore been translated into all the modern languages. This volume contains, among other things, "An Examination of Milton's Style"; "Explanatory and Critical Notes on Divers Passages of Milton and Shakspere"; "The Resurrection," a blank verse imitation of Milton by "a friend of the editor's in London," with analyses of "Lycidas," "Comus," "L'Allegro" and "Il Penseroso," and the "Nativity Ode." Peck defends Milton's rhymed poems against Dryden's strictures. "He was both a perfect master of rime and could also express something by it which nobody else ever thought of." He compares the verse paragraphs of "Lycidas" to musical bars and pronounces its system of "dispersed rimes" admirable and unique.

has not till very lately met with suitable regard. Shall I offend any rational admirer of Pope, by remarking that these juvenile descriptive poems of Milton, as well as his Latin elegies, are of a strain far more exalted than any the former author can boast?"

The first critical edition of the minor poems was published in 1785, by Thomas Warton, whose annotations have been of great service to all later editors. As late as 1779, Dr. Johnson spoke of these same poems with an absence of appreciation that now seems utterly astounding. "Those who admire the beauties of this great poet sometimes force their own judgment into false admiration of his little pieces, and prevail upon themselves to think that admirable which is only singular." Of Lycidas he says: "In this poem there is no nature, for there is no truth; there is no art, for there is nothing new. Its form is that of a pastoral, easy, vulgar, and therefore disgusting. . . Surely no man could have fancied that he read 'Lycidas' with pleasure, had he not known its author." He acknowledges that "L'Allegro" and "Il Penseroso" are "noble efforts of imagination"; and that, "as a series of lines," "Comus" "may be considered as worthy of all the admiration with which the votaries have received it." But he makes peevish objections to its dramatic probability, finds its dialogues and soliloquies tedious, and unmindful of the fate of Midas, solemnly pronounces the songs— "Sweet Echo" and "Sabrina fair"—"harsh in their diction and not very musical in their numbers"! Of the sonnets he says: "They deserve not any particular criticism; for of the best it can only be said that they are not bad."* Boswell reports that, Hannah

* "Life of Milton."

More having expressed her "wonder that the poet who had written 'Paradise Lost' should write such poor sonnets," Johnson replied: "Milton, madam, was a genius that could cut a colossus from a rock, but could not carve heads upon cherry stones."

The influence of Milton's minor poetry first becomes noticeable in the fifth decade of the century, and in the work of a new group of lyrical poets: Collins, Gray, Mason, and the brothers Joseph and Thomas Warton. To all of these Milton was master. But just as Thomson and Shenstone got original effects from Spenser's stanza, while West and Cambridge and Lloyd were nothing but echoes; so Collins and Gray— immortal names—drew fresh music from Milton's organ pipes, while for the others he set the tune. The Wartons, indeed, though imitative always in their verse, have an independent and not inconsiderable position in criticism and literary scholarship, and I shall return to them later in that connection. Mason, whose "English Garden" has been reviewed in chapter iv, was a very small poet and a somewhat absurd person. He aped, first Milton and afterward Gray, so closely that his work often seems like parody. In general the Miltonic revival made itself manifest in a more dispersed and indirect fashion than the Spenserian; but there was no lack of formal imitations, also, and it will be advisable to notice a few of these here in the order of their dates.

In 1740 Joseph Warton, then an Oxford undergraduate, wrote his blank-verse poem "The Enthusiast, or the Lover of Nature." The work of a boy of eighteen, it had that instinct of the future, of the set of the literary current, not uncommon in youthful

artists, of which Chatterton's precocious verses are a
remarkable instance. Composed only ten years later
than the completed "Seasons," and five years before
Shenstone began to lay out his miniature wildernesses
at the Leasowes, it is more distinctly modern and
romantic in its preference of wild nature to cultivated
landscape, and of the literature of fancy to the literature of reason.

> " What are the lays of artful Addison,
>   Coldly correct, to Shakspere's warblings wild ? "

asks the young enthusiast, in Milton's own phrase.
And again

> " Can Kent design like Nature ? . . .
>   Though he, by rules unfettered, boldly scorns
>   Formality and method, round and square
>   Disdaining, plans irregularly great ? . . .
>
>   Versailles
>   May boast a thousand fountains that can cast
>   The tortured waters to the distant heavens ;
>   Yet let me choose some pine-topped precipice
>   Abrupt and shaggy, whence a foamy stream,
>   Like Anio, tumbling roars ; or some black heath
>   Where straggling stands the mournful juniper,
>   Or yew tree scathed."

The enthusiast haunts "dark forests" and loves to
listen to "hollow winds and ever-beating waves" and
"sea-mew's clang." Milton appears at every turn,
not only in single epithets like "Lydian airs,"
"the level brine," "low-thoughted cares," "the light
fantastic dance," but in the entire spirit, imagery, and

diction of the poem. A few lines will illustrate this better than any description.

> " Ye green-robed Dryads, oft at dusky eve
>   By wondering shepherds seen ; to forests brown,
>   To unfrequented meads and pathless wilds
>   Lead me from gardens decked with art's vain
>   pomp. . .
>   But let me never fail in cloudless night,
>   When silent Cynthia in her silver car
>   Through the blue concave slides, . . .
>   To seek some level mead, and there invoke
>   Old midnight's sister, contemplation sage
>   (Queen of the rugged brow and stern-fixed eye),
>   To lift my soul above this little earth,
>   This folly-fettered world : to purge my ears,
>   That I may hear the rolling planets' song
>   And tuneful turning spheres."

Mason's Miltonic imitations, "Musæus," "Il Bellicoso" and "Il Pacifico" were written in 1744—according to the statement of their author, whose statements, however, are not always to be relied upon. The first was published in 1747; the second "surreptitiously printed in a magazine and afterward inserted in Pearch's miscellany," finally revised and published by the author in 1797; the third first printed in 1748 in the Cambridge verses on the peace of Aix-la-Chapelle. These pieces follow copy in every particular. "Il Bellicoso," *e. g.*, opens with the invocation.

> " Hence, dull lethargic Peace,
>   Born in some hoary beadsman's cell obscure ! "

The genealogies of Peace and War are recited, and contrasted pictures of peaceful and warlike pleasures presented in an order which corresponds as precisely as possible to Milton's in "L'Allegro" and "Il Penseroso."

> " Then, to unbend my mind, I'll roam
>   Amid the cloister's silent gloom ;
>   Or, where ranged oaks their shades diffuse,
>   Hold dalliance with my darling Muse,
>   Recalling oft some heaven-born strain
>   That warbled in Augustan reign;
>   Or turn, well pleased, the Grecian page,
>   If sweet Theocritus engage,
>   Or blithe Anacreon, mirthful wight,
>   Carol his easy love-lay light . . .
>   And joys like these, if Peace inspire,
>   Peace, with thee I string the lyre." *

"Musæus" was a monody on the death of Pope, employing the pastoral machinery and the varied irregular measure of "Lycidas." Chaucer, Spenser, and Milton, under the names of Tityrus, Colin Clout, and Thyrsis, are introduced as mourners, like Camus and St. Peter in the original. Tityrus is made to lament the dead shepherd in very incorrect Middle English. Colin Clout speaks two stanzas of the form used in the first eclogue of "The Shepherd's Calendar," and three stanzas of the form used in "The Faërie Queene." Thyrsis speaks in blank verse and is answered by the shade of Musæus (Pope) in heroic couplets. Verbal travesties of "Lycidas" abound— "laureate hearse," "forego each vain excuse," "without the loan of some poetic woe," etc.; and the closing passage is reworded thus:

* "Il Pacifico: Works of William Mason," London, 1811, Vol I. p. 166.

" Thus the fond swain his Doric oat essayed,
  Manhood's prime honors rising on his cheek:
  Trembling he strove to court the tuneful Maid,
  With stripling arts and dalliance all too weak,
  Unseen, unheard beneath an hawthorn shade.
  But now dun clouds the welkin 'gan to streak;
  And now down dropt the larks and ceased their strain:
  They ceased, and with them ceased the shepherd swain."

In 1746 appeared a small volume of odes, fourteen in number, by Joseph Warton, and another by William Collins.* The event is thus noticed by Gray in a letter to Thomas Wharton: "Have you seen the works of two young authors, a Mr. Warton and a Mr. Collins, both writers of odes? It is odd enough, but each is the half of a considerable man, and one the counterpart of the other. The first has but little invention, very poetical choice of expression and a good ear. The second, a fine fancy, modelled upon the antique, a bad ear, great variety of words and images with no choice at all. They both deserve to last some years, but will not." Gray's critical acuteness is not altogether at fault in this judgment, but half of his prophecy has failed, and his mention of Collins is singularly inappreciative. The names of Collins and Gray are now closely associated in literary history, but in life the two men were in no way connected. Collins and the Wartons, on the other hand, were personal friends. Joseph Warton and Collins had been schoolfellows at Winchester, and it was at first intended that their odes, which were issued in the same month (December), should be published in a volume together. Warton's collection was immedi-

* "Odes on Several Descriptive and Allegoric Subjects."

ately successful; but Collins' was a failure, and the author, in his disappointment, burned the unsold copies.

The odes of Warton which most nearly resemble Milton are "To Fancy," "To Solitude," and "To the Nightingale," all in the eight-syllabled couplet. A single passage will serve as a specimen of their quality:

> " Me, Goddess, by the right hand lead
> Sometimes through the yellow mead,
> Where Joy and white-robed Peace resort
> And Venus keeps her festive court:
> Where Mirth and Youth each evening meet,
> And lightly trip with nimble feet,
> Nodding their lily-crownëd heads;
> Where Laughter rose-lip'd Hebe leads," etc.*

Collins' "Ode to Simplicity" is in the stanza of the "Nativity Ode," and his beautiful "Ode to Evening," in the unrhymed sapphics which Milton had employed in his translation of Horace's "Ode to Pyrrha." There are Miltonic reminiscences like "folding-star," "religious gleams," "play with the tangles of her hair," and in the closing couplet of the "Ode to Fear,"

> " His cypress wreath my meed decree,
> And I, O Fear, will dwell with thee."

But, in general, Collins is much less slavish than Warton in his imitation.

Joseph Warton's younger brother, Thomas, wrote in 1745, and published in 1747, "The Pleasures of Melancholy," a blank-verse poem of three hundred and fifteen lines, made up, in nearly equal parts, of Milton

* " To Fancy."

and Akenside, with frequent touches of Thomson, Spenser, and Pope's "Epistle of Eloisa to Abelard." Warton was a lad of seventeen when his poem was written: it was published anonymously and was by some attributed to Akenside, whose "Pleasures of Imagination" (1744) had, of course, suggested the title. A single extract will suffice to show how well the young poet knew his Milton:

> "O lead me, queen sublime, to solemn glooms
> Congenial with my soul; to cheerless shades,
> To ruined seats, to twilight cells and bowers,
> Where thoughtful Melancholy loves to muse,
> Her favorite midnight haunts. . .
> Beneath yon ruined abbey's moss-grown piles
> Oft let me sit, at twilight hour of eve,
> When through some western window the pale moon
> *Pours her long-levelled rule of streaming light:*
> While sullen sacred silence reigns around,
> Save the lone screech-owl's note, who builds his bower
> Amid the moldering caverns dark and damp; *
> Or the calm breeze, that rustles in the leaves
> Of flaunting ivy, that with mantle green
> Invests some wasted tower. . .
> Then when the sullen shades of evening close
> Where *through the room* a blindly-glimmering gloom
> The *dying embers* scatter, far remote
> From Mirth's mad shouts, that through the illumined roof
> Resound with festive echo, let me sit
> Blessed with the lowly cricket's drowsy dirge. . .

> * *Cf.* Gray's "Elegy," first printed in 1751:

> "Save that, from yonder ivy-mantled tower,
> The moping owl does to the moon complain
> Of such as, wandering near her secret bower,
> Molest her ancient, solitary reign."

> This sober hour of silence will unmask
> False Folly's smile, that like the dazzling spells
> Of wily Comus cheat the unweeting eye
> With *blear illusion*, and persuade to drink
> That charmèd cup which *Reason's mintage fair*
> *Unmoulds*, and stamps the monster on the man."

I italicize the most direct borrowings, but both the Wartons had so saturated themselves with Milton's language, verse, and imagery that they ooze out of them at every pore. Thomas Warton's poems, issued separately from time to time, were first published collectively in 1777. They are all imitative, and most of them imitative of Milton. His two best odes, "On the First of April" and "On the Approach of Summer," are in the familiar octosyllabics.

> "Haste thee, Nymph! and hand in hand,
>   With thee lead a buxom band ;
>   Bring fantastic-footed joy,
>   With Sport, that yellow-tressèd boy," etc.*

In Gray and Collins, though one can hardly read a page without being reminded of Milton, it is commonly in subtler ways than this. Gray, for example, has been careful to point out in his notes his verbal obligations to Milton, as well as to Shakspere, Cowley, Dryden, Pindar, Vergil, Dante, and others; but what he could not well point out, because it was probably unconscious, was the impulse which Milton frequently gave to the whole exercise of his imagination. It is not often that Gray treads so closely in Milton's foot-

---

* "On the Approach of Summer." The "wattled cotes," "sweet-briar hedges," "woodnotes wild," "tanned haycock in the mead," and "valleys where mild whispers use," are transferred bodily into this ode from "L'Allegro."

steps as he does in the latest of his poems, the ode written for music, and performed at Cambridge in 1769 on the installation of the Duke of Grafton as Chancellor; in which Milton is made to sing a stanza in the meter of the "Nativity Ode":

> " Ye brown o'er-arching groves
> That Contemplation loves,
> Where willowy Camus lingers with delight;
> Oft at the blush of dawn
> I trod your level lawn,
> Oft wooed the gleam of Cynthia, silver bright,
> In cloisters dim, far from the haunts of Folly,
> With Freedom by my side, and soft-eyed Melancholy."

Not only the poets who have been named, but many obscure versifiers are witnesses to this Miltonic revival. It is usually, indeed, the minor poetry of an age which keeps most distinctly the "cicatrice and capable impressure" of a passing literary fashion. If we look through Dodsley's collection,* we find a *mélange* of satires in the manner of Pope, humorous fables in the manner of Prior, didactic blank-verse pieces after the fashion of Thomson and Akenside, elegiac quatrains on the model of Shenstone and Gray, Pindaric odes *ad nauseam*, with imitations of Spenser and Milton.†

* Three volumes appeared in 1748; a second edition, with Vol. IV. added in 1749, Vols. V. and VI. in 1758. There were new editions in 1765, 1770, 1775, and 1782. Pearch's continuations were published in 1768 (Vols. VII. and VIII.), and 1770 (Vols. IX. and X.); Mendez's independent collection in 1767; and Bell's "Fugitive Poetry," in 18 volumes, in 1790–97.

† The reader who may wish to pursue this inquiry farther will find the following list of Miltonic imitations useful: Dodsley's "Miscellany," I. 164, Pre-existence: "A Poem in Imitation of Milton," by Dr. Evans. This is in blank verse, and Gray, in a letter to Walpole, calls it "nonsense." II. 109, "The Institution of

To the increasing popularity of Milton's minor poetry is due the revival of the sonnet. Gray's solitary
sonnet, on the death of his friend Richard West, was
composed in 1742 but not printed till 1775, after the
author's death. This was the sonnet selected by
Wordsworth, to illustrate his strictures on the spurious
poetic diction of the eighteenth century, in the appendix to the preface to the second edition of "Lyrical
Ballads." The style is noble, though somewhat artificial: the order of the rhymes conforms neither to the
Shaksperian nor the Miltonic model. Mason wrote
fourteen sonnets at various times between 1748 and
1797; the earlier date is attached, in his collected
works, to "Sonnet I. Sent to a Young Lady with
Dodsley's Miscellanies." They are of the strict Italian or Miltonic form, and abound in Miltonic allusions

the Order of the Garter," by Gilbert West. This is a dramatic
poem, with a chorus of British bards, which is several times quoted
and commended in Joseph Warton's "Essay on Pope." West's
"Monody on the Death of Queen Caroline," is a "Lycidas" imitation. III. 214, "Lament for Melpomene and Calliope," by J. G.
Cooper; also a "Lycidas" poem. IV. 50, "Penshurst," by Mr. F.
Coventry: a very close imitation of "L'Allegro" and "Il Penseroso." IV. 181, "Ode to Fancy," by the Rev. Mr. Merrick: octo-
syllables. IV. 229, "Solitude, an Ode," by Dr. Grainger: octosyl-
lables. V. 283, "Prologue to Comus," performed at Bath, 1756.
VI. 148, "Vacation," by ———, Esq.: "L'Allegro," very close—

> "These delights, Vacation, give,
> And I with thee will choose to live."

IX. (Pearch) 199, "Ode to Health," by J. H. B., Esq.: "L'Allegro."
X. 5, "The Valetudinarian," by Dr. Marriott: "L'Allegro," very
close. X. 97, "To the Moon," by Robert Lloyd: "Il Penseroso,"
close. Parody is one of the surest testimonies to the prevalence of a
literary fashion, and in Vol. X. p. 269 of Pearch, occurs a humorous
"Ode to Horror," burlesquing "The Enthusiast" and "The Pleas-

and wordings. All but four of Thomas Edwards' fifty
sonnets, 1750–65, are on Milton's model. Thirteen
of them were printed in Dodsley's second volume.
They have little value, nor have those of Benjamin
Stillingfleet, some of which appear to have been written before 1750. Of much greater interest are the
sonnets of Thomas Warton, nine in number and all
Miltonic in form. Warton's collected poems were not
published till 1777, and his sonnets are undated, but
some of them seem to have been written as early as
1750. They are graceful in expression and reflect
their author's antiquarian tastes. They were praised
by Hazlitt, Coleridge, and Lamb; and one of them,
" To the River Lodon," has been thought to have
suggested Coleridge's " To the River Otter—"

" Dear native stream, wild streamlet of the west—"

ures of Melancholy,'' " in the allegoric, descriptive, alliterative, epi-
thetical, hyperbolical, and diabolical style of our modern ode-wrights
and monody-mongers," from which I extract a passage :

> " O haste thee, mild Miltonic maid,
> From yonder yew's sequestered shade. . .
> O thou whom wandering Warton saw,
> Amazed with more than youthful awe,
> As by the pale moon's glimmering gleam
> He mused his melancholy theme.
> O Curfew-loving goddess, haste !
> O waft me to some Scythian waste,
> Where, in Gothic solitude,
> Mid prospects most sublimely rude,
> Beneath a rough rock's gloomy chasm,
> Thy sister sits, Enthusiasm."

" Bell's Fugitive Poetry," Vol. XI. (1791), has a section devoted to
" poems in the manner of Milton," by Evans, Mason, T Warton
and a Mr. P. (L'Amoroso).

as well as, perhaps, more remotely Wordsworth's series, "On the River Duddon."

The poem of Milton which made the deepest impression upon the new school of poets was "Il Penseroso." This little masterpiece, which sums up in imagery of "Attic choice" the pleasures that Burton and Fletcher and many others had found in the indulgence of the atrabilious humor, fell in with a current of tendency. Pope had died in 1744, Swift in 1745, the last important survivors of the Queen Anne wits; and already the reaction against gayety had set in, in the deliberate and exaggerated solemnity which took possession of all departments of verse, and even invaded the theater; where Melpomene gradually crowded Thalia off the boards, until sentimental comedy—*la comédie larmoyante*—was in turn expelled by the ridicule of Garrick, Goldsmith, and Sheridan. That elegiac mood, that love of retirement and seclusion, which have been remarked in Shenstone, became now the dominant note in English poetry. The imaginative literature of the years 1740–60 was largely the literature of low spirits. The generation was persuaded, with Fletcher, that

" Nothing's so dainty sweet as lovely melancholy."

But the muse of their inspiration was not the tragic Titaness of Dürer's painting:

" The Melencolia that transcends all wit." *

rather the "mild Miltonic maid," Pensive Meditation.

There were various shades of somberness, from the

* See James Thomson's " City of Dreadful Night," xxi. Also the frontispiece to Mr. E. C. Stedman's " Nature of Poetry " (1892) and pp. 140–41 of the same.

delicate gray of the Wartons to the funereal sable of
Young's "Night Thoughts" (1742-44) and Blair's
"Grave" (1743).   Gosse speaks of Young as a "connecting link between this group of poets and their
predecessors of the Augustan age."   His poem does,
indeed, exhibit much of the wit, rhetorical glitter, and
straining after point familiar in Queen Anne verse, in
strange combination with a "rich note of romantic
despair. "*   Mr. Perry, too, describes Young's language as "adorned with much of the crude ore of
romanticism. . .   At this period the properties of
the poet were but few: the tomb, an occasional raven
or screech-owl, and the pale moon, with skeletons
and grinning ghosts. . .   One thing that the poets
were never tired of, was the tomb. . .   It was the
dramatic—can one say the melodramatic?—view of the
grave, as an inspirer of pleasing gloom, that was preparing readers for the romantic outbreak." †

It was, of course, in Gray's "Elegy Written in a
Country Churchyard " (1751), that this elegiac feeling
found its most perfect expression.   Collins, too, has
"more hearse-like airs than carols," and two of his
most heartfelt lyrics are the " Dirge in Cymbeline" and
the "Ode on the Death of Mr. Thomson."   And the
Wartons were perpetually recommending such themes,
both by precept and example.‡   Blair and Young,

* " Eighteenth Century Literature," pp. 209, 212.

† " English Literature in the Eighteenth Century," pp. 375, 379.

‡ Joseph mentions as one of Spenser's characteristics, "a certain
pleasing melancholy in his sentiments, the constant companion of an
elegant taste, that casts a delicacy and grace over all his composition," " Essay on Pope," Vol. II. p. 29.   In his review of Pope's
" Epistle of Eloisa to Abelard," he says: " the effect and influence
of Melancholy, who is beautifully personified, on every object that

however, are scarcely to be reckoned among the romanticists. They were heavy didactic-moral poets, for the most part, though they touched the string which, in the Gothic imagination, vibrates with a musical shiver to the thought of death. There is something that accords with the spirit of Gothic ecclesiastical architecture, with Gray's "ivy-mantled tower"—his "long-drawn aisle and fretted vault"— in the paraphernalia of the tomb which they accumulate so laboriously: the cypress and the yew, the owl and the midnight bell, the dust of the charnel-house, the nettles that fringe the grave-stones, the dim sepulchral lamp and gliding specters.

> " The wind is up.   Hark ! how it howls ! Methinks
> Till now I never heard a sound so dreary.
> Doors creak and windows clap, and night's foul bird,
> Rocked in the spire, screams loud : the gloomy aisles,
> Black-plastered and hung 'round with shreds of scutcheons
> And tattered coats-of-arms, send back the sound,
> Laden with heavier airs, from the low vaults,
> The mansions of the dead." *

Blair's mortuary verse has a certain impressiveness, in its gloomy monotony, not unlike that of Quarles' "Divine Emblems." Like the "Emblems," too, "The Grave" has been kept from oblivion by the art of the illustrator, the well-known series of engravings by Schiavonetti from designs by Wm. Blake.

But the thoughtful, scholarly fancy of the more

occurs and on every part of the convent, cannot be too much applauded, or too often read, as it is founded on nature and experience. That temper of mind casts a gloom on all things.

> " ' But o'er the twilight groves and dusky caves,' etc."
> —*Ibid.*, Vol. I. p. 314.

* " The Grave," by Robert Blair.

purely romantic poets haunted the dusk rather than
the ebon blackness of midnight, and listened more to
the nightingale than to the screech-owl.   They were
quietists, and their imagery was crepuscular.   They
loved the twilight, with its beetle and bat, solitude,
shade, the "darkening vale," the mossy hermitage,
the ruined abbey moldering in its moonlit glade,
grots, caverns, brooksides, ivied nooks, firelight
rooms, the curfew bell and the sigh of the æolian
harp.*   All this is exquisitely put in Collins' "Ode to
Evening."   Joseph Warton also wrote an "Ode to
Evening," as well as one "To the Nightingale."
Both Wartons wrote odes "To Solitude."   Dodsley's
"Miscellanies" are full of odes to Evening, Solitude,

---

* The æolian harp was a favorite property of romantic poets for a
hundred years. See Mason's "Ode to an Æolus's Harp" (Works,
Vol. I. p. 51). First invented by the Jesuit, Kircher, about 1650,
and described in his "Musurgia Universalis," Mason says that it
was forgotten for upwards of a century and "accidentally rediscov-
ered" in England by a Mr. Oswald. It is mentioned in "The
Castle of Indolence" (i. xl) as a novelty :

> "A certain music never known before
> Here lulled the pensive melancholy mind"—

a passage to which Collins alludes in his verses on Thomson's
death—

> "In yon deep bed of whispering reeds
> His airy harp shall now be laid."

See "The Lay of the Last Minstrel" I. 341-42 (1805.)

> "Like that wild harp whose magic tone
> Is wakened by the winds alone."

And Arthur Cleveland Coxe's (*Christian Ballads*, 1840)

> "It was a wind-harp's magic strong,
> Touched by the breeze in dreamy song,"

and the poetry of the Annals *passim*.

Silence, Retirement, Contentment, Fancy, Melancholy, Innocence, Simplicity, Sleep; of Pleasures of
Contemplation (Miss Whately, Vol. IX. p. 120) Triumphs of Melancholy (James Beattie, Vol. X. p. 77),
and similar matter.   Collins introduced a personified
figure of Melancholy in his ode, "The Passions."

> " With eyes upraised, as one inspired,
>   Pale Melancholy sat retired ;
>   And from her wild, sequestered seat,
>   In notes by distance made more sweet,
>   Poured through the mellow horn her pensive soul ;
>   And dashing soft from rocks around,
>   Bubbling runnels joined the sound ;
>   Through glades and glooms the mingled measure stole,
>   Or o'er some haunted stream, with fond delay,
>   Round a holy calm diffusing,
>   Love of peace and lonely musing,
>   In hollow murmurs died away."

Collins was himself afflicted with a melancholia
which finally developed into madness.   Gray, a shy,
fastidious scholar, suffered from inherited gout and a
lasting depression of spirits.   He passed his life as a
college recluse in the cloistered retirement of Cambridge, residing at one time in Pembroke, and at another in Peterhouse College.   He held the chair of
modern history in the university, but never gave a lecture.   He declined the laureateship after Cibber's
death.   He had great learning, and a taste most delicately correct; but the sources of creative impulse
dried up in him more and more under the desiccating
air of academic study and the increasing hold upon
him of his constitutional malady.   "Melancholy
marked him for her own."   There is a significant passage in one of his early letters to Horace Walpole

(1737): "I have, at the distance of half a mile, through a green lane, a forest (the vulgar call it a common) all my own, at least as good as so, for I spy no human thing in it but myself. It is a little chaos of mountains and precipices. . . Both vale and hill are covered with most venerable beeches and other very reverend vegetables that, like most other ancient people, are always dreaming out their old stories to the winds. . . At the foot of one of these, squats ME, I, (il penseroso) and there grow to the trunk for a whole morning." * To Richard West he wrote, in the same year, "Low spirits are my true and faithful companions"; and, in 1742, "Mine is a white Melancholy, or rather Leucocholy, for the most part . . . but there is another sort, black indeed, which I have now and then felt."

When Gray sees the Eton schoolboys at their sports, he is sadly reminded:

> " —how all around them wait
>   The ministers of human fate
>   And black Misfortune's baleful train." †

"Wisdom in sable garb," and "Melancholy, silent maid" attend the footsteps of Adversity; ‡ and to Contemplation's sober eye, the race of man resembles the insect race:

> " Brushed by the hand of rough mischance,
>   Or chilled by age, their airy dance
>   They leave, in dust to rest." §

* *Cf.* the " Elegy " :
    " There at the foot of yonder nodding beech," etc.
† " On a Distant Prospect of Eton College."
‡ " Hymn to Adversity."
§ " Ode on the Spring."

Will it be thought too trifling an observation that the poets of this group were mostly bachelors and *quo ad hoc,* solitaries? Thomson, Akenside, Shenstone, Collins, Gray, and Thomas Warton never married. Dyer, Mason, and Joseph Warton, were beneficed clergymen, and took unto themselves wives. The Wartons, to be sure, were men of cheerful and even convivial habits. The melancholy which these good fellows affected was manifestly a mere literary fashion. They were sad "only for wantonness," like the young gentlemen in France. "And so you have a garden of your own," wrote Gray to his young friend Nicholls, in 1769, "and you plant and transplant, and are dirty and amused; are you not ashamed of yourself? Why, I have no such thing, you monster; nor ever shall be either dirty or amused as long as I live." Gray never was; but the Wartons were easily amused, and Thomas, by all accounts, not unfrequently dirty, or at least slovenly in his dress, and careless and unpolished in his manners, and rather inclined to broad humor and low society.

Romantically speaking, the work of these Miltonic lyrists marks an advance upon that of the descriptive and elegiac poets, Thomson, Akenside, Dyer, and Shenstone. Collins is among the choicest of English lyrical poets. There is a flute-like music in his best odes—such as the one "To Evening," and the one written in 1746—"How sleep the brave," which are sweeter, more natural, and more spontaneous than Gray's. "The Muse gave birth to Collins," says Swinburne; "she did but give suck to Gray." Collins "was a solitary song-bird among many more or less excellent pipers and pianists. He could put more spirit of color into a single stroke, more breath of music into a single note, than could all the rest of the generation into all the labors of their lives." * Collins, like Gray, was a Greek scholar, and had projected a history of the revival of letters. There is a classical quality in his verse—not classical in the eighteenth-century sense—but truly Hellenic; a union, as in Keats, of Attic form with romantic sensibility; though in Collins, more than in Keats, the warmth seems to come from without; the statue of a nymph flushed with sunrise. "Collins," says Gosse, "has the touch of a sculptor; his verse is clearly cut and direct: it is marble pure, but also marble cold." † Lowell, however, thinks that Collins "was the first to bring back into poetry something of the antique flavor, and found again the long-lost secret of being classically elegant without being pedantically cold." ‡

These estimates are given for what they are worth. The coldness which is felt—or fancied—in some of Collins' poetry comes partly from the abstractness of his subjects and the artificial style which he inherited, in common with all his generation. Many of his odes are addressed to Fear, Pity, Mercy, Liberty, and similar abstractions. The pseudo-Pindaric ode, is, in itself, an exotic; and, as an art form, is responsible for some of the most tumid compositions in the history of English verse. Collins' most current ode, though by no means his best one, "The Passions," abounds in those personifications which, as has been said, constituted, in eighteenth-century poetry, a sort of feeble

---

* " Ward's English Poets," Vol. III. pp. 278-82.
† " Eighteenth Century Literature," p. 233.
‡ Essay on " Pope."

mythology: "wan Despair," "dejected **Pity,'**
"brown Exercise," and "Music sphere-descended
maid." It was probably the allegorical figures in Milton's "L'Allegro" and "Il Penseroso," "Sport that
wrinkled care derides," "spare Fast that oft with
gods doth diet," etc., that gave a new lease of life to
this obsolescent machinery which the romanticists
ought to have abandoned to the Augustan schools.

The most interesting of Collins' poems, from the
point of view of these inquiries, is his "Ode on the
Popular Superstitions of the Highlands of Scotland."
This was written in 1749, but as it remained in manuscript till 1788, it was of course without influence on
the minds of its author's contemporaries. It had been
left unfinished, and some of the printed editions contained interpolated stanzas which have since been
weeded away. Inscribed to Mr. John Home, the author of "Douglas," its purpose was to recommend to
him the Scottish fairy lore as a fit subject for poetry.
Collins justifies the selection of such "false themes"
by the example of Spenser, of Shakspere, (in "Macbeth"), and of Tasso

> " —whose undoubting mind
> Believed the magic wonders which he sung."

He mentions, as instances of popular beliefs that have
poetic capabilities, the kelpie, the will-o'-the-wisp,
and second sight. He alludes to the ballad of "Willie
Drowned in Yarrow," and doubtless with a line of
"The Seasons" running in his head,* conjures Home
to "forget not Kilda's race," who live on the eggs of
the solan goose, whose only prospect is the wintry

*See *ante*, p. 114.

main, and among whose cliffs the bee is never heard to murmur. Perhaps the most imaginative stanza is the ninth, referring to the Hebrides, the chapel of St. Flannan and the graves of the Scottish, Irish, and Norwegian kings in Icolmkill:

" Unbounded is thy range ; with varied skill
    Thy muse may, like those feathery tribes which spring
    From their rude rocks, extend her skirting wing,
Round the moist marge of each cold Hebrid isle,
    To that hoar pile which still its ruins shows ;
In whose small vaults a pygmy folk is found,
    Whose bones the delver with his spade upthrows,
And culls them, wondering, from the hallowed ground ;
Or thither, where, beneath the showery west,
    The mighty kings of three fair realms are laid ;
Once foes, perhaps, together now they rest,
    No slaves revere them and no wars invade.
Yet frequent now at midnight's solemn hour,
    The rifted mounds their yawning cells unfold,
And forth the monarchs stalk with sovereign power,
    In pageant robes, and wreathed with sheeny gold,
    And on their twilight tombs aërial council hold."

Collins' work was all done by 1749; for though he survived ten years longer, his mind was in eclipse. He was a lover and student of Shakspere, and when the Wartons paid him a last visit at the time of his residence with his sister in the cloisters of Chichester Cathedral, he told Thomas that he had discovered the source of the " Tempest," in a novel called " Aurelio and Isabella," printed in 1588 in Spanish, Italian, French, and English. No such novel has been found, and it was seemingly a figment of Collins' disordered fancy. During a lucid interval in the course of this visit, he read to the Wartons, from the manuscript,

his "Ode on the Superstitions of the Scottish Highlands"; and also a poem which is lost, entitled, "The
Bell of Arragon," founded on the legend of the great
bell of Saragossa that tolled of its own accord whenever a king of Spain was dying.

Johnson was also a friend of Collins, and spoke of
him kindly in his "Lives of the Poets," though he
valued his writings little. "He had employed his
mind chiefly upon works of fiction and subjects of
fancy; and by indulging some peculiar habits of
thought, was eminently delighted with those flights
of imagination which pass the bounds of nature, and
to which the mind is reconciled only by a passive
acquiescence in popular traditions. He loved fairies,
genii, giants, and monsters; he delighted to rove
through the meanders of enchantment, to gaze on the
magnificence of golden palaces, to repose by the
water-falls of Elysian gardens. This was, however,
the character rather of his inclination than his genius;
the grandeur of wildness and the novelty of extravagance were always desired by him, but were not always
attained." *

Thomas Gray is a much more important figure than
Collins in the intellectual history of his generation;
but this superior importance does not rest entirely upon
his verse, which is hardly more abundant than Collins',
though of a higher finish. His letters, journals, and
other prose remains, posthumously published, first
showed how long an arc his mind had subtended on
the circle of art and thought. He was sensitive to all
fine influences that were in the literary air. One of the
greatest scholars among English poets, his taste was

* " Life of Collins."

equal to his acquisitions. He was a sound critic of poetry, music, architecture, and painting. His mind and character both had distinction; and if there was something a trifle finical and old-maidish about his personality—which led the young Cantabs on one occasion to take a rather brutal advantage of his nervous dread of fire—there was also that nice reserve which gave to Milton, when *he* was at Cambridge, the nickname of the "the lady of Christ's."

A few of Gray's simpler odes, the "Ode on the Spring," the "Hymn to Adversity" and the Eton College ode, were written in 1742 and printed in Dodsley's collection in 1748. The "Elegy" was published in 1751; the two "sister odes," "The Progress of Poesy" and "The Bard," were struck off from Horace Walpole's private press at Strawberry Hill in 1757. Gray's popular fame rests, and will always rest, upon his immortal "Elegy." He himself denied somewhat impatiently that it was his best poem, and thought that its popularity was owing to its subject. There are not wanting critics of authority, such as Lowell and Matthew Arnold, who have pronounced Gray's odes higher poetry than his "Elegy." "'The Progress of Poesy,'" says Lowell, "overflies all other English lyrics like an eagle. . . It was the prevailing blast of Gray's trumpet that, more than anything else, called men back to the legitimate standard." * With all deference to such distinguished judges, I venture to think that the popular instinct on this point is right, and even that Dr. Johnson is not so wrong as usual. Johnson disliked Gray and spoke of him with surly injustice.

* Essay on " Pope."

Gray, in turn, could not abide Johnson, whom he
called *Ursa major.* Johnson said that Gray's odes
were forced plants, raised in a hot-house, and poor
plants at that. "Sir, I do not think Gray a first-rate
poet. He has not a bold imagination, nor much com-
mand of words. The obscurity in which he has
involved himself will not persuade us that he is
sublime. His 'Elegy in a Churchyard' has a happy
selection of images, but I don't like what are called
his great things." "He attacked Gray, calling him
a 'dull fellow.' Boswell: 'I understand he was reserved, and might appear dull in company; but surely
he was not dull in poetry.' Johnson: 'Sir, he was
dull in company, dull in his closet, dull everywhere.
He was dull in a new way and that made many people
think him GREAT. He was a mechanical poet.' He
then repeated some ludicrous lines, which have escaped
my memory, and said, 'Is not that GREAT, like his
odes?' . . . 'No, sir, there are but two good stanzas
in Gray's poetry, which are in his "Elegy in a Country
Churchyard." He then repeated the stanza—

"'For who, to dumb forgetfulness a prey,'" etc.

"In all Gray's odes," wrote Johnson, "there is a
kind of cumbrous splendor which we wish away. . .
These odes are marked by glittering accumulations
of ungraceful ornaments; they strike rather than
please; the images are magnified by affectation; the
language is labored into harshness. The mind of the
writer seems to work with unnatural violence. . .
His art and his struggle are too visible and there is
too little appearance of ease and nature. . . In the
character of his 'Elegy,' I rejoice to concur with the

common reader; for by the common sense of readers
uncorrupted with literary prejudices, after all the
refinements of subtlety and the dogmatism of learning,
must be finally decided all claims to poetical honors.
The 'Churchyard' abounds with images which find a
mirror in every mind, and with sentiments to which
every bosom returns an echo."

There are noble lines in Gray's more elaborate odes,
but they do make as a whole that mechanical, artificial
impression of which Johnson complains. They have
the same rhetorical ring, the worked-up fervor in
place of genuine passion, which was noted in Collins'
ode "On the Passions." Collins and Gray were perpetually writing about the passions; but they treated
them as abstractions and were quite incapable of
exhibiting them in action. Neither of them could
have written a ballad, a play, or a romance. Their
odes were bookish, literary, impersonal, retrospective.
They had too much of the ichor of fancy and too little
red blood in them.

But the "Elegy" is the masterpiece of this whole
"Il Penseroso" school, and has summed up for all
English readers, for all time, the poetry of the tomb.
Like the "Essay on Man," and "Night Thoughts"
and "The Grave," it is a poem of the moral-didactic
order, but very different in result from these. Its
moral is suffused with emotion and expressed concretely. Instead of general reflections upon the
shortness of life, the vanity of ambition, the leveling
power of death, and similar commonplaces, we have
the picture of the solitary poet, lingering among the
graves at twilight (*hora datur quieti*), till the place and
the hour conspire to work their effect upon the mind

and prepare it for the strain of meditation that follows. The universal appeal of its subject and the perfection of its style have made the "Elegy" known by heart to more readers than any other poem in the language. Parody is one proof of celebrity, if not of popularity, and the "sister odes" were presently parodied by Lloyd and Colman in an "Ode to Obscurity" and an "Ode to Oblivion." But the "Elegy" was more than celebrated and more than popular; it was the most admired and influential poem of the generation. The imitations and translations of it are innumerable, and it met with a response as immediate as it was general.* One effect of this was to consecrate the ten-syllabled quatrain to elegiac uses. Mason altered the sub-title of his "Isis" (written in 1748) from "An Elegy" to "A Monologue," because it was "not written in alternate rimes, which since Mr. Gray's exquisite 'Elegy in the Country Church-yard' has generally obtained, and seems to be more suited to that species of poem."† Mason's "Elegy written in a Church-yard in South Wales" (1787) is, of course, in Gray's stanza and, equally of course, introduces a tribute to the master:

> "Yes, had he paced this church-way path along,
>   Or leaned like me against this ivied wall,
>   How sadly sweet had flowed his Dorian song,
>   Then sweetest when it flowed at Nature's call."‡

* Mr. Perry enumerates, among English imitators, Falconer, T. Warton, James Graeme, Wm. Whitehead, John Scott, Henry Headly, John Henry Moore, and Robert Lovell, "Eighteenth Century Literature," p. 391. Among foreign imitations Lamartine's "Le Lac" is perhaps the most famous.

† "Mason's Works," Vol. I. p. 179.

‡ *Ibid.*, Vol. I. p. 114.

It became almost *de rigueur* for a young poet to try his hand at a churchyard piece. Thus Richard Cumberland, the dramatist, in his "Memoirs," records the fact that when he was an undergraduate at Cambridge in 1752 he made his "first small offering to the press, following the steps of Gray with another church-yard elegy, written on St. Mark's Eve, when, according to rural tradition, the ghosts of those who are to die within the year ensuing are seen to walk at midnight across the churchyard."* Goldsmith testifies to the prevalence of the fashion when, in his "Life of Parnell," he says of that poet's "Night Piece on Death" † that, "with very little amendment," it "might be made to surpass all those night-pieces and church-yard scenes that have since appeared." But in this opinion Johnson, who says that Parnell's poem "is indirectly preferred by Goldsmith to Gray's 'Churchyard,'" does not agree; nor did the public. ‡

Gray's correspondence affords a record of the progress of romantic taste for an entire generation. He set out with classical prepossessions—forming his verse, as he declared, after Dryden—and ended with translations from Welsh and Norse hero-legends, and

---

* *Cf.* Keats' unfinished poem, "The Eve of St. Mark."

† Parnell's collected poems were published in 1722.

‡ Not the least interesting among the progeny of Gray's "Elegy" was "The Indian Burying Ground" of the American poet, Philip Freneau (1752–1832). Gray's touch is seen elsewhere in Freneau, *e. g.*, in "The Deserted Farm-house."

> "Once in the bounds of this sequestered room
>   Perhaps some swain nocturnal courtship made :
> Perhaps some Sherlock mused amid the gloom,
>   Since Love and Death forever seek the shade.'

with an admiration for Ossian and Scotch ballads.   In
1739 he went to France and Italy with Horace Walpole.   He was abroad three years, though in 1741 he
quarreled with Walpole at Florence, separated from
him and made his way home alone in a leisurely manner.   Gray is one of the first of modern travelers to
speak appreciatively of Gothic architecture, and of the
scenery of the Alps, and to note those strange and
characteristic aspects of foreign life which we now call
picturesque, and to which every itinerary and guide-
book draws attention.   Addison, who was on his
travels forty years before, was quite blind to such
matters.   Not that he was without the feeling of the
sublime: he finds, *e. g.*, an "agreeable horror" in the
prospect of a storm at sea.*   But he wrote of his passage through Switzerland as a disagreeable and even
frightful experience: "a very troublesome journey
over the Alps.   My head is still giddy with mountains
and precipices; and you can't imagine how much I am
pleased with the sight of a plain."

"Let any one reflect," says the *Spectator*,† "on the
disposition of mind he finds in himself at his first
entrance into the Pantheon at Rome, and how his
imagination is filled with something great and amazing;
and, at the same time, consider how little, in proportion, he is affected with the inside of a Gothic cathedral, though it be five times larger than the other;
which can arise from nothing else but the greatness of
the manner in the one, and the meanness in the
other." ‡

* *Spectator*, No. 489.
† No. 415.
‡ John Hill Burton, in his " Reign of Queen Anne " gives a pas-

Gray describes the cathedral at Rheims as "a vast Gothic building of a surprising beauty and lightness, all covered over with a profusion of little statues and other ornaments"; and the cathedral at Siena, which Addison had characterized as "barbarous," and as an instance of "false beauties and affected ornaments," Gray commends as "labored with a Gothic niceness and delicacy in the old-fashioned way." It must be acknowledged that these are rather cold praises, but Gray was continually advancing in his knowledge of Gothic and his liking for it. Later in life he became something of an antiquarian and virtuoso. He corresponded with Rev. Thomas Wharton, about stained glass and paper hangings, which Wharton, who was refitting his house in the Gothic taste, had commissioned Gray to buy for him of London dealers. He describes, for Wharton's benefit, Walpole's new bedroom at Strawberry Hill as "in the best taste of anything he has yet done, and in your own Gothic way"; and he advises his correspondent as to the selection of patterns for staircases and arcade work. There was evidently a great stir of curiosity concerning Strawberry Hill in Gray's coterie, and a determination to be Gothic at all

sage from a letter of one Captain Burt, superintendent of certain road-making operations in the Scotch Highlands, by way of showing how very modern a person Carlyle's picturesque tourist is. The captain describes the romantic scenery of the glens as "horrid prospects." It was considerably later in the century that Dr. Johnson said, in answer to Boswell's timid suggestion that Scotland had a great many noble wild prospects, "I believe, sir, you have a great many. Norway, too, has noble wild prospects, and Lapland is remarkable for prodigious noble wild prospects. But, sir, let me tell you, the noblest prospect which a Scotchman ever sees is the high-road that leads him to England."

hazards; and the poet felt obliged to warn his friends that zeal should not outrun discretion. He writes to Wharton in 1754: "I rejoice to find you at last settled to your heart's content, and delight to hear you talk of giving your house some *Gothic ornaments* already. If you project anything, I hope it will be entirely within doors; and don't let me (when I come gaping into Coleman Street) be directed to the gentleman at the ten pinnacles, or with the church porch at his door." Again, to the same (1761): "It is mere pedantry in Gothicism to stick to nothing but altars and tombs, and there is no end to it, if we are to sit upon nothing but coronation chairs, nor drink out of nothing but chalices or flagons." Writing to Mason in 1758 about certain incongruities in one of the latter's odes, he gives the following Doresque illustration of his point. "If you should lead me into a superb Gothic building, with a thousand clustered pillars, each of them half a mile high, the walls all covered with fret-work, and the windows full of red and blue saints that had neither head nor tail, and I should find the Venus de Medici in person perked up in a long niche over the high altar, as naked as she was born, do you think it would raise or damp my devotions?"* He made it a favorite occupation to visit and take drawings from celebrated ruins and the great English cathedrals, particularly those in the Cambridge fens, Ely and Peterboro'. These studies he utilized in a

---

*See also Gray's letter to Rev. James Brown (1763) inclosing a drawing, in reference to a small ruined chapel at York Minster; and a letter (about 1765) to Jas. Bentham, Prebendary of Ely, whose "Essay on Gothic Architecture" had been wrongly attributed to Gray.

short essay on Norman architecture, first published by Mitford in 1814, and incorrectly entitled "Architectura Gothica."

Reverting to his early letters from abroad one is struck by the anticipation of the modern attitude, in his description of a visit to the Grande Chartreuse, which he calls "one of the most solemn, the most romantic, and the most astonishing scenes." * "I do not remember to have gone ten paces without an exclamation that there was no restraining. Not a precipice, not a torrent, not a cliff, but is pregnant with religion and poetry. . . One need not have a very fantastic imagination to see spirits there at noonday." † Walpole's letter of about the same date, also to West,‡ is equally ecstatic. It is written "from a hamlet among the mountains of Savoy. . . Here we are, the lonely lords of glorious desolate prospects. . . But the road, West, the road! Winding round a prodigious mountain, surrounded with others, all shagged with hanging woods, obscured with pines, or lost in clouds! Below a torrent breaking through cliffs, and tumbling through fragments of rocks! . . . Now and then an old foot bridge, with a broken rail, a leaning cross, a cottage or the ruin of an hermitage! This sounds too bombast and too romantic to one that has not seen it, too cold for one that has." Or contrast with Addison's Italian letters passages like these, which foretoken Rogers and Byron. We get nothing so sympathetic till at least a half century later. "It

* To Mrs. Dorothy Gray, 1739.

† To Richard West, 1739.

‡ Gray, Walpole, and West had been schoolfellows and intimates at Eton.

is the most beautiful of Italian nights. . . There is a
moon! There are stars for you! Do not you hear
the fountain? Do not you smell the orange flowers?
That building yonder is the convent of St. Isidore;
and that eminence with the cypress-tress and pines
upon it, the top of Mt. Quirinal." *   "The Neapoli-
tans work till evening: then take their lute or guitar
and walk about the city, or upon the sea shore with it,
to enjoy the *fresco*.   One sees their little brown children jumping about stark naked and the bigger ones
dancing with castanets, while others play on the cym-
bal to them." †   "Kennst du das Land," then already?
The

> " small voices and an old guitar,
> Winning their way to an unguarded heart " ?

And then, for a prophecy of Scott, read the description
of Netley Abbey,‡ in a letter to Nicholls in 1764.
"My ferryman," writes Gray in a letter to Brown
about the same ruin, "assured me that he would not
go near it in the night time for all the world, though
he knew much money had been found there.   The sun
was all too glaring and too full of gauds for such a
scene, which ought to be visited only in the dusk of
the evening."

> " If thou woulds't view fair Melrose aright
>   Go visit it by the pale moonlight,
>   For the gay beams of lightsome day
>   Gild, but to flout, the ruins, Gray."

* To West, 1740.

† To Mrs. Dorothy Gray, 1740.

‡ " Pearch's Collection " (VII. 138) gives an elegiac quatrain poem
on " The Ruins of Netley Abbey," by a poet with the suggestive name
of George Keate; and " The Alps," in heavy Thomsonian blank
verse (VII. 107) by the same hand.

In 1765 Gray visited the Scotch Highlands and sent enthusiastic histories of his trip to Wharton and Mason. "Since I saw the Alps, I have seen nothing sublime till now." "The Lowlands are worth seeing once, but the mountains are ecstatic, and ought to be visited in pilgrimage once a year. None but those monstrous creatures of God know how to join so much beauty with so much horror. A fig for your poets, painters, gardeners, and clergymen that have not been among them."

Again in 1770, the year before his death, he spent six weeks on a ramble through the western counties, descending the Wye in a boat for forty miles, and visiting among other spots which the muse had then, or has since, made illustrious, Hagley and the Leasowes, the Malvern Hills and Tintern Abbey. But the most significant of Gray's "Lilliputian travels," was his tour of the Lake Country in 1769. Here he was on ground that has since become classic; and the lover of Wordsworth encounters with a singular interest, in Gray's "Journal in the Lakes," written nearly thirty years before the "Lyrical Ballads," names like Grasmere, Winander, Skiddaw, Helvellyn, Derwentwater, Borrowdale, and Lodore. What distinguishes the entries in this journal from contemporary writing of the descriptive kind is a certain intimacy of comprehension, a depth of tone which makes them seem like nineteenth-century work. To Gray the landscape was no longer a picture. It had sentiment, character, meaning, almost personality. Different weathers and different hours of the day lent it expressions subtler than the poets had hitherto recognized in the broad, general changes of storm and calm, light and dark-

ness, and the successions of the seasons. He heard
Nature when she whispered, as well as when she spoke
out loud. Thomson could not have written thus, nor
Shenstone, nor even, perhaps, Collins. But almost
any man of cultivation and sensibility can write so
now; or, if not so well, yet with the same accent. A
passage or two will make my meaning clearer.

"To this second turning I pursued my way about
four miles along its borders [Ulswater], beyond a village scattered among trees and called Water Mallock,
in a pleasant, grave day, perfectly calm and warm,
but without a gleam of sunshine. Then, the sky
seeming to thicken, the valley to grow more desolate,
and evening drawing on, I returned by the way I came
to Penrith. . . While I was here, a little shower fell,
red clouds came marching up the hills from the east,
and part of a bright rainbow seemed to rise along the
side of Castle Hill. . . The calmness and brightness
of the evening, the roar of the waters, and the thump-
ing of huge hammers at an iron forge not far distant,
made it a singular walk. . . In the evening walked
alone down to the lake after sunset and saw the solemn
coloring of night draw on, the last gleam of sunshine
fading away on the hilltops, the deep serene of the
waters, and the long shadows of the mountains thrown
across them till they nearly touched the hithermost
shore. At distance heard the murmur of many water-
falls not audible in the day-time.* Wished for the
moon, but she was dark to me and silent, hid in her
vacant inter-lunar cave." †

> * " A soft and lulling sound is heard
>   Of streams inaudible by day."
>   — *The White Doe of Rylstone, Wordsworth.*
> † " Samson Agonistes."

"It is only within a few years," wrote Joseph Warton in 1782, "that the picturesque scenes of our own country, our lakes, mountains, cascades, caverns, and castles, have been visited and described."* It was in this very year that William Gilpin published his "Observations on the River Wye," from notes taken upon a tour in 1770. This was the same year when Gray made his tour of the Wye, and hearing that Gilpin had prepared a description of the region, he borrowed and read his manuscript in June, 1771, a few weeks before his own death. These "Observations" were the first of a series of volumes by Gilpin on the scenery of Great Britain, composed in a poetic and somewhat over-luxuriant style, illustrated by drawings in aquatinta, and all described on the title page as "Relative chiefly to Picturesque Beauty." They had great success, and several of them were translated into German and French.†

* "Essay on Pope" (5th ed.), Vol. II. p. 180.

† These were, in order of publication: "The Mountains and Lakes of Cumberland and Westmoreland" (2 vols.), 1789; "The Highlands of Scotland," 1789; "Remarks on Forest Scenery," 1791; "The Western Parts of England and the Isle of Wight," 1798; "The Coasts of Hampshire," etc., 1804; "Cambridge, Norfolk, Suffolk, Essex," etc., 1809. The last two were posthumously published. Gilpin, who was a prebendary of Salisbury, died in 1804. Pearch's "Collection" (VII. 23) has "A Descriptive Poem," on the Lake Country, in octosyllabic couplets, introducing Keswick, Borrowdale, Dovedale, Lodore, Derwentwater, and other familiar localities.

CHAPTER VI.

The School of Warton.

In the progress of our inquiries, hitherto, we have met with little that can be called romantic in the narrowest sense. Though the literary movement had already begun to take a retrospective turn, few distinctly mediæval elements were yet in evidence. Neither the literature of the monk nor the literature of the knight had suffered resurrection. It was not until about 1760 that writers began to gravitate decidedly toward the Middle Ages. The first peculiarly mediæval type that contrived to secure a foothold in eighteenth-century literature was the hermit, a figure which seems to have had a natural attraction, not only for romanticizing poets like Shenstone and Collins, but for the whole generation of verse writers from Parnell to Goldsmith, Percy and Beattie—each of whom composed a "Hermit"—and even for the authors of "Rasselas" and "Tom Jones," in whose fictions he becomes a stock character, as a fountain of wisdom and of moral precepts.†

† Dr. Johnson had his laugh at this popular person:
> "'Hermit hoar, in solemn cell
> Wearing out life's evening gray,
> Strike thy bosom, sage, and tell
> What is bliss, and which the way?'
>
> "Thus I spoke, and speaking sighed,
> Scarce suppressed the starting tear:
> When the hoary sage replied,
> '*Come, my lad, and drink some beer.*'"

A literary movement which reverts to the past for its inspiration is necessarily also a learned movement. Antiquarian scholarship must lead the way. The picture of an extinct society has to be pieced together from the fragments at hand, and this involves special research. So long as this special knowledge remains the exclusive possession of professional antiquaries like Gough, Hearne, Bentham, Perry, Grose,* it bears no fruit in creative literature. It produces only local histories, surveys of cathedrals and of sepulchral monuments, books about Druidic remains, Roman walls and coins, etc., etc. It was only when men of imagination and of elegant tastes were enlisted in such pursuits that the dry stick of antiquarianism put forth blossoms. The poets, of course, had to make studies of their own, to decipher manuscripts, learn Old English, visit ruins, collect ballads and ancient armor, familiarize themselves with terms of heraldry, architecture, chivalry, ecclesiology and feudal law, and in other such ways inform and stimulate their imaginations. It was many years before the joint labors of scholars and poets had reconstructed an image of mediæval society, sharp enough in outline and brilliant enough in color to impress itself upon the general public. Scott, indeed, was the first to popularize romance; mainly, no doubt, because of the greater power and fervor of his imagination; but also, in part, because an ampler store of materials had been already accumulated when he began work. He had fed on

* " Grose's Antiquities of Scotland " was published in 1791, and Burns wrote " Tam o' Shanter" to accompany the picture of Kirk Alloway in this work. See his poem, " On the late Captain Grose's Peregrinations through Scotland."

Percy's "Reliques" in boyhood; through Coleridge, his verse derives from Chatterton; and the line of Gothic romances which starts with "The Castle of Otranto" is remotely responsible for "Ivanhoe" and "The Talisman." But Scott too was, like Percy and Walpole, a virtuoso and collector; and the vast apparatus of notes and introductory matter in his metrical tales, and in the Waverley novels, shows how necessary it was for the romantic poet to be his own antiquary.

As was to be expected, the zeal of the first romanticists was not always a zeal according to knowledge, and the picture of the Middle Age which they painted was more of a caricature than a portrait. A large share of mediæval literature was inaccessible to the general reader. Much of it was still in manuscript. Much more of it was in old and rare printed copies, broadsides and black-letter folios, the treasures of great libraries and of jealously hoarded private collections. Much was in dialects little understood—forgotten forms of speech—Old French, Middle High German, Old Norse, mediæval Latin, the ancient Erse and Cymric tongues, Anglo-Saxon. There was an almost total lack of apparatus for the study of this literature. Helps were needed in the shape of modern reprints of scarce texts, bibliographies, critical editions, translations, literary histories and manuals, glossaries of archaic words, dictionaries and grammars of obsolete languages. These were gradually supplied by working specialists in different fields of investigation. Every side of mediæval life has received illustration in its turn. Works like Tyrwhitt's edition of Chaucer (1775–78); the collections of mediæval romances by Ellis (1805), Ritson (1802), and Weber (1810);

Nares' and Halliwell's "Archaic Glossary" (1822–46), Carter's "Specimens of Ancient Sculpture and Paintings" (1780-94), Scott's "Demonology and Witchcraft" (1830), Hallam's "Middle Ages" (1818), Meyrick's "Ancient Armour" (1824), Lady Guest's "Mabinogion" (1838), the publications of numberless individual scholars and of learned societies like the Camden, the Spenser, the Percy, the Chaucer, the Early English Text, the Roxburgh Club,—to mention only English examples, taken at random, and separated from each other by wide intervals of time,—are instances of the labors by which mediæval life has been made familiar to all who might choose to make acquaintance with it.

The history of romanticism, after the impulse had once been given, is little else than a record of the steps by which, one after another, new features of that vast and complicated scheme of things which we loosely call the Middle Ages were brought to light and made available as literary material. The picture was constantly having fresh details added to it, nor is there any reason to believe that it is finished yet. Some of the finest pieces of mediæval work have only within the last few years been brought to the attention of the general reader; *e. g.*, the charming old French story in prose and verse, "Aucassin et Nicolete," and the fourteenth-century English poem, "The Perle." The future holds still other phases of romanticism in reserve; the Middle Age seems likely to be as inexhaustible in novel sources of inspiration as classical antiquity has already proved to be. The past belongs to the poet no less than the present, and a great part of the literature of every generation will always be retrospective. The tastes and preferences of the individual artist will continue to find a wide field for selection in the rich quarry of Christian and feudal Europe.

It is not a little odd that the book which first aroused, in modern Europe, an interest in Norse mythology should have been written by a Frenchman. This was the "Introduction à l'Histoire de Danne-marc," published in 1755 by Paul Henri Mallet, a native of Geneva and sometime Professor of Belles Lettres in the Royal University at Copenhagen. The work included also a translation of the first part of the Younger Edda, with an abstract of the second part and of the Elder Edda, and versions of several Runic poems. It was translated into English, in 1770, by Thomas Percy, the editor of the "Reliques," under the title, "Northern Antiquities; or a Description of the Manners, Customs, Religion, and Laws of the An-cient Danes." A German translation had appeared a few years earlier and had inspired the Schleswig-Hol-steiner, Heinrich Wilhelm von Gerstenberg, to compose his "Gedicht eines Skalden," which introduced the old Icelandic mythology into German poetry in 1766. Percy had published independently in 1763 "Five Pieces of Runic Poetry, translated from the Ice-landic Language."

Gray did not wait for the English translation of Mallet's book. In a letter to Mason, dated in 1758, and inclosing some criticisms on the latter's "Caracta-cus" (then in MS.), he wrote: "I am pleased with the Gothic Elysium. Do you think I am ignorant about either that, or the *hell* before, or the *twilight*.*

* "Ragnarök," or "Götterdämmerung," the twilight of the Gods

I have been there and have seen it all in Mallet's
'Introduction to the History of Denmark' (it is in
French), and many other places." It is a far cry from
Mallet's "System of Runic Mythology" to William
Morris' "Sigurd the Volsung" (1877), but to Mallet
belongs the credit of first exciting that interest in
Scandinavian antiquity which has enriched the prose
and poetry not only of England but of Europe in
general. Gray refers to him in his notes on "The
Descent of Odin," and his work continued to be
popular authority on its subject for at least half a
century. Scott cites it in his annotations on "The
Lay of the Last Minstrel " (1805).

Gray's studies in Runic literature took shape in "The
Fatal Sisters " and "The Descent of Odin," written in
1761, published in 1768. These were paraphrases of
two poems which Gray found in the "De Causis Con-
temnendæ Mortis " (Copenhagen, 1689) of Thomas
Bartholin, a Danish physician of the seventeenth
century. The first of them describes the Valkyrie
weaving the fates of the Danish and Irish warriors in
the battle of Clontarf, fought in the eleventh century
between Sigurd, Earl of Orkney, and Brian, King of
Dublin; the second narrates the descent of Odin to
Niflheimer, to inquire of Hela concerning the doom
of Balder.* Gray had designed these for the intro-

---

* For a full discussion of Gray's sources and of his knowledge of
Old Norse, the reader should consult the appendix by Professor
G. L. Kittredge to Professor W. L. Phelps' " Selections from Gray "
(1894, pp. xl–l.) Professor Kittredge concludes that Gray had but
a slight knowledge of Norse, that he followed the Latin of Bartholin in his renderings ; and that he probably also made use of such
authorities as Torfæus' " Orcades " (1697), Ole Worm's " Literatura

ductory chapter of his projected history of English
poetry.   He calls them imitations, which in fact they
are, rather than literal renderings.   In spite of a tinge
of eighteenth-century diction, and of one or two
Shaksperian and Miltonic phrases, the translator
succeeded fairly well in reproducing the wild air of his
originals.   His biographer, Mr. Gosse, promises that
"the student will not fail . . . in the Gothic picturesqueness of 'The Descent of Odin,' to detect notes
and phrases of a more delicate originality than are to
be found even in his more famous writings; and will
dwell with peculiar pleasure on those passages in which
Gray freed himself of the trammels of an artificial and
conventional taste, and prophesied of the new romantic age that was coming."

Celtic antiquity shared with Gothic in this newly
aroused interest.   Here too, as in the phrase about
"the stormy Hebrides," "Lycidas" seems to have
furnished the spark that kindled the imaginations of
the poets.

> "Where were ye, nymphs, when the remorseless deep
>   Closed o'er the head of your loved Lycidas?
>   For neither were ye playing on the steep

Runica" (Copenhagen, 1636), Dr. George Hickes' monumental
"Thesaurus" (Oxford, 1705), and Robert Sheringham's "De An-
glorum Gentis Origine Disceptatio" (1716). Dryden's "Miscellany
Poems" (1716) has a verse translation, "The Waking of Angantyr,"
from the English prose of Hickes, of a portion of the "Hervarar
Saga." Professor Kittredge refers to Sir William Temple's essays
"Of Poetry" and "Of Heroic Virtue." "Nichols' Anecdotes"
(I. 116) mentions, as published in 1715, "The Rudiments of Grammar for the English Saxon Tongue ; with an Apology for the study
of Northern Antiquities." This was by Mrs. Elizabeth Elstob, and
was addressed to Hickes, the compiler of the "Thesaurus."

> Where your old bards, the famous Druids lie,
> Nor on the shaggy top of Mona high,
> Nor yet where Deva spreads her wizard stream."

Joseph Warton quotes this passage twice in his "Essay on Pope" (Vol. I. pp. 7 and 356, 5th ed.), once to assert its superiority to a passage in Pope's "Pastorals": "The mention of places remarkably romantic, the supposed habitation of Druids, bards and wizards, is far more pleasing to the imagination, than the obvious introduction of Cam and Isis." Another time, to illustrate the following suggestion: "I have frequently wondered that our modern writers have made so little use of the druidical times and the traditions of the old bards. . . Milton, we see, was sensible of the force of such imagery, as we may gather from this short but exquisite passage." As further illustrations of the poetic capabilities of similar themes, Warton gives a stanza from Gray's "Bard" and some lines from Gilbert West's "Institution of the Order of the Garter" which describe the ghosts of the Druids hovering about their ruined altars at Stonehenge:

> " —Mysterious rows
> Of rude enormous obelisks, that rise
> Orb within orb, stupendous monuments
> Of artless architecture, such as now
> Oft-times amaze the wandering traveller,
> By the pale moon discerned on Sarum's plain."

He then inserts two stanzas, in the Latin of Hickes' "Thesaurus," of an old Runic ode preserved by Olaus Wormius (Ole Worm) and adds an observation upon the Scandinavian heroes and their contempt of death. Druids and bards now begin to abound Collins'

"Ode on the Death of Mr. Thomson," *e. g.*, com-
mences with the line

> " In yonder grave a Druid lies."

In his " Ode to Liberty," he alludes to the tradition
that Mona, the druidic stronghold, was long covered
with an enchantment of mist—work of an angry
mermaid :

> " Mona, once hid from those who search the main,
>   Where thousand elfin shapes abide."

In Thomas Warton's " Pleasures of Melancholy,"
Contemplation is fabled to have been discovered, when
a babe, by a Druid

> " Far in a hollow glade of Mona's woods,"

and borne by him to his oaken bower, where she

> " —loved to lie
>   Oft deeply listening to the rapid roar
>   Of wood-hung Menai, stream of Druids old."

Mason's " Caractacus " (1759) was a dramatic poem on
the Greek model, with a chorus of British bards, and a
principal Druid for choragus. The scene is the sacred
grove in Mona. Mason got up with much care the
descriptions of druidic rites, such as the preparation of
the adder-stone and the cutting of the mistletoe with
a golden sickle, from Latin authorities like Pliny,
Tacitus, Lucan, Strabo, and Suetonius. Joseph Warton
commends highly the chorus on " Death " in this piece,
as well as the chorus of bards at the end of West's
" Institution of the Garter." For the materials of his
" Bard " Gray had to go no farther than historians
and chroniclers such as Camden, Higden, and Matthew

of Westminster, to all of whom he refers. Following a now discredited tradition, he represents the last survivor of the Welsh poetic guild, seated, harp in hand, upon a crag on the side of Snowdon, and denouncing judgment on Edward I. for the murder of his brothers in song.

But in 1764 Gray was incited, by the publication of Dr. Evans' "Specimens," * to attempt a few translations from the Welsh. The most considerable of these was "The Triumphs of Owen," published among Gray's collected poems in 1768. This celebrates the victory over the confederate fleets of Ireland, Denmark, and Normandy, won about 1160 by a prince of North Wales, Owen Ap Griffin, "the dragon son of Mona." The other fragments are brief but spirited versions of bardic songs in praise of fallen heroes: "Caràdoc" "Conan," and "The Death of Hoel." They were printed posthumously, though doubtless composed in 1764.

The scholarship of the day was not always accurate in discriminating between ancient systems of religion, and Gray, in his letters to Mason in 1758, when "Caractacus" was still in the works, takes him to task for mixing the Gothic and Celtic mythologies. He instructs him that Woden and his Valhalla belong

* " Some Specimens of the Poetry of the Ancient Welsh Bards, translated into English," by Rev. Evan Evans, 1764. The specimens were ten in number. The translations were in English prose. The originals were printed from a copy which Davies, the author of the Welsh dictionary, had made of an ancient vellum MS. thought to be of the times of Edward II., Edward III., and Henry V. The book included a Latin " Dissertatio de Bardis," together with notes, appendices, etc. The preface makes mention of Macpherson's recently published Ossianic poems.

to "the doctrine of the Scalds, not of the Bards";
but admits that, "in that scarcity of Celtic ideas we
labor under," it might be permissible to borrow from
the Edda, "dropping, however, all mention of Woden
and his Valkyrian virgins," and "without entering
too minutely on particulars"; or "still better, to
graft any wild picturesque fable, absolutely of one's
own invention, upon the Druid stock." But Gray
had not scrupled to mix mythologies in "The Bard,"
thereby incurring Dr. Johnson's censure. "The
weaving of the winding sheet he borrowed, as he
owns, from the northern bards; but their texture,
however, was very properly the work of female
powers, as the art of spinning the thread of life in
another mythology. Theft is always dangerous:
Gray has made weavers of the slaughtered bards, by a
fiction outrageous and incongruous."* Indeed Mallet
himself had a very confused notion of the relation
of the Celtic to the Teutonic race. He speaks constantly of the old Scandinavians as Celts. Percy
points out the difference, in the preface to his translation, and makes the necessary correction in the text,
where the word Celtic occurs—usually by substituting
"Gothic and Celtic" for the "Celtic" of the original.
Mason made his contribution to Runic literature,
"Song of Harold the Valiant," a rather insipid versification of a passage from the "Knytlinga Saga,"
which had been rendered by Bartholin into Latin,
from him into French by Mallet, and from Mallet into
English prose by Percy. Mason designed it for in-
sertion in the introduction to Gray's abortive history
of English poetry.

* "Life of Gray."

The true pioneers of the mediæval revival were the
Warton brothers. "The school of Warton" was a
term employed, not without disparaging implications,
by critics who had no liking for antique minstrelsy.
Joseph and Thomas Warton were the sons of Thomas
Warton, vicar of Basingstoke, who had been a fellow of
Magdalen and Professor of Poetry at Oxford; which
latter position was afterward filled by the younger of
his two sons. It is interesting to note that a volume
of verse by Thomas Warton, Sr., posthumously printed
in 1748, includes a Spenserian imitation and translations of two passages from the "Song of Ragner
Lodbrog," an eleventh-century Viking, after the
Latin version quoted by Sir Wm. Temple in his essay
"Of Heroic Virtue"; * so that the romantic leanings
of the Warton brothers seem to be an instance of
heredity. Joseph was educated at Winchester,—
where Collins was his schoolfellow—and both of the
brothers at Oxford. Joseph afterward became head-
master of Winchester, and lived till 1800, surviving
his younger brother ten years. Thomas was always
identified with Oxford, where he resided for forty-
seven years. He was appointed, in 1785, Camden
Professor of History in the university, but gave no
lectures. In the same year he was chosen to succeed
Whitehead, as Poet Laureate. Both brothers were
men of a genial, social temper. Joseph was a man of
some elegance; he was fond of the company of young
ladies, went into general society, and had a certain
renown as a drawing-room wit and diner-out. He
used to spend his Christmas vacations in London,
where he was a member of Johnson's literary club.

* See Phelps' "English Romantic Movement," pp. 73, 141–42.

Thomas, on the contrary, who waxed fat and indolent in college cloisters, until Johnson compared him to a turkey cock, was careless in his personal habits and averse to polite society. He was the life of the common room at Oxford, romped with the schoolboys when he visited Dr. Warton at Winchester, and was said to have a hankering after pipes and ale and the broad mirth of the taproom. Both Wartons had an odd passion for military parades; and Thomas—who was a believer in ghosts—used secretly to attend hangings. They were also remarkably harmonious in their tastes and intellectual pursuits, eager students of old English poetry, Gothic architecture, and British antiquities. So far as enthusiasm, fine critical taste, and elegant scholarship can make men poets, the Wartons were poets. But their work was quite unoriginal. Many of their poems can be taken to pieces and assigned, almost line by line and phrase by phrase, to Milton, Thomson, Spenser, Shakspere, Gray. They had all of our romantic poet Longfellow's dangerous gifts of sympathy and receptivity, without a tenth part of his technical skill, or any of his real originality as an artist. Like Longfellow, they loved the rich and mellow atmosphere of the historic past:

> " Tales that have the rime of age,
> And chronicles of eld."

The closing lines of Thomas Warton's sonnet, "Written in a Blank Leaf of Dugdale's Monasticon " *

* Wm. Dugdale published his " Monasticon Anglicanum," a history of English religious houses, in three parts, in 1655–62–73. It was accompanied with illustrations of the costumes worn by the ancient religious orders, and with architectural views. The latter,

—a favorite with Charles Lamb—might have been written by Longfellow:

> " Nor rough nor barren are the winding ways
> Of hoar Antiquity, but strewn with flowers."

Joseph Warton's pretensions, as a poet, are much less than his younger brother's. Much of Thomas Warton's poetry, such as his *facetiæ* in the "Oxford Sausage" and his "Triumph of Isis," had an academic flavor. These we may pass over, as foreign to our present inquiries. So, too, with most of his annual laureate odes, "On his Majesty's Birthday," etc. Yet even these official and rather perfunctory performances testify to his fondness for what Scott calls "the memorials of our forefathers' piety or splendor." Thus, in the birthday odes for 1787–88, and the New Year ode for 1787, he pays a tribute to the ancient minstrels and to early laureates like Chaucer and Spenser, and celebrates "the Druid harp" sounding "through the gloom profound of forests hoar "; the fanes and castles built by the Normans; and the

> "—bright hall where Odin's Gothic throne
> With the broad blaze of brandished falchions shone."

But the most purely romantic of Thomas Warton's poems are "The Crusade " and "The Grave of King Arthur." The former is the song which

> " The lion heart Plantagenet
> Sang, looking through his prison-bars,"

says Eastlake, were rude and unsatisfactory, but interesting to modern students, as "preserving representations of buildings, or portions of buildings, no longer in existence ; as, for instance, the *campanile*, or detached belfry of Salisbury, since removed, and the spire of Lincoln, destroyed in 1547."

when the minstrel Blondel came wandering in search
of his captive king. The latter describes how
Henry II., on his way to Ireland, was feasted at
Cilgarran Castle, where the Welsh bards sang to him
of the death of Arthur and his burial in Glastonbury
Abbey. The following passage anticipates Scott:

> " Illumining the vaulted roof,
> A thousand torches flamed aloof;
> From massy cups, with golden gleam,
> Sparkled the red metheglin's stream:
> To grace the gorgeous festival,
> Along the lofty-windowed hall
> The storied tapestry was hung;
> With minstrelsy the rafters rung
> Of harps that with reflected light
> From the proud gallery glittered bright:
> While gifted bards, a rival throng,
> From distant Mona, nurse of song,
> From Teivi fringed with umbrage brown,
> From Elvy's vale and Cader's crown,
> From many a shaggy precipice
> That shades Ierne's hoarse abyss,
> And many a sunless solitude
> Of Radnor's inmost mountains rude,
> To crown the banquet's solemn close
> Themes of British glory chose."

Here is much of Scott's skill in the poetic manipulation
of place-names, *e. g.*,

> " Day set on Norham's castled steep,
> And Tweed's fair river, broad and deep,
> And Cheviot's mountains lone "—

names which leave a far-resounding romantic rumble
behind them. Another passage in Warton's poem
brings us a long way on toward Tennyson's "wild

Tintagel by the Cornish sea " and his "island valley of Avilion."

> " O'er Cornwall's cliffs the tempest roared :
> High the screaming sea-mew soared:
> In Tintaggel's topmost tower
> Darksome fell the sleety shower :
> Round the rough castle shrilly sung
> The whirling blast, and wildly flung
> On each tall rampart's thundering side
> The surges of the tumbling tide,
> When Arthur ranged his red-cross ranks
> On conscious Camlan's crimsoned banks :
> By Mordred's faithless guile decreed
> Beneath a Saxon spear to bleed.
> Yet in vain a Paynim foe
> Armed with fate the mighty blow;
> For when he fell, an elfin queen,
> All in secret and unseen,
> O'er the fainting hero threw
> Her mantle of ambrosial blue,
> And bade her spirits bear him far,
> In Merlin's agate-axled car,
> To her green isle's enamelled steep
> Far in the navel of the deep."

Other poems of Thomas Warton touching upon his favorite studies are the " Ode Sent to Mr. Upton, on his Edition of the Faery Queene," the "Monody Written near Stratford-upon-Avon," the sonnets, "Written at Stonehenge," "To Mr. Gray," and "On King Arthur's Round Table," and the humorous epistle which he attributes to Thomas Hearne, the antiquary, denouncing the bishops for their recent order that fast-prayers should be printed in modern type instead of black letter, and pronouncing a curse upon the author

of "The Companion to the Oxford Guide Book" for
his disrespectful remarks about antiquaries.

> "May'st thou pore in vain
> For dubious doorways ! May revengeful moths
> Thy ledgers eat ! May chronologic spouts
> Retain no cypher legible ! May crypts
> Lurk undiscovered ! Nor may'st thou spell the names
> Of saints in storied windows, nor the dates
> Of bells discover, nor the genuine site
> Of abbots' pantries ! "

Warton was a classical scholar and, like most of the
forerunners of the romantic school, was a trifle shame-
faced over his Gothic heresies. Sir Joshua Reynolds
had supplied a painted window of classical design for
New College, Oxford; and Warton, in some complimentary verses, professes that those "portraitures
of Attic art" have won him back to the true taste; *
and prophesies that henceforth angels, apostles,
saints, miracles, martyrdoms, and tales of legendary
lore shall—

> " No more the sacred window's round disgrace,
> But yield to Grecian groups the shining space. . .
> Thy powerful hand has broke the Gothic chain,
> And brought my bosom back to truth again. . .
> For long, enamoured of a barbarous age,
> A faithless truant to the classic page—

* "Verses on Sir Joshua Reynolds' Painted Window." *Cf.* Poe,
"To Helen":

> " On desperate seas long wont to roam
> Thy hyacinth hair, thy classic face,
> Thy Naiad airs have brought me home
> To the glory that was Greece,
> And the grandeur that was Rome."

"Long have I loved to catch the simple chime
Of minstrel harps, and spell the fabling rime ;
To view the festive rites, the knightly play,
That decked heroic Albion's elder day ;
To mark the mouldering halls of barons bold,
And the rough castle, cast in giant mould ;
With Gothic manners, Gothic arts explore,
And muse on the magnificence of yore.
But chief, enraptured have I loved to roam,
A lingering votary, the vaulted dome,
Where the tall shafts, that mount in massy pride,
Their mingling branches shoot from side to side ;
Where elfin sculptors, with fantastic clew,
O'er the long roof their wild embroidery drew ;
Where Superstition, with capricious hand,
In many a maze, the wreathëd window planned,
With hues romantic tinged the gorgeous pane,
To fill with holy light the wondrous fane." *

The application of the word "romantic," in this
passage, to the mediæval art of glass-staining is
significant. The revival of the art in our own day is
due to the influence of the latest English school of
romantic poetry and painting, and especially to William Morris. Warton's biographers track his passion
for antiquity to the impression left upon his mind by a
visit to Windsor Castle, when he was a boy. He used
to spend his summers in wandering through abbeys and
cathedrals. He kept notes of his observations and is
known to have begun a work on Gothic architecture,

* This apology should be compared with Scott's verse epistle to
Wm. Erskine, prefixed to the third canto of " Marmion."

" For me, thus nurtured, dost thou ask
  The classic poet's well-conned task ? " etc.

Scott spoke of himself in Warton's exact language, as a " truant to
the classic page."

no trace of which, however, was found among his manuscripts. The Bodleian Library was one of his haunts, and he was frequently seen "surveying with quiet and rapt earnestness the ancient gateway of Magdalen College." He delighted in illuminated manuscripts and black-letter folios. In his "Observations on the Faëry Queene"* he introduces a digression of twenty pages on Gothic architecture, and speaks lovingly of a "very curious and beautiful folio manuscript of the history of Arthur and his knights in the Ashmolean Museum at Oxford, written on vellum, with illuminated initials and head-pieces, in which we see the fashion of ancient armor, building, manner of tilting and other particulars."

Another very characteristic poem of Warton's is the "Ode Written at Vale-Royal Abbey in Cheshire," a monastery of Cistercian monks, founded by Edward I. This piece is saturated with romantic feeling and written in the stanza and manner of Gray's "Elegy," as will appear from a pair of stanzas, taken at random:

> "By the slow clock, in stately-measured chime,
> That from the massy tower tremendous tolled,
> No more the plowman counts the tedious time,
> Nor distant shepherd pens the twilight fold.
>
> "High o'er the trackless heath at midnight seen,
> No more the windows, ranged in long array
> (Where the tall shaft and fretted nook between
> Thick ivy twines), the tapered rites betray."

It is a note of Warton's period that, though Fancy and the Muse survey the ruins of the abbey with pensive regret, "severer Reason"—the real eighteenth-century divinity—"scans the scene with philosophic ken," and

* See *ante*, pp. 99–101.

—being a Protestant—reflects that, after all, the monastic houses were " Superstition's shrine " and their demolition was a good thing for Science and Religion.

The greatest service, however, that Thomas Warton rendered to the studies that he loved was his " History of English Poetry from the Twelfth to the Close of the Sixteenth Century." This was in three volumes, published respectively in 1774, 1777, and 1781. The fragment of a fourth volume was issued in 1790. A revised edition in four volumes was published in 1824, under the editorship of Richard Price, corrected, augmented, and annotated by Ritson, Douce, Park, Ashby, and the editor himself. In 1871 appeared a new revision (also in four volumes) edited by W. Carew Hazlitt, with many additions, by the editor and by well-known English scholars like Madden, Skeat, Furnivall, Morris, and Thomas and Aldis Wright. It should never be forgotten, in estimating the value of Warton's work, that he was a forerunner in this field. Much of his learning is out of date, and the modern editors of his history—Price and Hazlitt—seem to the discouraged reader to be chiefly engaged, in their footnotes and bracketed interpellations, in taking back statements that Warton had made in the text. The leading position, *e. g.*, of his preliminary dissertation, " Of the Origin of Romantic Fiction in Europe "— deriving it from the Spanish Arabs—has long since been discredited. But Warton's learning was wide, if not exact; and it was not dry learning, but quickened by the spirit of a genuine man of letters. Therefore, in spite of its obsoleteness in matters of fact, his history remains readable, as a body of descriptive criticism, or a continuous literary essay. The best way to

read it is to read it as it was written—in the origi·
nal edition—disregarding the apparatus of notes,
which modern scholars have accumulated about it, but
remembering that it is no longer an authority and
probably needs correcting on every page.   Read thus,
it is a thoroughly delightful book, "a classic in its
way," as Lowell has said.   Southey, too, affirmed that
its publication formed an epoch in literary history;
and that, with Percy's " Reliques," it had promoted,
beyond any other work, the " growth of a better taste
than had prevailed for the hundred years preceding."

Gray had schemed a history of English poetry, but
relinquished the design to Warton, to whom he communicated an outline of his own plan.   The "Observations on English Metre " and the essay on the poet
Lydgate, among Gray's prose remains, are apparently
portions of this projected work.

Lowell, furthermore, pronounces Joseph Warton's
" Essay on the Genius and Writings of Pope " (1756)
"the earliest public official declaration of war against
the reigning mode."   The new school had its critics,
as well as its poets, and the Wartons were more effective
in the former capacity.   The war thus opened was by
no means as internecine as that waged by the French
classicists and romanticists of 1830.   It has never been
possible to get up a very serious conflict in England,
upon merely æsthetic grounds.   Yet the same opposition existed.   Warton's biographer tells us that the
strictures made upon his essay were "powerful
enough to damp the ardor of the essayist, who left
his work in an imperfect state for the long space of
twenty-six years," *i. e.*, till 1782, when he published the
second volume.

Both Wartons were personal friends of Dr. John son; they were members of the Literary Club and contributors to the *Idler* and the *Adventurer.* Thomas interested himself to get Johnson the Master's degree from Oxford, where the doctor made him a visit. Some correspondence between them is given in Boswell. Johnson maintained in public a respectful attitude toward the critical and historical work of the Wartons; but he had no sympathy with their antiquarian enthusiasm or their liking for old English poetry. In private he ridiculed Thomas' verses, and summed them up in the manner ensuing:

> " Wheresoe'er I turn my view,
>   All is strange yet nothing new;
>   Endless labor all along,
>   Endless labor to be wrong;
>   Phrase that time has flung away,
>   Uncouth words in disarray,
>   Tricked in antique ruff and bonnet,
>   Ode and elegy and sonnet."

And although he added, " Remember that I love the fellow dearly, for all I laugh at him," this saving clause failed to soothe the poet's indignant breast, when he heard that the doctor had ridiculed his lines. An estrangement resulted which Johnson is said to have spoken of even with tears, saying " that Tom Warton was the only man of genius he ever knew who wanted a heart."

Goldsmith, too, belonged to the conservative party, though Mr. Perry * detects romantic touches in " The Deserted Village," such as the line,

* " Eighteenth Century Literature," p. 397.

" Where wild Altama murmurs to their woe,"

or

" On Torno's cliffs or Pambamarca's side."

In his "Enquiry into the Present State of Polite
Learning" (1759) Goldsmith pronounces the age one
of literary decay; he deplores the vogue of blank
verse—which he calls an "erroneous innovation"—
and the "disgusting solemnity of manner" that it has
brought into fashion.   He complains of the revival of
old plays upon the stage.   "Old pieces are revived,
and scarcely any new ones admitted. . . The public
are again obliged to ruminate over those ashes of
absurdity which were disgusting to our ancestors even
in an age of ignorance. . . What must be done?
Only sit down contented, cry up all that comes before
us and advance even the absurdities of Shakspere.
Let the reader suspend his censure; I admire the
beauties of this great father of our stage as much as
they deserve, but could wish, for the honor of our
country, and for his own too, that many of his scenes
were forgotten.   A man blind of one eye should
always be painted in profile.   Let the spectator who
assists at any of these new revived pieces only ask
himself whether he would approve such a performance,
if written by a modern poet.   I fear he will find that
much of his applause proceeds merely from the sound
of a name and an empty veneration for antiquity.   In
fact the revival of those *pieces of forced humor, far-
fetched conceit and unnatural hyperbole which have been
ascribed to Shakspere,* is rather gibbeting than raising a
statue to his memory."

The words that I have italicized make it evident that

what Goldsmith was really finding fault with was the
restoration of the original text of Shakspere's plays,
in place of the garbled versions that had hitherto been
acted. This restoration was largely due to Garrick,
but Goldsmith's language implies that the reform was
demanded by public opinion and by the increasing
"veneration for antiquity." The next passage shows
that the new school had its *claque*, which rallied to
the support of the old British drama as the French
romanticists did, nearly a century later, to the support
of Victor Hugo's *melodrames.**

" What strange vamped comedies, farcical tragedies,
or what shall I call them—speaking pantomimes have
we not of late seen? . . . The piece pleases our
critics because it talks Old English; and it pleases the
galleries because it has ribaldry. . . A prologue
generally precedes the piece, to inform us that it was
composed by Shakspere or old Ben, or somebody else
who took them for his model. A face of iron could
not have the assurance to avow dislike; the theater
has its partisans who understand the force of combi-
nations trained up to vociferation, clapping of hands
and clattering of sticks; and though a man might
have strength sufficient to overcome a lion in single
combat, he may run the risk of being devoured by an
army of ants."

Goldsmith returned to the charge in " The Vicar of
Wakefield " (1766), where Dr. Primrose, inquiring
of the two London dames, " who were the present
theatrical writers in vogue, who were the Drydens and

* Lowell mentions the publication of Dodsley's " Old Plays,"
(1744) as, like Percy's " Reliques," a symptom of the return o the
past. Essay on " Gray."

Otways of the day," is surprised to learn that Dryden
and Rowe are quite out of fashion, that taste has gone
back a whole century, and that " Fletcher, Ben Jonson
and all the plays of Shakspere are the only things that
go down." "How," cries the good vicar, "is it
possible the present age can be pleased with that
antiquated dialect, that obsolete humor, those overcharged characters which abound in the works you
mention?" Goldsmith's disgust with this affectation
finds further vent in his " Life of Parnell " (1770).
" He [Parnell] appears to me to be the last of that
great school that had modeled itself upon the ancients,
and taught English poetry to resemble what the
generality of mankind have allowed to excel. . . His
productions bear no resemblance to those tawdry
things which it has, for some time, been the fashion to
admire. . . His poetical language is not less correct
than his subjects are pleasing. He found it at that
period in which it was brought to its highest pitch of
refinement; and ever since his time, it has been
gradually debasing. It is, indeed, amazing, after
what has been done by Dryden, Addison, and Pope, to
improve and harmonize our native tongue, that their
successors should have taken so much pains to involve
it into pristine barbarity. These misguided innovators
have not been content with restoring antiquated words
and phrases, but have indulged themselves in the most
licentious transpositions and the harshest construc-
tions; vainly imagining that, the more their writings
are unlike prose, the more they resemble poetry.
They have adopted a language of their own, and call
upon mankind for admiration. All those who do not
understand them are silent; and those who make out

their meaning are willing to praise, to show they understand." This last sentence is a hit at the alleged obscurity of Gray's and Mason's odes.

To illustrate the growth of a retrospective habit in literature Mr. Perry * quotes at length from an essay " On the Prevailing Taste for the Old English Poets," by Vicesimus Knox, sometime master of Tunbridge school, editor of " Elegant Extracts " and honorary doctor of the University of Pennsylvania. Knox's essays were written while he was an Oxford undergraduate, and published collectively in 1777. By this time the romantic movement was in full swing. " The Castle of Otranto " and Percy's "Reliques" had been out more than ten years: many of the Rowley poems were in print; and in this very year, Tyrwhitt issued a complete edition of them, and Warton published the second volume of his " History of English Poetry." Chatterton and Percy are both mentioned by Knox.

" The antiquarian spirit," he writes, "which was once confined to inquiries concerning the manners, the buildings, the records, and the coins of the ages that preceded us, has now extended itself to those poetical compositions which were popular among our forefathers, but which have gradually sunk into oblivion through the decay of language and the prevalence of a correct and polished taste. Books printed in the black letter are sought for with the same avidity with which the English antiquary peruses a monumental inscription, or treasures up a Saxon piece of money. The popular ballad, composed by some illiterate minstrel, and which has been handed down by tradition

* " Eighteenth Century Literature," pp. 401–03.

for several centuries, is rescued from the hands of the vulgar, to obtain a place in the collection of the man of taste.   Verses which, a few years past, were thought worthy the attention of children only, or of the lowest and rudest orders, are now admired for that artless simplicity which once obtained the name of coarseness and vulgarity." Early English poetry, continues the essayist, " has had its day, and the antiquary must not despise us if we cannot peruse it with patience.   He who delights in all such reading as is never read, may derive some pleasure from the singularity of his taste, but he ought still to respect the judgment of mankind, which has consigned to oblivion the works which he admires.   While he pores unmolested on Chaucer, Gower, Lydgate, and Occleve, let him not censure our obstinacy in adhering to Homer, Virgil, Milton, and Pope. . .   Notwithstanding the incontrovertible merit of many of our ancient relics of poetry, I believe it may be doubted whether any one of them would be tolerated as the production of a modern poet.   As a good imitation of the ancient manner, it would find its admirers; but, considered independently, as an original, it would be thought a careless, vulgar, inartificial composition.   There are few who do not read Dr. Percy's own pieces, and those of other late writers, with more pleasure than the oldest ballad in the collection of that ingenious writer." Mr. Perry quotes another paper of Knox in which he divides the admirers of English poetry into two parties: " On one side are the lovers and imitators of Spenser and Milton; and on the other, those of Dryden, Boileau, and Pope ": in modern phrase, the romanticists and the classicists.

Joseph Warton's " Essay on Pope " was an attempt

to fix its subject's rank among English poets. Following the discursive method of Thomas Warton's "Observations on the Faerie Queene," it was likewise an elaborate commentary on all of Pope's poems *seriatim*. Every point was illustrated with abundant learning, and there were digressions amounting to independent essays on collateral topics: one, *e. g.*, on Chaucer, one on early French metrical romances; another on Gothic architecture: another on the new school of landscape gardening, in which Walpole's essay and Mason's poem are quoted with approval, and mention is made of the Leasowes. The book was dedicated to Young; and when the second volume was published in 1782, the first was reissued in a revised form and introduced by a letter to the author from Tyrwhitt, who writes that, under the shelter of Warton's authority, "one may perhaps venture to avow an opinion that poetry is not confined to rhyming couplets, and that its greatest powers are not displayed in prologues and epilogues."

The modern reader will be apt to think Warton's estimate of Pope quite high enough. He places him, to be sure, in the second rank of poets, below Spenser, Shakspere, and Milton, yet next to Milton and above Dryden; and he calls the reign of Queen Anne the great age of English poetry. Yet if it be recollected that the essay was published only twelve years after Pope's death, and at a time when he was still commonly held to be, if not the greatest poet, at least the greatest artist in verse, that England had ever produced, it will be seen that Warton's opinions might well be thought revolutionary, and his challenge to the critics a bold one. These opinions can be best exhibited by quoting a few passages from his book, not consecutive, but taken here and there as best suits the purpose.

"The sublime and the pathetic are the two chief nerves of all genuine poesy. What is there transcendently sublime or pathetic in Pope? . . . He early left the more poetical provinces of his art, to become a moral, didactic, and satiric poet. . . And because I am, perhaps, unwilling to speak out in plain English, I will adopt the following passage of Voltaire, which, in my opinion, as exactly characterizes Pope as it does his model, Boileau, for whom it was originally designed. 'Incapable peut-être du sublime qui élève l'âme, et du sentiment qui l'attendrit, mais fait pour éclairer ceux à qui la nature accorda l'un et l'autre; laborieux, sévère, précis, pur, harmonieux, il devint enfin le poëte de la Raison.' . . . A clear head and acute understanding are not sufficient alone to make a poet; the most solid observations on human life, expressed with the utmost elegance and brevity, are morality and not poetry. . . It is a creative and glowing imagination, *acer spiritus ac vis*, and that alone, that can stamp a writer with this exalted and very uncommon character."

Warton believes that Pope's projected epic on Brutus, the legendary founder of Britain, "would have more resembled the 'Henriade' than the 'Iliad,' or even the 'Gierusalemme Liberata'; that it would have appeared (if this scheme had been executed) how much, and for what reasons, the man that is skillful in painting modern life, and the most secret foibles and follies of his contemporaries, is, THEREFORE, disqualified for representing the ages of heroism, and that simple life which alone epic poetry can gracefully de-

scribe. . . Wit and satire are transitory and perish-
able, but nature and passion are eternal." The largest
portion of Pope's work, says the author's closing summary, "is of the didactic, moral, and satiric kind; and
consequently not of the most poetic species of poetry;
whence it is manifest that good sense and judgment
were his characteristical excellencies, rather than fancy
and invention. . . He stuck to describing modern
manners; but those manners, because they are familiar,
uniform, artificial, and polished, are in their very nature, unfit for any lofty effort of the Muse. He gradually became one of the most correct, even, and exact
poets that ever wrote. . . Whatever poetical enthusiasm he actually possessed, he withheld and stifled.
The perusal of him affects not our minds with such
strong emotions as we feel from Homer and Milton;
so that no man of a true poetical spirit is master of
himself while he reads them. . . He who would think
the 'Faerie Queene,' 'Palamon and Arcite,' the
'Tempest' or 'Comus,' childish and romantic might
relish Pope. Surely it is no narrow and niggardly
encomium to say, he is the great poet of Reason, the
first of ethical authors in verse."

To illustrate Pope's inferiority in the poetry of nature and passion, Warton quotes freely by way of contrast, not only from Spenser and Milton, but from
such contemporaries of his own as Thomson, Akenside,
Gray, Collins, Dyer, Mason, West, Shenstone, and
Bedingfield. He complains that Pope's "Pastorals"
contains no new image of nature, and his "Windsor
Forest" no local color; while "the scenes of Thomson
are frequently as wild and romantic as those of Salvator Rosa, varied with precipices and torrents and

' castled cliffs ' and deep valleys, with piny mountains and the gloomiest caverns." "When Gray published his exquisite ode on Eton College . . . little notice was taken of it; but I suppose no critic can be found that will not place it far above Pope's ' Pastorals.' "

A few additional passages will serve to show that this critic's literary principles, in general, were consciously and polemically romantic.   Thus he pleads for the *mot précis*—that shibboleth of the nineteenth-century romanticists—for "*natural, little* circumstances " against "those who are fond of *generalities*"; for the "lively painting of Spenser and Shakspere," as contrasted with the lack of picturesqueness and imagery in Voltaire's "Henriade."   He praises "the fashion that has lately obtained, in all the nations of Europe, of republishing and illustrating their old poets." *
Again, commenting upon Pope's well-known triplet,

> " Waller was smooth, but Dryden taught to join
> The varying verse, the full-resounding line,
> The long majestic march and energy divine ! "

he exclaims: "What! Did Milton contribute nothing to the harmony and extent of our language? . . . Surely his verses vary and resound as much, and display as much majesty and energy, as any that can be found in Dryden.   And we will venture to say that he that studies Milton attentively, will gain a truer taste for genuine poetry than he that forms himself on French writers and their followers."   Elsewhere he

* It is curious, however, to find Warton describing Villon as " a pert and insipid ballad-monger, whose thoughts and diction were as low and illiberal as his life," Vol. II. p. 338 (Fifth Edition, 1806).

expresses a preference for blank verse over rhyme, in long poems on subjects of a dignified kind.*

" It is perpetually the nauseous cant of the French critics, and of their advocates and pupils, that the English writers are generally incorrect. If correctness implies an absence of petty faults, this perhaps may be granted: if it means that, because their tragedians have avoided the irregularities of Shakspere, and have observed a juster œconomy in their fables, therefore the 'Athalia,' for instance, is preferable to 'Lear,' the notion is groundless and absurd. Though the 'Henriade' should be allowed to be free from any very gross absurdities, yet who will dare to rank it with the 'Paradise Lost'? . . . In our own country the rules of the drama were never more completely understood than at present; yet what uninteresting, though faultless, tragedies have we lately seen! . . . Whether or no the natural powers be not confined and debilitated by that timidity and caution which is occasioned by a rigid regard to the dictates of art; or whether that philosophical, that geometrical and systematical spirit so much in vogue, which has spread itself from the sciences even into polite literature, by consulting only reason, has not diminished and destroyed sentiment, and made our poets write from and to the head rather than the heart; or whether, lastly, when just models, from which the rules have neces-

---

* Warton quotes the following bathetic opening of a " Poem in Praise of Blank Verse " by Aaron Hill, " one of the very first persons who took notice of Thomson, on the publication of ' Winter ' " :

> " Up from Rhyme's poppied vale ! and ride the storm
> That thunders in blank verse ! "

— Vol. II. p. 186.

sarily been drawn, have once appeared, succeeding writers, by vainly and ambitiously striving to surpass those . . . do not become stiff and forced." One of these uninteresting, though faultless tragedies was "Cato," which Warton pronounces a "sententious and declamatory drama" filled with "pompous Roman sentiments," but wanting action and pathos. He censures the tameness of Addison's "Letter from Italy." * "With what flatness and unfeelingness has he spoken of statuary and painting! Raphæl never received a more phlegmatic eulogy." He refers on the other hand to Gray's account of his journey to the Grande Chartreuse,† as worthy of comparison with one of the finest passages in the "Epistle of Eloisa to Abelard."

This mention of Addison recalls a very instructive letter of Gray on the subject of poetic style.‡ The romanticists loved a rich diction, and the passage might be taken as an anticipatory defense of himself against Wordsworth's strictures in the preface to the "Lyrical Ballads." "The language of the age," wrote Gray, "is never the language of poetry, except among the French, whose verse . . . differs in nothing from prose. Our poetry has a language peculiar to itself; to which almost everyone that has written has added something, by enriching it with foreign idioms and derivatives; nay, sometimes words of their own composition or invention. Shakspere and Milton have been great creators in this way . . . our language has an undoubted right to words of an hundred years old, provided antiquity have not rendered them

* See *ante*, p. 57.   † See *ante*, p. 181.
‡ To Richard West, April, 1742.

unintelligible. In truth Shakspere's language is one
of his principal beauties; and he has no less advantage
over your Addisons and Rowes in this, than in those
other great excellencies you mention. Every word in
him is a picture." He then quotes a passage from
"Richard III.," and continues, "Pray put me the
following lines into the tongue of our modern dramatics. To me they appear untranslatable, and if this be
the case, our language is greatly degenerated."

Warton further protests against the view which
ascribed the introduction of true taste in literature
to the French. "Shakspere and Milton imitated the
Italians and not the French." He recommends also
the reintroduction of the preternatural into poetry.
There are some, he says, who think that poetry has
suffered by becoming too rational, deserting fairyland,
and laying aside "descriptions of magic and enchantment," and he quotes, *à propos* of this the famous
stanza about the Hebrides in "The Castle of Indolence."* The false refinement of the French has made
them incapable of enjoying "the terrible graces of our
irregular Shakspere, especially in his scenes of magic
and incantations. These *Gothic* charms are in truth
more striking to the imagination than the classical. The magicians of Ariosto, Tasso, and Spenser
have more powerful spells than those of Apollonius,
Seneca, and Lucan. The enchanted forest of Ismeni
is more awfully and tremendously poetical than even
the grove which Cæsar orders to be cut down in
Lucan (i. iii. 400), which was so full of terrors that,
at noonday or midnight, the priest himself dared not
approach it—

        " ' Dreading the demon of the grove to meet.'

              * See *ante*, p. 94.

Who that sees the sable plumes waving on the pro
digious helmet in the Castle of Otranto, and the
gigantic arm on the top of the great staircase, is not
more affected than with the paintings of Ovid and
Apuleius? What a group of dreadful images do we
meet with in the Edda! The Runic poetry abounds
in them. Such is Gray's thrilling Ode on the ' Descent of Odin.' "

Warton predicts that Pope's fame as a poet will ultimately rest on his " Windsor Forest," his " Epistle
of Eloisa to Abelard," and " The Rape of the Lock."
To this prophecy time has already, in part, given
the lie. Warton preferred " Windsor Forest" and
" Eloisa " to the " Moral Essays " because they belonged to a higher kind of poetry. Posterity likes
the " Moral Essays" better because they are better of
their kind. They were the natural fruit of Pope's
genius and of his time, while the others were artificial.
We can go to Wordsworth for nature, to Byron for
passion, and to a score of poets for both, but Pope remains unrivaled in his peculiar field. In other words,
we value what is characteristic in the artist; the one
thing which he does best, the precise thing which he
can do and no one else can. But Warton's mistake is
significant of the changing literary standards of his
age; and his essay is one proof out of many that the
English romantic movement was not entirely without
self-conscious aims, but had its critical formulas and
its programme, just as Queen Anne classicism had.

CHAPTER VII.

The Gothic Revival.

ONE of Thomas Warton's sonnets was addressed to Richard Hurd, afterward Bishop of Lichfield and Coventry, and later of Worcester. Hurd was a friend of Gray and Mason, and his "Letters on Chivalry and Romance" (1762) helped to initiate the romantic movement. They perhaps owed their inspiration, in part, to Sainte Palaye's "Mémoires sur l'ancienne Chevalerie," the first volume of which was issued in 1759, though the third and concluding volume appeared only in 1781. This was a monumental work and, as a standard authority, bears much the same relation to the literature of its subject that Mallet's "Histoire de Dannemarc" bears to all the writing on Runic mythology that was done in Europe during the eighteenth-century. Jean Baptiste de la Curne de Sainte Palaye was a scholar of wide learning, not only in the history of mediæval institutions but in old French dialects. He went to the south of France to familiarize himself with Provençal: collected a large library of Provençal books and manuscripts, and published in 1774 his "Histoire des Troubadours." Among his other works are a "Dictionary of French Antiquities," a glossary of Old French, and an edition of "Aucassin et Nicolete." Mrs. Susannah Dobson, who wrote "Historical Anecdotes of Heraldry and Chivalry"

(1795), made an English translation of Sainte Palaye's
"History of the Troubadours" in 1779, and of his
"Memoirs of Ancient Chivalry" in 1784.

The purpose of Hurd's letters was to prove "the
pre-eminence of the Gothic manners and fictions, as
adapted to the ends of poetry, above the classic."
"The greatest geniuses of our own and foreign countries," he affirms, "such as Ariosto and Tasso in
Italy, and Spenser and Milton in England, were
seduced by these barbarities of their forefathers;
were even charmed by the Gothic romances. Was
this caprice and absurdity in them? Or may there not
be something in the Gothic Romance peculiarly suited
to the views of a genius and to the ends of poetry?
And may not the philosophic moderns have gone too
far in their perpetual ridicule and contempt of it?"
After a preliminary discussion of the origin of chivalry and knight-errantry and of the ideal knightly
characteristics, "Prowess, Generosity, Gallantry, and
Religion," which he derives from the military necessi-
ties of the feudal system, he proceeds to establish a
"remarkable correspondency between the manners of
the old heroic times, as painted by their great romancer, Homer, and those which are represented to us in
the books of modern knight-errantry." He compares,
e. g., the Læstrygonians, Cyclopes, Circes, and Calyp-
sos of Homer, with the giants, paynims, sorceresses
encountered by the champions of romance; the Greek
ἀοιδοί with the minstrels; the Olympian games with
tournaments; and the exploits of Hercules and Theseus, in quelling dragons and other monsters, with the
similar emprises of Lancelot and Amadis de Gaul.
The critic is daring enough to give the Gothic man-

ners the preference over the heroic. Homer, he says, if he could have known both, would have chosen the former by reason of "the improved gallantry of the feudal times, and the superior solemnity of their superstitions. The gallantry which inspirited the feudal times was of a nature to furnish the poet with finer scenes and subjects of description, in every view, than the simple and uncontrolled barbarity of the Grecian. . . There was a dignity, a magnificence, a variety in the feudal, which the other wanted."

An equal advantage, thinks Hurd, the romancers enjoyed over the pagan poets in the point of supernatural machinery. " For the more solemn fancies of witchcraft and incantation, the horrors of the Gothic were above measure striking and terrible. The mummeries of the pagan priests were childish, but the Gothic enchanters shook and alarmed all nature. . . You would not compare the Canidia of Horace with the witches in 'Macbeth.' And what are Virgil's myrtles, dropping blood, to Tasso's enchanted forest? . . . The fancies of our modern bards are not only more gallant, but . . . more sublime, more terrible, more alarming than those of the classic fables. In a word, you will find that the manners they paint, and the superstitions they adopt, are the more poetical for being Gothic."

Evidently the despised " Gothick " of Addison—as Mr. Howells puts it—was fast becoming the admired " Gothic " of Scott. This pronunciamento of very advanced romantic doctrine came out several years before Percy's "Reliques" and "The Castle of Otranto." It was only a few years later than Thomas Warton's " Observations on the Faërie Queene" and

Joseph's "Essay on Pope," but its views were much more radical. Neither of the Wartons would have ventured to pronounce the Gothic manners superior to the Homeric, as materials for poetry, whatever, in his secret heart, he might have thought.* To Johnson such an opinion must have seemed flat blasphemy. Hurd accounts for the contempt into which the Gothic had fallen on the ground that the feudal ages had never had the good fortune to possess a great poet, like Homer, capable of giving adequate artistic expression to their life and ideals. *Carent vate sacro.* Spenser and Tasso, he thinks, "came too late, and it was impossible for them to paint truly and perfectly what was no longer seen or believed. . . As it is, we may take a guess of what the subject was capable of affording to real genius from the rude sketches we have of it in the old romancers. . . The ablest writers of Greece ennobled the system of heroic manners, while it was fresh and flourishing; and their works being masterpieces of composition, so fixed the credit of it in the opinion of the world, that no revolution of time and taste could afterward shake it. Whereas the Gothic, having been disgraced in their infancy by bad writers, and a new set of manners springing up before there were any better to do them justice, they could never be brought into vogue by the attempts of later poets." Moreover, "the Gothic manners of chivalry, as springing out of the feudal system, were as singular as that system itself; so that when that political constitution vanished out of Europe, the manners that belonged to it were no

* But compare the passage last quoted with the one from Warton's essay *ante*, p. 219.

longer seen or understood. There was no example
of any such manners remaining on the face of the
earth. And as they never did subsist but once, and
are never likely to subsist again, people would be led
of course to think and speak of them as romantic and
unnatural."

Even so, he thinks that the Renaissance poets,
Ariosto and Spenser, owe their finest effects not to
their tinge of classical culture but to their romantic
materials. Shakspere "is greater when he uses
Gothic manners and machinery, than when he employs classical." Tasso, to be sure, tried to trim
between the two, by giving an epic form to his
romantic subject-matter, but Hurd pronounces his
imitations of the ancients "faint and cold and
almost insipid, when compared with his original
fictions. . . If it was not for these *lies* [*magnan-
ima mensogna*] of Gothic invention, I should scarcely
be disposed to give the 'Gierusalemme Liberata'
a second reading." Nay, Milton himself, though
finally choosing the classic model, did so only after
long hesitation. "His favorite subject was Arthur
and the Knights of the Round Table. On this he had
fixed for the greater part of his life. What led him
to change his mind was partly, as I suppose, his
growing fanaticism; partly his ambition to take a
different route from Spenser; but chiefly, perhaps, the
discredit into which the stories of chivalry had now
fallen by the immortal satire of Cervantes. Yet we
see through all his poetry, where his enthusiasm
flames out most, a certain predilection for the legends
of chivalry before the fables of Greece." Hurd says
that, if the "Faërie Queene" be regarded as a Gothic

poem, it will be seen to have true unity of design,
a merit which even the Wartons had denied it.
"When an architect examines a Gothic structure by
Grecian rules he finds nothing but deformity. But
the Gothic architecture has its own rules by which,
when it comes to be examined, it is seen to have its
merit, as well as the Grecian."

The essayist complains that the Gothic fables fell
into contempt through the influence of French critics
who ridiculed and disparaged the Italian romancers,
Ariosto and Tasso. The English critics of the
Restoration—Davenant, Hobbes, Shaftesbury—took
their cue from the French, till these pseudo-classical
principles "grew into a sort of a cant, with which
Rymer and the rest of that school filled their flimsy
essays and rumbling prefaces. . . The exact but
cold Boileau happened to say something about the
clinquant of Tasso," and "Mr. Addison,* who gave
the law in taste here, took it up and sent it about," so
that "it became a sort of watchword among the
critics." "What we have gotten," concludes the
final letter of the series, "by this revolution, is a
great deal of good sense. What we have lost is a
world of fine fabling, the illusion of which is so grate-
ful to the *charméd spirit* that, in spite of philosophy
and fashion 'Faery' Spenser still ranks highest
among the poets; I mean with all those who are
either come of that house, or have any kindness
for it."

We have seen that, during the classical period,
"Gothic," as a term in literary criticism, was synonymous with barbarous, lawless, and tawdry. Addison

* See *ante*, p. 49.

instructs his public that "the taste of most of our English poets, as well as readers, is extremely Gothic." * After commending the French critics, Bouhours and Boileau, for their insistence upon good sense, justness of thought, simplicity, and naturalness he goes on as follows: "Poets who want this strength of genius, to give that majestic simplicity to nature which we so much admire in the works of the ancients, are forced to hunt after foreign ornaments, and not to let any piece of wit, of what kind soever, escape them. I look upon these writers as Goths in poetry, who, like those in architecture, not being able to come up to the beautiful simplicity of the old Greeks and Romans, have endeavored to supply its place with all the extravagances of an irregular fancy." In the following paper (No. 63), an "allegorical vision of the encounter of True and False Wit," he discovers, "in a very dark grove, a monstrous fabric, built after the Gothic manner and covered with innumerable devices in that barbarous kind of sculpture." This temple is consecrated to the God of Dullness, who is "dressed in the habit of a monk." In his essay "On Taste" (No. 409) he says, "I have endeavored, in several of my speculations, to banish this Gothic taste which has taken possession among us."

The particular literary vice which Addison strove to correct in these papers was that conceited style which infected a certain school of seventeenth-century poetry, running sometimes into such puerilities as anagrams, acrostics, echo-songs, rebuses, and verses in the shape of eggs, wings, hour-glasses, etc. He

* *Spectator*, No. 62.

names, as special representatives of this affectation, Herbert, Cowley, and Sylvester. But it is significant that Addison should have described this fashion as Gothic. It has in reality nothing in common with the sincere and loving art of the old builders. He might just as well have called it classic; for, as he acknowledges, devices of the kind are to be found in the Greek anthology, and Ovid was a poet given to conceits. Addison was a writer of pure taste, but the coldness and timidity of his imagination, and the maxims of the critical school to which he belonged, made him mistake for spurious decoration the efflorescence of that warm, creative fancy which ran riot in Gothic art. The grotesque, which was one expression of this sappy vigor, was abhorrent to Addison. The art and poetry of his time were tame, where Gothic art was wild; dead where Gothic was alive. He could not sympathize with it, nor understand it. "Vous ne pouvez pas le comprendre; vous avez toujours haï la vie."

I have quoted Vicesimus Knox's complaint that the antiquarian spirit was spreading from architecture and numismatics into literature.* We meet with satire upon antiquaries many years before this; in Pope, in Akenside's Spenserian poem "The Virtuoso (1737); in Richard Owen Cambridge's "Scribleriad" (1751):

> " See how her sons with generous ardor strive,
> Bid every long-lost Gothic art revive, . . .
> Each Celtic character explain, or show
> How Britons ate a thousand years ago;
> On laws of jousts and tournaments declaim,
> Or shine, the rivals of the herald's fame.

* See *ante*, p. 211.

> But chief the Saxon wisdom be your care,
> Preserve their idols and their fanes repair;
> And may their deep mythology be shown
> By Seater's wheel and Thor's tremendous throne." *

The most notable instance that we encounter of virtuosity invading the neighboring realm of literature is in the case of Strawberry Hill and "The Castle of Otranto." Horace Walpole, the son of the great prime minister, Robert Walpole, was a person of varied accomplishments and undoubted cleverness. He was a man of fashion, a man of taste, and a man of letters; though, in the first of these characters, he entertained or affected a contempt for the last, not uncommon in dilettante authors and dandy artists, who belong to the *beau monde* or are otherwise socially of high place, *teste* Congreve, and even Byron, that "rhyming peer." Walpole, as we have seen, had been an Eton friend of Gray and had traveled—and quarreled—with him upon the Continent. Returning home, he got a seat in Parliament, the entrée at court, and various lucrative sinecures through his father's influence. He was an assiduous courtier, a keen and spiteful observer, a busy gossip and retailer of social tattle. His feminine turn of mind made him a capital letter-writer; and his corre-

---

* "Works of Richard Owen Cambridge," pp. 198–99. Cambridge was one of the Spenserian imitators. See *ante*, p. 89, *note*. In Lady Luxborough's correspondence with Shenstone there is much mention of a Mr. Miller, a neighboring proprietor, who was devoted to Gothic. On the appearance of "The Scribleriad," she writes (January 28, 1751), "I imagine this poem is not calculated to please Mr. Miller and the rest of the Gothic gentlemen; for this Mr. Cambridge expresses a dislike to the introducing or reviving tastes and fashions that are inferior to the modern taste of our country."

spondence, particularly with Sir Horace Mann, English ambassador at Florence, is a running history of back-stairs diplomacy, court intrigue, subterranean politics, and fashionable scandal during the reigns of the second and third Georges. He also figures as an historian of an amateurish sort, by virtue of his "Catalogue of Royal and Noble Authors," "Anecdotes of Painting," and "Historic Doubts on Richard III." Our present concern with him, however, lies quite outside of these.

It was about 1750 that Walpole, who had bought a villa at Strawberry Hill, on the Thames near Windsor, which had formerly belonged to Mrs. Chenevix, the fashionable London toy-woman, began to turn his house into a miniature Gothic castle, in which he is said to have "outlived three sets of his own battlements." These architectural experiments went on for some twenty years. They excited great interest and attracted many visitors, and Walpole may be regarded as having given a real impetus to the revival of pointed architecture. He spoke of Strawberry Hill as a castle, but it was, in fact, an odd blend of ecclesiastical and castellated Gothic applied to domestic uses. He had a cloister, a chapel, a round tower, a gallery, a "refectory," a stair-turret with Gothic balustrade, stained windows, mural scutcheons, and Gothic paper-hangings. Walpole's mock-gothic became something of a laughing-stock, after the true principles of mediæval architecture were better understood. Since the time when Inigo Jones, court architect to James I., came back from Italy, where he had studied the works of Palladio; and especially since the time when his successor, Sir Christopher Wren, had rebuilt St. Paul's in the Italian Renaissance style,

after the great fire of London in 1664, Gothic had
fallen more and more into disuse. "If in the history
of British art," says Eastlake, "there is one period
more distinguished than another for the neglect of
Gothic, it was certainly the middle of the eighteenth
century." But architecture had this advantage over
other arts, it had left memorials more obvious and imposing. Mediæval literature was known only to the
curious, to collectors of manuscript romances and
black-letter ballads. The study of mediæval arts like
tempera painting, illuminating, glass-staining, wood-
carving, tapestry embroidery; of the science of
blazonry, of the details of ancient armor and costumes, was the pursuit of specialists. But Westminster Abbey, the Tower of London, Salisbury
Cathedral, and York Minster, ruins such as Melrose
and Fountain Abbeys, Crichton Castle, and a hundred
others were impressive witnesses for the civilization
that had built them and must, sooner or later, demand
respectful attention. Hence it is not strange that the
Gothic revival went hand in hand with the romantic
movement in literature, if indeed it did not give it its
original impulse.

"It is impossible," says Eastlake,* speaking of
Walpole, "to peruse either the letters or the romances
of this remarkable man, without being struck by the
unmistakable evidence which they contain of his
mediæval predilections. His 'Castle of Otranto'
was perhaps the first modern work of fiction which
depended for its interest on the incidents of a chivalrous age, and it thus became the prototype of that
class of novel which was afterward imitated by Mrs.

* " History of the Gothic Revival," p. 43.

Radcliffe and perfected by Sir Walter Scott. The feudal tyrant, the venerable ecclesiastic, the forlorn but virtuous damsel, the castle itself with its moats and drawbridge, its gloomy dungeons and solemn corridors, are all derived from a mine of interest which has since been worked more efficiently and to better profit. But to Walpole must be awarded the credit of its discovery and first employment."

Walpole's complete works* contain elaborate illustrations and ground plans of Strawberry Hill. Eastlake gives a somewhat technical account of its constructive features, its gables, buttresses, finials, lath and plaster parapets, wooden pinnacles and, what its proprietor himself describes as his "lean windows fattened with rich saints." From this I extract only the description of the interior, which was "just what one might expect from a man who possessed a vague admiration for Gothic without the knowledge necessary for a proper adaptation of its features. Ceilings, screens, niches, etc., are all copied, or rather parodied, from existing examples, but with utter disregard for the original purpose of the design. To Lord Orford, Gothic was Gothic, and that sufficed. He would have turned an altar-slab into a hall-table, or made a cupboard of a piscina, with the greatest complacency, if it only served his purpose. Thus we find that in the north bed-chamber, when he wanted a model for his chimney-piece, he thought he could not do better than adopt the form of Bishop Dudley's tomb in Westminster Abbey. He found a pattern for the piers of his garden gate in the choir of Ely Cathedral."

* "Works of Horace Walpole, Earl of Orford," in five volumes, 1798. "A Description of Strawberry Hill," Vol. II. pp. 395–516.

The ceiling of the gallery borrowed a design from
Henry VII.'s Chapel; the entrance to the same apartment from the north door of St. Alban's; and one side
of the room from Archbishop Bourchier's tomb at
Canterbury. Eastlake's conclusion is that Walpole's
Gothic, "though far from reflecting the beauties of
a former age, or anticipating those which were
destined to proceed from a re-development of the
style, still holds a position in the history of English
art which commands our respect, for it served to
sustain a cause which had otherwise been well-nigh
forsaken."

James Fergusson, in his "History of the Modern
Styles of Architecture," says of Walpole's structures:
"We now know that these are very indifferent specimens of the true Gothic art, and are at a loss to
understand how either their author or his contemporaries could ever fancy that these very queer carvings were actual reproductions of the details of York
Minster, or other equally celebrated buildings, from
which they were supposed to have been copied."
Fergusson adds that the fashion set by Walpole soon
found many followers both in church and house architecture, "and it is surprising what a number of castles
were built which had nothing castellated about them
except a nicked parapet and an occasional window in
the form of a cross." That school of bastard Gothic
illustrated by the buildings of Batty Langley, and
other early restorers of the style, bears an analogy
with the imitations of old English poetry in the last
century. There was the same prematurity in both,
the same defective knowledge, crudity, uncertainty,
incorrectness, feebleness of invention, mixture of

ancient and modern manners. It was not until the
time of Pugin * that the details of the mediæval building art were well enough understood to enable the
architect to work in the spirit of that art, yet not as
a servile copyist, but with freedom and originality.
Meanwhile, one service that Walpole and his followers
did, by reviving public interest in Gothic, was to
arrest the process of dilapidation and save the crum-
bling remains of many a half-ruinous abbey, castle, or
baronial hall.   Thus, "when about a hundred years
since, Rhyddlan Castle, in North Wales, fell into the
possession of Dr. Shipley, Dean of St. Asaph, the
massive walls had been prescriptively used as stone
quarries, to which any neighboring occupier who
wanted building materials might resort; and they are
honey-combed all round as high as a pick-ax could
reach." †   "Walpole," writes Leslie Stephen, "is
almost the first modern Englishman who found out
that our old cathedrals were really beautiful.   He discovered that a most charming toy might be made of
mediævalism.   Strawberry Hill, with all its gimcracks,
its pasteboard battlements and stained-paper carvings,
was the lineal ancestor of the new law-courts.   The
restorers of churches, the manufacturers of stained
glass, the modern decorators and architects of all
varieties, the Ritualists and the High Church party,
should think of him with kindness. . .   That he was

* Pugin's " True Principles of Gothic Architecture " was published in 1841.

† "Sketches of Eminent Statesmen and Writers," A. Hayward
(1880). In a note to " Marmion " (1808) Scott said that the ruins of
Crichton Castle, remarkable for the richness and elegance of its
stone carvings, were then used as a cattle-pen and a sheep-fold.

quite conscious of the necessity for more serious study, appears in his letters; in one of which, *e. g.*, he proposes a systematic history of Gothic architecture such as has since been often executed." * Mr. Stephen adds that Walpole's friend Gray "shared his Gothic tastes, with greatly superior knowledge."

Walpole did not arrive at his Gothicism by the gate of literature. It was merely a specialized development of his tastes as a virtuoso and collector. The museum of curiosities which he got together at Strawberry Hill included not only suits of armor, stained glass, and illuminated missals, but a miscellaneous treasure of china ware, enamels, faïence, bronzes, paintings, engravings, books, coins, bric-a-brac, and memorabilia such as Cardinal Wolsey's hat, Queen Elizabeth's glove, and the spur that William III. wore at the Battle of the Boyne. Walpole's romanticism was a thin veneering; underneath it, he was a man of the eighteenth century. His opinions on all subjects were, if not inconsistent, at any rate notoriously whimsical and ill-assorted. Thus in spite of his admiration for Gray and his—temporary—interest in Ossian, Chatterton, and Percy's ballads, he ridiculed Mallet's and Gray's Runic experiments, spoke contemptuously of Spenser, Thomson, and Akenside, compared Dante to "a Methodist parson in bedlam," and pronounced "A Midsummer Night's Dream" "forty times more nonsensical than the worst translation of any Italian opera-books." † He said that poetry died with Pope, whose measure and manner he

* " Hours in a Library," Second Series: article, " Horace Walpole."

† Letter to Bentley, February 23, 1755.

employed in his own verses. It has been observed that, in all his correspondence, he makes but a single mention of Froissart's "Chronicle," and that a sneer at Lady Pomfret for translating it.

Accordingly we find, on turning to "The Castle of Otranto," that, just as Walpole's Gothicism was an accidental "sport" from his general virtuosity; so his romanticism was a casual outgrowth of his architectural amusements. Strawberry Hill begat "The Castle of Otranto," whose title is fitly chosen, since it is the castle itself that is the hero of the book. The human characters are naught. "Shall I even confess to you," he writes to the Rev. William Cole (March 9, 1765), "what was the origin of this romance? I waked one morning in the beginning of last June from a dream, of which all I could recover was, that I had thought myself in an ancient castle (a very natural dream for a head filled, like mine, with Gothic story), and that, on the uppermost banister of a great staircase, I saw a gigantic hand in armor. In the evening I sat down and began to write, without knowing in the least what I intended to say or relate. The work grew on my hands. . . In short, I was so engrossed with my tale, which I completed in less than two months, that one evening I wrote from the time I had drunk my tea, about six o'clock, till half an hour after one in the morning."

"The Castle of Otranto, A Gothic Story," was published in 1765.* According to the title page, it was translated from the original Italian of Onuphrio Muralto—a sort of half-pun on the author's surname

---

* Five hundred copies, says Walpole, were struck off December 24, 1764.

—by W. Marshall, Gent. This mystification was kept up in the preface, which pretended that the book had been printed at Naples in black-letter in 1529, and was found in the library of an old Catholic family in the north of England. In the preface to his second edition Walpole described the work as "an attempt to blend the two kinds of romance, the ancient and the modern": declared that, in introducing humorous dialogues among the servants of the castle, he had taken nature and Shakspere for his models; and fell foul of Voltaire for censuring the mixture of buffoonery and solemnity in Shakspere's tragedies. Walpole's claim to having created a new species of romance has been generally allowed. "His initiative in literature," says Mr. Stephen, "has been as fruitful as his initiative in art. 'The Castle of Otranto,' and the 'Mysterious Mother,' were the progenitors of Mrs. Radcliffe's romances, and probably had a strong influence upon the author of 'Ivanhoe.' Frowning castles and gloomy monasteries, knights in armor and ladies in distress, and monks, and nuns, and hermits; all the scenery and characters that have peopled the imagination of the romantic school, may be said to have had their origin on the night when Walpole lay down to sleep, his head crammed full of Wardour Street curiosities, and dreamed that he saw a gigantic hand in armor resting on the banisters of his staircase."

It is impossible at this day to take "The Castle of Otranto" seriously, and hard to explain the respect with which it was once mentioned by writers of authority. Warburton called it "a master-piece in the Fable, and a new species likewise. . . The scene is laid in

Gothic chivalry; where a beautiful imagination, sup‹
ported by strength of judgment, has enabled the
reader to go beyond his subject and effect the full
purpose of the ancient tragedy; *i. e.*, to purge the
passions by pity and terror, in coloring as great and
harmonious as in any of the best dramatic writers."
Byron called Walpole the author of the last tragedy *
and the first romance in the language.   Scott wrote of
"The Castle of Otranto": "This romance has been
justly considered, not only as the original and model
of a peculiar species of composition attempted and
successfully executed by a man of great genius, but
as one of the standard works of our lighter literature."
Gray in a letter to Walpole (December 30, 1764),
acknowledging the receipt of his copy, says: "It
makes some of us cry a little, and all in general afraid
to go to bed o' nights."   Walpole's masterpiece can no
longer make anyone cry even a little; and instead of
keeping us out of bed, it sends us there—or would, if
it were a trifle longer.   For the only thing that is
tolerable about the book is its brevity, and a certain
rapidity in the action.   Macaulay, who confesses its
absurdity and insipidity, says that no reader, probably,
ever thought it dull.   "The story, whatever its value
may be, never flags for a single moment.   There are
no digressions, or unreasonable descriptions, or long
speeches.   Every sentence carries the action forward.
The excitement is constantly renewed."   Excitement
is too strong a word to describe any emotion which
"The Castle of Otranto" is now capable of arousing.
But the same cleverness which makes Walpole's correspondence always readable saves his romance from the

* "The Mysterious Mother," begun 1766, finished 1768.

unpardonable sin—in literature—of tediousness. It does go along and may still be read without a too painful effort.

There is nothing very new in the plot, which has all the stock properties of romantic fiction, as common in the days of Sidney's " Arcadia " as in those of Sylvanus Cobb. Alfonso, the former lord of Otranto, had been poisoned in Palestine by his chamberlain Ricardo, who forged a will making himself Alfonso's heir. To make his peace with God, the usurper founded a church and two convents in honor of St. Nicholas, who "appeared to him in a dream and promised that Ricardo's posterity should reign in Otranto until the rightful owner should be grown too large to inhabit the castle." When the story opens, this prophecy is about to be fulfilled. The tyrant Manfred, grandson of the usurper, is on the point of celebrating the marriage of his only son, when the youth is crushed to death by a colossal helmet that drops, from nobody knows where, into the court-yard of the castle. Gigantic armor haunts the castle piecemeal: a monstrous gauntlet is laid upon the banister of the great staircase; a mailed foot appears in one apartment; a sword is brought into the court-yard on the shoulders of a hundred men. And finally the proprietor of these fragmentary apparitions, in " the form of Alfonso, dilated to an immense magnitude," throws down the walls of the castle, pronounces the words " Behold in Theodore the true heir of Alfonso," and with a clap of thunder ascends to heaven. Theodore is, of course, the young peasant, grandson of the crusader by a fair Sicilian secretly espoused *en route* for the Holy Land; and he is identified by the strawberry mark of old romance, in this instance the figure of a bloody arrow impressed upon his shoulder. There are other supernatural portents, such as a skeleton with a cowl and a hollow voice, a portrait which descends from its panel, and a statue that bleeds at the nose.

The novel feature in the "Castle of Otranto" was its Gothic setting; the "wind whistling through the battlements"; the secret trap-door, with iron ring, by which Isabella sought to make her escape. "An awful silence reigned throughout those subterraneous regions, except now and then some blasts of wind that shook the doors she had passed, and which, grating on the rusty hinges, were re-echoed through that long labyrinth of darkness. The wind extinguished her candle, but an imperfect ray of clouded moonshine gleamed through a cranny in the roof of the vault and fell directly on the spring of the trap-door." But Walpole's mediævalism was very thin. He took some pains with the description of the feudal cavalcade entering the castle gate with the great sword, but the passage is incorrect and poor in detail compared with similar things in Scott. The book was not an historical romance, and the manners, sentiments, language, all were modern. Walpole knew little about the Middle Ages and was not in touch with their spirit. At bottom he was a trifler, a fribble; and his incurable superficiality, dilettantism, and want of seriousness, made all his real cleverness of no avail when applied to such a subject as "The Castle of Otranto.*

* "The Castle of Otranto" was dramatized by Robert Jephson, under the title "The Count of Narbonne," put on at Covent Garden Theater in 1781, and afterward printed, with a dedication to Walpole.

Walpole's tragedy, "The Mysterious Mother," has not even that degree of importance which secures his romance a niche in literary history. The subject was too unnatural to admit of stage presentation. Incest, when treated in the manner of Sophocles (Walpole justified himself by the example of "Œdipus"), or even of Ford, or of Shelley, may possibly claim a place among the themes which art is not quite forbidden to touch; but when handled in the prurient and crudely melodramatic fashion of this particular artist, it is merely offensive. "The Mysterious Mother," indeed, is even more absurd than horrible. Gothic machinery is present, but it is of the slightest. The scene of the action is a castle at Narbonne and the *châtelaine* is the heroine of the play. The other characters are knights, friars, orphaned damsels, and feudal retainers; there is mention of cloisters, drawbridges, the Vaudois heretics, and the assassination of Henri III. and Henri IV.; and the author's Whig and Protestant leanings are oddly evidenced in his exposure of priestly intrigues.

"The Castle of Otranto" was not long in finding imitators. One of the first of these was Clara Reeve's "Champion of Virtue" (1777), styled on its title-page "A Gothic Story," and reprinted the following year as "The Old English Baron." Under this latter title it has since gone through thirteen editions, the latest of which, in 1883, gave a portrait of the author. Miss Reeve had previously published (1772) "The Phœnix," a translation of "Argenis," "a romance written in Latin about the beginning of the seventeenth century, by John Barclay, a Scotchman, and supposed to contain an allegorical account of the civil wars of France during

the reign of Henry III."* " Pray," inquires the author
of " The Champion of Virtue " in her address to the
reader, " did you ever read a book called, ' The Castle
of Otranto'? If you have, you will willingly enter with
me into a review of it. But perhaps you have not
read it? However, you have heard that it is an attempt
to blend together the most attractive and interesting
circumstances of the ancient romance and modern
novel. . . The conduct of the story is artful and
judicious; the characters are admirably drawn and
supported; the diction polished and elegant; yet with
all these brilliant advantages, it palls upon the
mind. . . The reason is obvious; the machinery is so
violent that it destroys the effect it is intended to excite. Had the story been kept within the utmost *verge*
of probability, the effect had been preserved. . . For
instance, we can conceive and allow of the appearance
of a ghost; we can even dispense with an enchanted
sword and helmet, but then they must keep within
certain limits of credibility. A sword so large as to
require a hundred men to lift it, a helmet that by its
own weight forces a passage through a court-yard into
an arched vault, . . . when your expectation is
wound up to the highest pitch, these circumstances
take it down with a witness, destroy the work of imagination, and, instead of attention, excite laughter. . .
In the course of my observations upon this singular
book, it seemed to me that it was possible to compose
a work upon the same plan, wherein these defects
might be avoided."

Accordingly Miss Reeve undertook to admit only a

* James Beattie, " Dissertation on Fable and Romance." " Argenis," was printed in 1621.

rather mild dose of the marvelous in her romance.
Like Walpole she professed to be simply the editor of
the story, which she said that she had transcribed or
translated from a manuscript in the Old English language, a now somewhat threadbare device. The
period was the fifteenth century, in the reign of Henry
VI., and the scene England. But, in spite of the
implication of its sub-title, the fiction is much less
" Gothic " than its model, and its modernness of sentiment and manners is hardly covered with even the
faintest wash of mediævalism. As in Walpole's book,
there are a murder and a usurpation, a rightful heir
defrauded of his inheritance and reared as a peasant.
There are a haunted chamber, unearthly midnight
groans, a ghost in armor, and a secret closet with its
skeleton. The tale is infinitely tiresome, and is full
of that edifying morality, fine sentiment and stilted
dialogue—that "old perfumed, powdered D'Arblay
conversation," as Thackeray called it—which abound
in " Evelina," " Thaddeus of Warsaw," and almost all
the fiction of the last quarter of the last century.
Still it was a little unkind in Walpole to pronounce his
disciple's performance tedious and insipid, as he did.

This same lady published, in 1785, a work in two
volumes entitled "The Progress of Romance," a sort
of symposium on the history of fiction in a series of
evening conversations. Her purpose was to claim for
the prose romance an honorable place in literature; a
place beside the verse epic. She discusses the definitions of romance given in the current dictionaries,
such as Ainsworth's and Littleton's *Narratio ficta—
Scriptum eroticum—Splendida fabula;* and Johnson's
" A military fable of the Middle Ages—A tale of wild

adventures of war and love." She herself defines it as "An heroic fable," or "An epic in prose." She affirms that Homer is the father of romance and thinks it astonishing that men of sense "should despise and ridicule romances, as the most contemptible of all kinds of writing, and yet expatiate in raptures on the beauties of the fables of the old classic poets—on stories far more wild and extravagant and infinitely more incredible." After reviewing the Greek romances, like Heliodorus' "Theagenes and Chariclea," she passes on to the chivalry tales of the Middle Ages, which, she maintains, "were by no means so contemptible as they have been represented by later writers." Our poetry, she thinks, owes more than is imagined to the spirit of romance. "Chaucer and all our old writers abound with it. Spenser owes perhaps his immortality to it; it is the Gothic imagery that gives the principal graces to his work . . . Spenser has made more poets than any other writer of our country." Milton, too, had a hankering after the romances; and Cervantes, though he laughed Spain's chivalry away, loved the thing he laughed at and preferred his serious romance "Persiles and Sigismonda" to all his other works.

She gives a list, with conjectural dates, of many mediæval romances in French and English, verse and prose; but the greater part of the book is occupied with contemporary fiction, the novels of Richardson, Fielding, Smollett, Crébillon, Marivaux, Rousseau, etc. She commends Thomas Leland's historical romance "Longsword, Earl of Salisbury" (1762), as "a romance in reality, and not a novel:—a story like those of the Middle Ages, composed of chivalry, love, and religion." To her second volume she appended the "History of Charoba, Queen of Egypt," englished from the French of Vattier, professor of Arabic to Louis XIV., who had translated it from a history of ancient Egypt written in Arabic. This was the source of Landor's poem, "Gebir." When Landor was in Wales in 1797, Rose Aylmer—

> " Rose Aylmer, whom these wakeful eyes,
> May weep but never see "—

lent him a copy of Miss Reeve's "Progress of Romance," borrowed from a circulating library at Swansea. And so the poor forgotten thing retains a vicarious immortality, as the prompter of some of the noblest passages in modern English blank verse and as associated with one of the tenderest passages in Landor's life.

Miss Reeve quotes frequently from Percy's "Essay on the Ancient Minstrels," mentions Ossian and Chatterton and refers to Hurd, Warton, and other authorities. "It was not till I had completed my design," she writes in her preface, "that I read either Dr. Beattie's 'Dissertation on Fable and Romance' or Mr. Warton's 'History of English Poetry.'" The former of these was an essay of somewhat more than a hundred pages by the author of "The Minstrel." It is of no great importance and follows pretty closely the lines of Hurd's "Letters on Chivalry and Romance," to which Beattie repeatedly refers in his footnotes. The author pursues the beaten track in inquiries of the kind: discusses the character of the Gothic tribes, the nature of the feudal system, and the institutions of chivalry and knight-errantry. Romance, it seems, was " one of the consequences of chivalry. The first writers in this way exhibited a species of fable different from all that had hitherto appeared. They undertook to describe the adventures of those heroes who professed knight-errantry. The world was then ignorant and credulous and passionately fond of wonderful adventures and deeds of valor. They believed in giants, dwarfs, dragons, enchanted castles, and every imaginable species of necromancy. These form the materials of the old romance. The knight-errant was described as courteous, religious, valiant, adventurous, and temperate. Some enchanters befriended and others opposed him. To do his mistress honor, and to prove himself worthy of her, he was made to encounter the warrior, hew down the giant, cut the dragon in pieces, break the spell of the necromancer, demolish the enchanted castle, fly through the air on wooden or winged horses, or, with some magician for his guide, to descend unhurt through the opening earth and traverse the caves in the bottom of the ocean. He detected and punished the false knight, overthrew or converted the infidel, restored the exiled monarch to his dominions and the captive damsel to her parents; he fought at the tournament, feasted in the hall, and bore a part in the warlike processions."

There is nothing very startling in these conclusions. Scholars like Percy, Tyrwhitt, and Ritson, who, as collectors and editors, rescued the fragments of ancient minstrelsy and gave the public access to concrete specimens of mediæval poetry, performed a more useful service than mild clerical essayists, such as Beattie and Hurd, who amused their leisure with general speculations about the origin of romance and whether it came in the first instance from the troubadours or the Saracens or the Norsemen. One more passage, however, may be transcribed from Beattie's "Dissertation," because it seems clearly a suggestion from "The Castle of Otranto." "The castles of the greater barons, reared in a rude but grand style of architecture, full of dark and winding passages, of secret apartments, of long uninhabited galleries, and of chambers supposed to be haunted with spirits, and undermined by subterraneous labyrinths as places of retreat in extreme danger; the howling of winds through the crevices of old walls and other dreary vacuities; the grating of heavy doors on rusty hinges of iron; the shrieking of bats and the screaming of owls and other creatures that resort to desolate or half-inhabited buildings; these and the like circumstances in the domestic life of the people I speak of, would multiply their superstitions and increase their credulity; and among warriors who set all danger at defiance, would encourage a passion for wild adventure and difficult enterprise."

One of the books reviewed by Miss Reeve is worth mentioning, not for its intrinsic importance, but for its early date. "Longsword, Earl of Salisbury, An Historical Romance," in two volumes, and published two years before "The Castle of Otranto," is probably the first fiction of the kind in English literature. Its author was Thomas Leland, an Irish historian and doctor of divinity.* "The outlines of the following story," begins the advertisement, "and some of the

* "The Dictionary of National Biography" miscalls it "Earl of *Canterbury*," and attributes it, though with a query, to *John* Leland.

incidents and more minute circumstances, are to be found in some of the ancient English historians." The period of the action is the reign of Henry III. The king is introduced in person, and when we hear him swearing "by my Halidome," we rub our eyes and ask, "Can this be Scott?" But we are soon disabused, for the romance, in spite of the words of the advertisement, is very little historical, and the fashion of it is thinly wordy and sentimental. The hero is the son of Henry II. and Fair Rosamond, but his speech is Grandisonian. The adventures are of the usual kind: the *dramatis personæ* include gallant knights who go a-tilting with their ladies' gloves upon their casques, usurpers, villains, pirates, a wicked monk who tries to poison the hero, an oppressed countess, a distressed damsel disguised as a page, a hermit who has a cave in a mountain side, etc. The Gothic proporties are few; though the frontispiece to the first volume represents a cowled monk raising from the ground the figure of a swooning knight in complete armor, in front of an abbey church with an image of the Virgin and Child sculptured in a niche above the door; and the building is thus described in the text: "Its windows crowded with the foliage of their ornaments, and dimmed by the hand of the painter; its numerous spires towering above the roof, and the Christian ensign on its front, declared it a residence of devotion and charity." An episode in the story narrates the death of a father by the hand of his son in the Barons' War of Henry III. But no farther advantage is taken of the historic background afforded by this civil conflict, nor is Simon de Montfort so much as named in the whole course of the book.

Clara Reeve was the daughter of a clergyman. She lived and died at Ipswich (1725–1803). Walter Scott contributed a memoir of her to "Ballantyne's Novelists' Library," in which he defended Walpole's frank use of the supernatural against her criticisms, quoted above, and gave the preference to Walpole's method.* She acknowledged that her romance was a "literary descendant of 'Otranto';" but the author of the latter, evidently nettled by her strictures, described "The Old English Baron," as "Otranto reduced to reason and probability," and declared that any murder trial at the Old Bailey would have made a more interesting story. Such as it is, it bridges the interval between its model and the novels of Mrs. Radcliffe, Lewis' "Monk" (1795), and Maturin's "Fatal Revenge, or the Family of Montorio" (1807).†

Anne Radcliffe—born Ward in 1764, the year of "Otranto"—was the wife of an editor, who was necessarily absent from home much of the time until late at night. A large part of her writing was done to amuse her loneliness in the still hours of evening; and the wildness of her imagination, and the romantic love of night and solitude which pervades her books, are sometimes accounted for in this way. In 1809 it was currently reported and believed that Mrs. Radcliffe was dead. Another form of the rumor was that she had been made insane by continually poring over visions of horror and mystery. Neither

---

* See also, for a notice of this writer, Julia Kavanagh's " English Women of Letters."

† Maturin's " Melmoth the Wanderer " (1820) had some influence on the French romantic school and was utilized, in some particulars, by Balzac.

report was true; she lived till 1823, in full possession of her faculties, although she published nothing
after 1797. The circulation of such stories shows
how retired, and even obscure, a life this very popular
writer contrived to lead.

It would be tedious to give here an analysis of these
once famous fictions *seriatim.** They were very long,
very much alike, and very much overloaded with
sentiment and description. The plots were complicated and abounded in the wildest improbabilities and
in those incidents which were once the commonplaces
of romantic fiction and which realism has now turned
out of doors: concealments, assassinations, duels,
disguises, kidnapings, escapes, elopements, intrigues,
forged documents, discoveries of old crimes, and identi-
fications of lost heirs. The characters, too, were of
the conventional kind. There were dark-browed,
crime-stained villains—forerunners, perhaps, of Manfred and Lara, for the critics think that Mrs. Radcliffe's stories were not without important influence
on Byron.† There were high-born, penitent dames
who retired to convents in expiation of sins which
are not explained until the general raveling of clews
in the final chapter. There were bravoes, banditti,
feudal tyrants, monks, inquisitors, soubrettes, and
simple domestics *à la* Bianca, in Walpole's romance.
The lover was of the type adored by our great-grand-

---

* Following is a list of Mrs. Radcliffe's romances : " The Castles
of Athlin and Dunbayne" (1789) ; "Sicilian Romance" (1790) ;
"Romance of the Forest" (1791) ; "Mysteries of Udolpho (1794) ;
" The Italian" (1797) ; "Gaston de Blondville" (1826). Collections of her poems were published in 1816, 1834, and 1845.

† See " Childe Harold," canto iv, xviii.

mothers, handsome, melancholy, passionate, respectful but desperate, a user of most choice English; with
large black eyes, smooth white forehead, and jetty
curls, now sunk, Mr. Perry says, to the covers of
prune boxes. The heroine, too, was sensitive and
melancholy. When alone upon the seashore or in
the mountains, at sunset or twilight, or under the
midnight moon, or when the wind is blowing, she
overflows into stanza or sonnet, "To Autumn," "To
Sunset," "To the Bat," "To the Nightingale," "To
the Winds," "To Melancholy," "Song of the Evening Hour." We have heard this pensive music drawing near in the strains of the Miltonic school, but in
Mrs. Radcliffe the romantic gloom is profound and all-
pervading. In what pastures she had fed is manifest
from the verse captions that head her chapters, taken
mainly from Blair, Thomson, Warton, Gray, Collins,
Beattie, Mason, and Walpole's "Mysterious Mother."
Here are a few stanzas from her ode "To Melancholy":

> " Spirit of love and sorrow, hail!
>   Thy solemn voice from far I hear,
>   Mingling with evening's dying gale:
>   Hail, with thy sadly pleasing tear!

> " O at this still, this lonely hour—
>   Thine own sweet hour of closing day—
>   Awake thy lute, whose charmful power
>   Shall call up fancy to obey:

> " To paint the wild, romantic dream
>   That meets the poet's closing eye,
>   As on the bank of shadowy stream
>   He breathes to her the fervid sigh.

" O lonely spirit, let thy song
    Lead me through all thy sacred haunt,
The minster's moonlight aisles along
    Where spectres raise the midnight chant."

In Mrs. Radcliffe's romances we find a tone that is
absent from Walpole's: romanticism plus sentimentalism.   This last element had begun to infuse itself into
general literature about the middle of the century, as a
protest and reaction against the emotional coldness of
the classical age.   It announced itself in Richardson,
Rousseau, and the youthful Goethe; in the *comédie
larmoyante*, both French and English; found its clever-
est expression in Sterne, and then, becoming a universal vogue, deluged fiction with productions like
Mackenzie's "Man of Feeling," Miss Burney's
" Evelina," and the novels of Jane Porter and Mrs.
Opie.   Thackeray said that there was more crying in
"Thaddeus of Warsaw " than in any novel he ever
remembered to have read.*   Emily, in the " Mysteries of Udolpho " cannot see the moon, or hear a guitar
or an organ or the murmur of the pines, without
weeping.   Every page is bedewed with the tear of
sensibility; the whole volume is damp with it, and
ever and anon a chorus of sobs goes up from the
entire company.   Mrs. Radcliffe's heroines are all de-
scendants of Pamela and Clarissa Harlowe, but under
more romantic circumstances.   They are beset with a
thousand difficulties; carried off by masked ruffians,
immured in convents, held captive in robber castles,
encompassed with horrors natural and supernatural,

* " Roundabout Papers," " A Peal of Bells." " Monk " Lewis
wrote at sixteen a burlesque novel, " Effusions of Sensibility," which
remained in MS.

persecuted, threatened with murder and with rape. But though perpetually sighing, blushing, trembling, weeping, fainting, they have at bottom a kind of toughness that endures through all. They rebuke the wicked in stately language, full of noble sentiments and moral truths. They preserve the most delicate feelings of propriety in situations the most discouraging. Emily, imprisoned in the gloomy castle of Udolpho, in the power of ruffians whose brawls and orgies fill night and day with horror, in hourly fear for her virtue and her life, sends for the lord of the castle,— whom she believes to have murdered her aunt,—and reminds him that, as her protectress is now dead, it would not be proper for her to stay any longer under his roof thus unchaperoned, and will he please, therefore, send her home?

Mrs. Radcliffe's fictions are romantic, but not usually mediæval in subject. In the " Mysteries of Udolpho," the period of the action is the end of the sixteenth century; in the "Romance of the Forest," 1658; in " The Italian," about 1760. But her machinery is prevailingly Gothic and the real hero of the story is commonly, as in Walpole, some haunted building. In the " Mysteries of Udolpho " it is a castle in the Apennines; in the "Romance of the Forest," a deserted abbey in the depth of the woods; in "The Italian," the cloister of the Black Penitents. The moldering battlements, the worm-eaten tapestries, the turret staircases, secret chambers, underground passages, long, dark corridors where the wind howls dismally, and distant doors which slam at midnight all derive from "Otranto." So do the supernatural fears which haunt these abodes of desolation; the strains of mysterious music, the apparitions which glide through the shadowy apartments, the hollow voices that warn the tyrant to beware. But her method here is quite different from Walpole's; she tacks a natural explanation to every unearthly sight or sound. The hollow voices turn out to be ventriloquism; the figure of a putrefying corpse which Emily sees behind the black curtain in the ghost chamber at Udolpho is only a wax figure, contrived as a *memento mori* for a former penitent. After the reader has once learned this trick he refuses to be imposed upon again, and, whenever he encounters a spirit, feels sure that a future chapter will embody it back into flesh and blood.

There is plenty of testimony to the popularity of these romances. Thackeray says that a lady of his acquaintance, an inveterate novel reader, names Valancourt as one of the favorite heroes of her youth. " 'Valancourt? And who was he?' cry the young people. Valancourt, my dears, was the hero of one of the most famous romances which ever was published in this country. The beauty and elegance of Valancourt made your young grandmammas' gentle hearts to beat with respectful sympathy. He and his glory have passed away. . . Enquire at Mudie's or the London Library, who asks for the 'Mysteries of Udolpho' now." * Hazlitt said that he owed to Mrs.

---

* "O Radcliffe, thou once wert the charmer
    Of girls who sat reading all night :
 Thy heroes were striplings in armor,
    Thy heroines, damsels in white."
        —*Songs, Ballads and other Poems.*
     By Thos. Haynes Bayly, London, 1857, p 141.

Radcliffe his love of moonlight nights, autumn leaves and decaying ruins. It was, indeed, in the melo-dramatic manipulation of landscape that this artist was most original. "The scenes that savage Rosa dashed" seem to have been her model, and critics who were fond of analogy called her the Salvator Rosa of fiction. It is here that her influence on Byron and Chateaubriand is most apparent.* Mrs. Radcliffe's scenery is not quite to our modern taste, any more than are Salvator's paintings. Her Venice by moon-light, her mountain gorges with their black pines and foaming torrents, are not precisely the Venice and the Alps of Ruskin; rather of the operatic stage. Still they are impressive in their way, and in this depart-ment she possessed genuine poetic feeling and a real mastery of the art of painting in distemper. Witness the picture of the castle of Udolpho, on Emily's first sight of it, and the hardly less striking description, in the "Romance of the Forest," of the ruined abbey

> "A novel now is nothing more
> Than an old castle and a creaking door,
> A distant hovel,
> Clanking of chains, a gallery, a light,
> Old armor and a phantom all in white,
> And there's a novel."
> —*George Colman,* "*The Will.*"

* Several of her romances were dramatized and translated into French. It is curious, by the way, to find that Goethe was not unaware of Walpole's story. See his quatrain "Die Burg von Otranto," first printed in 1837.

"Sind die Zimmer sämmtlich besetzt der Burg von Otranto:
Kommt, voll innigen Grimmes, der erste Riesenbesitzer
Stückweis an, und verdrängt die neuen falschen Bewohner.
Wehe! den Fliehenden, weh! den Bleibenden also geschiet es.

in which the La Motte family take refuge: "He approached and perceived the Gothic remains of an abbey: it stood on a kind of rude lawn, overshadowed by high and spreading trees, which seemed coeval with the building, and diffused a romantic gloom around. The greater part of the pile appeared to be sinking into ruins, and that which had withstood the ravages of time showed the remaining features of the fabric more awful in decay. The lofty battlements, thickly enwreathed with ivy, were half demolished and become the residence of birds of prey. Huge fragments of the eastern tower, which was almost demolished, lay scattered amid the high grass, that waved slowly in the breeze. 'The thistle shook its lonely head: the moss whistled to the wind.' * A Gothic gate, richly ornamented with fretwork, which opened into the main body of the edifice, but which was now obstructed with brushwood, remained entire. Above the vast and magnificent portal of this gate arose a window of the same order, whose pointed arches still exhibited fragments of stained glass, once the pride of monkish devotion. La Motte, thinking it possible it might yet shelter some human being, advanced to the gate and lifted a massy knocker. The hollow sounds rung through the emptiness of the place. After waiting a few minutes, he forced back the gate, which was heavy with iron-work, and creaked harshly on its hinges. . . From this chapel he passed into the nave of the great church, of which one window, more perfect than the rest, opened upon a long vista of the forest, through which was seen the rich coloring of evening, melting by imperceptible gradations into the solemn gray of upper air."

* Ossian.

Mrs. Radcliffe never was in Italy or Switzerland or the south of France; she divined the scenery of her romances from pictures and descriptions at second hand. But she accompanied her husband in excursions to the Lakes and other parts of England, and in 1794 made the tour of the Rhine.* The passages in her diary, recording these travels, are much superior in the truthfulness and local color of their nature sketching to anything in her novels. Mrs. Radcliffe is furthermore to be credited with a certain skill in producing terror, by the use of that favorite weapon in the armory of the romanticists, mystery. If she did not invent a new shudder, as Hugo said of Baudelaire, she gave at least a new turn to the old-fashioned ghost story. She creates in her readers a feeling of impending danger, suspense, foreboding. There is a sense of unearthly presences in these vast, empty rooms; the silence itself is ominous; echoes sound like footfalls, ghostly shadows lurk in dark corners, whispers come from behind the arras, as it stirs in the gusts of wind.† The heroine is afraid to look in the glass lest she should see another face there beside her own; her lamp expires and leaves her in the dark just as she is coming to the critical point in the manuscript which she has found in an old chest, etc., etc. But the tale loses its impressiveness as soon as it strays beyond the shade of the battlements. The

---

* See her " Journey through Holland," etc. (1795).
† *Cf.* Keats, " The Eve of Saint Agnes ":

> " The arras rich with hunt and horse and hound
>   Fluttered in the besieging wind's uproar,
>   And the long carpets rose along the gusty floor."

Gothic castle or priory is still, as in Walpole, the nucleus of the story.

Two of these romances, the earliest and the latest, though they are the weakest of the series, have a special interest for us as affording points of comparison with the Waverley novels. " The Castles of Athlin and Dunbayne" is the narrative of a feud between two Highland clans, and its scene is the northeastern coast of Scotland, "in the most romantic part of the Highlands," where the castle of Athlin—like Uhland's "Schloss am Meer"—stood "on the summit of a rock whose base was in the sea." This was a fine place for storms. " The winds burst in sudden squalls over the deep and dashed the foaming waves against the rocks with inconceivable fury. The spray, notwithstanding the high situation of the castle, flew up with violence against the windows. . . The moon shone faintly by intervals, through broken clouds, upon the waters, illumining the white foam which burst around. . . The surges broke on the distant shores in deep resounding murmurs, and the solemn pauses between the stormy gusts filled the mind with enthusiastic awe." Perhaps the description slightly reminds of the picture, in " Marmion," of Tantallon Castle, the hold of the Red Douglases on the German Ocean, a little north of Berwick, whose frowning towers have recently done duty again in Stevenson's " David Balfour." The period of the action is but vaguely indicated; but, as the weapons used in the attack on the castle are bows and arrows, we may regard the book as mediæval in intention. Scott says that the scene of the romance was Scotland in the dark ages, and complains that the author evidently knew nothing of Scottish life or scenery. This is true; her castles might have stood anywhere. There is no mention of the pipes or the plaid. Her rival chiefs are not Gaelic caterans, but just plain feudal lords. Her baron of Dunbayne is like any other baron; or rather, he is unlike any baron that ever was on sea or land or anywhere else except in the pages of a Gothic romance.

" Gaston de Blondville " was begun in 1802 and published posthumously in 1826, edited by Sergeant Talfourd. Its inspiring cause was a visit which the author made in the autumn of 1802 to Warwick Castle and the ruins of Kenilworth. The introduction has the usual fiction of an old manuscript found in an oaken chest dug up from the foundation of a chapel of Black Canons at Kenilworth: a manuscript richly illuminated with designs at the head of each chapter—which are all duly described—and containing a " trew chronique of what passed at Killingworth, in Ardenn, when our Soveren Lord the Kynge kept ther his Fest of Seynt Michel: with ye marveylous accident that ther befel at the solempnissacion of the marriage of Gaston de Blondeville. With divers things curious to be known thereunto purtayning. With an account of the grete Turney there held in the year MCCLVI. Changed out of the Norman tongue by Grymbald, Monk of Senct Marie Priori in Killingworth." Chatterton's forgeries had by this time familiarized the public with imitations of early English. The finder of this manuscript pretends to publish a modernized version of it, while endeavoring " to preserve somewhat of the air of the old style." This he does by a poor reproduction, not of thirteenth-century, but of sixteenth-century English, consisting chiefly in inversions of phrase and the occasional use of a *certes* or *naithless.* Two words in particular seem to have struck Mrs. Radcliffe as most excellent archaisms: *ychon* and *his-self,* which she introduces at every turn.

"Gaston de Blondville," then, is a tale of the time of Henry III. The king himself is a leading figure and so is Prince Edward. Other historical personages are brought in, such as Simon de Montfort and Marie de France, but little use is made of them. The book is not indeed, in any sense, an historical novel like Scott's "Kenilworth," the scene of which is the same, and which was published in 1821, five years before Mrs. Radcliffe's. The story is entirely fictitious. What differences it from her other romances is the conscious attempt to portray feudal manners. There are elaborate descriptions of costumes, upholstery, architecture, heraldic bearings, ancient military array, a tournament, a royal hunt, a feast in the great hall at Kenilworth, a visit of state to Warwick Castle, and the session of a baronial court. The ceremony of the "voide," when the king took his spiced cup, is rehearsed with a painful accumulation of particulars. For all this she consulted Leland's "Collectanea," Warton's "History of English Poetry," the "Household Book of Edward IV.," Pegge's "Dissertation on the Obsolete Office of Esquire of the King's Body," the publications of the Society of Antiquaries and similar authorities, with results that are infinitely tedious. Walter Scott's archæology is not always correct, nor his learning always lightly borne; but, upon the whole, he had the art to make his cumbrous materials contributory to his story rather than obstructive of it.

In these two novels we meet again all the familiar

apparatus of secret trap-doors, sliding panels, spiral
staircases in the thickness of the walls, subterranean
vaults conducting to a neighboring priory or a cavern
in the forest, ranges of deserted apartments where the
moon looks in through mullioned casements, ruinous
turrets around which the night winds moan and
howl. Here, too, once more are the wicked uncle who
seizes upon the estates of his deceased brother's wife,
and keeps her and her daughter shut up in his dungeon for the somewhat long period of eighteen years;
the heroine who touches her lute and sings in pensive
mood, till the notes steal to the ear of the young earl
imprisoned in the adjacent tower; the maiden who is
carried off on horseback by bandits, till her shrieks
bring ready aid; the peasant lad who turns out to be
the baron's heir. "His surprise was great when the
baroness, reviving, fixed her eyes mournfully upon
him and asked him to uncover his arm." Alas! the
surprise is not shared by the reader, when " 'It is—it
is my Philip!' said she, with strong emotion; 'I have
indeed found my long-lost child: that strawberry,' " *
etc., etc. "Gaston de Blondville" has a ghost which
is a real ghost—not explained away in the end according to Mrs. Radcliffe's custom. It is the spirit of
Reginald de Folville, Knight Hospitaller of St. John,
murdered in the Forest of Arden by Gaston de Blondville and the prior of St. Mary's. He is a most
robust apparition, and is by no means content with
revisiting the glimpses of the moon, but goes in and
out at all hours of the day, and so often as to become
somewhat of a bore. He ultimately destroys both
first and second murderer: one in his cell, the other

* " Castles of Athlin and Dunbayne."

in open tournament, where his exploits as a mysterious knight in black armor may have given Scott a hint for his black knight at the lists of Ashby-de-la-Zouche in "Ivanhoe" (1819). His final appearance is in the chamber of the king, with whom he holds quite a long conversation. "The worm is my sister," he says: "the mist of death is on me. My bed is in darkness. The prisoner is innocent. The prior of St. Mary's is gone to his account. Be warned." It is not explained why Mrs. Radcliffe refrained from publishing this last romance of hers. Perhaps she recognized that it was belated and that the time for that sort of thing had gone by. By 1802 Lewis' "Monk" was in print, as well as several translations from German romances; Scott's early ballads were out, and Coleridge's "Ancient Mariner." That very year saw the publication of the "Minstrelsy of the Scottish Border." By 1826 the Waverley novels had made all previous fiction of the Gothic type hopelessly obsolete. In 1834 two volumes of her poems were given to the world, including a verse romance in eight cantos, "St. Alban's Abbey," and the verses scattered through her novels. By this time Scott and Coleridge were dead; Byron, Shelley, and Keats had been dead for years, and Mrs. Radcliffe's poesies fell upon the unheeding ears of a new generation. A sneer in "Waverley" (1814) at the "Mysteries of Udolpho" had hurt her feelings; * but Scott made amends in the handsome things which he said of her in his "Lives of the Novelists." It is interesting to note that when the "Mysteries" was issued, the venerable Joseph Warton was so much entranced that he sat up the greater part of the night to finish it.

* See Julia Kavanagh's "English Women of Letters."

The warfare between realism and romance, which went on in the days of Cervantes, as it does in the days of Zola and Howells, had its skirmishes also in Mrs. Radcliffe's time. Jane Austen's "Northanger Abbey," written in 1803 but published only in 1817, is gently satirical of Gothic fiction. The heroine is devoted to the "Mysteries of Udolpho," which she discusses with her bosom friend. "While I have 'Udolpho' to read, I feel as if nobody could make me miserable. O the dreadful black veil! My dear Isabella, I am sure there must be Laurentina's skeleton behind it."

"When you have finished 'Udolpho,'" replies Isabella, "we will read 'The Italian' together; and I have made out a list of ten or twelve more of the same kind for you. . . I will read you their names directly. Here they are in my pocket-book. 'Castle of Wolfenbach,' 'Clermont,' 'Mysterious Warnings,' 'Necromancer of the Black Forest,' 'Midnight Bell,' 'Orphan of the Rhine,' and 'Horrid Mysteries.'"

When introduced to her friend's brother, Miss Morland asks him at once, "Have you ever read 'Udolpho,' Mr. Thorpe?" But Mr. Thorpe, who is not a literary man, but much given to dogs and horses, assures her that he never reads novels; they are "full of nonsense and stuff; there has not been a tolerably decent one come out since 'Tom Jones,' except the 'Monk.'" The scenery about Bath reminds Miss Morland of the south of France and "the country that Emily and her father traveled through in the 'Mysteries of Udolpho.'" She is enchanted at the prospect of a drive to Blaize Castle, where she hopes to have "the happiness of being stopped in their way along narrow, winding vaults by a low, grated door; or even of having their lamp—their only lamp—extinguished by a sudden gust of wind and of being left in total darkness." She visits her friends, the Tilneys, at their country seat, Northanger Abbey, in Gloucestershire; and, on the way thither, young Mr. Tilney teases her with a fancy sketch of the Gothic horrors which she will unearth there: the "sliding panels and tapestry"; the remote and gloomy guest-chamber, which will be assigned her, with its ponderous chest, and its portrait of a knight in armor: the secret door, with massy bars and padlocks, that she will discover behind the arras, leading to a "small vaulted room," and eventually to a "subterraneous communication between your apartment and the chapel of St. Anthony scarcely two miles off." Arrived at the abbey, she is disappointed at the modern appearance of her room, but contrives to find a secret drawer in an ancient ebony cabinet, and in this a roll of yellow manuscript which, on being deciphered, proves to be a washing bill. She is convinced, notwithstanding, that a mysterious door at the end of a certain gallery conducts to a series of isolated chambers where General Tilney, who is supposed to be a widower, is keeping his unhappy wife immured and fed on bread and water. When she finally gains admission to this Bluebeard's chamber and finds it nothing but a suite of modern rooms, "the visions of romance were over. . . Charming as were all Mrs. Radcliffe's works, and charming even as were the works of all her imitators, it was not in them, perhaps, that human nature, at least in the midland counties of England was to be looked for."

CHAPTER VIII.

Percy and the Ballads.

THE regeneration of English poetic style at the close of the last century came from an unexpected quarter. What scholars and professional men of letters had sought to do by their imitations of Spenser and Milton, and their domestication of the Gothic and the Celtic muse, was much more effectually done by Percy and the ballad collectors. What they had sought to do was to recall British poetry to the walks of imagination and to older and better models than Dryden and Pope. But they could not jump off their own shadows: the eighteenth century was too much for them. While they anxiously cultivated wildness and simplicity, their diction remained polished, literary, academic to a degree. It is not, indeed, until we reach the boundaries of a new century that we encounter a Gulf Stream of emotional, creative impulse strong enough and hot enough to thaw the classical icebergs till not a floating spiculum of them is left.

Meanwhile, however, there occurred a revivifying contact with one department, at least, of early verse literature, which did much to clear the way for Scott and Coleridge and Keats. The decade from 1760 to 1770 is important in the history of English romanticism, and its most important title is Thomas Percy's "Reliques of Ancient English Poetry: Consisting of

Old Heroic Ballads, Songs, and Other Pieces of our
Earlier Poets," published in three volumes in 1765.
It made a less immediate and exciting impression upon
contemporary Europe than MacPherson's "Poems of
Ossian," but it was more fruitful in enduring results.
The Germans make a convenient classification of
poetry into *Kunstpoesie* and *Volkspoesie*, terms which
may be imperfectly translated as literary poetry and
popular poetry. The English *Kunstpoesie* of the
Middle Ages lay buried under many superincumbent
layers of literary fashion. Oblivion had overtaken
Gower and Occleve, and Lydgate and Stephen Hawes,
and Skelton, and Henryson and James I. of Scotland, and
well-nigh Chaucer himself—all the mediæval poetry of
the schools, in short. But it was known to the curious
that there was still extant a large body of popular
poetry in the shape of narrative ballads, which had
been handed down chiefly by oral transmission, and
still lived in the memories and upon the lips of the
common people. Many of these went back in their
original shapes to the Middle Ages, or to an even
remoter antiquity, and belonged to that great store of
folk-lore which was the common inheritance of the
Aryan race. Analogues and variants of favorite English and Scottish ballads have been traced through
almost all the tongues of modern Europe. Danish
literature is especially rich in ballads and affords
valuable illustrations of our native ministrelsy.* It
was, perhaps, due in part to the Danish settlements in
Northumbria and to the large Scandinavian admixture
in the Northumbrian blood and dialect, that "the

* Svend Grundtvig's great collection, "Danmarks Gamle Folkeviser," was published in five volumes in 1853–90.

north countrie " became *par excellence* the ballad land:
Lowland Scotland—particularly the Lothians—and the
English bordering counties, Northumberland, Westmoreland, and Cumberland; with Yorkshire and Not-
tinghamshire, in which were Barndale and Sherwood
Forests, Robin Hood's haunts. It is not possible to
assign exact dates to these songs. They were seldom
reduced to writing till many years after they were
composed. In the Middle Ages they were sung to
the harp by wandering minstrels. In later times they
were chanted or recited by ballad-singers at fairs,
markets, ale-houses, street-corners, sometimes to the
accompaniment of a fiddle or crowd. They were
learned by ancient dames, who repeated them in
chimney corners to children and grandchildren. In
this way some of them were preserved in an unwrit-
ten state, even to the present day, in the tenacious
memory of the people, always at bottom conservative
and, under a hundred changes of fashion in the literary
poetry which passes over their heads, clinging obsti-
nately to old songs and beliefs learned in childhood,
and handing them on to posterity. Walter Scott got
much of the material for his " Ministrelsy of the Border " from the oral recitation of pipers, shepherds, and
old women in Ettrick Forest. Professor Child's—the
latest and fullest ballad collection—contains pieces
never before given in print or manuscript, some of
them obtained in America! *

Leading this subterranean existence, and generally
thought unworthy the notice of educated people, they

* Francis James Child's " English and Scottish Popular Ballads,"
issued in ten parts in 1882–98 is one of the glories of American
scholarship.

naturally underwent repeated changes; so that we have numerous versions of the same story, and incidents, descriptions, and entire stanzas are borrowed and lent freely among the different ballads. The circumstance, *e. g.*, of the birk and the briar springing from the graves of true lovers and intertwisting their branches occurs in the ballads of " Fair Margaret and Sweet William," "Lord Thomas and Fair Annet," "Lord Lovel," "Fair Janet," and many others. The knight who was carried to fairyland through an entrance in a green hillside, and abode seven years with the queen of fairy, recurs in " Tam Lin," " Thomas Rymer," * etc. Like all folk-songs, these ballads are anonymous and may be regarded not as the composition of any one poet, but as the property, and in a sense the work, of the people as a whole. Coming out of an uncertain past, based on some dark legend of heart-break or blood-shed, they bear no author's name, but are *feræ naturæ* and have the flavor of wild game. They were common stock, like the national speech; everyone could contribute toward them: generations of nameless poets, minstrels, ballad-singers modernized their language to suit new times, altered their dialect to suit new places, accommodated their details to different audiences, English or Scotch, and in every way that they thought fit added, retrenched, corrupted, improved, and passed them on.

Folk-poetry is conventional; it seems to be the production of a guild, and to have certain well understood and commonly expected tricks of style and verse. Freshness and sincerity are almost always attributes of the poetry of heroic ages, but individuality belongs

---

* *Cf.* The Tannhäuser legend and the Venusberg.

to a high civilization and an advanced literary culture. Whether the "Iliad" and the "Odyssey" are
the work of one poet or of a cycle of poets, doubtless
the rhetorical peculiarities of the Homeric epics, such
as the recurrent phrase and the conventional epithet
(the rosy-fingered dawn, the well-greaved Greeks, the
swift-footed Achilles, the much-enduring Odysseus,
etc.) are due to this communal or associative character of ancient heroic song. As in the companies of
architects who built the mediæval cathedrals, or in
the schools of early Italian painters, masters and disciples, the manner of the individual artist was subdued
to the tradition of his craft.

The English and Scottish popular ballads are in
various simple stanza forms, the commonest of all
being the old *septenarius* or "fourteener," arranged
in a four-lined stanza of alternate eights and sixes,
thus:

> " Up then crew the red, red cock,
>   And up and crew the gray;
>   The eldest to the youngest said
>   ' 'Tis time we were away.' " *

This is the stanza usually employed by modern ballad
imitators, like Coleridge in "The Ancient Mariner,"
Scott in "Jock o' Hazeldean," Longfellow in "The
Wreck of the Hesperus," Macaulay in the "Lays of
Ancient Rome," Aytoun in the "Lays of the Scottish
Cavaliers." Many of the stylistic and metrical peculiarities of the ballads arose from the fact that they were
made to be sung or recited from memory. Such are
perhaps the division of the longer ones into fits, to rest
the voice of the singer; and the use of the burden or

* " The Wife of Usher's Well."

refrain for the same purpose, as also to give the listen-
ers and bystanders a chance to take up the chorus,
which they probably accompanied with a few dancing
steps.* Sometimes the burden has no meaning in
itself and serves only to mark time with a *Hey derry
down* or an *O lilly lally* and the like.   Sometimes it has
more or less reference to the story, as in " The Two
Sisters ":

> " He has ta'en three locks o' her yellow hair—
>   Binnorie, O Binnorie—
> And wi' them strung his harp sae rare—
>   By the bonnie mill-dams of Binnorie."

Again it has no discoverable relation to the context, as
in " Riddles Wisely Expounded "—

> " There was a knicht riding frae the east—
>   *Jennifer gentle and rosemarie—*
> Who had been wooing at monie a place—
>   *As the dew flies over the mulberry tree."*

Both kinds of refrain have been liberally employed by
modern balladists.   Thus Tennyson in " The Sisters ":

> " We were two sisters of one race,
>   *The wind is howling in turret and tree;*
> She was the fairer in the face,
>   *O the earl was fair to see."*

While Rossetti and Jean Ingelow and others have
rather favored the inconsequential burden, an affectation travestied by the late Mr. C. S. Calverley:

* It should never be forgotten that the ballad (derived from *ballare*
—to dance) was originally not a written poem, but a song and dance.
Many of the old tunes are preserved.   A number are given in Chap-
pell's " Popular Music of the Olden Time," and in the appendix to
Motherwell's " Minstrelsy, Ancient and Modern " (1827).

" The auld wife sat at her ivied door,
　　(Butter and eggs and a pound of cheese)
　A thing she had frequently done before;
　　And her spectacles lay on her aproned knees.

" The farmer's daughter hath soft brown hair
　　(Butter and eggs and a pound of cheese),
　And I met with a ballad, I can't say where,
　　Which wholly consisted of lines like these." *

A musical or mnemonic device akin to the refrain was
that sing-song species of repetend so familiar in ballad language:

　　" She had na pu'd a double rose,
　　　A rose but only twa."

　　" They had na sailed a league, a league,
　　　A league but barely three."

　　" How will I come up ?　How can I come up?
　　　How can I come to thee ? "

An answer is usually returned in the identical words
of the question; and as in Homer, a formula of narration or a commonplace of description does duty again
and again.　Iteration in the ballads is not merely for
economy, but stands in lieu of the metaphor and other
figures of literary poetry:

　　" 'O Marie, put on your robes o' black,
　　　Or else your robes o' brown,
　　For ye maun gang wi' me the night,
　　　To see fair Edinbro town.'

　　' I winna put on my robes o' black,
　　　Nor yet my robes o' brown;
　　But I'll put on my robes o' white,
　　　To shine through Edinbro town.' "

* " A Ballad."　One theory explains these meaningless refrains as
remembered fragments of older ballads.

Another mark of the genuine ballad manner, as of Homer and *Volkspoesie* in general, is the conventional epithet. Macaulay noted that the gold is always red in the ballads, the ladies always gay, and Robin Hood's men are always his merry men.   Doughty Douglas, bold Robin Hood, merry Carlisle, the good greenwood, the gray goose wing, and the wan water are other inseparables of the kind.   Still another mark is the frequent retention of the Middle English accent on the final syllable in words like contrié, barón, dinére, feláwe, abbáy, rivére, monéy, and its assumption by words which never properly had it, such as ladý, harpér, weddíng, watér, etc.*   Indeed, as Percy pointed out in his introduction, there were " many phrases and idioms which the minstrels seem to have appropriated to themselves, . . a cast of style and measure very different from that of contemporary poets of a higher class."

Not everything that is called a ballad belongs to the class of poetry that we are here considering.   In its looser employment the word has signified almost any kind of song: " a woeful ballad made to his mistress' eyebrow," for example.   " Ballade " was also the name of a somewhat intricate French stanza form, employed by Gower and Chaucer, and recently reintroduced into English verse by Dobson, Lang, Gosse, and others, along with the virelay, rondeau, triolet, etc. There is also a numerous class of popular ballads—in

* Reproduced by Rossetti and other moderns. See them parodied in Robert Buchanan's " Fleshly School of Poets " :

> " When seas do roar and skies do pour,
>   Hard is the lot of the sailór
>   Who scarcely, as he reels, can tell
>   The sidelights from the binnacle."

the sense of something made *for* the people, though not *by* the people—which are without relation to our subject. These are the street ballads, which were and still are hawked about by ballad-mongers, and which have no literary character whatever. There are satirical and political ballads, ballads versifying passages in Scripture or chronicle, ballads relating to current events, or giving the history of famous murders and other crimes, of prodigies, providences, and all sorts of happenings that teach a lesson in morals: about George Barnwell and the "Babes in the Wood," and "Whittington and his Cat," etc.: ballads like Shenstone's "Jemmy Dawson" and Gay's "Black-eyed Susan." Thousands of such are included in manuscript collections like the "Pepysian," or printed in the publications of the Roxburghe Club and the Ballad Society. But whether entirely modern, or extant in black-letter broadsides, they are nothing to our purpose. We have to do here with the folk-song, the *traditional* ballad, product of the people at a time when the people was homogeneous and the separation between the lettered and unlettered classes had not yet taken place: the true minstrel ballad of the Middle Ages, or of that state of society which in rude and primitive neighborhoods, like the Scottish border, prolonged mediæval conditions beyond the strictly mediæval period.

In the form in which they are preserved, few of our ballads are older than the seventeenth or the latter part of the sixteenth century, though in their origin many of them are much older. Manuscript versions of "Robin Hood and the Monk" and "Robin Hood and the Potter" exist, which are referred to the last years of the fifteenth century.   The "Lytel Geste of Robyn Hode" was printed by Wynkyn de Worde in 1489.   The "Not-Brown Maid" was printed in "Arnold's Chronicle" in 1502.   "The Hunting of the Cheviot"—the elder version of "Chevy Chase"—was mentioned by Philip Sidney in his "Defence of Poesie" in 1580.*   The ballad is a narrative song, naïve, impersonal, spontaneous, objective.   The singer is lost in the song, the teller in the tale.   That is its essence, but sometimes the story is told by the lyrical, sometimes by the dramatic method.   In "Helen of Kirkconnell" it is the bereaved lover who is himself the speaker: in "Waly Waly," the forsaken maid. These are monologues; for a purely dialogue ballad it will be sufficient to mention the powerful and impressive piece in the "Reliques" entitled "Edward." Herder translated this into German; it is very old, with Danish, Swedish, and Finnish analogues.   It is a story of parricide, and is narrated in a series of questions by the mother and answers by the son.   The commonest form, however, was a mixture of epic and dramatic, or direct relation with dialogue.   A frequent feature is the abruptness of the opening and the transitions.   The ballad-maker observes unconsciously Aristotle's rule for the epic poet, to begin *in medias res.*   Johnson noticed this in the instance of "Johnny Armstrong," but a stronger example is found in "The Banks of Yarrow:"

* "I never heard the old song of Percie and Douglas that I found not my heart moved more than with a trumpet; and yet it is sung but by some blind crouder, with no rougher voice than rude style; which being so evil apparelled in the dust and cobwebs of that uncivil age, what would it work, trimmed in the gorgeous eloquence of Pindar!"

> " Late at e'en, drinking the wine,
>   And ere they paid the lawing,
>   They set a combat them between,
>   To fight it in the dawing."

With this, an indirect, allusive way of telling the story, which Goethe mentions in his prefatory note to " Des Sängers Fluch," as a constant note of the " Volkslied." The old ballad-maker does not vouchsafe explanations about persons and motives; often he gives the history, not expressly nor fully, but by hints and glimpses, leaving the rest to conjecture; throwing up its salient points into a strong, lurid light against a background of shadows. The knight rides out a-hunting, and by and by his riderless horse comes home, and that is all:

> " Toom* hame cam the saddle
>   But never cam he. "

Or the knight himself comes home and lies down to die, reluctantly confessing, under his mother's questioning, that he dined with his true-love and is poisoned.† And again that is all. Or

> " —In behint yon auld fail ‡ dyke,
>   I wot there lies a new-slain knight ;
>   And naebody kens that he lies there,
>   But his hawk, his hound, and lady fair.

> " His hound is to the hunting gane,
>   His hawk to fetch the wild-fowl hame,
>   His lady's ta'en another mate,
>   So we may mak our dinner sweet."

A whole unuttered tragedy of love, treachery, and murder lies back of these stanzas. This method of

---

* Empty : " Bonnie George Campbell."   † " Lord Randall."
‡ Turf : " The Twa Corbies."

narration may be partly accounted for by the fact
that the story treated was commonly some local
country-side legend of family feud or unhappy
passion, whose incidents were familiar to the ballad-
singer's audience and were readily supplied by
memory.   One theory holds that the story was partly
told and partly sung, and that the links and exposi-
tions were given in prose.   However this may be, the
artless art of these popular poets evidently included
a knowledge of the uses of mystery and suggestion.
They knew that, for the imagination, the part is sometimes greater than the whole.   Gray wrote to Mason in
1757, " I have got the old Scotch ballad [Gil Maurice]
on which ' Douglas ' [Home's tragedy, first played at
Edinburgh in 1756] was founded.   It is divine. . .
Aristotle's best rules are observed in it in a manner
which shews the author never had heard of Aristotle.
It begins in the fifth act of the play.   You may read
it two-thirds through without guessing what it is
about; and yet, when you come to the end, it is impossible not to understand the whole story."

It is not possible to recover the conditions under
which these folk-songs "made themselves," * as it
were, or grew under the shaping hands of generations
of nameless bards.   Their naïve, primitive quality
cannot be acquired: the secret is lost.   But Walter

* I use this phrase without any polemic purpose.   The question of
origins is not here under discussion.   Of course at some stage in the
history of any ballad the poet, the individual artist, is present,
though the precise ratio of his agency to the communal element in
the work is obscure.   For an acute and learned review of this topic,
see the Introduction to " Old English Ballads," by Professor Francis
B. Gummere (Athenæum Press Series), Boston, 1894.

Scott, who was steeped to the lips in balladry, and whose temper had much of the healthy objectivity of an earlier age, has succeeded as well as any modern. Some of his ballads are more perfect artistically than his long metrical romances; those of them especially which are built up from a burden or fragment of old minstrel song, like " Jock o' Hazeldean " * and the song in " Rokeby ":

> " He turned his charger as he spake
> Upon the river shore,
> He gave the bridle-reins a shake,
> Said ' Adieu for evermore,
> My love !
> And adieu for evermore.' "

Here Scott catches the very air of popular poetry, and the dovetailing is done with most happy skill. " Proud Maisie is in the Wood " is a fine example of the ballad manner of story-telling by implication.†

As regards their subject-matter, the ballads admit of a rough classification into the historical, or *quasi*-historical, and the purely legendary or romantic. Of the former class were the " riding-ballad " of the Scottish border, where the forays of moss-troopers,

---

* From " Jock o' Hazel Green." " Young Lochinvar " is derived from " Katherine Janfarie" in the " Minstrelsy of the Scottish Border."

† " Scott has given us nothing more complete and lovely than this little song, which unites simplicity and dramatic power to a wildwood music of the rarest quality. No moral is drawn, far less any conscious analysis of feeling attempted : the pathetic meaning is left to be suggested by the mere presentment of the situation. Inexperienced critics have often named this, which may be called the Homeric manner, superficial from its apparent simple facility."— *Palgrave : ' Golden Treasury* " (Edition of 1866), p. 392.

the lifting of blackmail, the raids and private warfare of the Lords of the Marches, supplied many traditions of heroism and adventure like those recorded in "The Battle of Otterburn," "The Hunting of the Cheviot," "Johnnie Armstrong," "Kinmont Willie," "The Rising in the North" and "Northumberland Betrayed by Douglas." Of the fictitious class, some were shortened, popularized, and generally degraded versions of the chivalry romances, which were passing out of favor among educated readers in the sixteenth century and fell into the hands of the ballad-makers. Such, to name only a few included in the "Reliques," were "Sir Lancelot du Lake," "The Legend of Sir Guy," "King Arthur's Death" and "The Marriage of Sir Gawaine." But the substance of these was not of the genuine popular stuff, and their personages were simply the old heroes of court poetry in reduced circumstances. Much more impressive are the original folk-songs, which strike their roots deep into the ancient world of legend and even of myth.

In this true ballad world there is a strange commingling of paganism and Catholic Christianity. It abounds in the supernatural and the marvelous. Robin Hood is a pious outlaw. He robs the fat-headed monks, but will not die unhouseled and has great devotion to Our Blessed Lady; who appears also to Brown Robyn, when he is cast overboard, hears his confession and takes his soul to Heaven.* When mass has been sung and the bells of merry Lincoln have rung, Lady Maisry goes seeking her little Hugh, who has been killed by the Jew's daughter

* " Brown Robyn's Confession." Robin Hood risks his life to take the sacrament. " Robin Hood and the Monk."

and thrown into Our Lady's draw-well fifty fathom deep, and the boy answers his mother miraculously from the well.* Birds carry messages for lovers † and dying men,‡ or show the place where the body lies buried and the corpse-candles shine.§ The harper strings his harp with three golden hairs of the drowned maiden, and the tune that he plays upon them reveals the secret of her death.‖ The ghosts of the sons that have perished at sea come home to take farewell of their mother.¶ The spirit of the forsaken maid visits her false lover at midnight;** or "the dead comes for the quick,"†† as in Bürger's weird poem. There are witches, fairies, and mermaidens ‡‡ in the ballads: omens, dreams, spells,§§ enchantments, transformations,‖‖ magic rings and charms, "gramarye"¶¶ of many sorts; and all these things are more effective here than in poets like Spenser and Collins, because they are matters of belief and not of make-believe.

The ballads are prevailingly tragical in theme, and the tragic passions of pity and fear find an elementary force of utterance.   Love is strong as death, jealousy

* "Sir Hugh."   *Cf.* Chaucer's "Prioresse Tale."
† "The Gay Goshawk."
‡ "Johnnie Cock."
§ "Young Hunting."
‖ "The Twa Sisters."
¶ "The Wife of Usher's Well."
** "Fair Margaret and Sweet William."
†† "Sweet William's Ghost."
‡‡ "Clerk Colven."
§§ "Willie's Lady."
‖‖ "Kemp Owyne" and "Tam Lin."
¶¶ "King Estmere."

cruel as the grave.   Hate, shame, grief, despair speak
here with their native accent:

> " There are seven forsters at Pickeram Side,
>   At Pickeram where they dwell,
> And for a drop of thy heart's bluid
>   They wad ride the fords of hell." *

> " O little did my mother think,
>   The day she cradled me,
> What lands I was to travel through,
>   What death I was to dee." †

The maiden asks her buried lover:

> " Is there any room at your head, Sanders?
>   Is there any room at your feet?
> Or any room at your twa sides,
>   Where fain, fain would I sleep? " ‡

> " O waly, waly, but love be bonny
>   A little time while it is new; §
> But when 'tis auld it waxeth cauld
>   And fades awa' like morning dew. . .

> " And O! if my young babe were born,
>   And set upon the nurse's knee,
> And I mysel' were dead and gane,
>   And the green grass growing over me! "

Manners in this world are of a primitive savagery.
There are treachery, violence, cruelty, revenge; but
there are also honor, courage, fidelity, and devotion

* " Johnnie Cock."
† " Mary Hamilton."
‡ " Sweet William's Ghost."
§ " The Forsaken Bride."   *Cf*. Chaucer:
>   " Love is noght old as whan that it is newe."
>> —*Clerkes* **Tale.**

that endureth to the end. "Child Waters" and "Fair Annie" do not suffer on a comparison with Tennyson's "Enid" and Chaucer's story of patient Griselda ("The Clerkes Tale") with which they have a common theme. It is the mediæval world. Marauders, pilgrims, and wandering gleemen go about in it. The knight stands at his garden pale, the lady sits at her bower window, and the little foot page carries messages over moss and moor. Marchmen are riding through the Bateable Land "by the hie light o' the moon." Monks are chanting in St. Mary's Kirk, trumpets are blowing in Carlisle town, castles are burning; down in the glen there is an ambush and swords are flashing; bows are twanging in the greenwood; four and twenty ladies are playing at the ball, and four and twenty milk-white calves are in the woods of Glentanner—all ready to be stolen. About Yule the round tables begin; the queen looks over the castle-wall, the palmer returns from the Holy Land, Young Waters lies deep in Stirling dungeon, but Child Maurice is in the silver wood, combing his yellow locks with a silver comb.

There is an almost epic coherence about the ballads of the Robin Hood cycle. This good robber, who with his merry men haunted the forests of Sherwood and Barnsdale, was the real ballad hero and the darling of the popular fancy which created him. For though the names of his confessor, Friar Tuck; his mistress, Maid Marian; and his companions, Little John, Scathelock, and Much the miller's son, have an air of reality,—and though the tradition has associated itself with definite localities,—there is nothing historical about Robin Hood. Langland, in the fourteenth century, mentions "rhymes of Robin Hood"; and efforts have been made to identify him with one of the dispossessed followers of Simon de Montfort, in "the Barons' War," or with some still earlier freebooter, of Hereward's time, who had taken to the woods and lived by plundering the Normans. Myth as he is, he is a thoroughly national conception. He had the English love of fair play; the English readiness to shake hands and make up when worsted in a square fight. He killed the King's venison, but was a loyal subject. He took from the rich and gave to the poor, executing thus a kind of wild justice. He defied legal authority in the person of the proud sheriff of Nottingham, thereby appealing to that secret sympathy with lawlessness which marks a vigorous, free yeomanry.* He had the knightly virtues of courtesy and hospita!ity, and the yeomanly virtues of good temper and friendliness. And finally, he was a mighty archer with the national weapons, the long-bow and the cloth-yard shaft; and so appealed to the national love of sport in his free and careless life under the greenwood tree. The forest scenery gives a poetic background to his exploits, and though the ballads, like folk-poetry in general, seldom linger over natural description, there is everywhere a consciousness of this background and a wholesome, outdoor feeling:

> " In somer, when the shawes be sheyne,
>   And leves be large and long,
> Hit is full mery in feyre foreste
>   To here the foulys song:

* What character so popular as a wild prince—like Prince Hal— who breaks his own laws, and the heads of his own people, in a democratic way ?

" To se the dere draw to the dale,
    And leve the hillis hee,
  And shadow hem in the levës grene,
    Under the grene-wode tre." *

Although a few favorite ballads such as "Johnnie Armstrong," "Chevy Chase," "The Children in the Wood," and some of the Robin Hood ones had long been widely, nay almost universally familiar, they had hardly been regarded as literature worthy of serious attention. They were looked upon as nursery tales, or at best as the amusement of peasants and unlettered folk, who used to paste them up on the walls of inns, cottages, and ale-houses. Here and there an educated man had had a sneaking fondness for collecting old ballads—much as people nowadays collect postage stamps. Samuel Pepys, the diarist, made such a collec tion, and so did John Selden, the great legal antiquary and scholar of Milton's time. "I have heard," wrote Addison, "that the late Lord Dorset, who had the greatest wit tempered with the greatest candor, and was one of the finest critics as well as the best poets of his age, had a numerous collection of old English ballads, and a particular pleasure in the reading of them. I can affirm the same of Mr. Dryden." Dryden's "Miscellany Poems" (1684) gave "Gilde- roy," "Johnnie Armstrong," "Chevy Chase," "The Miller and the King's Daughter," and "Little Mus- grave and the Lady Barnard." The last named, as well as "Lady Anne Bothwell's Lament" and "Fair Margaret and Sweet William," † was quoted in Beau-

* " Robin Hood and the Monk."

† For a complete exposure of David Mallet's impudent claim to the authorship of this ballad, see Appendix II. to Professor Phelps' " English Romantic Movement."

mont and Fletcher's "Knight of the Burning **Pestle,**" (1611). Scraps of them are sung by one of the *dramatis personæ*, old Merrythought, whose specialty is a damnable iteration of ballad fragments. References to old ballads are numerous in the Elizabethan plays. Percy devoted the second book of his first series to "Ballads that Illustrate Shakspere." In the seventeenth century a few ballads were printed entire in poetic miscellanies entitled "Garlands," higgledy-piggledy with pieces of all kinds. Professor Child enumerates nine ballad collections before Percy's. The only ones of any importance among these were "A Collection of Old Ballads" (Vols. I. and II. in 1723, Vol. III. in 1725), ascribed to Ambrose Philips; and the Scotch poet, Allan Ramsay's, "Tea Table Miscellany," (in 4 vols., 1714–40) and "Evergreen" (2 vols., 1724). The first of these collections was illustrated with copperplate engravings and supplied with introductions which were humorous in intention. The editor treated his ballads as trifles, though he described them as "corrected from the best and most ancient copies extant"; and said that Homer himself was nothing more than a blind ballad-singer, whose songs had been subsequently joined together and formed into an epic poem. Ramsay's ballads were taken in part from a manuscript collection of some eight hundred pages, made by George Bannatyne about 1570 and still preserved in the Advocates' Library at Edinburgh.

In Nos. 70, 74, and 85, of the *Spectator*, Addison had praised the naturalness and simplicity of the popular ballads, selecting for special mention "Chevy Chase"—the later version—"which," he wrote, "is the favorite ballad of the common people of England; and

Ben Jonson used to say he had rather have been the author of it than of all his works "; and "the 'Two Children in the Wood,' which is one of the darling songs of the common people, and has been the delight of most Englishmen in some part of their age." Addison justifies his liking for these humble poems by classical precedents. "The greatest modern critics have laid it down as a rule that an heroic poem should be founded upon some important precept of morality adapted to the constitution of the country in which the poet writes. Homer and Virgil have formed their plans in this view." Accordingly he thinks that the author of "Chevy Chase" meant to point a moral as to the mischiefs of private war. As if it were not precisely the *gaudium certaminis* that inspired the old border ballad-maker! As if he did not glory in the fight! The passage where Earl Percy took the dead Douglas by the hand and lamented his fallen foe reminds Addison of Æneas' behavior toward Lausus. The robin red-breast covering the children with leaves recalls to his mind a similar touch in one of Horace's odes. But it was much that Addison, whose own verse was so artificial, should have had a taste for the wild graces of folk-song. He was severely ridiculed by his contemporaries for these concessions. "He descended now and then to lower disquisitions," wrote Dr. Johnson, "and by a serious display of the beauties of 'Chevy Chase,' exposed himself to the ridicule of Wagstaff, who bestowed a like pompous character on 'Tom Thumb'; and to the contempt of Dennis, who, considering the fundamental position of his criticism, that 'Chevy Chase' pleases and ought to please because it is natural, observes that 'there is a way of deviating from nature . . . by imbecility, which degrades nature by faintness and diminution' . . . In 'Chevy Chase' . . . there is a chill and lifeless imbecility. The story cannot possibly be told in a manner that shall make less impression on the mind." *

Nicholas Rowe, the dramatist and Shakspere editor, had said a good word for ballads in the prologue to "Jane Shore" (1713):

> "Let no nice taste despise the hapless dame
>   Because recording ballads chant her name.
>   Those venerable ancient song enditers
>   Soared many a pitch above our modern writers. . .
>   Our numbers may be more refined than those,
>   But what we've gained in verse, we've lost in prose.
>   Their words no shuffling double meaning knew :
>   Their speech was homely, but their hearts were true. . .
>   With rough, majestic force they moved the heart,
>   And strength and nature made amends for art."

Ballad forgery had begun early. To say nothing of appropriations, like Mallet's, of "William and Margaret," Lady Wardlaw put forth her "Hardyknut" in 1719 as a genuine old ballad, and it was reprinted as such in Ramsay's "Evergreen." Gray wrote to Walpole in 1760, "I have been often told that the poem called 'Hardicanute' (which I always admired and still admire) was the work of somebody that lived a few years ago. This I do not at all believe, though it has evidently been retouched by some modern hand." Before Percy no concerted or intelligent effort had been made toward collecting, preserving, and editing the *corpus poetarum* of English minstrelsy.

* " Life of Addison."

The great mass of ancient ballads, so far as they were in print at all, existed in "stall copies," *i. e.*, single sheets or broadsides, struck off for sale by ballad-mongers and the keepers of book-stalls.

Thomas Percy, the compiler of the "Reliques," was a parish clergyman, settled at the retired hamlet of Easton Maudit, Northamptonshire. For years he had amused his leisure by collecting ballads. He numbered among his acquaintances men of letters like Johnson, Goldsmith, Garrick, Grainger, Farmer, and Shenstone. It was the last who suggested the plan of the "Reliques" and who was to have helped in its execution, had not his illness and death prevented. Johnson spent a part of the summer of 1764 on a visit to the vicarage of Easton Maudit, on which occasion Percy reports that his guest "chose for his regular reading the old Spanish romance of 'Felixmarte of Hircania,' in folio, which he read quite through." He adds, what one would not readily suspect, that the doctor, when a boy, "was immoderately fond of reading romances of chivalry, and he retained his fondness for them through life. . . I have heard him attribute to these extravagant fictions that unsettled turn of mind which prevented his ever fixing in any profession." Percy talked over his project with Johnson, who would seem to have given his approval, and even to have added his persuasions to Shenstone's. For in the preface to the first edition of the "Reliques," the editor declared that "he could refuse nothing to such judges as the author of the *Rambler* and the late Mr. Shenstone"; and that "to the friendship of Mr. Johnson he owes many valuable hints for the conduct of his work." And after Ritson had questioned the existence of the famous "folio manuscript," Percy's nephew in the advertisement to the fourth edition (1794), cited "the appeal publicly made to Dr. Johnson . . . so long since as in the year 1765, and never once contradicted by him."

In spite of these amenities, the doctor had a low opinion of ballads and ballad collectors. In the *Rambler* (No. 177) he made merry over one Cantilenus, who "turned all his thoughts upon old ballads, for he considered them as the genuine records of the natural taste. He offered to show me a copy of 'The Children in the Wood,' which he firmly believed to be of the first edition, and by the help of which the text might be freed from several corruptions, if this age of barbarity had any claim to such favors from him." "The conversation," says Boswell, "having turned on modern imitations of ancient ballads, and someone having praised their simplicity, he treated them with that ridicule which he always displayed when that subject was mentioned." Johnson wrote several stanzas in parody of the ballads; *e. g.*,

> " The tender infant, meek and mild,
>   Fell down upon a stone:
> The nurse took up the squealing child,
>   But still the child squealed on."

And again:

> " I put my hat upon my head
>   And walked into the Strand;
> And there I met another man
>   Whose hat was in his hand."

This is quoted by Wordsworth,* who compares it with a stanza from " The Children in the Wood ":

* Preface to second edition of the " Lyrical Ballads."

> " Those pretty babes, with hand in hand,
>   Went wandering up and down;
> But never more they saw the man
>   Approaching from the town. "

He says that in both of these stanzas the language is that of familiar conversation, yet one stanza
is admirable and the other contemptible, because the
matter of it is contemptible. In the essay supple-
mentary to his preface, Wordsworth asserts that the
" Reliques " was " ill suited to the then existing taste
of city society, and Dr. Johnson . . . was not sparing
in his exertions to make it an object of contempt";
and that " Dr. Percy was so abashed by the ridicule
flung upon his labors . . . that, though while he was
writing under a mask he had not wanted resolution to
follow his genius into the regions of true simplicity
and genuine pathos (as is evinced by the exquisite
ballad of ' Sir Cauline ' and by many other pieces),
yet when he appeared in his own person and character
as a poetical writer, he adopted, as in the tale of ' The
Hermit of Warkworth,' a diction scarcely distin-
guishable from the vague, the glossy and unfeeling
language of his day." Wordsworth adds that he
esteems the genius of Dr. Percy in this kind of writing
superior to that of any other modern writer; and that
even Bürger had not Percy's fine sensibility. He
quotes, in support of this opinion, two stanzas from
" The Child of Elle " in the " Reliques," and contrasts them with the diluted and tricked-out version
of the same in Bürger's German.

Mr. Hales does not agree in this high estimate of
Percy as a ballad composer. Of this same " Child of
Elle " he says: " The present fragment of a version

may be fairly said to be now printed for the first time, as in the ' Reliques ' it is buried in a heap of 'polished' verses composed by Percy. That worthy prelate, touched by the beauty of it—he had a soul—was unhappily moved to try his hand at its completion. A wax-doll-maker might as well try to restore Milo's Venus. There are thirty-nine lines here. There are two hundred in the thing called the ' Child of Elle ' in the ' Reliques.' But in those two hundred lines all the thirty-nine originals do not appear. . . On the whole, the union of the genuine and the false—of the old ballad with Percy's tawdry feebleness—makes about as objectionable a *mésalliance* as that in the story itself is in the eyes of the father." * The modern ballad scholars, in their zeal for the purity of the text, are almost as hard upon Percy as Ritson himself was. They say that he polished " The Heir of Linne " till he could see his own face in it; and swelled out its 126 lines to 216—" a fine flood of ballad and water." † The result of this piecing and tinkering in " Sir Cauline "—which Wordsworth thought exquisite—they regard as a heap of tinsel, though they acknowledge that " these additional stanzas show, indeed, an extensive acquaintance with old balladry and a considerable talent of imitation."

From the critical or scholarly point of view, these strictures are doubtless deserved. It is an editor's duty to give his text as he finds it, without interpolations or restorations; and it is unquestionable that

* " Bishop Percy's Folio Manuscript " (1867), Vol. II. Introductory Essay by J. W. Hales on " The Revival of Ballad Poetry in the Eighteenth Century."

† *Ibid.*

Percy's additions to fragmentary pieces are full of
sentimentalism, affectation, and the spurious poetic
diction of his age. An experienced ballad amateur
can readily separate, in most cases, the genuine portions from the insertions. But it is unfair to try
Percy by modern editorial canons. That sacredness
which is now imputed to the *ipsissima verba* of an
ancient piece of popular literature would have been
unintelligible to men of that generation, who regarded
such things as trifles at best, and mostly as barbarous
trifles—something like wampum belts, or nose-rings,
or antique ornaments in the *goût barbare et charmant
des bijoux goths.* Percy's readers did not want torsos
and scraps; to present them with acephalous or bob-
tailed ballads—with *cetera desunt* and constellations of
asterisks—like the manuscript in Prior's poem, the
conclusion of which was eaten by the rats—would
have been mere pedantry. Percy knew his public,
and he knew how to make his work attractive to it.
The readers of that generation enjoyed their ballad
with a large infusion of Percy. If the scholars of this
generation prefer to take theirs without, they know
where to get it.

The materials for the "Reliques" were drawn partly
from the Pepys collection at Magdalen College,
Cambridge; from Anthony Wood's, made in 1676, in
the Ashmolean Museum at Oxford; from manuscript
and printed ballads in the Bodleian, the British
Museum, the archives of the Antiquarian Society,
and private collections. Sir David Dalrymple sent
a number of Scotch ballads, and the editor
acknowledged obligations to Thomas Warton and
many others. But the nucleus of the whole was a

certain folio manuscript in a handwriting of Charles
I.'s time, containing 191 songs and ballads, which
Percy had begged, when still very young, from his
friend Humphrey Pitt, of Prior's-Lee in Shropshire.
When he first saw this precious document, it was torn,
unbound, and mutilated, "lying dirty on the floor
under a bureau in the parlor, being used by the maids
to light the fire." The first and last leaves were
wanting, and "of 54 pages near the beginning, half
of every leaf hath been torn away."* Percy had it
bound, but the binders trimmed off the top and bottom
lines in the process. From this manuscript he professed to have taken "the greater part" of the pieces
in the "Reliques." In truth he took only 45 of the
176 poems in his first edition from this source.

Percy made no secret of the fact that he filled
lacunæ in his originals with stanzas, and, in some
cases, with nearly entire poems of his own composition. But the extent of the liberties that he took
with the text, although suspected, was not certainly
known until Mr. Furnivall finally got leave to have
the folio manuscript copied and printed.† Before this
time it had been jealously guarded by the Percy family,
and access to it had been denied to scholars. "Since
Percy and his nephew printed their fourth edition of
the 'Reliques' from the manuscript in 1794," writes
Mr. Furnivall in his "Forewords," "no one has
printed any piece from it except Robert Jamieson—to
whom Percy supplied a copy of 'Child Maurice' and
'Robin Hood and the Old Man' for his 'Popular
Ballads and Songs' (1806)—and Sir Frederic Madden,

* "Advertisement to the Fourth Edition."
† In four volumes, 1867–68.

who was allowed—by one of Percy's daughters—to print 'The Grene Knight,' 'The Carle of Carlisle' and 'The Turk and Gawin' in his 'Syr Gawaine' for the Bannatyne Club, 1839." Percy was furiously assailed by Joseph Ritson for manipulating his texts; and in the 1794 edition he made some concessions to the latter's demand for a literal rescript, by taking off a few of the ornaments in which he had tricked them. Ritson was a thoroughly critical, conscientious student of poetic antiquities and held the right theory of an editor's functions. In his own collections of early English poetry he rendered a valuable service to all later inquirers. These included "Pieces of Ancient Popular Poetry," 1791; "Ancient Songs," 1792; "Scottish Songs," 1794; "Robin Hood," 1795; besides editions of Laurence Minot's poems, and of "Gammer Gurton's Needle," as well as other titles. He was an ill-tempered and eccentric man: a vegetarian, a free-thinker, a spelling reformer, * and latterly a Jacobin. He attacked Warton as well as Percy, and used to describe any clerical antagonist as a "stinking priest." He died insane in 1803. Ritson took issue with the theory maintained in Percy's introductory "Essay on the Ancient Minstrels," viz.: that the minstrels were not only the singers, but likewise the authors of the ballads. This is a question chiefly interesting to antiquaries. But Ritson went so far in his rage against Percy as to deny the existence of the sacred Folio Manuscript, until convinced by abundant testimony

---

* Spelling reform has been a favorite field for cranks to disport themselves upon. Ritson's particular vanity was the past participle of verbs ending in *e*: *e. g.*, *perceiveed*. *Cf.* Landor's notions of a similar kind.

that there was such a thing.   It was an age of forgeries, and Ritson was not altogether without justification in supposing that the author of "The Hermit of Warkworth " belonged in the same category with Chatterton, Ireland, and MacPherson.

Percy, like Warton, took an apologetic tone toward his public.   " In a polished age, like the present," he wrote, " I am sensible that many of these reliques of antiquity will require great allowances to be made for them.   Yet have they, for the most part, a pleasing simplicity and many artless graces, which, in the opinion of no mean critics, have been thought to compensate for the want of higher beauties."   Indeed how should it have been otherwise?   The old ballads were everything which the eighteenth century was not. They were rough and wild, where that was smooth and tame; they dealt, with fierce sincerity, in the elementary passions of human nature.   They did not moralize, or philosophize, or sentimentalize; were never subtle, intellectual, or abstract.   They used plain English, without finery or elegance.   They had certain popular mannerisms, but none of the conventional figures of speech or rhetorical artifices like personification, periphrasis, antithesis, and climax, so dear to the Augustan heart.   They were intent on the story—not on the style—and they just told it and let it go for what it was worth.

Moreover, there are ballads and ballads.   The best of them are noble in expression as well as feeling, unequaled by anything in our mediæval poetry outside of Chaucer; unequaled by Chaucer himself in point of intensity, in occasional phrases of a piercing beauty:

" The swans-fethars that his arrowe bar
    With his hart-blood they were wet." *

" O cocks are crowing a merry mid-larf,
        A wat the wild fule boded day ;
    The salms of Heaven will be sung,
        And ere now I'll be missed away." †

" If my love were an earthly knight,
        As he's an elfin gray,
    A wad na gie my ain true love
        For no lord that ye hae." ‡

" She hang ae napkin at the door,
        Another in the ha,
    And a' to wipe the trickling tears,
        Sae fast as they did fa." §

" And all is with one chyld of yours,
        I feel stir at my side:
    My gowne of green, it is too strait:
        Before it was too wide." ‖

Verse of this quality needs no apology. But of many
of the ballads, Dennis' taunt, repeated by Dr. Johnson, is true; they are not merely rude, but weak and
creeping in style. Percy knew that the best of them
would savor better to the palates of his contemporaries if he dressed them with modern sauces. Yet he
must have loved them, himself, in their native simplicity, and it seems almost incredible that he could have
spoken as he did about Prior's insipid paraphrase of
the " Nut Brown Maid." " If it had no other merit,"
he says of that most lovely ballad, "than the having
afforded the ground-work to Prior's ' Henry and

---

* " The Hunting of the Cheviot."   ‡ " Tam Lin."
† " Sweet William's Ghost."   § " Fair Annie."
        ‖ " Child Waters."

Emma,' this ought to preserve it from oblivion."
Prior was a charming writer of epigram, society verse,
and the humorous *conte* in the manner of La Fontaine;
but to see how incapable he was of the depth and sweetness of romantic poetry, compare a few lines of the
original with the "hubbub of words" in his modernized version, in heroic couplets:

> " O Lord, what is this worldes blisse
> That changeth as the mone!
> The somer's day in lusty May
> Is derked before the none.
> I hear you say farewel. Nay, nay,
> We departe not so soon:
> Why say ye so? Wheder wyle ye goo?
> Alas! what have ye done?
> Alle my welfare to sorrow and care
> Shulde change if ye were gon;
> For in my minde, of all mankynde,
> I love but you alone."

Now hear Prior, with his Venus and flames and god of
love:

> " What is our bliss that changeth with the moon,
> And day of life that darkens ere 'tis noon?
> What is true passion, if unblest it dies?
> And where is Emma's joy, if Henry flies?
> If love, alas! be pain, the pain I bear
> No thought can figure and no tongue declare.
> Ne'er faithful woman felt, nor false one feigned
> The flames which long have in my bosom reigned.
> The god of love himself inhabits there
> With all his rage and dread and grief and care,
> His complement of stores and total war.
> O cease then coldly to suspect my love,
> And let my deed at least my faith approve.
> Alas! no youth shall my endearments share
> Nor day nor night shall interrupt my care;

No future story shall with truth upbraid
The cold indifference of the nut-brown maid;
Nor to hard banishment shall Henry run
While careless Emma sleeps on beds of down.
View me resolved, where'er thou lead'st, to go:
Friend to thy pain and partner of thy woe;
For I attest fair Venus and her son
That I, of all mankind, will love but thee alone."

There could be no more striking object lesson than this of the plethora from which English poetic diction was suffering, and of the sanative value of a book like the " Reliques."

" To atone for the rudeness of the more obsolete poems," and " to take off from the tediousness of the longer narratives," Percy interspersed a few modern ballads and a large number of "little elegant pieces of the lyric kind " by Skelton, Hawes, Gascoigne, Raleigh, Marlowe, Shakspere, Jonson, Warner, Carew, Daniel, Lovelace, Suckling, Drayton, Beaumont and Fletcher, Wotton, and other well-known poets.   Of the modern ballads the only one with any resemblance to folk-poetry was " The Braes o' Yarrow " by William Hamilton of Bangour, a Scotch gentleman who was "out in the forty-five." The famous border stream had watered an ancient land of song and story, and Hamilton's ballad, with its "strange, fugitive melody," was not unworthy of its traditions.   Hamilton belongs to the Milton imitators by virtue of his octosyllabics "Contemplation."*   His "Braes o' Yarrow " had been given already in Ramsay's "Tea Table Miscellany." The opening lines—

" Busk ye, busk ye, my bonny, bonny bride,
    Busk ye, busk ye, my winsome marrow "—

* See Phelps' " English Romantic Movement," pp. 33–35.

are quoted in Wordsworth's "Yarrow Unvisited," as well as a line of the following stanza:

> " Sweet smells the birk, green grows, green grows the grass,
>   Yellow on Yarrow's bank the gowan:
> Fair hangs the apple frae the rock,
>   Sweet the wave of Yarrow flowin'."

The first edition of the "Reliques" included one acknowledged child of Percy's muse, " The Friar of Orders Grey," a short, narrative ballad made up of song snatches from Shakspere's plays. Later editions afforded his longer poem, " The Hermit of Warkworth," first published independently in 1771.

With all its imperfections—perhaps partly in consequence of its imperfections—the " Reliques " was an epoch-making book. The nature of its service to English letters is thus stated by Macaulay, in the introduction to his " Lays of Ancient Rome ": "We cannot wonder that the ballads of Rome should have altogether disappeared, when we remember how very narrowly, in spite of the invention of printing, those of our own country and those of Spain escaped the same fate. There is, indeed, little doubt that oblivion covers many English songs equal to any that were published by Bishop Percy; and many Spanish songs as good as the best of those which have been so happily translated by Mr. Lockhart. Eighty years ago England possessed only one tattered copy of ' Child Waters ' and ' Sir Cauline,' and Spain only one tattered copy of the noble poem of the ' Cid.' The snuff of a candle, or a mischievous dog, might in a moment have deprived the world forever of any of those fine compositions. Sir Walter Scott, who united to the fire of a great poet the minute curiosity and patient diligence of a great antiquary, was but just in time to save the precious reliques of the Minstrelsy of the Border."

But Percy not only rescued, himself, a number of ballads from forgetfulness; what was equally important, his book prompted others to hunt out and publish similar relics before it was too late. It was the occasion of collections like Herd's (1769), Scott's (1802–03), and Motherwell's (1827), and many more, resting on purer texts and edited on more scrupulous principles than his own. Furthermore, his ballads helped to bring about a reform in literary taste and to inspire men of original genius. Wordsworth, Coleridge, Southey, Scott, all acknowledged the greatest obligations to them. Wordsworth said that English poetry had been "absolutely redeemed" by them. "I do not think there is a writer in verse of the present day who would not be proud to acknowledge his obligations to the 'Reliques.' I know that it is so with my friends; and, for myself, I am happy in this occasion to make a public avowal of my own." * Without the "Reliques," "The Ancient Mariner," "The Lady of the Lake," "La Belle Dame sans Merci," "Stratton Water," and "The Haystack in the Floods" might never have been. Perhaps even the "Lyrical Ballads" might never have been, or might have been something quite unlike what they are. Wordsworth, to be sure, scarcely ranks among romantics, and he expressly renounces the romantic machinery:

> " The dragon's wing,
> The magic ring,
> I shall not covet for my dower." †

* Appendix to the Preface to the 2d edition of " Lyrical Ballads."
† " Peter Bell."

What he learned from the popular ballad was the power of sincerity and of direct and homely speech.

As for Scott, he has recorded in an oft-quoted passage the impression that Percy's volumes made upon him in his school-days: "I remember well the spot where I read these volumes for the first time. It was beneath a huge plantain tree in the ruins of what had been intended for an old-fashioned arbor in the garden I have mentioned. The summer day sped onward so fast that, notwithstanding the sharp appetite of thirteen, I forgot the hour of dinner, was sought for with anxiety, and was still found entranced in my intellectual banquet. To read and to remember was, in this instance, the same thing; and henceforth I overwhelmed my school-fellows, and all who would hearken to me, with tragical recitations from the ballads of Bishop Percy. The first time, too, I could scrape a few shillings together, I bought unto myself a copy of these beloved volumes; nor do I believe I ever read a book so frequently, or with half the enthusiasm."

The "Reliques" worked powerfully in Germany, too. It was received in Lessing's circle with universal enthusiasm,* and fell in with that newly aroused interest in "Volkslieder" which prompted Herder's "Stimmen der Völker" (1778–79). †   Gottfried August

---

* Scherer: "Geschichte der Deutschen Literatur," p. 445.

† In his third book Herder gave translations of over twenty pieces in the "Reliques," besides a number from Ramsay's and other collections. His selections from Percy included "Chevy Chase," "Edward," "The Boy and the Mantle," "King Estmere," "Waly, Waly," "Sir Patrick Spens," "Young Waters," "The Bonny Earl of Murray," "Fair Margaret and Sweet William," "Sweet William's Ghost," "The Nut-Brown Maid," "The Jew's Daughter," etc., etc.;

Bürger, in particular, was a poet who may be said to have been made by the English ballad literature, of which he was an ardent student. His poems were published in 1778, and included five translations from Percy: "The Child of Elle" ("Die Entführung"), "The Friar of Orders Grey" ("Graurock"), "The Wanton Wife of Bath" ("Frau Schnips"), "King John and the Abbot of Canterbury" ("Der Kaiser und der Abt"), and "Child Waters" ("Graf Walter"). A. W. Schlegel says that Bürger did not select the more ancient and genuine pieces in the "Reliques"; and, moreover, that he spoiled the simplicity of the originals in his translations. It was doubtless in part the success of the "Reliques" that is answerable for many collections of old English poetry put forth in the last years of the century. Tyrwhitt's "Chaucer" and Ritson's publications have been already mentioned. George Ellis, a friend and correspondent of Walter Scott, and a fellow of the Society of Antiquaries, who was sometimes called "the Sainte Palaye of England," issued his "Specimens of Early English Poets" in 1790; edited in 1796 G. L. Way's translations from French *fabliaux* of the twelfth and thirteenth centuries; and printed in 1805 three volumes of "Early English Metrical Romances."

but none of the Robin Hood ballads. Herder's preface testifies that the "Reliques" was the starting-point and the kernel of his whole undertaking. "Der Anblick dieser Sammlung giebts offenbar dass ich eigentlich von *Englischen* Volksliedern ausging und auf sie zurückkomme. Als vor zehn und mehr Jahren die 'Reliques of Ancient Poetry' mir in die Hände fielen, freuten mich einzelne Stücke so sehr, dass ich sie zu übersetzen versuchte."—*Vorrede zu den Volksliedern. Herder's Sämmtliche Werke*, Achter Theil, s. 89 (Carlsruhe, 1821).

It is pleasant to record that Percy's labors brought him public recognition and the patronage of those whom Dr. Johnson used to call "the great." He had dedicated the "Reliques" to Elizabeth Percy, Countess of Northumberland. Himself the son of a grocer, he liked to think that he was connected by blood with the great northern house whose exploits had been sung by· the ancient minstrels that he loved. He became chaplain to the Duke of Northumberland, and to King George III.; and, in 1782, Bishop of Dromore in Ireland, in which see he died in 1811.

This may be as fit a place as any to introduce some mention of "The Minstrel, or the Progress of Genius," by James Beattie; a poem once widely popular, in which several strands of romantic influence are seen twisted together. The first book was published in 1771, the second in 1774, and the work was never completed. It was in the Spenserian stanza, was tinged with the enthusiastic melancholy of the Wartons, followed the landscape manner of Thomson, had elegiac echoes of Gray, and was perhaps not unaffected, in its love of mountain scenery, by MacPherson's "Ossian." But it took its title and its theme from a hint in Percy's "Essay on the Ancient Minstrels." * Beattie was Professor of Moral Philosophy in the University of Aberdeen. He was an amiable, sensitive, deeply religious man. He was fond of music and of nature, and was easily moved to tears; had "a young girl's nerves," says Taine, "and an old maid's hobbies." Gray, who met him in 1765, when on a visit to the Earl

* Stanzas 44–46, book i., bring in references to ballad literature in general and to "The Nut-Brown Maid" and "The Children in the Wood" in particular.

of Strathmore at Glammis Castle, esteemed him
highly. So did Dr. Johnson, partly because of his
"Essay on Truth" (1770), a shallow invective against
Hume, which gained its author an interview with
George III. and a pension of two hundred pounds a
year. Beattie visited London in 1771, and figured there
as a champion of orthodoxy and a heaven-inspired
bard. Mrs. Montagu patronized him extensively.
Sir Joshua Reynolds painted his portrait, with his
"Essay on Truth" under his arm, and Truth itself in
the background, an allegoric angel holding the bal-
ances in one hand, and thrusting away with the other
the figures of Prejudice, Skepticism, and Folly. Old
Lord Lyttelton had the poet out to Hagley, and
declared that he was Thomson come back to earth, to
sing of virtue and of the beauties of nature. Oxford
made him an LL.D.: he was urged to take orders in
the Church of England; and Edinburgh offered him
the chair of Moral Philosophy. Beattie's head was
slightly turned by all this success, and he became
something of a tuft-hunter. But he stuck faithfully
to Aberdeen, whose romantic neighborhood had first
inspired his muse. The biographers tell a pretty
story of his teaching his little boy to look for the hand
of God in the universe, by sowing cress in a garden
plot in the shape of the child's initials and leading him
by this gently persuasive analogy to read design in the
works of nature.

The design of "The Minstrel" is to "trace the progress of a Poetical Genius, born in a rude age," a
youthful shepherd who "lived in Gothic days." But
nothing less truly Gothic or mediæval could easily be
imagined than the actual process of this young poet's

education.　Instead of being taught to carve and ride and play the flute, like Chaucer's squire who

> " Cowde songes make and wel endite,
>   Juste and eek daunce, and wel purtraye and write,"

Edwin wanders alone upon the mountains and in solitary places and is instructed in history, philosophy, and science—and even in Vergil—by an aged hermit, who sits on a mossy rock, with his harp beside him, and delivers lectures.　The subject of the poem, indeed, is properly the education of nature; and in a way it anticipates Wordsworth's " Prelude," as this hoary sage does the "Solitary" of " The Excursion."　Beattie justifies his use of Spenser's stanza on the ground that it " seems, from its Gothic structure and original, to bear some relation to the subject and spirit of the poem."　He makes no attempt, however, to follow Spenser's "antique expressions."　The following passage will illustrate as well as any the romantic character of the whole:

> " When the long-sounding curfew from afar
>   Loaded with loud lament the lonely gale,
>   Young Edwin, lighted by the evening star,
>   Lingering and listening, wandered down the vale.
>   There would he dream of graves and corses pale,
>   And ghosts that to the charnel-dungeon throng,
>   And drag a length of clanking chain, and wail,
>   Till silenced by the owl's terrific song,
>   Or blast that shrieks by fits the shuddering aisles along.

> " Or when the setting moon, in crimson dyed,
>   Hung o'er the dark and melancholy deep,
>   To haunted stream, remote from man, he hied,
>   Where fays of yore their revels wont to keep;
>   And there let Fancy rove at large, till sleep
>   A vision brought to his entrancèd sight.

And first a wildly murmuring wind gan creep
Shrill to his ringing ear; then tapers bright,
With instantaneous gleam, illumed the vault of night.

" Anon in view a portal's blazing arch
Arose ; the trumpet bids the valves unfold ;
And forth a host of little warriors march,
Grasping the diamond lance and targe of gold.
Their look was gentle, their demeanour bold,
And green their helms, and green their silk attire ;
And here and there, right venerably old,
The long-robed minstrels wake the warbling wire,
And some with mellow breath the martial pipe inspire." *

The influence of Thomson is clearly perceptible in these stanzas. "The Minstrel," like "The Seasons," abounds in insipid morality, the commonplaces of denunciation against luxury and ambition, and the praise of simplicity and innocence. The titles alone of Beattie's minor poems are enough to show in what school he was a scholar: "The Hermit," "Ode to Peace," "The Triumph of Melancholy," "Retirement," etc., etc. "The Minstrel" ran through four editions before the publication of its second book in 1774.

* Book I. stanzas 32–34.

CHAPTER IX.

Ossian.

IN 1760 appeared the first installment of MacPherson's "Ossian." * Among those who received it with the greatest curiosity and delight was Gray, who had recently been helping Mason with criticisms on his "Caractacus," published in 1759. From a letter to Walpole (June, 1760) it would seem that the latter had sent Gray two manuscript bits of the as yet unprinted "Fragments," communicated to Walpole by Sir David Dalrymple, who furnished Scotch ballads to Percy. "I am so charmed," wrote Gray, "with the two specimens of Erse poetry, that I cannot help giving you the trouble to inquire a little farther about them; and should wish to see a few lines of the original, that I may form some slight idea of the language, the measures and the rhythm. Is there anything known of the author or authors; and of what antiquity are they supposed to be? Is there any more to be had of equal beauty, or at all approaching it?"

In a letter to Stonehewer (June 29,) he writes: "I have received another Scotch packet with a third specimen . . . full of nature and noble wild imagina-

* "Fragments of Ancient Poetry collected in the Highlands of Scotland, and translated from the Gaelic or Erse language." Edinburgh, MDCCLX. 70 pp.

tion." * And in the month following he writes to
Wharton: "If you have seen Stonehewer, he has
probably told you of my old Scotch (or rather Irish)
poetry. I am gone mad about them. They are said
to be translations (literal and in prose) from the *Erse*
tongue, done by one MacPherson, a young clergyman
in the Highlands. He means to publish a collection
he has of these specimens of antiquity, if it be antiquity; but what plagues me, is, I cannot come at any
certainty on that head. I was so struck, so *extasié*
with their infinite beauty, that I writ into Scotland to
make a thousand enquiries." This is strong language
for a man of Gray's coolly critical temper; but all his
correspondence of about this date is filled with references to Ossian which enable the modern reader to
understand in part the excitement that the book
created among Gray's contemporaries. The letters
that he got from MacPherson were unconvincing,
"ill-wrote, ill-reasoned, calculated to deceive, and yet
not cunning enough to do it cleverly." The external
evidence disposed him to believe the poems counterfeit; but the impression which they made was such
that he was "resolved to believe them genuine, spite
of the Devil and the Kirk. It is impossible to convince me that they were invented by the same man
that writes me these letters. On the other hand, it is
almost as hard to suppose, if they are original, that he
should be able to translate them so admirably."

On August 7 he writes to Mason that the Erse
fragments have been published five weeks ago in Scotland, though he had not received his copy till the last

* This was sent him by MacPherson and was a passage not given in
the " Fragments."

week.   "I continue to think them genuine, though
my reasons for believing the contrary are rather
stronger than ever."   David Hume, who afterward
became skeptical as to their authenticity, wrote to
Gray, assuring him that these poems were in everybody's mouth in the Highlands, and had been handed
down from father to son, from an age beyond all
memory and tradition.   Gray's final conclusion is very
much the same with that of the general public, to
which the Ossianic question is even yet a puzzle.   " I
remain still in doubt about the authenticity of these
poems, tho' inclining rather to believe them genuine
in spite of the world.   Whether they are the inventions of antiquity, or of a modern Scotchman, either
case is to me alike unaccountable.   *Je m'y perds.*"

We are more concerned here with the impression
which MacPherson's books, taking them just as they
stand, made upon their contemporary Europe, than
with the history of the controversy to which they gave
rise, and which is still unsettled after more than a
century and a quarter of discussion.   Nevertheless, as
this controversy began immediately upon their publication, and had reference not only to the authenticity
of the Ossianic poems, but also to their literary value;
it cannot be altogether ignored in this account.   The
principal facts upon which it turned may be given in a
nut-shell.   In 1759 Mr. John Home, author of the
tragedy of " Douglas," who had become interested in
the subject of Gaelic poetry, met in Dumfriesshire a
young Scotchman, named James MacPherson, who
was traveling as private tutor to Mr. Graham of Bal-
gowan.   MacPherson had in his possession a number
of manuscripts which, he said, were transcripts of

Gaelic poems taken down from the recital of old people in the Highlands. He translated two of these for Home, who was so much struck with them that he sent or showed copies to Dr. Hugh Blair, Professor of Rhetoric in the University of Edinburgh. At the solicitation of Dr. Blair and Mr. Home, MacPherson was prevailed upon to make further translations from the materials in his hands; and these, to the number of sixteen, were published in the "Fragments" already mentioned, with a preface of eight pages by Blair. They attracted so much attention in Edinburgh that a subscription was started, to send the compiler through the Highlands in search of more Gaelic poetry.

The result of these researches was " Fingal, an Ancient Epic Poem in Six Books: Together with several other poems, composed by Ossian the son of Fingal. Translated from the Gaelic language by James Mac-Pherson," London, 1762; together with "Temora, an Ancient Epic Poem in Eight Books," etc., etc., London, 1763. MacPherson asserted that he had made his versions from Gaelic poems ascribed to Ossian or Oisin, the son of Fingal or Finn MacCumhail, a chief renowned in Irish and Scottish song and popular legend. Fingal was the king of Morven, a district of the western Highlands, and head of the ancient warlike clan or race of the Feinne or Fenians. Tradition placed him in the third century and connected him with the battle of Gabhra, fought in 281. His son, Ossian, the warrior-bard, survived all his kindred. Blind and old, seated in his empty hall, or the cave of the rock; alone save for the white-armed Malvina, bride of his dead son, Oscar, he struck the harp and sang the memories of his youth: "a tale of the times of old."

MacPherson translated—or composed—his "Ossian" in an exclamatory, abrupt, rhapsodical prose, resembling somewhat the English of Isaiah and others of the books of the prophets.   The manners described were heroic, the state of society primitive.   The properties were few and simple; the cars of the heroes, their spears, helmets, and blue shields; the harp, the shells from which they drank in the hall, etc.   Conventional compound epithets abound, as in Homer: the "dark-bosomed" ships, the "car-borne" heroes, the "white-armed" maids, the "long-bounding" dogs of the chase.   The scenery is that of the western Highlands; and the solemn monotonous rhythm of MacPherson's style accorded well with the tone of his descriptions, filling the mind with images of vague sublimity and desolation: the mountain torrent, the dark rock in the ocean, the mist on the hills, the ghosts of heroes half seen by the setting moon, the thistle in the ruined courts of chieftains, the grass whistling on the windy heath, the blue stream of Lutha, and the cliffs of sea-surrounded Gormal.   It was noticed that there was no mention of the wolf, common in ancient Caledonia; nor of the thrush or lark or any singing bird; nor of the salmon of the sea-lochs, so often referred to in modern Gaelic poetry. But the deer, the swan, the boar, eagle, and raven occur repeatedly.

But a passage or two will exhibit the language and imagery of the whole better than pages of description.   "I have seen the walls of Balclutha, but they were desolate.   The fire had resounded in the halls, and the voice of the people is heard no more. The stream of Clutha was removed from its place by the fall of the walls. The thistle shook there its lonely head; the moss whistled to the wind. The fox looked out from the windows, the rank grass of the wall waved round its head. Desolate is the dwelling of Moina, silence is in the house of her fathers. Raise the song of mourning, O bards, over the land of strangers. They have but fallen before us; for, one day, we must fall. Why dost thou build the hall, son of the winged days? Thou lookest from thy towers to-day; yet a few years, and the blast of the desert comes; it howls in thy empty court, and whistles round thy half-worn shield."* "They rose rustling like a flock of sea-fowl when the waves expel them from the shore. Their sound was like a thousand streams that meet in Cona's vale, when, after a stormy night, they turn their dark eddies beneath the pale light of the morn. As the dark shades of autumn fly over hills of grass; so, gloomy, dark, successive came the chiefs of Lochlin's † echoing woods. Tall as the stag of Morven, moved stately before them the King.‡ His shining shield is on his side, like a flame on the heath at night; when the world is silent and dark, and the traveler sees some ghost sporting in the beam. Dimly gleam the hills around, and show indistinctly their oaks. A blast from the troubled ocean removed the settled mist. The sons of Erin appear, like a ridge of rocks on the coast; when mariners, on shores unknown are trembling at veering winds." §

The authenticity of the "Fragments" of 1760 had

* From " Carthon."   ‡ An unconscious hexameter.
† Scandinavia.   § From " Fingal " book ii

not passed without question; but when MacPherson
brought forward entire epics which, he asserted, were
composed by a Highland bard of the third century,
handed down through ages by oral tradition, and
finally committed—at least in part—to writing and
now extant in manuscripts in his possession, there
ensued at once a very emphatic expression of in-
credulity.   Among the most truculent of the disbe-
lievers was Dr. Johnson.   He had little liking for
Scotland, still less for the poetry of barbarism.   In
his tour of the Western Islands with Boswell in 1773,
he showed an insensibility, and even a kind of hostility, to the wild beauties of Highland scenery, which
gradually affects the reader with a sense of the ludicrous as he watches his sturdy figure rolling along on
a small Highland pony by sequestered Loch Ness,
with its fringe of birch trees, or between the prodigious
mountains that frown above Glensheal; or seated in a
boat off the Mull of Cantyre, listening to the Erse
songs of the rowers:

> " Breaking the silence of the seas
> Among the farthest Hebrides."

"Dr. Johnson," says Boswell, "owned he was now in
a scene of as wild nature as he could see; but he corrected me sometimes in my inaccurate observations.
'There,'said I, 'is a mountain like a cone.'   Johnson:
'No, sir.   It would be called so in a book, but when
a man comes to look at it, he sees it is not so.   It is
indeed pointed at the top, but one side of it is larger
than the other.'   Another mountain I called immense.
Johnson: 'No; it is no more than a considerable
protuberance.'"

Johnson not only disputed the antiquity of Mac-Pherson's "Ossian," but he denied it any poetic merit. Dr. Blair having asked him whether he thought any man of a modern age could have written such poems, he answered: "Yes, sir: many men, many women and many children." "Sir," he exclaimed to Reynolds, "a man might write such stuff forever, if he would *abandon* his mind to it." To Mr. Mac-Queen, one of his Highland hosts, he said: "I look upon MacPherson's 'Fingal' to be as gross an imposition as ever the world was troubled with." Johnson's arguments were mostly *a priori.* He asserted that the ancient Gael were a barbarous people, incapable of producing poetry of the kind. Long epics, such as "Fingal" and "Temora," could not be preserved in memory and handed down by word of mouth. As to ancient manuscripts which MacPherson pretended to have, there was not a Gaelic manuscript in existence a hundred years old.

It is now quite well established that Dr. Johnson was wrong on all these points. To say nothing of the Homeric poems, the ancient Finns, Scandinavians, and Germans were as barbarous as the Gael; yet they produced the Kalewala, the Edda, and the Nibelungen Lied. The Kalewala, a poem of 22,793 lines—as long as the Iliad—was transmitted orally from a remote antiquity and first printed in 1849. As to Gaelic manuscripts, there are over sixty in the Advocates' Library at Edinburgh, varying in age from three hundred to five hundred years.* There is, *e. g.,* the

* See the dissertation by Rev. Archibald Clerk in his "Poems of Ossian in the Original Gaelic, with a literal translation into English." 2 vols., Edinburgh, 1870.

"Glenmasan Manuscript" of the year 1238, containing the story of "Darthula,"* which is the ground-
work of the same story in MacPherson's "Ossian."
There is the important "Dean of Lismore's Book," a
manuscript collection made by Dean MacGregor of
Lismore, Argyleshire, between 1512 and 1529, containing 11,000 lines of Gaelic poetry, some of which is
attributed to Ossian or Oisin. One of the poems is
identical in substance with the first book of MacPherson's "Temora;" although Mr. Campbell says,
"There is not one line in the Dean's book that I can
identify with any line in MacPherson's Gaelic." †

Other objections to the authenticity of Mac Pherson's translations rested upon internal evidence, upon
their characteristics of thought and style. It was
alleged that the "peculiar tone of sentimental grandeur and melancholy" which distinguishes them, is
false to the spirit of all known early poetry, and is
a modern note. In particular, it was argued, Mac-
Pherson's heroes are too sensitive to the wild and
sublime in nature. Professor William R. Sullivan,
a high authority on Celtic literature, says that in the
genuine and undoubted remains of old Irish poetry
belonging to the Leinster or Finnian Cycle and
ascribed to Oisin, there is much detail in descriptions
of arms, accouterments, and articles of indoor use

---

* This story has been retold, from Irish sources, in Dr. R. D.
Joyce's poem of "Deirdrè," Boston, 1876.

† See "Leabhar na Feinne, Heroic Gaelic Ballads, Collected in
Scotland, chiefly from 1512 to 1871. Arranged by J. F. Campbell."
London, 1872. Selections from "The Dean of Lismore's Book"
were edited and published at Edinburgh in 1862, by Rev. Thomas
MacLauchlan, with a learned introduction by Mr. W. F. Skene.

and ornament, but very little in descriptions of outward nature.* On the other hand, the late Principal
Shairp regards this "sadness of tone in describing
nature" as a strong proof of authenticity. "Two
facts," he says, "are enough to convince me of the
genuineness of the ancient Gaelic poetry. The truthfulness with which it reflects the melancholy aspects
of Highland scenery, the equal truthfulness with
which it expresses the prevailing sentiment of the
Gael, and his sad sense of his people's destiny. I need
no other proofs that the Ossianic poetry is a native
formation, and comes from the primeval heart of the
Gaelic race." † And he quotes, in support of his
view, a well-known passage from Matthew Arnold's
"Study of Celtic Literature": "The Celts are the
prime authors of this vein of piercing regret and
passion, of this Titanism in poetry. A famous book,
MacPherson's 'Ossian,' carried, in the last century,
this vein like a flood of lava through Europe. I am
not going to criticise MacPherson's 'Ossian' here.
Make the part of what is forged, modern, tawdry,
spurious in the book as large as you please; strip
Scotland, if you like, of every feather of borrowed
plumes which, on the strength of MacPherson's 'Ossian,' she may have stolen from that *vetus et major
Scotia*—Ireland; I make no objection. But there will
still be left in the book a residue with the very soul of
the Celtic genius in it; and which has the proud distinction of having brought this soul of the Celtic
genius into contact with the nations of modern

* Article on "Celtic Literature" in the " Encyclopædia Britannica."
† " Aspects of Poetry," by J. C. Shairp, 1872, pp. 244-45 (American Edition).

Europe, and enriched all our poetry by it. Woody
Morven, and echoing Lora, and Selma with its silent
halls! We all owe them a debt of gratitude, and when
we are unjust enough to forget it, may the Muse forget us! Choose any one of the better passages in
MacPherson's 'Ossian,' and you can see, even at this
time of day, what an apparition of newness and of
power such a strain must have been in the eighteenth
century."

But from this same kind of internal evidence,
Wordsworth draws just the opposite conclusion.
"The phantom was begotten by the snug embrace of
an impudent Highlander upon a cloud of tradition.
It traveled southward, where it was greeted with
acclamation, and the thin consistence took its course
through Europe upon the breath of popular applause.*
. . Open this far-famed book! I have done so at random, and the beginning of the epic poem 'Temora,'
in eight books, presents itself. 'The blue waves of
Ullin roll in light. The green hills are covered with
day. Trees shake their dusky heads in the breeze.
Gray torrents pour their noisy streams. Two green
hills with aged oaks surround a narrow plain. The
blue course of a stream is there. On its banks stood
Cairbar of Atha. His spear supports the king: the
red eyes of his fear are sad. Cormac rises on his soul
with all his ghastly wounds. . .' Having had the good
fortune to be born and reared in a mountainous coun-

---

* Appendix to the Preface to the Second Edition of "Lyrical Ballads." Taine says that Ossian "with Oscar, Malvina, and his whole
troop, made the tour of Europe; and, about 1830, ended by furnishing
baptismal names for French *grisettes* and *perruquiers*."—*English
Literature*, Vol. II. p. 220 (American Edition).

try, from my very childhood I have felt the falsehood that pervades the volumes imposed upon the world under the name of Ossian. From what I saw with my own eyes, I knew that the imagery was spurious. In nature everything is distinct, yet nothing defined into absolute, independent singleness. In MacPherson's work it is exactly the reverse: everything (that is not stolen) is in this manner defined, insulated, dislocated, deadened, yet nothing distinct. It will always be so when words are substituted for things. To say that the characters never could exist; that the manners are impossible; and that a dream has more substance than the whole state of society, as there depicted, is doing nothing more than pronouncing a censure which MacPherson defied. . . Yet, much as these pretended treasures of antiquity have been admired, they have been wholly uninfluential upon the literature of the country. No succeeding writer appears to have caught from them a ray of inspiration; no author in the least distinguished has ventured formally to imitate them, except the boy Chatterton, on their first appearance. . . This incapability to amalgamate with the literature of the Island is, in my estimation, a decisive proof that the book is essentially unnatural; nor should I require any other to demonstrate it to be a forgery, audacious as worthless. Contrast, in this respect, the effect of MacPherson's publication with the 'Reliques' of Percy, so unassuming, so modest in their pretensions."

Other critics have pointed out a similar indistinctness in the human actors, no less than in the landscape features of "Fingal" and "Temora." They have no dramatic individuality, but are all alike, and all ex-

tremely shadowy.   " Poor, moaning, monotonous Mac
Pherson" is Carlyle's alliterative description of the
translator of "Ossian"; and it must be confessed
that, in spite of the deep poetic feeling which pervades these writings, and the undeniable beauty of
single passages, they have damnable iteration.   The
burden of their song is a burden in every sense.   Mr.
Malcolm Laing, one of MacPherson's most persistent
adversaries, who published " Notes and Illustrations to
Ossian " in 1805, essayed to show, by a minute analysis
of the language, that the whole thing was a fabrication, made up from Homer, Milton, the English Bible,
and other sources.   Thus he compared MacPherson's
" Like the darkened moon when she moves, a dim
circle, through heaven, and dreadful change is expected
by men," with Milton's

> " Or from behind the moon,
> In dim eclipse, disastrous twilight sheds
> On half the nations, and with fear of change
> Perplexes monarchs."

Laing's method proves too much and might be applied
with like results to almost any literary work.   And,
in general, it is hazardous to draw hard and fast conclusions from internal evidence of the sort just reviewed.   Taken altogether, these objections do leave
a strong bias upon the mind, and were one to
pronounce upon the genuineness of MacPherson's
" Ossian," as a whole, from impressions of tone and
style, it might be guessed that whatever element
of true ancient poetry it contains, it had been thoroughly steeped in modern sentiment before it was
put before the public.   But remembering Beowulf and

the Norse mythology, one might hesitate to say that the songs of primitive, heroic ages are always insensible to the sublime in nature; or to admit that melancholy is a Celtic monopoly.

The most damaging feature of MacPherson's case was his refusal or neglect to produce his originals. The testimony of those who helped him in collecting and translating leaves little doubt that he had materials of some kind; and that these consisted partly of old Gaelic manuscripts, and partly of transcriptions taken down in Gaelic from the recitation of aged persons in the Highlands. These testimonies may be read in the " Report of the Committee of the Highland Society," Edinburgh, 1805.* It is too voluminous to examine here, and it leaves unsettled the point as to the precise use which MacPherson made of his materials, whether, *i. e.*, he gave literal renderings of them, as he professed to do; or whether he manipulated them—and to what extent—by piecing fragments together, lopping, dove-tailing, smoothing, interpolating, modernizing, as Percy did with his ballads. He was challenged to show his Gaelic

---

* The Committee found that Gaelic poems, and fragments of poems, which they had been able to obtain, contained often the substance, and sometimes the " literal expression (the *ipsissima verba*)" of passages given by MacPherson. " But," continues the " Report," " the Committee has not been able to obtain any one poem the same in title and tenor with the poems published by him. It is inclined to believe that he was in use to supply chasms and to give connection, by inserting passages which he did not find ; and to add what he conceived to be dignity and delicacy to the original composition, by striking out passages, by softening incidents, by refining the language: in short, by changing what he considered as too simple or too rude for a modern ear."

manuscripts, and Mr. Clerk says that he accepted the challenge. "He deposited the manuscripts at his publishers', Beckett and De Hondt, Strand, London. He advertised in the newspapers that he had done so; offered to publish them if a sufficient number of subscribers came forward; and in the *Literary Journal* of the year 1784, Beckett certifies that the manuscripts had lain in his shop for the space of a whole year." *

But this was more than twenty years after. Mr. Clerk does not show that Johnson or Laing or Shaw or Pinkerton, or any of MacPherson's numerous critics, ever saw any such advertisement, or knew where the manuscripts were to be seen; or that— being ignorant of Gaelic—it would have helped them if they had known; and he admits that "MacPherson's subsequent conduct, in postponing from time to time the publication, when urged to it by friends who had liberally furnished him with means for the purpose . . . is indefensible." In 1773 and 1775, *e. g.*, Dr. Johnson was calling loudly for the production of the manuscripts. "The state of the question," he wrote to Boswell, February 7, 1775, "is this. He and Dr. Blair, whom I consider as deceived, say that he copied the poem from old manuscripts. His copies, if he had them—and I believe him to have none—are nothing. Where are the manuscripts? They can be shown if they exist, but they were never shown. *De non existentibus et non apparentibus eadem est ratio.*" And during his Scotch trip in 1773, at a dinner at Sir Alexander Gordon's, Johnson said: "If the poems were really translated, they were certainly first

* "Dissertation on the Authenticity of the Poems." See *ante*, p. 313

written down. Let Mr. MacPherson deposit the manuscripts in one of the colleges at Aberdeen, where there are people who can judge; and if the professors certify their authenticity, then there will be be an end of the controversy. If he does not take this obvious and easy method, he gives the best reason to doubt."

Indeed the subsequent history of these alleged manuscripts casts the gravest suspicion on MacPherson's good faith. A thousand pounds were finally subscribed to pay for the publication of the Gaelic texts. But these MacPherson never published. He sent the manuscripts which were ultimately published in 1807 to his executor, Mr. John Mackenzie; and he left one thousand pounds by his will to defray the expense of printing them. After MacPherson's death in 1796, Mr. Mackenzie "delayed the publication from day to day, and at last handed over the manuscripts to the Highland Society," * which had them printed in 1807, nearly a half century after the first appearance of the English Ossian.† These, however, were not the identical manuscripts which MacPherson had found, or said that he had found, in his tour of exploration through the Highlands. They were all in his own handwriting or in that of his amanuenses. Moreover the Rev. Thomas Ross was employed by the society to transcribe them

* Clerk.

† "The Poems of Ossian in the Original Gaelic, with a Literal Translation into Latin by the late Robert Macfarland, etc., Published under the Sanction of the Highland Society of London," 3 vols., London, 1807. The work included dissertations on the authenticity of the poems by Sir Jno. Sinclair, and the Abbé Cesarotti (translated). Four hundred and twenty-three lines of Gaelic, being the alleged original of the seventh book of "Temora," had been published with that epic in 1763.

and conform the spelling to that of the Gaelic Bible, which is modern. The printed text of 1807, therefore, does not represent acurately even MacPherson's Gaelic. Whether the transcriber took any further liberties than simply modernizing the spelling cannot be known, for the same mysterious fate that overtook MacPherson's original collections followed his own manuscript. This, after being at one time in the Advocates' Library, has now utterly disappeared. Mr. Campbell thinks that under this double process of distillation—a copy by MacPherson and then a copy by Ross—"the ancient form of the language, if it was ancient, could hardly survive." * "What would become of Chaucer," he asks, "so maltreated and finally spelt according to modern rules of grammar and orthography? I have found by experience that an alteration in 'spelling' may mean an entire change of construction and meaning, and a substitution of whole words."

But the Gaelic text of 1807 was attacked in more vital points than its spelling. It was freely charged with being an out-and-out fabrication, a translation of MacPherson's English prose into modern Gaelic. This question is one which must be settled by Gaelic scholars, and these still disagree. In 1862 Mr. Campbell wrote: "When the Gaelic 'Fingal,' published in 1807, is compared with any one of the translations which purport to have been made from it, it seems to me incomparably superior. It is far simpler in diction. It has a peculiar rhythm and assonance which seem to repel the notion of a mere translation from English,

* "Popular Tales of the West Highlands," J. F. Campbell, Edinburgh, 1862. Vol. IV. p. 156.

as something almost absurd. It is impossible that it can be a translation from MacPherson's English, unless there was some clever Gaelic poet * then alive, able and willing to write what Eton schoolboys call 'full-sense verses.'" The general testimony is that MacPherson's own knowledge of Gaelic was imperfect. Mr. Campbell's summary of the whole matter— in 1862—is as follows: "My theory then is, that about the beginning of the eighteenth century, or the end of the seventeenth, or earlier, Highland bards may have fused floating popular traditions into more complete forms, engrafting their own ideas on what they found; and that MacPherson found their works, translated and altered them; published the translation in 1760; † made the Gaelic ready for the press; published some of it in 1763, ‡ and made away with the evidence of what he had done, when he found that his conduct was blamed. I can see no other way out of the maze of testimony." But by 1872 Mr. Campbell had come to a conclusion much less favorable to the claims of the Gaelic text. He now considers that the English was first composed by MacPherson and that "he and other translators afterward worked at it and made a Gaelic equivalent whose merit varies according to the translator's skill and knowledge of Gaelic." § On the other hand, two of the foremost authorities in Gaelic, Mr. W. F. Skene and Mr. Archibald Clerk, are confident that the Gaelic is the original and the

---

* He suggests Lachlan MacPherson of Strathmashie, one of Mac-Pherson's helpers. " Popular Tales of the West Highlands."

† " Fragments," etc.

‡ Seventh book of " Temora." See *ante*, p. 321.

§ " Leabhar Na Feinne," p. xii.

English the translation. Mr. Clerk, who reprinted
the Highland Society's text in 1870,* with a literal
translation of his own on alternate pages and Mac-
Pherson's English at the foot of the page, believes
implicitly in the antiquity and genuineness of the
Gaelic originals. "MacPherson," he writes, "got
much from manuscripts and much from oral recitation. It is most probable that he has given the minor
poems exactly as he found them. He may have made
considerable changes in the larger ones in giving
them their present form; although I do not believe
that he, or any of his assistants, added much even
in the way of connecting links between the various
episodes."

To a reader unacquainted with Gaelic, comparing
MacPherson's English with Mr. Clerk's, it certainly
looks unlikely that the Gaelic can be merely a translation from the former. The reflection in a mirror
cannot be more distinct than the object it reflects; and
if Mr. Clerk's version can be trusted (it appears to be
more literal though less rhetorical than MacPherson's)
the Gaelic is often concrete and sharp where Mac-
Pherson is general; often plain where he is figura-
tive or ornate; and sometimes of a meaning quite
different from his rendering. Take, *e. g.*, the closing passage of the second "Duan," or book, of
"Fingal."

"An arrow found his manly breast. He sleeps
with his loved Galbina at the noise of the sounding
surge. Their green tombs are seen by the mariner,
when he bounds on the waves of the north."—
MacPherson.

* See *ante*, p. 313, note.

" A ruthless arrow found his breast.
His sleep is by thy side, Galbina,
Where wrestles the wind with ocean.
The sailor sees their graves as one,
When rising on the ridge of the waves."

—Clerk.

But again Mr. Archibald Sinclair, a Glasgow publisher, a letter from whom is given by Mr. Campbell
in his "Tales of the West Highlands," has "no hesitation in affirming that a considerable portion of the
Gaelic which is published as the original of his
[MacPherson's] translation, is actually translated
back from the English." And Professor Sullivan
says: " The so-called originals are a very curious
kind of mosaic, constructed evidently with great labor
afterward, in which sentences or parts of sentences of
genuine poems are cemented together in a very inferior
word-paste of MacPherson's own." *

It is of course no longer possible to maintain what
Mr. Campbell says is the commonest English opinion,
viz., that MacPherson invented the characters and
incidents of his "Ossian," and that the poems had no
previous existence in any shape. The evidence is
overwhelming that there existed, both in Ireland and
the Scottish Highlands traditions, tales, and poems
popularly attributed to Oisin, the son of Finn Mac-
Cumhail. But no poem has been found which corresponds exactly to any single piece in MacPherson; and
Sullivan cites, as one proof of the modern and spurious
character of these versions, the fact that they mingle
names from the ancient hero-cycle, like Darthula,
Cuthullin, and Conlach, with names belonging to

* " Encylopædia Britannica" : " Celtic Literature."

the Finnian cycle, as is never the case in the authentic and undoubted remains of Celtic poetry. Between 1760, the date of MacPherson's "Fragments," and 1807, the date of the Highland Society's text, there had been published independently nine hundred lines of Ossianic verse in Gaelic in Gillie's collection, 1786, and Stewart's, 1804. In 1780 Dr. Smith had published his "Ancient Lays," a free translation from Gaelic fragments, which he subsequently printed (1787) under the title "Sean Dàna," Smith frankly took liberties with his originals, such as we may suppose that MacPherson took with his; but he made no secret of this and, by giving the Gaelic on which his paraphrase rested, he enabled the public to see how far his "Ancient Lays," were really ancient, and how far they were built up into poetic wholes by his own editorial labors.*

Wordsworth's assertion of the failure of Mac-Pherson's "Ossian" to "amalgamate with the literature of the island" needs some qualification. That it did not enter into English literature in a formative way, as Percy's ballads did, is true enough, and is easy of explanation. In the first place, it was professedly a prose translation from poetry in another tongue, and could hardly, therefore, influence the verse and diction of English poetry directly. It could not even work upon them as directly as many foreign literatures have worked; as the ancient classical literatures, *e. g.*, have always worked; or as Italian

---

* For a further account of the state of the "authenticity" question, see Archibald McNeil's "Notes on the Authenticity of Ossian's Poems," 1868; and an article on "Ossian" in *Macmillan's Magazine*, XXIV. 113–25.

and French and German have at various times worked;
for the Gaelic was practically inaccessible to all but
a few special scholars. Whatever its beauty or
expressiveness, it was in worse case than a dead
language, for it was marked with the stigma of
barbarism. In its palmiest days it had never been
what the Germans call a *Kultursprache;* and now it
was the idiom of a few thousand peasants and moun-
taineers, and was rapidly becoming extinct even in its
native fastnesses.

Whatever effect was to be wrought by the Ossianic
poems upon the English mind, was to be wrought in
the dress which MacPherson had given them. And
perhaps, after all, the tumid and rhetorical cast of
MacPherson's prose had a great deal to do with
producing the extraordinary enthusiasm with which
his "wild paraphrases," as Mr. Campbell calls them,
were received by the public. The age was tired of
polish, of wit, of over-civilization; it was groping
toward the rude, the primitive, the heroic; had begun
to steep itself in melancholy sentiment and to feel a
dawning admiration of mountain solitudes and the
hoary past. Suddenly here was what it had been
waiting for—"a tale of the times of old"; and the
solemn, dirge-like chant of MacPherson's sentences,
with the peculiar manner of his narrative, its repetitions, its want of transitions, suited well with his
matter. "Men had been talking under their breath,
and in a mincing dialect so long," says Leslie Stephen,
"that they were easily gratified and easily imposed
upon by an affectation of vigorous and natural
sentiment."

The impression was temporary, but it was immediate and powerful.   Wordsworth was wrong when he said that no author of distinction except Chatterton had ventured formally to imitate Ossian.   A generation after the appearance of the "Fragments" we find the youthful Coleridge alluding to "Ossian" in the preface * to his first collection of poems (1793), which contains two verse imitations of the same, as *ecce signum* :

> "How long will ye round me be swelling,
>   O ye blue-tumbling waves of the sea?
> Not always in caves was my dwelling,
>   Nor beneath the cold blast of the tree," etc., etc. †

In Byron's "Hours of Idleness" (1807), published when he was a Cambridge undergraduate, is a piece of prose founded on the episode of Nisus and Euryalus in the "Æneid" and entitled "The Death of Calmar and Orla—An Imitation of MacPherson's Ossian." "What form rises on the roar of clouds? Whose dark ghost gleams in the red stream of tempests? His voice rolls on the thunder. 'Tis Orla, the brown chief of Orthona . . . Lovely wast thou, son of blue-eyed Morla," etc. After reading several pages of such stuff, one comes to feel that Byron could do this sort of thing about as well as MacPherson himself; and indeed, that Johnson was not so very far wrong when he said that anyone could do it if he would abandon his mind to it.   Chatterton applied the Ossianic verbiage in a number of pieces which he pretended to have translated from the Saxon: "Ethelgar," "Ken-

---

* "The sweet voice of Cona never sounds so sweetly as when it speaks of itself."

† "The Complaint of Ninathoma."

rick," "Cerdick," and "Gorthmund"; as well as in a composition which he called "Godred Crovan," from the Manx dialect, and one from the ancient British, which he entitled "The Heilas." He did not catch the trick quite so successfully as Byron, as a passage or two from "Kenrick" will show: "Awake, son of Eldulph! Thou that sleepest on the white mountain, with the fairest of women; no more pursue the dark brown wolf: arise from the mossy bank of the falling waters: let thy garments be stained in blood, and the streams of life discolor thy girdle . . . Cealwulf of the high mountain, who viewed the first rays of the morning star, swift as the flying deer, strong as a young oak, fiery as an evening wolf, drew his sword; glittering like the blue vapors in the valley of Horso: terrible as the red lightning bursting from the dark-brown clouds, his swift bark rode over the foaming waves like the wind in the tempest."

In a note on his Ossianic imitation, Byron said that Mr. Laing had proved Ossian an impostor, but that the merit of MacPherson's work remained, although in parts his diction was turgid and bombastic.* A poem in the "Hours of Idleness," upon the Scotch mountain "Lachin Y Gair," has two Ossianic lines in quotation points—

> " Shades of the dead! have I not heard your voices
> Rise on the night-rolling breath of the gale ? "

Byron attributed much importance to his early recollections of Highland scenery, which he said had prepared him to love the Alps and "blue Friuli's

---

* For some MS. notes of Byron in a copy of " Ossian," see Phelps' " English Romantic Movement," pp. 153–54.

mountains," and "the Acroceraunian mountains of old name." But the influence of Ossian upon Byron and his older contemporaries was manifested in subtler ways than in formal imitations. It fell in with that current of feeling which Carlyle called "Wertherism," and helped to swell it. It chimed with the tone that sounds through the German *Sturm und Drang* period; that impatience of restraint, that longing to give full swing to the claims of the elementary passions, and that desperation when these are checked by the arrangements of modern society, which we encounter in Rousseau and the young Goethe. Hence the romantic gloom, the Byronic *Zerrissenheit*, to use Heine's word, which drove the poet from the rubs of social life to waste places of nature and sometimes to suicide. In such a mood the mind recurred to the language of Ossian, as the fit expression of its own indefinite and stormy griefs.

"Homer," writes Werther, "has been superseded in my heart by the divine Ossian. Through what a world does this angelic bard carry me! With him I wander over barren wastes and frightful wilds; surrounded by whirlwinds and hurricanes, trace by the feeble light of the moon the shades of our noble ancestors; hear from the mountainous heights, intermingled with the roaring of waves and cataracts, their plaintive tones stealing from cavernous recesses; while the pensive monody of some love-stricken maiden, who heaves her departing sighs over the moss-clad grave of the warrior by whom she was adored, makes up the inarticulate concert. I trace this bard, with his silver locks, as he wanders in the valley and explores the footsteps of his fathers. Alas! no vestige remains

but their tombs. His thought then hangs on the
silver moon, as her sinking beams play upon the rip-
pling main; and the remembrance of deeds past and
gone recurs to the hero's mind—deeds of times when
he gloried in the approach of danger, and emulation
nerved his whole frame; when the pale orb shone upon
his bark, laden with the spoils of his enemy, and illuminated his triumphant return. When I see depicted
on his countenance a bosom full of woe; when I behold his heroic greatness sinking into the grave, and
he exclaims, as he throws a glance at the cold sod
which is to lie upon him: 'Hither will the traveler
who is sensible of my worth bend his weary steps, and
seek the soul-enlivening bard, the illustrious son of
Fingal; his foot will tread upon my tomb, but his eyes
shall never behold me'; at this time it is, my dear
friend, that, like some renowned and chivalrous
knight, I could instantly draw my sword; rescue my
prince from a long, irksome existence of languor and
pain; and then finish by plunging the weapon into my
own breast, that I might accompany the demi-god
whom my hand had emancipated." *

In his last interview with Charlotte, Werther, who
had already determined upon suicide, reads aloud to
her, from "The Songs of Selma," "that tender passage wherein Armin deplores the loss of his beloved
daughter. 'Alone on the sea-beat rocks, my daughter
was heard to complain. Frequent and loud were her
cries. What could her father do? All night I stood
on the shore. I saw her by the faint beam of the
moon,'" etc. The reading is interrupted by a mutual
flood of tears. "They traced the similitude of their

* "Sorrows of Werther," Letter lxviii.

own misfortune in this unhappy tale. . . The pointed
allusion of those words to the situation of Werther
rushed with all the electric rapidity of lightning to the
inmost recesses of his soul."

It is significant that one of Ossian's most fervent
admirers was Chateaubriand, who has been called the
inventor of modern melancholy and of the primeval
forest. Here is a passage from his "Génie du
Christianisme": * "Under a cloudy sky, on the coast
of that sea whose tempests were sung by Ossian, their
Gothic architecture has something grand and somber.
Seated on a shattered altar in the Orkneys, the traveler
is astonished at the dreariness of those places: sudden
fogs, vales where rises the sepulchral stone, streams
flowing through wild heaths, a few reddish pine trees,
scattered over a naked desert studded with patches of
snow; such are the only objects which present themselves to his view. The wind circulates among the
ruins, and their innumerable crevices become so many
tubes, which heave a thousand sighs. Long grasses
wave in the apertures of the domes, and beyond these
apertures you behold the flitting clouds and the soar-
ing sea-eagle. . . Long will those four stones which
mark the tombs of heroes on the moors of Caledonia,
long will they continue to attract the contemplative
traveler. Oscar and Malvina are gone, but nothing is
changed in their solitary country. 'Tis no longer the
hand of the bard himself that sweeps the harp; the
tones we hear are the slight trembling of the strings,
produced by the touch of a spirit, when announcing at
night, in a lonely chamber, the death of a hero. . .
So when he sits in the silence of noon in the valley of

* "Caledonia, or Ancient Scotland," book ii. chapter vii. part iv.

his breezes is the murmur of the mountain to Ossian's ear: the gale drowns it often in its course, but the pleasant sound returns again."

In Byron's passion for night and tempest, for the wilderness, the mountains, and the sea, it is of course impossible to say how large a share is attributable directly to MacPherson's "Ossian," or more remotely, through Chateaubriand and other inheritors of the Ossianic mood. The influence of any particular book becomes dispersed and blended with a hundred currents that are in the air. But I think one has often a consciousness of Ossian in reading such passages as the famous apostrophe to the ocean in "Childe Harold "—

> " Roll on, thou deep and dark blue ocean, roll ! "— .

which recalls the address to the sun in Carthon—"O thou that rollest above, round as the shield of my fathers,"—perhaps the most hackneyed *locus classicus* in the entire work; or as the lines beginning,

> " O that the desert were my dwelling place ; " *

or the description of the storm in the Jura:

> " And this is in the night : Most glorious night !
> Thou wert not sent for slumber. Let me be
> A sharer in thy fierce and far delight
> A portion of the tempest and of thee." *

Walter Scott, while yet a lad, made acquaintance with Ossian through Dr. Blacklock, and was at first delighted; but "the tawdry repetitions of the Ossianic phraseology," he confesses, "disgusted me

* " Childe Harold," canto iii.

rather sooner than might have been expected from my age." He afterward contributed an essay on the authenticity of the poems to the proceedings of the Speculative Club of Edinburgh. In one sense of the word Scott was the most romantic of romanticists; but in another sense he was very little romantic, and there was not much in his sane, cheerful, and robust nature upon which such poetry as Ossian could fasten.*
It is just at this point, indeed, that definitions diverge and the two streams of romantic tendency part company. These Carlyle has called "Wertherism" and "Götzism": † *i. e.*, sentimentalism and mediæval-ism, though so mild a word as sentimentalism fails to express adequately the morbid despair to which "Werther" gave utterance, and has associations with works of a very different kind, such as the fictions of Richardson and Sterne. In England, Scott became the foremost representative of "Götzism," and Byron of "Wertherism." The pessimistic, sardonic heroes of "Manfred," "Childe Harold," and "The Corsair" were the latest results of the "Il Penseroso" literature, and their melodramatic excesses already foretokened a reaction.

Among other testimonies to Ossian's popularity in England are the numerous experiments at versify-ing MacPherson's prose. These were not over-sucessful and only a few of them require mention here. The Rev. John Wodrow, a Scotch minister,

---

* The same is true of Burns, though references to Cuthullin's dog Luath, in "The Twa Dogs"; to "Caric-thura" in "The Whistle"; and to "Cath-Loda" in the notes on "The Vision," show that Burns knew his Ossian.

† From Goethe's "Götz von Berlichingen."

"attempted" "Carthon," "The Death of Cuthullin" and "Darthula" in heroic conplets, in 1769; and "Fingal" in 1771. In the preface to his "Fingal," he maintained that there was no reasonable doubt of the antiquity and authenticity of MacPherson's "Ossian." "Fingal"—which seems to have been the favorite—was again turned into heroic couplets by Ewen Cameron, in 1776, prefaced by the attestations of a number of Highland gentlemen to the genuineness of the originals; and by an argumentative introduction, in which the author quotes Dr. Blair's *dictum* that Ossian was the equal of Homer and Vergil "in strength of imagination, in grandeur of sentiment, and in native majesty of passion." National pride enlisted most of the Scotch scholars on the affirmative side of the question, and made the authenticity of Ossian almost an article of belief. Wodrow's heroics were merely respectable. The quality of Cameron's may be guessed from a half dozen lines:

> "When Moran, one commissioned to explore
> The distant seas, came running from the shore
> And thus exclaimed—'Cuthullin, rise ! The ships
> Of snowy Lochlin hide the rolling deeps.
> Innumerable foes the land invade,
> And Swaran seems determined to succeed.'"

Whatever impressiveness belonged to MacPherson's cadenced prose was lost in these metrical versions, which furnish a perfect *reductio ad absurdum* of the critical folly that compared Ossian with Homer. Homer could not be put in any dress through which the beauty and interest of the original would not appear. Still again, in 1786, "Fingal" was done into

heroics by a Mr. R. Hole, who varied his measures
with occasional ballad stanzas, thus:

> " But many a fair shall melt with woe
>   At thy soft strain in future days,
> And many a manly bosom glow,
>   Congenial to thy lofty lays."

These versions were all emitted in Scotland.   But as
late as 1814 " Fingal " appeared once more in verse,
this time in London, and in a variety of meters by Mr.
George Harvey; who, in his preface, expressed the
hope that Walter Scott would feel moved to cast
" Ossian " into the form of a metrical romance, like
" Marmion " or " The Lay of the Last Minstrel."
The best English poem constructed from MacPherson
is " The Six Bards of Ossian Versified," by Sir Egerton Brydges (dated in 1784).* The passage selected
was the one which Gray so greatly admired,† from a
note to " Croma," in the original " Fragments."   Six
bards who have met at the hall of a chieftain, on an
October night, go out one after another to observe the
weather, and return to report their observations, each
ending with the refrain " Receive me from the night,
my friends."   The whole episode is singularly arrest-
ing, and carries a conviction of reality too often wanting in the epic portions of MacPherson's collection.

Walpole, at first, was nearly as much charmed by
the " Fragments " as Gray had been.   He wrote to
Dalrymple that they were real poetry, natural poetry,
like the poetry of the East.   He liked particularly the

---

* See " Poems by Saml. Egerton Brydges," 4th ed., London, 1807.
pp. 87–96.

† See *ante*, p. 117.

synonym for an echo—"son of the rock"; and in a later letter he said that all doubts which he might once have entertained as to their genuineness had disappeared. But Walpole's literary judgments were notoriously capricious. In his subsequent correspondence with Mason and others, he became very contemptuous of MacPherson's "cold skeleton of an epic poem, that is more insipid than 'Leonidas.'" "Ossian," he tells Mason, in a letter dated March, 1783, has become quite incredible to him; but Mrs. Montagu—the founder of the Blue Stocking Club—still "holds her feast of shells in her feather dressing-room."

The Celtic Homer met with an even warmer welcome abroad than at home. He was rendered into French,* German, Italian, Spanish, Dutch, Polish, and possibly other languages. Bonaparte was a great lover of Ossian, and carried about with him a copy of Cesarotti's Italian version. A resemblance has been fancied between MacPherson's manner and the grandiloquent style of Bonaparte's bulletins and dispatches.† In Germany Ossian naturally took most strongly. He was translated into hexameters by a Vienna Jesuit named Michael Denis‡ and produced many imitations. Herder gave three translations from "Ossian" in his "Stimmen der Völker" (1778–79) and prefixed to the whole collection an essay

---

* There were French translations by Letourneur in 1777 and 1810: by Lacaussade in 1842 ; and an imitation by Baour-Lormian in 1801.

† See Perry's "Eighteenth Century Literature," p. 417.

‡ One suspects this translator to have been of Irish descent. He was born at Schärding, Bavaria, in 1729.

"Ueber Ossian und die Lieder alter Völker" written in 1773. Schiller was one of the converts; Klopstock and his circle called themselves "bards"; and an exclamatory and violent mannerism came into vogue, known in German literary history as *Bardengebrüll*. MacPherson's personal history need not be followed here in detail. In 1764 he went to Pensacola as secretary to Governor Johnston. He was afterward a government pamphleteer, writing against Junius and in favor of taxing the American colonies. He was appointed agent to the Nabob of Arcot; sat in Parliament for the borough of Camelford, and built a handsome Italian villa in his native parish; died in 1796, leaving a large fortune, and was buried in Westminster Abbey. In 1773 he was ill-advised enough to render the "Iliad" into Ossianic prose. The translation was overwhelmed with ridicule, and probably did much to increase the growing disbelief in the genuineness of "Fingal" and "Temora."

CHAPTER X.

Thomas Chatterton.

THE history of English romanticism has its tragedy: the life and death of Thomas Chatterton—

> " The marvelous boy,
> The sleepless soul that perished in his pride." *

The story has been often told, but it may be told again here; for, aside from its dramatic interest, and leaving out of question the absolute value of the Rowley poems, it is most instructive as to the conditions which brought about the romantic revival. It shows by what process antiquarianism became poetry.

The scene of the story was the ancient city of Bristol—old Saxon *Bricgestowe*, "place of the bridge"—bridge, namely, over the Avon stream, not far above its confluence with the Severn. Here Chatterton was born in 1752, the posthumous son of a dissipated schoolmaster, whose ancestors for a hundred and fifty years had been, in unbroken succession, sextons to the church of St. Mary Redcliffe. Perhaps it may be more than an idle fancy to attribute to heredity the bent which Chatterton's genius took spontaneously and almost from infancy; to guess that some mysterious ante-natal influence—"striking the electric

* Wordsworth, " Resolution and Independence."

chain wherewith we are darkly bound "—may have set
vibrating links of unconscious association running
back through the centuries. Be this as it may, Chatterton was the child of Redcliffe Church. St. Mary
stood by his cradle and rocked it; and if he did not
inherit with his blood, or draw in with his mother's
milk a veneration for her ancient pile; at least the
waters of her baptismal font * seemed to have signed
him with the token of her service. Just as truly as
" The Castle of Otranto " was sprung from Strawberry
Hill, the Rowley poems were born of St. Mary's
Church.

Chatterton's father had not succeeded to the sexton-
ship, but he was a sub-chanter in Bristol Cathedral,
and his house and school in Pile Street were only a
few yards from Redcliffe Church. In this house
Chatterton was born, under the eaves almost of the
sanctuary; and when his mother removed soon after
to another house, where she maintained herself by
keeping a little dame's school and doing needle work,
it was still on Redcliffe Hill and in close neighborhood to St. Mary's. The church itself—" the pride
of Bristowe and the western land "—is described as
"one of the finest parish churches in England," †
a rich specimen of late Gothic or " decorated " style;
its building or restoration dating from the middle of
the fifteenth century. Chatterton's uncle by marriage,
Richard Phillips, had become sexton in 1748, and the
boy had the run of the aisles and transepts. The

* January 1, 1753.

† " The Poetical Works of Thos. Chatterton. With an Essay on
the Rowley Poems by the Rev. Walter W. Skeat and a Memoir by
Edward Bell "; in two volumes. London, 1871, Vol, I. p. xv.

stone effigies of knights, priests, magistrates, and other ancient civic worthies stirred into life under his intense and brooding imagination; his mind took color from the red and blue patterns thrown on the pavement by the stained glass of the windows; and he may well have spelled out much of the little Latin that he knew from "the knightly brasses of the tombs" and " cold *hic jacets* of the dead."

It is curious how early his education was self-determined to its peculiar ends. A dreamy, silent, solitary child, given to fits of moodiness, he was accounted dull and even stupid. He would not, or could not, learn his letters until, in his seventh year, his eye was caught by the illuminated capitals in an old music folio. From these his mother taught him the alphabet, and a little later he learned to read from a black-letter Bible. "Paint me an angel with wings and a trumpet," he answered, when asked what device he would choose for the little earthenware bowl that had been promised him as a gift.* Colston's Hospital, where he was put to school, was built on the site of a demolished monastery of Carmelite Friars; the scholars wore blue coats, with metal plates on their breasts stamped with the image of a dolphin, the armorial crest of the founder, and had their hair cropped short in imitation of the monkish tonsure. As the boy grew into a youth, there were numbered among his near acquaintances, along with the vintners, sugar-bakers, pipe-makers, apothecaries, and other tradesmen of the Bristol *bourgeoisie,* two church organists, a miniature painter, and an engraver of coats-of-arms—

* Willcox's edition of " Chatterton's Poetical Works," Cambridge, 1842, Vol. I. p. xxi.

figures quaintly suggestive of that mingling of munic-
ipal life and ecclesiastical-mediæval art which is reproduced in the Rowley poems.

"Chatterton," testifies one of his early acquaintances, "was fond of walking in the fields, particularly
in Redcliffe meadows, and of talking of his manuscripts,
and sometimes reading them there. There was one
spot in particular, full in view of the church, in which
he seemed to take a peculiar delight. He would frequently lay himself down, fix his eyes upon the church,
and seem as if he were in a kind of trance. Then on
a sudden he would tell me: 'That steeple was burnt
down by lightning: that was the place where they
formerly acted plays.'" "Among his early studies," we
are told, "antiquities, and especially the surroundings
of mediæval life, were the favorite subjects; heraldry
seems especially to have had a fascination for him.
He supplied himself with charcoal, black-lead, ochre,
and other colors; and with these it was his delight to
delineate, in rough and quaint figures, churches,
castles, tombs of mailed warriors, heraldic emblazon-
ments, and other like belongings of the old world." *

Is there not a breath of the cloister in all this, reminding one of the child martyr in Chaucer's "Prioresse Tale," the "litel clergeon, seven yeer of age"?

> " This litel child his litel book lerninge,
>   As he sat in the scole at his prymer,
>   He ' Alma redemptoris ' herde singe,
>   As children lerned hir antiphoner."

A choir boy bred in cathedral closes, catching his
glimpses of the sky not through green boughs, but

* " Memoir by Edward Bell," p. **xxiv.**

through the treetops of the episcopal gardens dis-
colored by the lancet windows of the clear-stories;
dreaming in the organ loft in the pauses of the music,
when

> " The choristers, sitting with faces aslant,
> Feel the silence to consecrate more than the chant."

Thus Chatterton's sensitive genius was taking the
impress of its environment. As he pored upon the
antiquities of his native city, the idea of its life did
sweetly creep into his study of imagination; and he
gradually constructed for himself a picture of fifteenth-
century Bristol, including a group of figures, partly
historical and partly fabulous, all centering about
Master William Canynge. Canynge was the rich
Bristol merchant who founded or restored St. Mary
Redcliffe's; was several times mayor of the city in
the reigns of Henry VI. and Edward IV., and once
represented the borough in Parliament. Chatterton
found or fabled that he at length took holy orders and
became dean of Westbury College. About Canynge
Chatterton arranged a number of *dramatis personæ*,
some of whose names he discovered in old records
and documents, such as Carpenter, Bishop of Worcester, and Sir Theobald Gorges, a knight of Wraxhall,
near Bristol; together with others entirely of his own
invention—as John a Iscam, whom he represents to
have been a canon of St. Augustine's Abbey in Bristol;
and especially one Thomas Rowley, parish priest of
St. John's, employed by Canynge to collect manuscripts and antiquities. He was his poet laureate and
father confessor, and to him Chatterton ascribed most
of the verses which pass under the general name of
the Rowley poems. But Iscam was also a poet and

Master Canynge himself sometimes burst into song. Samples of the Iscam and the Canynge muse diversify the collection. The great Bristol merchant was a mediæval Mæcenas, and at his house, "nempned the Red Lodge," were played interludes—"Aella," "Goddwyn," and "The Parliament of Sprites"—composed by Rowley, or by Rowley and Iscam collaborating. Canynge sometimes wrote the prologues; and Rowley fed his patron with soft dedication and complimentary verses: "On Our Lady's Church," "Letter to the dygne Master Canynge," "The Account of W. Canynges Feast," etc. The well-known fifteenth-century poet Lydgate is also introduced into this literary *cénacle*, as John Ladgate, and made to exchange verse epistles with Rowley in eighteenth-century fashion. Such is the remarkable fiction which the marvelous boy erected, as a scaffolding for the fabric of sham-antique poetry and prose, which he built up during the years 1767 to 1770, *i. e.*, from the fifteenth to the eighteenth year of his age.

There is a wide distance between the achievements of this untaught lad of humble birth and narrow opportunities, and the works of the great Sir Walter, with his matured powers and his stores of solid antiquarian lore. But the impulse that conducted them to their not dissimilar tasks was the same. In "Yarrow Revisited," Wordsworth uses, *à propos* of Scott, the expression "localized romance." It was, indeed, the absorbing local feeling of Scott, his patriotism, his family pride, his attachment to the soil, that brought passion and poetry into his historical pursuits. With Chatterton, too, this absorption in the past derived its intensity from his love of place.

Bristol was his world; in "The Battle of Hastings,"
he did not forget to introduce a Bristowan contingent,
led by a certain fabulous Alfwold, and performing
prodigies of valor upon the Normans. The image of
mediæval life which he succeeded in creating was, of
course, a poor, faint *simulacrum*, compared with Scott's.
He lacked knowledge, leisure, friends, long life—
everything that was needed to give his work solidity.
All that he had was a creative, though undisciplined
imagination, together with an astonishing industry,
persistence, and secretiveness. Yet with all his disadvantages, his work, with all its imperfections, is far
more striking than the imitative verse of the Wartons,
or the thin, diffused mediævalism of Walpole and
Clara Reeve. It is the product of a more original
mind and a more intense conception.

In the muniment room over the north porch of
St. Mary Redcliffe's were several old chests filled
with parchments: architectural memoranda, church-
wardens' accounts, inventories of vestments, and
similar parish documents. One of these chests,
known as Master Canynge's coffer, had been broken
open some years before, and whatever was of value
among its contents removed to a place of safety. The
remainder of the parchments had been left scattered
about, and Chatterton's father had carried a number
of them home and used them to cover copy-books.
The boy's eye was attracted by these yellow sheep-
skins, with their antique script; he appropriated them
and kept them locked up in his room.

How early he conceived the idea of making this
treasure-trove responsible for the Rowley myth, which
was beginning to take shape in his mind, is uncertain.

According to the testimony of a schoolfellow, by
name Thistlethwaite, Chatterton told him in the
summer of 1764 that he had a number of old manuscripts, found in a chest in Redcliffe Church, and
that he had lent one of them to Thomas Philips, an
usher in Colston's Hospital.   Thistlethwaite says that
Philips showed him this manuscript, a piece of vellum
pared close around the edge, on which was traced in
pale and yellow writing, as if faded with age, a poem
which he thinks identical with " Elinoure and Juga,"
afterward published by Chatterton in the *Town and
Country Magazine* for May, 1769.   One is inclined to
distrust this evidence.   " The Castle of Otranto " was
first published in December, 1764, and the " Reliques,"
only in the year following.   The latter was certainly
known to Chatterton; many of the Rowley poems,
" The Bristowe Tragedie," *e. g.*, and the minstrel
songs in " Aella," show ballad influence *; while it
seems not unlikely that Chatterton was moved to take
a hint from the disguise—slight as it was—assumed by
Walpole in the preface to his romance.†   But perhaps
this was not needed to suggest to Chatterton that the
surest way to win attention to his poems would be to
ascribe them to some fictitious bard of the Middle
Ages.   It was the day of literary forgery; the Ossian
controversy was raging, and the tide of popular favor

---

* *Cf.* (" Battle of Hastings," i. xx)

> " The grey-goose pinion, that thereon was set,
>   Eftsoons with smoking crimson blood was wet "

with the lines from " Chevy Chase " (*ante*, p. 295).   To be sure the
ballad was widely current before the publication of the " Reliques."

† See *ante*, p. 237.

set strongly toward the antique. A series of avowed imitations of old English poetry, however clever, would have had small success. But the discovery of a hitherto unknown fifteenth-century poet was an announcement sure to interest the learned and perhaps a large part of the reading public. Besides, instances are not rare where a writer has done his best work under a mask. The poems composed by Chatterton in the disguise of Rowley—a dramatically imagined *persona* behind which he lost his own identity—are full of a curious attractiveness; while his acknowledged pieces are naught. It is not worth while to bear down very heavily on the moral aspects of this kind of deception. The question is one of literary methods rather than of ethics. If the writer succeeds by the skill of his imitations, and the ingenuity of the evidence that he brings to support them, in actually imposing upon the public for a time, the success justifies the attempt. The artist's purpose is to create a certain impression, and the choice of means must be left to himself.

In the summer of 1764 Chatterton was barely twelve, and wonderful as his precocity was, it is doubtful whether he had got so far in the evolution of the Rowley legend as Thistlethwaite's story would imply. But it is certain that three years later, in the spring of 1767, Chatterton gave Mr. Henry Burgum, a worthy pewterer of Bristol, a parchment emblazoned with the "de Bergham," coat-of-arms, which he pretended to have found in St. Mary's Church, furnishing him also with two copy-books, in which were transcribed the "de Bergham," pedigree, together with three poems in pseudo-antique spelling. One of these, "The

Tournament," described a joust in which figured one Sir Johan de Berghamme, a presumable ancestor of the gratified pewterer. Another of them, "The Romaunte of the Cnyghte," purported to be the work of this hero of the tilt-yard, "who spent his whole life in tilting," but notwithstanding found time to write several books and translate "some part of the Iliad under the title ' Romance of Troy.'"

All this stuff was greedily swallowed by Burgum, and the marvelous boy next proceeded to befool Mr. William Barrett, a surgeon and antiquary who was engaged in writing a history of Bristol. To him he supplied copies of supposed documents in the muniment room of Redcliffe Church: "Of the Auntiaunte Forme of Monies," and the like: deeds, bills, letters, inscriptions, proclamations, accounts of churches and other buildings, collected by Rowley for his patron, Canynge: many of which this singularly uncritical historian incorporated in his "History of Bristol," published some twenty years later. He also imparted to Barrett two Rowleian poems, "The Parliament of Sprites," and "The Battle of Hastings " (in two quite different versions). In September, 1768, a new bridge was opened at Bristol over the Avon; and Chatterton, who had now been apprenticed to an attorney, took advantage of the occasion to send anonymously to the printer of *Farley's Bristol Journal* a description of the mayor's first passing over the old bridge in the reign of Henry II. This was composed in obsolete language and alleged to have been copied from a contemporary manuscript. It was the first published of Chatterton's fabrications. In the years 1768-69 he produced and gave to Mr. George

Catcott the long tragical interlude "Aella," "The Bristowe Tragedie," and other shorter pieces, all of which he declared to be transcripts from manuscripts in Canynge's chest, and the work of Thomas Rowley, a secular priest of Bristol, who flourished about 1460. Catcott was a local book-collector and the partner of Mr. Burgum. He was subsequently nicknamed "Rowley's midwife."

In December, 1768, Chatterton opened a correspondence with James Dodsley, the London publisher, saying that several ancient poems had fallen into his hands, copies of which he offered to supply him, if he would send a guinea to cover expenses. He inclosed a specimen of "Ælla." "The motive that actuates me to do this," he wrote, "is to convince the world that the monks (of whom some have so despicable an opinion) were not such blockheads as generally thought, and that good poetry might be wrote in the dark days of superstition, as well as in these more enlightened ages." Dodsley took no notice of the letters, and the owner of the Rowley manuscripts next turned to Horace Walpole, whose tastes as a virtuoso, a lover of Gothic, and a romancer might be counted on to enlist his curiosity in Chatterton's find. The document which he prepared for Walpole was a prose paper entitled "The Ryse of Peyncteynge yn Englande, wroten by T. Rowleie, 1469, for Mastre Canynge," and containing *inter alia*, the following extraordinary "anecdote of painting" about Afflem, an Anglo-Saxon glass-stainer of Edmond's reign who was taken prisoner by the Danes. "Inkarde, a soldyer of the Danes, was to slea hym; onne the Nete before the Feeste of Deathe hee founde Afflem to bee hys Broder

Affrighte chaynede uppe hys soule. Gastnesse dwelled yn his Breaste. Oscarre, the greate Dane, gave hest hee shulde bee forslagene with the commeynge Sunne: no tears colde availe; the morne cladde yn roabes of ghastness was come, whan the Danique Kynge behested Oscarre to arraie hys Knyghtes eftsoones for Warre. Afflem was put yn theyre flyeynge Battailes, sawe his Countrie ensconced wyth Foemen, hadde hys Wyfe ande Chyldrenne brogten Capteeves to hys Shyppe, ande was deieynge wythe Soorowe, whanne the loude blautaunte Wynde hurled the Battayle agaynste an Heck. Forfraughte wythe embolleynge waves, he sawe hys Broder, Wyfe and Chyldrenne synke to Deathe: himself was throwen onne a Banke ynne the Isle of Wyghte, to lyve hys lyfe forgard to all Emmoise: thus moche for Afflem." *

This paper was accompanied with notes explaining queer words and giving short biographical sketches of Canynge, Rowley, and other imaginary characters, such as John, second abbot of St. Austin's Minster, who was the first English painter in oils and also the greatest poet of his age. "Take a specimen of his poetry, 'On King Richard I.':

> "' Harte of Lyone! shake thie Sworde,
> Bare thie mortheynge steinede honde,' etc."

The whole was inclosed in a short note to Walpole, which ran thus:

* Walter Scott quotes this passage in his review of Southey and Cottle's edition of Chatterton in the Edinburgh *Review* for April, 1804, and comments as follows: " While Chatterton wrote plain narrative, he imitated with considerable success the dry, concise style of an antique annalist; but when anything required a more dignified or sentimental style, he mounted the fatal and easily recognized car of the son of Fingal."

" Sir, Being versed a little in antiquitys, I have met with several curious manuscripts, among which the following may be of Service to you, in any future Edition of your truly entertaining Anecdotes of Painting.* In correcting the mistakes (if any) in the Notes, you will greatly oblige

"Your most humble Servant,

" THOMAS CHATTERTON."

Walpole replied civilly, thanking his correspondent for what he had sent and for his offer of communicating his manuscripts, but disclaiming any ability to correct Chatterton's notes. "I have not the happiness of understanding the Saxon language, and, without your learned notes, should not have been able to comprehend Rowley's text." He asks where Rowley's poems are to be found, offers to print them, and pronounces the Abbot John's verses "wonderful for their harmony and spirit." This encouragement called out a second letter from Chatterton, with another and longer extract from the "Historie of Peyncteynge yn Englande," including translations into the Rowley dialect of passages from a pair of mythical Saxon poets: Ecca, Bishop of Hereford, and Elmar, Bishop of Selseie, "fetyve yn Workes of ghastlienesse," as *ecce signum*:

" Nowe maie alle Helle open to golpe thee downe," etc.

But by this time Walpole had begun to suspect imposture. He had been lately bitten in the Ossian business and had grown wary in consequence. More-

---

* Publication begun 1761: 2d edition 1768. Chatterton's letter was dated March 25 [1769].

over, Chatterton had been incautious enough to show his hand in his second letter (March 30). "He informed me," said Walpole, in his history of the affair, "that he was the son of a poor widow . . . that he was clerk or apprentice to an attorney, but had a taste and turn for more elegant studies; and hinted a wish that I would assist him with my interest in emerging out of so dull a profession, by procuring him some place." Meanwhile, distrusting his own scholarship, Walpole had shown the manuscripts to his friends Gray and Mason, who promptly pronounced them modern fabrications and recommended him to return them without further notice. But Walpole, good-naturedly considering that it was no "grave crime in a young bard to have forged false notes of hand that were to pass current only in the parish of Parnassus," wrote his ingenious correspondent a letter of well-meant advice, counseling him to stick to his profession, and saying that he "had communicated his transcripts to much better judges, and that they were by no means satisfied with the authenticity of his supposed manuscripts." Chatterton then wrote for his manuscripts, and after some delay—Walpole having been absent in Paris for several months—they were returned to him.

In 1769 Chatterton had begun contributing miscellaneous articles, in prose and verse, to the *Town and Country Magazine*, a London periodical. Among these appeared the eclogue of "Elinoure and Juga," * the only one of the Rowley poems printed during its author's lifetime. He had now turned his pen to the service of politics, espousing the side of Wilkes and

* See *ante*, p. 346.

liberty. In April, 1770, he left Bristol for London, and cast himself upon the hazardous fortunes of a literary career. Most tragical is the story of the poor, unfriended lad's struggle against fate for the next few months. He scribbled incessantly for the papers, receiving little or no pay. Starvation confronted him; he was too proud to ask help, and on August 24 he took poison and died, at the age of seventeen years and nine months.

With Chatterton's acknowledged writings we have nothing here to do; they include satires in the manner of Churchill, political letters in the manner of Junius, squibs, lampoons, verse epistles, elegies, "African eclogues," a comic burletta, "The Revenge"—played at Marylebone Gardens shortly after his death—with essays and sketches in the style that the *Spectator* and *Rambler* had made familiar: "The Adventures of a Star," "The Memoirs of a Sad Dog," and the like. They exhibit a precocious cleverness, but have no value and no interest to-day. One gets from Chatterton's letters and miscellanies an unpleasant impression of his character. There is not only the hectic quality of too early ripeness which one detects in Keats' correspondence; and the defiant swagger, the affectation of wickedness and knowingness that one encounters in the youthful Byron, and that is apt to attend the stormy burst of irregular genius upon the world; but there are things that imply a more radical unscrupulousness. But it would be harsh to urge any such impressions against one who was no more than a boy when he perished, and whose brief career had struggled through cold obstruction to its bitter end. The best traits in Chatterton's character appear to have been his proud spirit of independence and his warm family affections.

The death of an obscure penny-a-liner, like young Chatterton, made little noise at first. But gradually it became rumored about in London literary coteries that manuscripts of an interesting kind existed at Bristol, purporting to be transcripts from old English poems; and that the finder, or fabricator, of the same was the unhappy lad who had taken arsenic the other day, to anticipate a slower death from hunger. It was in April, 1771, that Walpole first heard of the fate of his would-be *protégé*. "Dining," he says, "at the Royal Academy, Dr. Goldsmith drew the attention of the company with an account of a marvelous treasure of ancient poems lately discovered at Bristol, and expressed enthusiastic belief in them; for which he was laughed at by Dr. Johnson, who was present. I soon found this was the *trouvaille* of my friend Chatterton, and I told Dr. Goldsmith that this novelty was known to me, who might, if I had pleased, have had the honor of ushering the great discovery to the learned world. You may imagine, sir, we did not all agree in the measure of our faith; but though his credulity diverted me, my mirth was soon dashed; for, on asking about Chatterton, he told me he had been in London and had destroyed himself."

With the exception of "Elinour and Juga," already mentioned, the Rowley poems were still unprinted. The manuscripts, in Chatterton's handwriting, were mostly in the possession of Barrett and Catcott. They purported to be copies of Rowley's originals; but of these alleged originals, the only specimens brought forward by Chatterton were a few scraps of parchment containing, in one instance, the first thirty-four lines of the poem entitled " The Storie of William Canynge "; in another a prose account of one " Symonne de Byrtonne," and, in still others, the whole of the short-verse pieces, " Songe to Aella " and " The Accounte of W. Canynge's Feast." These scraps of vellum are described as about six inches square, smeared with glue or brown varnish, or stained with ochre, to give them an appearance of age. Thomas Warton had seen one of them, and pronounced it a clumsy forgery; the script not of the fifteenth century, but unmistakably modern. Southey describes another as written, for the most part, in an attorney's regular engrossing hand. Mr. Skeat " cannot find the slightest indication that Chatterton had ever seen a MS. of early date; on the contrary, he never uses the common contractions, and he was singularly addicted to the use of capitals, which in old MSS. are rather scarce."

Boswell tells how he and Johnson went down to Bristol in April, 1776, "where I was entertained with seeing him inquire upon the spot into the authenticity of Rowley's poetry, as I had seen him inquire upon the spot into the authenticity of Ossian's poetry. Johnson said of Chatterton, 'This is the most extraordinary young man that has encountered my knowledge. It is wonderful how the whelp has written such things.'"

In 1777, seven years after Chatterton's death, his Rowley poems were first collected and published by Thomas Tyrwhitt, the Chaucerian editor, who gave, in an appendix, his reasons for believing that Chatterton was their real author, and Rowley a myth.*

* " Poems supposed to have been written at Bristol by Thomas Rowley and others in the fifteenth century. The greatest part now

These reasons are convincing to any modern scholar. Tyrwhitt's opinion was shared at the time by all competent authorities—Gray, Thomas Warton, and Malone, the editor of the *variorum* Shakspere, among others. Nevertheless, a controversy sprang up over Rowley, only less lively than the dispute about Ossian, which had been going on since 1760. Rowley's most prominent champions were the Rev. Dr. Symmes, who wrote in the *London Review;* the Rev. Dr. Sherwin, in the *Gentleman's Magazine;* Dr. Jacob Bryant,* and Jeremiah Milles, D. D., Dean of Exeter, who published a sumptuous quarto edition of the poems in 1782.† These asserters of Rowley belonged to the class of amateur scholars whom Edgar Poe used to speak of as "cultivated old clergymen." They had the usual classical training of Oxford and Cambridge graduates, but no precise knowledge of old English literature. They had the benevolent curiosity of Mr. Pickwick, and the gullibility—the large, easy swallow —which seems to go with the clerico-antiquarian habit of mind.

Nothing is so extinct as an extinct controversy; and, unlike the Ossian puzzle, which was a harder nut to crack, this Rowley controversy was really settled from

first published from the most authentic copies, with engraved specimens of one of the MSS. To which are added a preface, an introductory account of the several pieces, and a glossary. London: Printed for T. Payne & Son at the Mews Gate. MDCCLXXVII."

"* Observations upon the Poems of Thomas Rowley," 2 vols. 1781.

"† Poems supposed to have been written at Bristol in the fifteenth century by Thomas Rowley, Priest, etc. With a commentary in which the antiquity of them is considered and defended."

the start. It is not essential to our purpose to give any extended history of it. The evidence relied upon by the supporters of Rowley was mainly of the external kind: personal testimony, and especially the antecedent unlikeliness that a boy of Chatterton's age and imperfect education could have reared such an elaborate structure of deceit; together with the inferiority of his acknowledged writings to the poems that he ascribed to Rowley. But Tyrwhitt was a scholar of unusual thoroughness and acuteness; and, having a special acquaintance with early English, he was able to bring to the decision of the question evidence of an internal nature which became more convincing in proportion as the knowledge necessary to understand his argument increased; *i. e.,* as the number of readers increased, who knew something about old English poetry. Indeed, it was nothing but the general ignorance of the spelling, flexions, vocabulary, and scansion of Middle English verse, that made the controversy possible.

Tyrwhitt pointed out that the Rowleian dialect was not English of the fifteenth century, nor of any century, but a grotesque jumble of archaic words of very different periods and dialects. The orthography and grammatical forms were such as occurred in no old English poet known to the student of literature. The fact that Rowley used constantly the possessive pronominal form *itts,* instead of *his;* or the other fact that he used the termination *en* in the singular of the verb, was alone enough to stamp the poems as spurious. Tyrwhitt also showed that the syntax, diction, idioms, and stanza forms were modern; that if modern words were substituted throughout for the antique, and the

spelling modernized, the verse would read like eighteenth-century work.   " If anyone," says Scott, in his
review of the Southey and Cottle edition, "resists the
internal evidence of the style of Rowley's poems, we
make him welcome to the rest of the argument; to his
belief that the Saxons imported heraldry and gave
armorial bearings (which were not known till the time
of the Crusades); that Mr. Robert [*sic*] Canynge, in
the reign of Edward IV., encouraged drawing and had
private theatricals."   In this article Scott points out
a curious blunder of Chatterton's which has become
historic, though it is only one of a thousand.   In the
description of the cook in the General Prologue to the
" Canterbury Tales," Chaucer had written:

> " But gret harm was it, as it thoughte me,
>   That on his schyne a mormal hadde he,
>   For blankmanger he made with the beste."

Mormal, in this passage, means a cancerous sore, and
blankmanger is a certain dish or confection—the
modern *blancmange*.   But a confused recollection of
the whole was in Chatterton's mind, when, among the
fragments of paper and parchment which he covered
with imitations of ancient script, and which are now
in the British Museum,—" The Yellow Roll," " The
Purple Roll," etc.,—he inserted the following title in
" The Rolls of St. Bartholomew's Priory," purporting
to be old medical prescriptions: " The cure of mor-
malles and the waterie leprosie; the rolle of the blacke
mainger "; turning Chaucer's innocent *blankmanger*
into some kind of imaginary *black mange.*

Skeat believes that Chatterton had read very little
of Chaucer, probably only a small portion of the Pro-

logue to the "Canterbury Tales." "If he had really taken pains," he thinks, "to *read* and *study* Chaucer or Lydgate or any old author earlier than the age of Spenser, the Rowley poems would have been very different. They would then have borne some resemblance to the language of the fifteenth century, whereas they are rather less like the language of that period than of any other. The spelling of the words is frequently too late, or too bizarre, whilst many of the words themselves are too archaic or too uncommon." *
But this internal evidence, which was so satisfactory to Scott, was so little convincing to Chatterton's contemporaries that Tyrwhitt felt called upon to publish in 1782 a "Vindication" of his appendix; and Thomas Warton put forth in the same year an "Enquiry," in which he reached practically the same conclusions with Tyrwhitt. And yet Warton had devoted the twenty-sixth section of the second volume of his "History of English Poetry" (1778,) to a review of the Rowley poems, on the ground that "as they are held to be real by many respectable critics, it was his duty to give them a place in this series": a curious testimony to the uncertainty of the public mind on the question, and a half admission that the poems might possibly turn out to be genuine. †

Tyrwhitt proved clearly enough that Chatterton wrote the Rowley poems, but it was reserved for Mr. Skeat to show just *how* he wrote them. The *modus operandi* was about as follows: Chatterton first made,

---

* " Essay on the Rowley Poems : " Skeat's edition of "Chatterton's Poetical Works," Vol. II. p. xxvii.

† For a bibliography of the Rowley controversy, consult the article on Chatterton in the " Dictionary of National Biography."

for his private use, a manuscript glossary, by copying out the words in the glossary to Speght's edition of Chaucer, and those marked as old in Bailey's and Kersey's English Dictionaries. Next he wrote his poem in modern English, and finally rewrote it, substituting the archaic words for their modern equivalents, and altering the spelling throughout into an exaggerated imitation of the antique spelling in Speght's Chaucer. The mistakes that he made are instructive, as showing how closely he followed his authorities, and how little independent knowledge he had of genuine old English. Thus, to give a few typical examples of the many in Mr. Skeat's notes: in Kersey's dictionary occurs the word *gare*, defined as "cause." This is the verb *gar*, familiar to all readers of Burns,* and meaning to cause, to make; but Chatterton, taking it for the *noun*, cause, employs it with grotesque incorrectness in such connections as these:

> " Perchance in Virtue's gare rhyme might be then " :
> " If in this battle luck deserts our gare."

Again the Middle English *howten* (Modern English, *hoot*) is defined by Speght as "hallow," *i. e.*, halloo. But Kersey and Bailey misprint this " hollow "; and Chatterton, entering it so in his manuscript list of old words, evidently takes it to be the *adjective* "hollow " and uses it thus in the line:

> " Houten are wordes for to telle his doe," *i. e.*,
> Hollow are words to tell his doings.

Still again, in a passage already quoted,† it is told how

* " Ah, gentle dames ! it gars me greet."
                                        — *Tam o' Shanter*
† *Ante*, p. 350.

the "Wynde hurled the Battayle"—Rowleian for a small boat—"agaynste an Heck." *Heck* in this and other passages was a puzzle. From the context it obviously meant "rock," but where did Chatterton get it? Mr. Skeat explains this. *Heck* is a provincial word signifying "rack," *i. e.*, "hay-rack"; but Kersey misprinted it "rock," and Chatterton followed him. A typical instance of the kind of error that Chatterton was perpetually committing was his understanding the "Listed, bounded," *i. e.*, *edged* (as in the "list" or selvage of cloth) for "bounded" in the sense of *jumped*, and so coining from it the verb "to liss" = to jump:

> " The headed javelin lisseth here and there."

Every page in the Rowley poems abounds in forms which would have been as strange to an Englishman of the fifteenth as they are to one of the nineteenth century. Adjectives are used for nouns, nouns for verbs, past participles for present infinitives; and derivatives and variants are employed which never had any existence, such as *hopelen* = hopelessness, and *anere* = another. Skeat says, that "an analysis of the glossary in Milles's edition shows that the *genuine* old English words correctly used, occurring in the Rowleian dialect, amount to only about *seven* per cent. of all the old words employed." It is probable that, by constant use of his manuscript glossary, the words became fixed in Chatterton's memory and he acquired some facility in composing at first hand in this odd jargon. Thus he uses the archaic words quite freely as rhyme words, which he would not have been likely to do unless he had formed the habit of thinking. to some degree, in Rowleian.

The question now occurs, apart from the tragic interest of Chatterton's career, from the mystery connected with the incubation and hatching of the Rowley poems, and from their value as records of a very unusual precocity—what independent worth have they as poetry, and what has been the extent of their literary influence? The dust of controversy has long since settled, and what has its subsidence made visible? My own belief is that the Rowley poems are interesting principally as literary curiosities—the work of an infant phenomenon—and that they have little importance in themselves, or as models and inspirations to later poets. I cannot help thinking that, upon this subject, many critics have lost their heads. Malone, *e. g.*, pronounced Chatterton the greatest genius that England had produced since Shakspere. Professor Masson permits himself to say: "These antique poems of Chatterton are perhaps as worthy of being read consecutively as many portions of the poetry of Byron, Shelley, or Keats. There are passages in them, at least, quite equal to any to be found in these poets." * Mr. Gosse seems to me much nearer the truth: "Our estimate of the complete originality of the Rowley poems must be tempered by a recollection of the existence of 'The Castle of Otranto' and 'The Schoolmistress,' of the popularity of Percy's 'Reliques' and the 'Odes' of Gray, and of the revival of a taste for Gothic literature and art which dates from Chatterton's infancy. Hence the claim which has been made for Chatterton as the father of the romantic school, and as having influenced the actual

* "Chatterton. A Story of the Year 1770," by David Masson London, 1874.

style of Coleridge and Keats, though supported with great ability, appears to be overcharged. So also the positive praise given to the Rowley poems, as artistic productions full of rich color and romantic melody, may be deprecated without any refusal to recognize these qualities in measure. There are frequent flashes of brilliancy in Chatterton, and one or two very perfectly sustained pieces; but the main part of his work, if rigorously isolated from the melodramatic romance of his career, is surely found to be rather poor reading, the work of a child of exalted genius, no doubt, yet manifestly the work of a child all through." *

Let us get a little closer to the Rowley poems, as they stand in Mr. Skeat's edition, stripped of their sham-antique spelling and with their language modernized wherever possible; and we shall find, I think, that, tried by an absolute standard, they are markedly inferior not only to true mediæval work like Chaucer's poems and the English and Scottish ballads, but also to the best modern work conceived in the same spirit: to "Christabel" and "The Eve of St. Agnes," and "Jock o' Hazeldean" and "Sister Helen," and "The Haystack in the Flood." The longest of the Rowley poems is "Aella," "a tragycal enterlude or discoorseynge tragedie" in 147 stanzas, and generally regarded as Chatterton's masterpiece.† The scene of this tragedy is Bristol and the neighboring Watchet

---

* "Eighteenth Century Literature," p. 334.

† A recent critic, the Hon. Roden Noel ("Essays on Poetry and Poets," London, 1886), thinks that "'Aella' is a drama worthy of the Elizabethans" (p. 44). "As to the Rowley series," as a whole, he does "not hesitate to say that they contain some of the finest poetry in our language" (p. 39). The choric "Ode to Freedom" in "Goddwyn" appears to Mr. Noel to be the original of a much

Mead; the period, during the Danish invasions. The hero is the warden of Bristol Castle.* While he is absent on a victorious campaign against the Danes, his bride, Bertha, is decoyed from home by his treacherous lieutenant, Celmond, who is about to ravish her in the forest, when he is surprised and killed by a band of marauders. Meanwhile Aella has returned home, and, finding that his wife has fled, stabs himself mortally. Bertha arrives in time to hear his dying speech and make the necessary explanations, and then dies herself on the body of her lord. It will be seen that the plot is sufficiently melodramatic; the sentiments and dialogue are entirely modern, when translated out of Rowleian into English. The verse is a modified form of the Spenserian, a ten-line stanza which Mr. Skeat says is an invention of Chatterton and a striking instance of his originality.† It answers very well in descriptive passages and soliloquies; not so well in the "discoorseynge" parts. As this is Chatterton's favorite stanza, in which "The Battle of Hastings," "Goddwyn," "English Metamorphosis" and others of the Rowley series are written, an example of it may be cited here, from "Aella."

> *Scene*, Bristol. Celmond, *alone.*
>
> The world is dark with night ; the winds are still,
> Faintly the moon her pallid light makes gleam;
> The risen sprites the silent churchyard fill,

admired passage in "Childe Harold," in which war is personified, " and at any rate is finer " !

* See in Wm. Howitt's " Homes of the Poets," Vol. I. pp. 264–307, the description of a drawing of this building in 1138, done by Chatterton and inserted in Barrett's " History."

† For some remarks on Chatterton's metrical originality, see " Ward's English Poets," Vol. III. pp. 400–403.

With elfin fairies joining in the dream ;
The forest shineth with the silver leme ;
Now may my love be sated in its treat ;
Upon the brink of some swift running stream,
At the sweet banquet I will sweetly eat.
This is the house ; quickly, ye hinds, appear.

Enter a servant.

Cel. Go tell to Bertha straight, a stranger waiteth here.

The Rowley poems include, among other things, a number of dramatic or quasi-dramatic pieces, " Goddwyn," " The Tournament," " The Parliament of Sprites "; the narrative poem of " The Battle of Hastings," and a collection of " eclogues." These are all in long-stanza forms, mostly in the ten-lined stanza. " English Metamorphosis " is an imitation of a passage in " The Faërie Queene," (book ii. canto x. stanzas 5–19). " The Parliament of Sprites " is an interlude played by Carmelite friars at William Canynge's house on the occasion of the dedication of St. Mary Redcliffe's. One after another the *antichi spiriti dolenti* rise up and salute the new edifice: Nimrod and the Assyrians, Anglo-Saxon ealdormen and Norman knights templars, and citizens of ancient Bristol. Among others, " Elle's sprite speaks ":

" Were I once more cast in a mortal frame,
To hear the chantry-song sound in mine ear,
To hear the masses to our holy dame,
To view the cross-aisles and the arches fair !
Through the half-hidden silver-twinkling glare
Of yon bright moon in foggy mantles dressed,
I must content this building to aspere,*
Whilst broken clouds the holy sight arrest ;
Till, as the nights grow old, I fly the light.
Oh ! were I man again, to see the sight ! "

* Look at.

Perhaps the most engaging of the Rowley poems are "An Excelente Balade of Charitie," written in the rhyme royal; and "The Bristowe Tragedie," in the common ballad stanza, and said by Tyrwhitt to be founded on an historical fact: the execution at Bristol, in 1461, of Sir Baldwin Fulford, who fought on the Lancastrian side in the Wars of the Roses. The best quality in Chatterton's verse is its unexpectedness,— sudden epithets or whole lines, of a wild and artless sweetness,—which goes far to explain the fascination that he exercised over Coleridge and Keats. I mean such touches as these:

> " Once as I dozing in the witch-hour lay."

> " Brown as the filbert dropping from the shell."

> " My gorme emblanchèd with the comfreie plant."

> " Where thou may'st here the sweetè night-lark chant,
> Or with some mocking brooklet sweetly glide."

> " Upon his bloody carnage-house he lay,
> Whilst his long shield did gleam with the sun's rising ray."

> " The red y-painted oars from the black tide,
> Carved with devices rare, do shimmering rise."

> " As elfin fairies, when the moon shines bright,
> In little circles dance upon the green ;
> All living creatures fly far from their sight,
> Nor by the race of destiny be seen ;
> For what he be that elfin fairies strike,
> Their souls will wander to King Offa's dyke."

The charming wildness of Chatterton's imagination —which attracted the notice of that strange, visionary genius William Blake *—is perhaps seen at its best in

---

* Blake was an early adherent of the "Gothic artists who built the Cathedrals in the so-called Dark Ages . . . of whom the world was

one of the minstrel songs in "Aella." This is obviously an echo of Ophelia's song in "Hamlet," but Chatterton gives it a weird turn of his own:

> " Hark ! the raven flaps his wing
> In the briared dell below ;
> Hark ! the death-owl loud doth sing
> To the nightmares, as they go.
> My love is dead.
> Gone to his death-bed
> All under the willow tree.

> " See the white moon shines on high,*
> Whiter is my true-love's shroud,
> Whiter than the morning sky,
> Whiter than the evening cloud.
> My love is dead," etc.

It remains to consider briefly the influence of Chatterton's life and writings upon his contemporaries and successors in the field of romantic poetry. The dramatic features of his personal career drew, naturally, quite as much if not more attention than his literary legacy to posterity. It was about nine years after his death that a clerical gentleman, Sir Herbert Croft, went to Bristol to gather materials for a biography. He talked with Barrett and Catcott, and with many of the poet's schoolmates and fellow-townsmen, and visited his mother and sister, who told him anecdotes of the marvelous boy's childhood and gave him

not worthy." Mr. Rossetti has pointed out his obligations to Ossian and possibly to " The Castle of Otranto." See Blake's poems " Fair Eleanor " and " Gwin, King of Norway."

* Chatterton's sister testifies that he had the romantic habit of sitting up all night and writing by moonlight. Cambridge Ed. p. lxi.

some of his letters.   Croft also traced Chatterton's footsteps in London, where he interviewed, among others, the coroner who had presided at the inquest over the suicide's body.   The result of these inquiries he gave to the world in a book entitled "Love and Madness" (1780).*   Southey thought that Croft had treated Mrs. Chatterton shabbily, in making her no pecuniary return from the profits of his book; and arraigned him publicly for this in the edition of Chatterton's works which he and Joseph Cottle—both native Bristowans—published in three volumes in 1803.   This was at first designed to be a subscription edition for the benefit of Chatterton's mother and sister, but, the subscriptions not being numerous enough, it was issued in the usual way, through "the trade."

It was in 1795, just a quarter of a century after Chatterton's death, that Southey and Coleridge were married in St. Mary Redcliffe's Church to the Misses Edith and Sara Fricker.   Coleridge was greatly interested in Chatterton.   In his "Lines on Observing a Blossom on the First of February, 1796," he compares the flower to

> " Bristowa's bard, the wondrous boy,
>   An amaranth which earth seemed scarce to own,
>   Blooming 'mid poverty's drear wintry waste."

And a little earlier than this, when meditating his pantisocracy scheme with Southey and Lovell, he had addressed the dead poet in his indignant "Monody on the Death of Chatterton," associating him in

* Other standard lives of Chatterton are those by Gregory, 1789, (reprinted and prefixed to the Southey and Cottle edition): Dix, 1837 ; and Wilson, 1869.

imagination with the abortive community on the Susquehannah:

> " O Chatterton, that thou wert yet alive !
> Sure thou would'st spread thy canvas to the gale,
> And love with us the tinkling team to drive
> O'er peaceful freedom's undivided dale ;
> And we at sober eve would round thee throng,
> Hanging enraptured on thy stately song,
> And greet with smiles the young-eyed poesy
> All deftly masked as hoar antiquity. . .
> Yet will I love to follow the sweet dream
> Where Susquehannah pours his untamed stream ;
> And on some hill, whose forest-frowning side
> Waves o'er the murmurs of his calmer tide,
> Will raise a solemn cenotaph to thee,
> Sweet harper of time-shrouded minstrelsy."

It might be hard to prove that the Rowley poems had very much to do with giving shape to Coleridge's own poetic output. Doubtless, without them, "Christabel," and "The Ancient Mariner," and "The Darke Ladye" would still have been; and yet it is possible that they might not have been just what they are. In "The Ancient Mariner" there is the ballad strain of the "Reliques," but *plus* something of Chatterton's. In such lines as these:

> " The bride hath paced into the hall
> Red as a rose is she :
> Nodding their heads before her, goes
> The merry minstrelsy; "

or as these:

> " The wedding guest here beat his breast,
> For he heard the loud bassoon : "

one catches a far-away reverberation from certain stanzas of " The Bristowe Tragedie : " this, *e. g.*,

> " Before him went the council-men
>   In scarlet robes and gold,
>   And tassels spangling in the sun,
>   Much glorious to behold ; "

and this :

> " In different parts a godly psalm
>   Most sweetly they did chant :
>   Behind their backs six minstrels came,
>   Who tuned the strung bataunt." *

Among all the young poets of the generation that succeeded Chatterton, there was a tender feeling of comradeship with the proud and passionate boy, and a longing to admit him of their crew.   Byron, indeed, said that he was insane; but Shelley, in " Adonais," classes him with Keats among "the inheritors of unful-filled renown."   Lord Houghton testifies that Keats had a prescient sympathy with Chatterton in his early death.   He dedicated " Endymion " to his memory. In his epistle " To George Felton Mathew," he asks him to help him find a place

> " Where we may soft humanity put on,
>   And sit, and rhyme, and think on Chatterton." †

Keats said that he always associated the season of autumn with the memory of Chatterton.   He asserted,

---

* Rowleian : there is no such instrument known unto men.   The romantic love of *color* is observable in this poem, and is strong every-where in Chatterton.

† See also the sonnet : " O Chatterton, how very sad thy fate "— given in Lord Houghton's memoir.   " Life and Letters of John Keats " : By R.   Monckton Milnes, p. 20 (American Edition, New York, 1848).

somewhat oddly, that he was the purest writer in the
English language and used " no French idiom or parti-
cles, like Chaucer." In a letter from Jane Porter to
Keats about the reviews of his " Endymion," she wrote:
" Had Chatterton possessed sufficient manliness of
mind to know the magnanimity of patience, and been
aware that great talents have a commission from
Heaven, he would not have deserted his post, and his
name might have been paged with Milton."

Keats was the poetic child of Spenser, but some
traits of manner—hard to define, though not to feel—
he inherited from Chatterton. In his unfinished
poem, " The Eve of St. Mark," there is a Rowleian
accent in the passage imitative of early English, and
in the loving description of the old volume of saints'
legends whence it is taken, with its

> " —pious poesies
> Written in smallest crow-quill size
> Beneath the text."

And we cannot but think of the shadow of St. Mary
Redcliffe falling across another young life, as we
read how

> " Bertha was a maiden fair
> Dwelling in th' old Minster-square ;
> From her fireside she could see,
> Sidelong, its rich antiquity,
> Far as the Bishop's garden-wall " ;

and of the footfalls that pass the echoing minster-gate,
and of the clamorous daws that fall asleep in the
ancient belfry to the sound of the drowsy chimes.
Rossetti, in so many ways a continuator of Keats'
artistry, devoted to Chatterton the first of his sonnet-

group, "Five English Poets," * of which the sestet
runs thus:

> " Thy nested home-loves, noble Chatterton ;
>   The angel-trodden stair thy soul could trace
>   Up Redcliffe's spire ; and in the world's armed space
>   Thy gallant sword-play:—these to many an one
>   Are sweet for ever ; as thy grave unknown
>   And love-dream of thine unrecorded face."

The story of Chatterton's life found its way into
fiction and upon the stage. Alfred de Vigny, one of
the French romanticists, translator of " Othello" and
" The Merchant of Venice," introduced it as an episode into his romance, " Stello ou les Diables Bleus,"
afterward dramatized as "Chatterton," and first played
at Paris on February 12, 1835, with great success. De
Vigny made a love tragedy out of it, inventing a
sweetheart for his hero, in the person of Kitty Bell,
a rôle which became one of Madame Dorval's chief
triumphs. On the occasion of the revival of De Vigny's
drama in December, 1857, Théophile Gautier gave,
in the *Moniteur*,† some reminiscences of its first performance, twenty-two years before.

" The parterre before which Chatterton declaimed
was full of pale, long-haired youths, who firmly believed that there was no other worthy occupation on
earth but the making of verses or of pictures—art, as
they called it; and who looked upon the bourgeois
with a disdain to which the disdain of the Heidelberg
or Jena 'fox' for the 'philistine' hardly approaches. . .

---

* Chatterton, Blake, Coleridge, Keats, Shelley. " The absolutely
miraculous Chatterton," Rossetti elsewhere styles him.

† " Histoire du Romantisme," pp. 153–54.

As to money, no one thought of it.   More than one, as in that assembly of impossible professions which Theodore de Banville describes with so resigned an irony, could have cried without falsehood ' I am a lyric poet and I live by my profession.'   One who has not passed through that mad, ardent, over-excited but generous epoch, cannot imagine to what a forgetfulness of material existence the intoxication, or, if you prefer, infatuation of art pushed the obscure and fragile victims who would rather have died than renounce their dream.   One actually heard in the night the crack of solitary pistols.   Judge of the effect produced in such an environment by M. Alfred Vigny's ' Chatterton '; to which, if you would comprehend it, you must restore the contemporary atmosphere." *

* " Chatterton," a drama by Jones and Herman, was played at the Princess' Theater, London, May 22, 1884.

CHAPTER XI.

Zbe German Tributary.

Up to the last decade of the eighteenth century the romantic movement in Great Britain had been self-developed and independent of foreign influence, except for such stimulus as it had found, once and again, in the writings of continental scholars like Sainte Palaye and Mallet. But now the English literary current began to receive a tributary stream from abroad. A change had taken place in the attitude of the German mind which corresponds quite closely to that whose successive steps we have been following. In Germany, French classicism had got an even firmer hold than in England. It is well-known that Frederick the Great (1740–86) regarded his mother-tongue as a barbarous dialect, hardly fit for literary use. In his own writings, prose and verse, he invariably employed French; and he boasted to Gottsched that from his youth up he had not read a German book.*

But already before the middle of the century, and just about the time of the publication of Thomson's "Seasons," the so-called Swiss school, under the leadership of the Züricher, Johann Jacob Bodmer, had begun a national movement and an attack upon Gallic influences. Bodmer fought under Milton's banner,

* Scherer's " History of German Literature," Conybeare's Translation, Vol. II. p. 26.

and in the preface to his prose translation of " Paradise Lost " (1732), he praised Shakspere as the English Sophocles. In his "Abhandlung von dem Wunderbaren " ("Treatise on the Marvelous," 1740) he asserted the claims of freedom, nature, and the inspired imagination against the rules of French critics, very much as the Wartons and Bishop Hurd did a few years later in England. *Deutscheit, Volkspoesie,* the German past, the old Teutonic hero-age, with the *Kaiserzeit* and the Middle Ages in general, soon came into fashion. "As early as 1748 Bodmer had published specimens from the Minnesingers, in 1757 he had brought out a part of the Nibelungenlied, in 1758 and 1759 a more complete collection of the Minnesingers, and till 1781, till just before his death, he continued to produce editions of the Middle High-German poems. Another Swiss writer, Christian Heinrich Myller, a pupil of Bodmer's . . . published in 1784 and 1785 the whole of the Nibelungenlied and the most important of the chivalrous epics. Lessing, in his preface to Gleim's 'War-songs,' called attention to the Middle High German poets, of whom he continued to be throughout his life an ardent admirer. Justus Möser took great interest in the Minnesingers. About the time when 'Götz' appeared, this enthusiasm for early German poetry was at its strongest, and Bürger, Voss, Miller, and Höltz wrote Minnesongs, in which they imitated the old German lyric poets. In 1773 Gleim published 'Poems after the Minnesingers,' and in 1779 'Poems after Walther von der Vogelweide.' Some enthusiasts had already hailed the Nibelungenlied as the German Iliad, and Bürger, who vied hard with the rest, but without

much success, in turning Homer into German, insisted
on dressing up the Greek heroes a little in the
Nibelungen style.   He and a few other poets loved to
give their ballads a chivalrous character.   Fritz Stolberg wrote the beautiful song of a German boy,
beginning, 'Mein Arm wird stark und gross mein
Muth, gib, Vater, mir ein Schwert'; and the song of
the old Swabian knight—'Sohn, da hast du meinen
Speer; meinem Arm wird er zu schwer.'   Lessing's
'Nathan,' too, appealed to this enthusiasm for the
times of chivalry, and must have strengthened the
feeling.   An historian like the Swiss, Johannes
Müller, began to show the Middle Ages in a fairer
light, and even to ascribe great merits to the Papacy.
But in doing so, Johannes Müller was only following
in Herder's steps.   Herder . . . had written against
the self-conceit of his age, its pride in its enlighten-
ment and achievements.   He found in the Middle
Ages the realization of his æsthetic ideas, namely,
strong emotion, stirring life and action, everything
guided by feeling and instinct, not by morbid thought:
religious ardor and chivalrous honor, boldness in love
and strong patriotic feeling." *

When the founders of a truly national literature in
Germany cut loose from French moorings, they had
an English pilot aboard; and in the translations from
German romances, dramas, and ballads that were
made by Scott, Coleridge, Taylor, Lewis, and others,
English literature was merely taking back with usury
what it had lent its younger sister.   Mention has
already been made of Bürger's and Herder's renderings from Percy's " Reliques," † an edition of which

*Scherer, Vol. II. pp. 123-24.   † See *ante*, pp. 300-301.

was published at Göttingen in 1767; as well as of the strong excitement aroused in Germany by MacPherson's "Ossian." * This last found—besides the Viennese Denis—another translator in Fritz Stolberg, who carried his mediævalism so far as to join the Roman Catholic Church in 1800. Klopstock's "Kriegslied," written as early as 1749, was in the meter of "Chevy Chase," which Klopstock knew through Addison's *Spectator* papers. Through Mallet, the Eddaic literature made an impression in Germany as in England; and Gersternberg's "Gedicht eines Skalden" (1766), one of the first-fruits of the German translation of the "Histoire de Dannemarc," preceded by two years the publication—though not the composition—of Gray's poems from the Norse.

But the spirit which wrought most mightily upon the new German literature was Shakspere's. During the period of French culture there had been practically no knowledge of Shakspere in Germany. In 1741 Christian von Borck, Prussian ambassador to London, had translated "Julius Cæsar." This was followed, a few years later, by a version of "Romeo and Juliet." In 1762–66 Wieland translated, in whole or in part, twenty-two of Shakspere's plays. His translation was in prose and has been long superseded by the Tieck-Schlegel translation (1797–1801–1810). Goethe first made acquaintance with Shakspere, when a student at Leipsic, through the detached passages given in "Dodd's Beauties of Shakspere." † He afterward got

* See *ante*, pp. 337–38.
† "The Beauties of Shakspere. Regularly selected from each Play. With a general index. Digesting them under proper heads." By the Rev. Wm. Dodd, 1752.

hold of Wieland's translation, and when he went to Strassburg he fell under the influence of Herder, who inspired him with his own enthusiasm for "Ossian," and the *Volkslieder*, and led him to study Shakspere in the original.

Young Germany fastened upon and appropriated the great English dramatist with passionate conviction. He became an object of worship, an article of faith. The Shakspere *cultus* dominated the whole *Sturm- und Drangperoide*. The stage domesticated him: the poets imitated him; the critics exalted him into the type and representative (*Urbild*) of Germanic art, as opposed to and distinguished from the art of the Latin races, founded upon a false reproduction of the antique.* It was a recognition of the essential kinship between the two separated branches of the great Teutonic stock. The enthusiastic young patriots of the Göttinger *Hain*,—who hated everything French and called each other by the names of ancient bards,—accustomed themselves to the use of Shaksperian phrases in conversation; and on one occasion celebrated the dramatist's birthday so uproariously that they were pounced upon by the police and spent the night in the lockup. In Goethe's circle at Strassburg, which num-

* " Es war nicht blos die Tiefe der Poesie, welche sie zu Shakespeare zog, es war ebenso sehr das sichere Gefühl, das hier germanische Art und Kunst sei."—*Hettner's Geschichte der deutschen Literatur*, 3.3.1. s. 51. " Ist zu sagen, dass die Abwendung von den Franzosen zu den stammverwandten Engländern . . . in ihrem geschichtlichen Ursprung und Wachsthum wesentlich die Auflehnung des erstarkten germanischen Volksnaturells gegen die erdrückende Uebermacht der romanischen Formenwelt war," etc.—*Ibid.* s. 47. See also, ss. 389–95, for a review of the interpretation of the great Shaksperian rôles by German actors like Schröder and Fleck.

bered, among others, Lenz, Klinger, and H. L. Wagner, this Shakspere mania was *de rigueur*. Lenz, particularly, who translated " Love's Labour's Lost," excelled in whimsical imitations of " such conceits as clownage keeps in pay." * Upon his return to Frankfort, Goethe gave a feast in Shakspere's honor at his father's house (October 14, 1771), in which healths were drunk to the " Will of all Wills," and the youthful host delivered an extravagant eulogy. " The first page of Shakspere's that I read," runs a sentence of this oration, " made me his own for life, and when I was through with the first play, I stood like a man born blind, to whom sight has been given by an instant's miracle. I had a most living perception of the fact that my being had been expanded a whole infinitude. Everything was new and strange; my eyes ached with the unwonted light." †

Lessing, in his onslaught upon the French theater in his " Hamburgische Dramaturgie " (1767–69), maintained that there was a much closer agreement between Sophocles and Shakspere in the essentials of dramatic art than between Sophocles and Racine or Voltaire in their mechanical copies of the antique. In their own plays, Lessing, Goethe, and Schiller all took Shakspere as their model. But while beginning with imitation, they came in time to work freely in the

---

* " Wir hören einen Nachklang jener fröhlichen Unterhaltungen, in denen die Freunde sich ganz und gar in Shakespear'schen Wendungen und Wortwitzen ergingen, in seiner Uebersetzung von Shakespeare's ' Love's Labour's Lost.' "—*Hettner*, s. 244.

† See the whole oration (in Hettner, s. 120,) which gives a most vivid expression of the impact of Shakspere upon the newly aroused mind of Germany.

spirit of Shakspere rather than in his manner. Thus the first draught of Goethe's " Götz von Berlichingen " conforms in all externals to the pattern of a Shaksperian " history." The unity of action went overboard along with those of time and place; the scene was shifted for a monologue of three lines or a dialogue of six; tragic and comic were interwoven; the stage was thronged with a motley variety of figures, humors, and conditions—knights, citizens, soldiers, horse-boys, peasants; there was a courtjester; songs and lyric passages were interspersed; there were puns, broad jokes, rant, Elizabethan metaphors, and swollen trunk-hose hyperboles, with innumerable Shakesperian reminiscences in detail. But the advice of Herder, to whom he sent his manuscript, and the example of Lessing, whose " Emilia Galotti" had just appeared, persuaded Goethe to recast the piece and give it a more independent form.

Scherer * says that the pronunciamento of the new national movement in German letters was the " small, badly printed anonymous book " entitled " Von Deutscher Art und Kunst, einige fliegende Blätter " ("Some Loose Leaves about German Style and Art "), which appeared in 1773 and contained essays by Justus Möser, who "upheld the liberty of the ancient Germans as a vanished ideal"; by Johann Gottfried Herder, who "celebrated the merits of popular song, advocated a collection of the German *Volkslieder*, extolled the greatness of Shakspere, and prophesied the advent of a German Shakspere "; and Johann Wolfgang Goethe, who praised the Strassburg Minster

* " German Literature," Vol. II. pp. 82–83.

and Gothic architecture* in general, and "asserted that art, to be true, must be characteristic. The reform, or revolution, which this little volume announced was connected with hostility to France, and with a friendly attitude toward England. . . This great movement was, in fact, a revulsion from the spirit of Voltaire to that of Rousseau, from the artificiality of society to the simplicity of nature, from doubt and rationalism to feeling and faith, from *a priori* notions† to history, from hard and fast æsthetic rules to the freedom of genius. Goethe's 'Götz' was the first revolutionary symptom which really attracted much attention, but the 'Fly-sheets on German Style and Art' preceded the publication of 'Götz,' as a kind of programme or manifesto." Even Wieland, the mocking and French-minded, the man of consummate talent but shallow genius, the representative of the *Aufklärung* (*Éclaircissement*, Illumination) was carried away by this new stream of tendency, and saddled his hippogriff for a ride *ins alte romantische Land.* He availed himself of the new "Library of Romance" which Count Tressan began publishing in France in 1775, studied Hans Sachs and Hartmann von Aue, experimented with Old German meters, and enriched his vocabulary from Old German sources. He poetized popular fairy tales, chivalry stories, and motives from the Arthurian epos, such as "Gandalin" and "Geron der Adeliche" ("Gyron le Courteois").

---

* "Unter allen Menschen des Achtzehnten Jahrhunderts war Goethe wieder der Erste, welcher die lang verachtete Herrlichkeit der gothischen Baukunst empfand und erfasste."—*Hettner*, 3.3.1., s. 120.

† *Construirtes Ideal.*

But his best and best-known work in this temper was " Oberon " (1780) a rich composite of materials from Chaucer, "A Midsummer Night's Dream," and the French romance of "Huon of Bordeaux." *

From this outline—necessarily very imperfect and largely at second hand—of the course of the German romantic movement in the eighteenth century, it will nevertheless appear that it ran parallel to the English most of the way. In both countries the reaction was against the *Aufklärung, i. e.,* against the rationalistic, prosaic, skeptical, common-sense spirit of the age, represented in England by deistical writers like Shaftesbury, Mandeville, Bolingbroke, and Tindal in the department of religious and moral philosophy; and by writers like Addison, Swift, Prior, and Pope in polite letters; and represented most brilliantly in the literatures of Europe by Voltaire. In opposition to this spirit, an effort was now made to hark back to the ages of faith; to recover the point of view which created mythology, fairy lore, and popular superstitions; to *believe,* at all hazards, not only in God and the immortal soul of man, but in the old-time corollaries of these beliefs, in ghosts, elves, demons, and witches.

In both countries, too, the revolution, as it concerned form, was a break with French classicism and with that part of the native literature which had followed academic traditions. Here the insurrection was far more violent in Germany than in England,†

---

*Scherer, II. 129–31. " Oberon " was englished by William Sotheby in 1798.

† " Vor den classischen Dichtarten fängt mich bald an zu ekeln," wrote Bürger in 1775. " Charakteristiken ": von Erich Schmidt (Berlin, 1886) s. 205. " O, das verwünschte Wort: Klassisch! "

partly because Gallic influence had tyrannized there more completely and almost to the supplanting of the vernacular by the foreign idiom, for literary uses; and partly because Germany had nothing to compare with the shining and solid achievements of the Queen Anne classics in England. It was easy for the new school of German poets and critics to brush aside *perruques* like Opitz, Gottsched, and Gellert—authors of the fourth or fifth class. But Swift and Congreve, and Pope and Fielding, were not thus to be disposed of. We have noted the cautious, respectful manner in which such innovators as Warton and Percy ventured to question Pope's supremacy and to recommend older English poets to the attention of a polite age; and we have seen that Horace Walpole's Gothic enthusiasms were not inconsistent with literary prejudices more conservative than radical, upon the whole. In England, again, the movement began with imitations of Spenser and Milton, and, gradually only, arrived at the resuscitation of Chaucer and mediæval poetry and the translation of Bardic and Scaldic remains. But in Germany there was no Elizabethan literature to mediate between the modern mind and the Middle Age, and so the Germans resorted to England and Shakspere for this.

In Germany, as in England, though for different reasons, the romantic revival did not culminate until the nineteenth century, until the appearance of the

exclaims Herder. " Dieses Wort war es, das alle wahre Bildung nach den Alten als noch lebenden Mustern verdrängte. . . Dies Wort hat manches Genie unter einen Schutt von Worten vergraben. . . Es hat dem Vaterland blühende Fruchtbäume entzogen!"—*Hettner* 3. 3. I. s. 50.

Romantische Schule in the stricter sense—of Tieck, Novalis, the Schlegel brothers, Wackenroder, Fouqué, Von Arnim, Brentano, and Uhland. In England this was owing less to arrested development than to the absence of genius. There the forerunners of Scott, Coleridge, and Keats were writers of a distinctly inferior order: Akenside, Shenstone, Dyer, the Wartons, Percy, Walpole, Mrs. Radcliffe, "Monk" Lewis, the boy Chatterton. If a few rise above this level, like Thomson, Collins, and Gray, the slenderness of their performance, and the somewhat casual nature of their participation in the movement, diminish their relative importance. Gray's purely romantic work belongs to the last years of his life. Collins' derangement and early death stopped the unfolding of many buds of promise in this rarely endowed lyrist. Thomson, perhaps, came too early to reach any more advanced stage of evolution than Spenserism. In Germany, on the contrary, the pioneers were men of the highest intellectual stature, Lessing, Herder, Goethe, Schiller. But there the movement was checked for a time by counter-currents, or lost in broader tides of literary life. English romanticism was but one among many contemporary tendencies: sentimentalism, naturalism, realism. German romanticism was simply an incident of the *Sturm- und Drangperiode*, which was itself but a temporary phase of the swift and many-sided unfolding of the German mind in the latter half of the last century; one element in the great intellectual ferment which threw off, among other products, the Kantian philosophy, the "Laocoön," "Faust," and "Wilhelm Meister"; Winckelmann's "Geschichte der Kunst des Alterthums" and

Schiller's "Wallenstein" and "Wilhelm Tell." Men like Goethe and Schiller were too broad in their culture, too versatile in their talents, too multifarious in their mental activities and sympathies to be classified with a school. The temper which engendered "Götz" and "Die Räuber" was only a moment in the history of their *Entwickelung;* they passed on presently into other regions of thought and art.

In Goethe especially there ensued, after the time of his *Italienische Reise,* a reversion to the classic; not the exploded pseudo-classic of the eighteenth-century brand, but the true Hellenic spirit which expressed itself in such work as "Iphigenie auf Tauris," "Hermann und Dorothea," and the "Schöne Helena" and "Classische Walpurgis-Nacht" episodes in the second part of "Faust." "In his youth," says Scherer, "a love for the historical past of Germany had seized on the minds of many. Imaginative writers filled the old Teutonic forests with Bards and Druids and cherished an enthusiastic admiration for Gothic cathedrals and for the knights of the Middle Ages and of the sixteenth century. . . In Goethe's mature years, on the contrary, the interest in classical antiquity dwarfed all other æsthetic interests, and Germany and Europe were flooded by the classical fashion for which Winckelmann had given the first strong impulse. The churches became ancient temples, the mechanical arts strove after classical forms, and ladies affected the dress and manners of Greek women. The leaders of German poetry, Goethe and Schiller, both attained the summit of their art in the imitation of classical models." * Still the ground

* "German Literature," Vol. II. p. 230.

recovered from the Middle Age was never again entirely lost; and in spite of this classical prepossession, Goethe and Schiller, even in the last years of the century, vied with one another in the composition of romantic ballads, like the former's "Der Erlkönig," "Der Fischer," "Der Todtentanz," and "Der Zauberlehrling," and the latter's "Ritter Toggenburg," "Der Kampf mit dem Drachen," and "Der Gang nach dem Eisenhammer."

On comparing the works of a romantic temper produced in England and in Germany during the last century, one soon becomes aware that, though the original impulse was communicated from England, the continental movement had greater momentum. The *Gründlichkeit*, the depth and thoroughness of the German mind, impels it to base itself in the fine arts, as in politics and religion, on foundation principles; to construct for its practice a theoria, an *æsthetik*. In the later history of German romanticism, the mediæval revival in letters and art was carried out with a philosophic consistency into other domains of thought and made accessory to reactionary statecraft and theology, to Junkerism and Catholicism. Meanwhile, though the literary movement in Germany in the eighteenth century did not quite come to a head, it was more critical, learned, and conscious of its own purposes and methods than the kindred movement in England. The English mind, in the act of creation, works practically and instinctively. It seldom seeks to bring questions of taste or art under the domain of scientific laws. During the classical period it had accepted its standards of taste from France, and when it broke away from these, it did so upon impulse and gave either no reasons, or very superficial ones, for its new departure. The elegant dissertations of Hurd and Percy, and the Wartons, seem very dilettantish when set beside the imposing systems of æsthetics propounded by Kant, Fichte, and Schelling; or beside thorough-going *Abhandlungen* like the "Laocoön," the "Hamburgische Dramaturgie," Schiller's treatise "Ueber naive und sentimentalische Dichtung," or the analysis of Hamlet's character in "Wilhelm Meister." There was no criticism of this kind in England before Coleridge; no Shakspere criticism, in particular, to compare with the papers on that subject by Lessing, Herder, Gerstenberg, Lenz, Goethe, and many other Germans. The only eighteenth-century Englishman who would have been capable of such was Gray. He had the requisite taste and scholarship, but even he wanted the philosophic breadth and depth for a fundamental and *eingehend* treatment of underlying principles.

Yet even in this critical department, German literary historians credit England with the initiative. Hettner * mentions three English critics, in particular, as predecessors of Herder in awakening interest in popular poetry. These were Edward Young, the author of "Night Thoughts," whose "Conjectures on Original Composition" was published in 1759: Robert Wood, whose "Essay on the Original Genius and Writings of Homer" (1768) was translated into German, French, Spanish, and Italian; and Robert Lowth, Bishop of Oxford, who as Professor of Poetry at Oxford delivered there in 1753 his "Prælectiones de Sacra Poesi Hebræorum," translated into English

* "Literaturgeschichte," 3.3. 1. s. 30–31.

and German in 1793. The significance of Young's brilliant little essay, which was in form a letter addressed to the author of "Sir Charles Grandison," lay in its assertion of the superiority of genius to learning and of the right of genius to be free from rules and authorities. It was a sort of literary declaration of independence; and it asked, in substance, the question asked in Emerson's "Nature": "Why should not we also enjoy an original relation to the universe?" Pope had said, in his "Essay on Criticism," * "follow Nature," and in order to follow Nature, learn the rules and study the ancients, particularly Homer. "Nature and Homer were the same." Contrariwise, Young says: "The less we copy the renowned ancients, we shall resemble them the more. . . Learning . . . is a great lover of rules and boaster of famed examples . . . and sets rigid bounds to that liberty to which genius often owes its supreme glory. . . Born *originals*, how comes it to pass that we die *copies?* . . Let not great examples or authorities browbeat thy reason into too great a diffidence of thyself. . . While the true genius is crossing all public roads into fresh untrodden ground; he [the imitative writer], up to the knees in antiquity, is treading the sacred footsteps of great examples with the blind veneration of a bigot saluting the sacred toe." Young asserts that Shakspere is equal in greatness to the ancients: regrets that Pope did not employ blank verse in his translation of Homer, and calls Addison's "Cato" "a piece of statuary."

Robert Wood, who visited and described the ruins of Balbec and Palmyra, took his Iliad to the Troad and

* See *ante*, p. 48.

read it on the spot. He sailed in the track of Mene-
laus and the wandering Ulysses; and his acquaintance
with Eastern scenery and life helped to substitute a
fresher apprehension of Homer for the somewhat conventional conception that had prevailed through the
classical period. What most forcibly struck Herder
and Goethe in Wood's essay was the emphasis laid
upon the simple, unlettered, and even barbaric state
of society in the heroic age: and upon the primitive
and popular character (*Urspünglichkeit, Volksthüm-
lichkeit*) of the Homeric poems.* This view of
Homer, as essentially a minstrel or ballad-maker, has
been carried so far in Professor Newman's translations as to provoke remonstrance from Matthew
Arnold, who insists upon Homer's "nobility" and
"grand style." † But with whatever exaggeration it
may have latterly been held, it was wholesomely
corrective and stimulating when propounded in
1768.

Though the final arrival of German romanticism, in
its fullness, was postponed too late to modify the
English movement, before the latter had spent its first
strength, yet the prelude was heard in England and
found an echo there. In 1792 Walter Scott was a
young lawyer at Edinburgh and had just attained his
majority.

---

* "Our polite neighbors the French seem to be most offended at
certain pictures of primitive simplicity, so unlike those refined modes
of modern life in which they have taken the lead; and to this we may
partly impute the rough treatment which our poet received from
them."—*Essay on Homer* (Dublin Edition, 1776), p. 127.

† See Francis W. Newman's "Iliad" (1856) and Arnold's "Lectures
on Translating Homer" (1861).

" Romance who loves to nod and sing
With drowsy head and folded wing,
To *him* a painted paroquet
Had been—a most familiar bird—
Taught *him* his alphabet to say,
To lisp his very earliest word." *

He had lain from infancy "in the lap of legends old,"
and was already learned in the antiquities of the
Border.   For years he had been making his collection
of *memorabilia;* claymores, suits of mail, Jedburgh
axes, border horns, etc.   He had begun his annual
raids into Liddesdale, in search of ballads and folk
lore, and was filling notebooks with passages from
the Edda, records of old Scotch law-cases, copies
of early English poems, notes on the "Morte Dar-
thur," on the second sight, on fairies and witches;
extracts from Scottish chronicles, from the Books of
Adjournal, from Aubrey, and old Glanvil of superstitious memory; tables of the Mœso-Gothic, Anglo-
Saxon, and Runic alphabets and transcripts relating
to the history of the Stuarts.   In the autumn or early
winter of that year, a class of six or seven young men
was formed at Edinburgh for the study of German, and
Scott joined it.   In his own account of the matter he
says that interest in German literature was first
aroused in Scotland by a paper read before the Royal
Society of Edinburgh in April, 1788, by Henry Mackenzie, the "Addison of the North," and author of
that most sentimental of fictions, "The Man of Feeling."   "The literary persons of Edinburgh were then
first made aware of the existence of works of genius
in a language cognate with the English, and possessed

* " Romance," Edgar Poe.

of the same manly force of expression; they learned
at the same time that the taste which dictated the
German compositions was of a kind as nearly allied to
the English as their language; those who were from
their youth accustomed to admire Shakspere and
Milton became acquainted for the first time with a
race of poets who had the same lofty ambition to
spurn the flaming boundaries of the universe and
investigate the realms of Chaos and old Night; and
of dramatists who, disclaiming the pedantry of the
unities, sought, at the expense of occasional improbabilities and extravagance, to present life on the stage
in its scenes of wildest contrast, and in all its bound-
less variety of character. . . Their fictitious narratives, their ballad poetry, and other branches of their
literature which are particularly apt to bear the stamp
of the extravagant and the supernatural, began also to
occupy the attention of the British literati." Scott's
German studies were much assisted by Alexander
Frazer Tytler, whose version of Schiller's "Robbers"
was one of the earliest English translations from the
German theater.*

In the autumn of 1794 Miss Aikin, afterward Mrs.
Barbauld, entertained a party at Dugald Stewart's
by reading a translation of Bürger's ghastly ballad
"Lenore." The translation was by William Taylor
of Norwich; it had not yet been published, and Miss
Aikin read it from a manuscript copy. Scott was not
present, but his friend Mr. Cranstoun described the
performance to him; and he was so much impressed
by his description that he borrowed a volume of Bürger's poems from his young kinswoman by marriage,

* "Lockhart's Life of Scott," Vol. I. p. 163.

Mrs. Scott of Harden, a daughter of Count Brühl of
Martkirchen, formerly Saxon ambassador at London,
who had a Scotchwoman for his second wife, the
dowager Countess of Egremont.   Scott set to work in
1795 to make a translation of the ballad for himself,
and succeeded so well in pleasing his friends that he
had a few copies struck off for private circulation in
the spring of 1796.   In the autumn of the same year
he published his version under the title " William and
Helen," together with " The Chase," a translation of
Bürger's " Der Wilde Jäger."   The two poems made
a thin quarto volume.   It was printed at Edinburgh,
was anonymous, and was Walter Scott's first published
book.   Meanwhile Taylor had given his rendering to
the public in the March number of the *Monthly
Magazine,* introducing it with a notice of Bürger's
poems; and the very same year witnessed the appearance of three other translations, one by J. T. Stanley
(with copperplate engravings), one by Henry James
Pye, the poet laureate, and one by the Hon. William
Robert Spencer,—author of " Beth Gélert," " Too
Late I Stayed," etc.,—with designs by Lady Diana
Beauclerc.   (A copy of this last, says Allibone, in
folio, on vellum, sold at Christie's in 1804 for £25 4s.)
A sixth translation, by the Rev. James Beresford, who
had lived some time in Berlin, came out about 1800;
and Schlegel and Brandl unite in pronouncing this the
most faithful, if not the best, English version of the
ballad.*

---

* For full titles and descriptions of these translations, as well as for
the influence of Bürger's poems in England, see Alois Brandl: " Lenore in England," in " Charakteristiken," by Erich Schmidt (Berlin,
1886) ss. 244–48.   Taylor said in 1830 that no German poem had

The poem of which England had taken such manifold possession, under the varied titles "Lenore," "Leonore," "Leonora," "Lenora," "Ellenore," "Helen," etc., was indeed a noteworthy one. In the original, it remains Bürger's masterpiece, and in its various English dresses it gained perhaps as many graces as it lost. It was first printed at Göttingen in Boie's "Musen Almanach" in 1773. It was an uncanny tale of a soldier of Frederick the Great, who had perished in the Seven Years' War, and who came at midnight on a spectral steed to claim his lady-love and carry her off a thousand miles to the bridal bed. She mounts behind him and they ride through the phantasms of the night till, at cock-crow, they come to a churchyard. The charger vanishes in smoke, the lover's armor drops from him, green with the damps of the grave, revealing a skeleton within, and the maiden finds that her nuptial chamber

been so often translated: "eight different versions are lying on my table and I have read others." He claimed his to be the earliest, as written in 1790, though not printed till 1796. "Lenore" won at once the honors of parody—surest proof of popularity. Brandl mentions two—"Miss Kitty," Edinburgh, 1797, and "The Hussar of Magdeburg, or the Midnight Phaeton," Edinburgh, 1800, and quotes Mathias' satirical description of the piece ("Pursuits of Literature," 1794–97) as "diablerie tudesque" and a "'Blue Beard' story for the nursery." The bibliographies mention a new translation in 1846 by Julia M. Cameron, with illustrations by Maclise; and I find a notice in Allibone of "The Ballad of Lenore: a Variorum Monograph," 4to, containing thirty metrical versions in English, announced as about to be published at Philadelphia in 1866 by Charles Lukens. *Quære* whether this be the same as Henry Clay Lukens ("Erratic Enrico"), who published "Lean 'Nora" (Philadelphia, 1870; New York, 1878), a title suggestive of a humorous intention, but a book which I have not seen.

is the charnel vault, and her bridegroom is Death.
"This poem," says Scherer, "leaves on us, to some
degree, the impression of an unsolved mystery; all the
details are clear, but at the end we have to ask ourselves what has really happened; was it a dream of the
girl, a dream in which she died, or did the ghost really
appear and carry her away?" *   The story is man-
aged, indeed, with much of that subtle art which Coleridge used in "The Ancient Mariner" and "Christabel"; so that the boundary between the earthly and the
unearthly becomes indefinite, and the doubt continually
occurs whether we are listening to a veritable ghost-
story, or to some finer form of allegory.   "Lenore"
drew for its materials upon ballad motives common
to many literatures.   It will be sufficient to mention
"Sweet William's Ghost," as an English example of
the class.

Scott's friends assured him that his translation was
superior to Taylor's, and Taylor himself wrote to him:
"The ghost nowhere makes his appearance so well
as with you, or his exit so well as with Mr. Spencer."
But Lewis was right in preferring Taylor's version,
which has a wildness and quaintness not found in
Scott's more literal and more polished rendering, and
is wonderfully successful in catching the *Grobheit*, the
rude, rough manner of popular poetry.   A few stanzas
from each will illustrate the difference:

[From Scott's " William and Helen."]

" Dost fear? dost fear? The moon shines clear:—
Dost fear to ride with me ?
Hurrah! hurrah! the dead can ride "—
"O William, let them be!"

* History of German Literature," Vol. II. p. 123.

" See there! see there!   What yonder swings
    And creaks 'mid whistling rain ? "
" Gibbet and steel, the accursed wheel;
    A murd'rer in his chain.

" Halloa! Thou felon, follow here:
    To bridal bed we ride;
And thou shalt prance a fetter dance
    Before me and my bride."

And hurry! hurry! clash, clash, clash!
    The wasted form descends,*
And fleet as wind through hazel bush
    The wild career attends.*

Tramp, tramp! along the land they rode,
    Splash, splash! along the sea:
The scourge is red, the spur drops blood,
    The flashing pebbles flee.

[From Taylor's "Lenora."]

Look up, look up, an airy crewe
    In roundel dances reele.
The moone is bryghte and blue the night,
    May'st dimly see them wheel.†

" Come to, come to, ye ghostlie crewe,
    Come to and follow me.
And daunce for us the wedding daunce
    Wnen we in bed shall be."

And brush, brush, brush, the ghostlie crew
    Come wheeling o'er their heads,
All rustling like the withered leaves
    That wyde the whirlwind spreads.

* These are book phrases, not true ballad diction.
† *Cf.* The " Ancient Mariner ":

        " The feast is set, the guests are met,
            May'st hear the merry din."

> Halloo! halloo! away they goe
>   Unheeding wet or drye,
> And horse and rider snort and blowe,
>   And sparkling pebbles flye.
>
> And all that in the moonshyne lay
>   Behynde them fled afar;
> And backward scudded overhead
>   The skye and every star.
>
> Tramp, tramp across the land they speede,
>   Splash, splash across the sea:
> " Hurrah! the dead can ride apace,
>   Dost fear to ride with me ? "

It was this last stanza which fascinated Scott, as repeated from memory by Mr. Cranstoun; and he
retained it without much change in his version.
There is no mention of the sea in Bürger, whose
hero is killed in the battle of Prague and travels
only by land. But Taylor nationalized and individual-
ized the theme by making his William a knight of
Richard the Lion Heart's, who had fallen in Holy
Land. Scott followed him and made his a crusader
in the army of Frederic Barbarossa. Bürger's poem
was written in an eight-lined stanza, but Taylor and
Scott both chose the common English ballad verse,
with its folkloreish associations, as the best vehicle
for reproducing the grewsome substance of the story;
and Taylor gave an archaic cast to his diction, still
further to heighten the effect. Lewis considered his
version a masterpiece of translation, and, indeed,
"far superior, both in spirit and in harmony, to the
German." Taylor showed almost equal skill in his
rendering of Bürger's next most popular ballad, " Des
Pfarrer's Tochter von Taubenhain," first printed in

the *Monthly Magazine* for April, 1796, under the somewhat odd title of "The Lass of Fair Wone."

Taylor of Norwich did more than any man of his
generation, by his translations and critical papers in
the *Monthly Magazine* and *Monthly Review*, to spread a
knowledge of the new German literature in England.
When a lad of sixteen he had been sent to study at
Detmold, Westphalia, and had spent more than a year
(1781–82) in Germany, calling upon Goethe at Weimar,
with a letter of introduction, on his way home to
England. "When his acquaintance with this literature
began," wrote Lucy Aikin, "there was probably no
English translation of any German author but through
the medium of the French, and he is very likely to
have been the first Englishman of letters to read
Goethe, Wieland, Lessing, and Bürger in the originals." * Some years before the publication of his
"Lenora" he had printed for private distribution
translations of Lessing's "Nathan der Weise (1791)
and Goethe's "Iphigenie auf Tauris" (1793). In
1829–30 he gathered up his numerous contributions to
periodicals and put them together in a three-volume
"Historic Survey of German Poetry," which was
rather roughly, though not disrespectfully, handled by
Carlyle in the *Edinburgh Review*. Taylor's tastes were
one-sided, not to say eccentric; he had not kept up
with the later movement of German thought; his critical opinions were out of date, and his book was sadly
wanting in unity and a proper perspective. Carlyle
was especially scandalized by the slight space accorded

---

* "Memoir of Wm. Taylor of Norwich," by J. W. Robberds
(1843), Vol. II. p. 573.

to Goethe.* But Taylor's really brilliant talent in
translation, and his important service as an introducer
and interpreter of German poetry to his own country-
men, deserve always to be gratefully remembered.
"You have made me hunger and thirst after German
poetry," wrote Southey to him, February 24, 1799.†

The year 1796, then, marks the confluence of the
English and German romantic movements. It seems
a little strange that so healthy a genius as Walter
Scott should have made his *début* in an exhibition of
the horrible. Lockhart reports him, on the authority
of Sir Alexander Wood, as reading his "William and
Helen" over to that gentleman "in a very slow and
solemn tone," and then looking at the fire in silence
and presently exclaiming, "I wish to Heaven I could
get a skull and two crossbones." Whereupon Sir Alexander accompanied him to the house of John Bell,
surgeon, where the desired articles were obtained and
mounted upon the poet's bookcase. During the next
few years, Scott continued to make translations of
German ballads, romances, and chivalry dramas.
These remained for the present in manuscript; and
some of them, indeed, such as his versions of Babo's
"Otto von Wittelsbach" (1796–97) and Meier's "Wol-
fred von Dromberg" (1797) were never permitted
to see the light. His second publication (February,
1799) was a free translation of Goethe's tragedy, "Götz
von Berlichingen mit der Eisernen Hand." The original
was a most influential work in Germany. It had been
already twenty-six years before the public and had

---

* For Taylor's opinion of Carlyle's papers on Goethe in the *Foreign
Review*, see "Historic Survey," Vol. III. pp. 378–79.

† "Memoir of Taylor," Vol. I. p. 255.

produced countless imitations, with some of which Scott had been busy before he encountered this, the fountain head of the whole flood of *Ritterschauspiele.* * Götz was an historical character, a robber knight of Franconia in the fifteenth century, who had championed the rights of the free knights to carry on private warfare and had been put under the ban of the empire for engaging in feuds. "It would be difficult," wrote Carlyle, "to name two books which have exercised a deeper influence on the subsequent literature of Europe"—than "The Sorrows of Werther" and "Götz." "The fortune of 'Berlichingen with the Iron Hand,' though less sudden "—than Werther's—"was by no means less exalted. In his own country 'Götz,' though he now stands solitary and childless, became the parent of an innumerable progeny of chivalry plays, feudal delineations, and poetico-antiquarian performances; which, though long ago deceased, made noise enough in their day and generation; and with ourselves his influence has been perhaps still more remarkable. Sir Walter Scott's first literary enterprise was a translation of 'Götz von Berlichingen'; and if genius could be communicated, like instruction, we might call this work of Goethe's the prime cause of 'Marmion' and 'The Lady of the Lake,' with all that has since followed from the same creative hand. . . How far 'Götz von Berlichingen' actually affected Scott's literary destination, and whether with-

---

* Among the most notable of these was "Maler" (Friedrich) Müller's "Golo und Genoveva" (written 1781; published 1811); Count Törring's "Agnes Bernauerin" (1780); and Jacob Meyer's "Sturm von Borberg" (1778), and "Fust von Stromberg" (1782). Several of these were very successful on the stage.

out it the rhymed romances, and then the prose romances of the author of Waverley, would not have followed as they did, must remain a very obscure question; obscure and not important. Of the fact, however, there is no doubt, that these two tendencies, which may be named Götzism and Wertherism, of the former of which Scott was representative with us, have made and are still in some quarters making the tour of all Europe. In Germany, too, there was this affectionate, half-regretful looking-back into the past: Germany had its buff-belted, watch-tower period in literature, and had even got done with it before Scott began." *

Elsewhere Carlyle protests against the common English notion that German literature dwells "with peculiar complacency among wizards and ruined towers, with mailed knights, secret tribunals, monks, specters, and banditti. . . If any man will insist on taking Heinse's ' Ardinghello ' and Miller's ' Siegwart,' the works of Veit Weber the Younger, and above all the everlasting Kotzebue,† as his specimens of German literature, he may establish many things.   Black Forests and the glories of Lubberland, sensuality and horror, the specter nun and the charmed moonshine shall not be wanting.   Boisterous outlaws also, with huge whiskers and the most cat-o'-mountain aspect; tear-stained sentimentalists, the grimmest man-haters,

* " Essay on Walter Scott."

† Kotzebue's "The Stranger " ("Menschenhass und Reue") still keeps the English stage. Sheridan's " Pizarro "—a version of Kotzebue's " Spaniards in Peru "—was long a favorite; and " Monk " Lewis made another translation of the same in 1799, entitled "Rolla," which, however, was never acted.

ghosts and the like suspicious characters will be found in abundance. We are little read in this bowl-and-dagger department; but we do understand it to have been at one time rather diligently cultivated; though at present it seems to be mostly relinquished. . . What should we think of a German critic that selected his specimens of British literature from 'The Castle Specter,' Mr. Lewis' 'Monk,' or the 'Mysteries of Udolpho,' and 'Frankenstein, or the Modern Prometheus'? . . . 'Faust,' for instance, passes with many of us for a mere tale of sorcery and art magic. It would scarcely be more unwise to consider 'Hamlet' as depending for its main interest on the ghost that walks in it." *

Now for the works here named, as for the whole class of melodramas and melodramatic romances which swarmed in Germany during the last quarter of the century and made their way into English theaters and circulating libraries, in the shape of translations, adaptations, imitations, two plays were remotely responsible: Goethe's "Götz" (1773), with its robber knights, secret tribunal, imperialist troopers, gypsies, and insurgent peasants; and Schiller's "Die Räuber" (1781), with its still more violent situations and more formidable *dramatis personæ.* True, this spawn of the *Sturm- und Drangzeit,* with its dealings in banditti, monks, inquisitors, confessionals, torture and poison, dungeon and rack, the haunted tower, the yelling ghost, and the solitary cell, had been anticipated in England by Walpole's "Castle of Otranto" and "Mysterious Mother"; but this slender native stream was now quite overwhelmed in the turbid flood of

* "State of German Literature."

sensational matter from the Black Forest and the
Rhine.   Mrs. Radcliffe herself had drunk from foreign
sources.   In 1794 she made the tour of the Rhine and
published a narrative of her journey in the year following.   The knightly river had not yet become hackneyed; Brentano had not invented nor Heine sung
the seductive charms of the Lürlei; nor Byron mused
upon "the castled crag of Drachenfels."   The
French armies were not far off, and there were
alarums and excursions all along the border.   But the
fair traveler paused upon many a spot already sacred
to legend and song: the Mouse Tower and Roland-
seck and the Seven Mountains.   She noted the peasants, in their picturesque costumes, carrying baskets
of soil to the steep vineyard terraces: the ruined keeps
of robber barons on the heights, and the dark sweep
of the romantic valleys, bringing in their tributary
streams from north and south.

Lockhart says that Scott's translation of "Götz"
should have been published ten years sooner to have
had its full effect.   For the English public had already
become sated with the melodramas and romances of
Kotzebue and the other German *Kraftmänner;* and
the clever parody of "The Robbers," under the title
of "The Rovers," which Canning and Ellis had published in the *Anti-Jacobin,* had covered the entire
species with ridicule.   The vogue of this class of
fiction, the chivalry romance, the feudal drama, the
robber play and robber novel, the monkish tale and
the ghost story (*Ritterstück, Ritterroman, Räuberstück,
Räuberroman, Klostergeschichte, Gespensterlied*) both in
Germany and England, satisfied, however crudely, the
longing of the time for freedom, adventure, strong

action, and emotion. As Lowell said of the transcendental movement in New England, it was a breaking of windows to get at the fresh air. Laughable as many of them seem to-day, with their improbable plots and exaggerated characters, they met a need which had not been met either by the rationalizing wits of the Augustan age or by the romanticizing poets who followed them with their elegiac refinement, and their unimpassioned strain of reflection and description. They appeared, for the moment, to be the new avatar of the tragic muse whereof Akenside and Collins and Warton had prophesied, the answer to their demand for something wild and primitive, for the return into poetry of the *Naturton*, and the long-absent power of exciting the tragic emotions, pity and terror. This spirit infected not merely the department of the chivalry play and the Gothic romance, but prose fiction in general. It is responsible for morbid and fantastic creations like Beckford's "Vathek," Godwin's "St. Leon" and "Caleb Williams," Mrs. Shelley's "Frankenstein," Shelley's "Zastrozzi" and "St. Irvine the Rosicrucian," and the American Charles Brockden Brown's "Ormond" and "Wieland," forerunners of Hawthorne and Poe; tales of sleep-walkers and ventriloquists, of persons who are in pursuit of the *elixir vitæ*, or who have committed the unpardonable sin, or who manufacture monsters in their laboratories, or who walk about in the Halls of Eblis, carrying their burning hearts in their hands.

Lockhart, however, denies that "Götz von Berlichingen" had anything in common with the absurdities which Canning made fun of in the *Anti-Jacobin*. He says that it was a "broad, bold, free, and most picturesque delineation of real characters, manners, and events." He thinks that in the robber barons of the Rhine, with "their forays upon each other's domains, the besieged castles, the plundered herds, the captive knights, the brow-beaten bishop and the baffled liege-lord," Scott found a likeness to the old life of the Scotch border, with its moss-troopers, cattle raids, and private warfare; and that, as Percy's "Reliques" prompted the "Minstrelsy of the Scottish Border," so "Götz" prompted the "Lay of the Last Minstrel" and "Marmion." He quotes the passage from "Götz" where Selbiss is borne in, wounded, by two troopers who ascend a watch-tower and describe to their leader the further progress of the battle; and he asks "who does not recognize in Goethe's drama the true original of the death scene in 'Marmion' and the storm in 'Ivanhoe'?"

A singular figure now comes upon our stage, Matthew Gregory Lewis, commonly nicknamed "Monk" Lewis, from the title of his famous romance. It is a part of the irony of things that so robust a muse as Walter Scott's should have been nursed in infancy by a little creature like Lewis. His "Monk" had been published in 1795, when the author was only twenty. In 1798 Scott's friend William Erskine met Lewis in London. The latter was collecting materials for his "Tales of Wonder," and when Erskine showed him Scott's "William and Helen" and "The Wild Huntsman," and told him that he had other things of the kind in manuscript, Lewis begged that Scott would contribute to his collection. Erskine accordingly put him in communication with Scott, who felt highly flattered by the Monk's request, and wrote to him that

his ballads were quite at his service. Lewis replied,
thanking him for the offer. "A ghost or a witch," he
wrote, "is a *sine qua non* ingredient in all the dishes
of which I mean to compose my hobgoblin repast."
Later in the same year Lewis came to Edinburgh and
was introduced to Scott, who found him an odd contrast to the grewsome horrors of his books, being a
cheerful, foppish, round-faced little man, a follower of
fashion and an assiduous tuft-hunter. "Mat had
queerish eyes," writes his *protégé:* "they projected
like those of some insects, and were flattish on the
orbit. His person was extremely small and boyish—
he was indeed the least man I ever saw, to be strictly
well and neatly made. . . This boyishness went
through life with him. He was a child and a spoiled
child, but a child of high imagination; and so he wasted
himself on ghost stories and German romances. He
had the finest ear for rhythm I ever met with—finer
than Byron's."

Byron, by the way, had always a kindly feeling for
Lewis, though he laughed at him in "English Bards
and Scotch Reviewers":

> "O wonder-working Lewis, Monk or Bard,
> Who fain would'st make Parnassus a churchyard ;
> Lo ! wreaths of yew, not laurel, bind thy brow ;
> Thy muse a sprite, Apollo's sexton thou ;
> Whether on ancient tombs thou tak'st thy stand,
> By gibbering spectres hailed, thy kindred band,
> Or tracest chaste descriptions on thy page,
> To please the females of our modest age—
> All hail, M. P.,* from whose infernal brain
> Thin-sheeted phantoms glide, a grisly train ;

* Lewis sat in Parliament for Hindon, Wilts, succeeding Beckford
of "Vathek" and Fonthill Abbey fame.

> At whose command grim women throng in crowds,
> And kings of fire, of water and of clouds,
> With ' small gray men,' wild yagers and what not,
> To crown with honor thee and Walter Scott ! "

In 1816, while on his way to Italy, Lewis sojourned for a space with Byron and Shelley in their Swiss retreat and set the whole company composing goblin stories. The most remarkable outcome of this queer symposium was Mrs. Shelley's abnormal romance, "Frankenstein." The signatures of Byron and Shelley are affixed, as witnesses, to a codicil to Lewis' will, which he drew at this time and dated at Maison Diodati, Geneva; a somewhat rhetorical document in which he provided for the protection of the slaves on his Jamaica plantations. It was two years after this, and on his return voyage from a visit to these West Indian estates, that Lewis died of yellow fever and was buried at sea. Byron made this note of it in his diary:

> " ' I'd give the lands of Deloraine
>   Dark Musgrave were alive again,'

that is,

> " I would give many a sugar cane
>   Monk Lewis were alive again."

Scott's modesty led him to depreciate his own verses as compared with Lewis', some of which he recited to Ballantyne, in 1799, speaking of their author, says Lockhart, "with rapture." But however fine an ear for rhythm Lewis may have had, his verse is for the most part execrable; and his jaunty, jigging anapæsts and pragmatic manner are ludicrously out of keeping with the horrors of his tale, increasing the air of bathos which distinguishes his poetry:

> " A toad still alive in the liquor she threw,
>   And loud shrieked the toad as in pieces it flew:
>   And ever, the cauldron as over she bent,
>   She muttered strange words of mysterious intent : "

or this from the same ballad: *

> " Wild laughing, the Fiend caught the hand from the floor,
>   Releasing the babe, kissed the wound, drank the gore ;
>   A little jet ring from her finger then drew,
>   Thrice shrieked a loud shriek and was borne from their view."

Lewis would appear to have inherited his romantic turn from his mother, a sentimental little dame whose youthful looks caused her often to be taken for Mat's sister, and whose reading was chiefly confined to novels. The poor lady was something of a blue-stocking and aspired, herself, to literary honors. Lewis' devotion to her is very charming, and the elder-brotherly tone of his letters to her highly amusing. But he had a dislike of "female authorship"; and the rumor having reached his ear that his mother had written a novel and a tragedy and was preparing to print them, he wrote to her in alarm, begging her to stay her hand. "I hold that a woman has no business to be a public character, and that, in proportion as she acquires notoriety, she loses delicacy. I always consider a female author as a sort of half-man." He was also, quite properly, shocked at some gossip which attributed " The Monk," to his mother instead of to his mother's son.

We read in the "Life and Correspondence of

* " The Grim White Woman," in " Tales of Wonder."

Matthew Gregory Lewis" (2 vols., London, 1839),
that one of Mrs. Lewis' favorite books was "Glanvil
on Witches." Glanvil was the seventeenth-century
writer whose "Vanity of Dogmatizing," * and "Sad-
duceismus Triumphatus" rebuked the doubter and
furnished arguments for Cotton Mather's "Wonders
of the Invisible World" (1693), an apology for
his share in the Salem witchcraft trials; and whose
description of a ghostly drum, that was heard to
beat every night in a Wiltshire country house, gave
Addison the hint for his comedy of "The Drummer."
Young Lewis gloated with a pleasing horror over
Glanvil's pages and the wonderful copperplates which
embellished them; particularly the one which represents the devil beating his airy tympanum over Mr.
Mompesson's house. In the ancient mansion of Stan-
stead Hall, belonging to a kinsman of his father,
where the boy spent a part of his childhood, there was
a haunted chamber known as the cedar room. "In
maturer years," says his biographer, "Lewis has frequently been heard to declare that at night, when he
was conducted past that gloomy chamber, on the way
to his dormitory, he would cast a glance of terror over
his shoulder, expecting to see the huge and strangely
carved folding doors fly open and disclose some of
those fearful shapes that afterward resolved themselves
into the ghastly machinery of his works."

Lewis' first and most celebrated publication was
"Ambrosio, or the Monk" (1795), a three-volume
romance of the Gothic type, and a lineal descendant
of Walpole and Mrs. Radcliffe. He began it at Oxford

* Matthew Arnold's lovely "Scholar Gypsy" was suggested by
a passage in this.

in 1792, describing it in a letter to his mother as "a romance in the style of 'The Castle of Otranto.'" But in the summer of the same year he went to Germany and took up his residence at Weimar, where he was introduced to Goethe and made eager acquaintance with the bizarre productions of the *Sturm- und Drang-periode.* For years Lewis was one of the most active intermediaries between the German purveyors of the terrible and the English literary market. He fed the stage with melodramas and operas, and stuffed the closet reader with ballads and prose romances.* Meanwhile, being at The Hague in the summer of 1794, he resumed and finished his "Monk," in ten weeks. "I was induced to go on with it," he wrote to his mother, "by reading the 'Mysteries of Udolpho,' which is, in my opinion, one of the most interesting books that has ever been published. . . When you read it, tell me whether you think there is any resemblance between the character given of Montoni . . . and my own. I confess that it struck me." This innocent vanity of fancying a likeness between Anne Radcliffe's dark-browed villain and his own cherubic

* The following is a list of his principal translations: "The Minister" (1797), from Schiller's "Kabale und Liebe"; played at Covent Garden in 1803, as "The Harper's Daughter." "Rolla" (1799), from Kotzebue's "Spaniards in Peru." "Adelmorn, or the Outlaw" (1800), played at Drury Lane, 1801. "Tales of Terror" (1801) and "Tales of Wonder" (1801). (There seems to be some doubt as to the existence of the alleged Kelso editions of these in 1799 and 1800, respectively. See article on Lewis in the "Dict. Nat. Biog.") "The Bravo of Venice" (1804), a prose romance, dramatized and played at Covent Garden, as "Rugantino," in 1805. "Feudal Tyrants" (1807), a four-volume romance. "Romantic Tales" (1808), 4 vols. from German and French.

personality recalls Scott's story about the picture of
Lewis, by Saunders, which was handed round at
Dalkeith House.   "The artist had ingeniously flung a
dark folding-mantle around the form, under which was
half-hid a dagger, a dark lantern, or some cut-throat
appurtenance; with all this, the features were preserved and ennobled.   It passed from hand to hand
into that of Henry, Duke of Buccleuch, who, hearing
the general voice affirm that it was very like, said
aloud, ' Like Mat Lewis!   Why, that picture's like a
man.'"   "The Monk" used, and abused, the now
familiar apparatus of Gothic romance.   It had Spanish grandees, heroines of dazzling beauty, bravoes
and forest banditti, foolish duennas and gabbling
domestics, monks, nuns, inquisitors, magic mirrors,
enchanted wands, midnight incantations, sorcerers,
ghosts, demons; haunted chambers, wainscoated in
dark oak; moonlit castles with ruined towers and
ivied battlements, whose galleries rang with the
shrieks and blasphemies of guilty spirits, and from
whose portals issued, when the castle clock tolled
one, the specter of a bleeding nun, with dagger and
lamp in hand.   There were poisonings, stabbings, and
ministrations of sleeping potions; beauties who
masqueraded as pages, and pages who masqueraded
as wandering harpers; secret springs that gave
admittance to winding stairs leading down into the
charnel vaults of convents, where erring sisters were
immured by cruel prioresses and fed on bread and
water among the loathsome relics of the dead.

With all this, "The Monk" is a not wholly contemptible work.   There is a certain narrative power
about it which puts it much above the level of "The

Castle of Otranto." And though it partakes of the stilted dialogue and false conception of character that abound in Mrs. Radcliffe's romances, it has neither the excess of scenery nor of sentiment which distinguishes that very prolix narrator. There is nothing strictly mediæval about it. The knight in armor cuts no figure and the historical period is not precisely indicated. But the ecclesiastical features lend it a semblance of mediævalism; and one is reminded, though but faintly, by the imprisonment of the offending sister in the sepulcher of the convent, of the scene in "Marmion" where Constance is immured in the vaults of Lindisfarne—a frank anachronism, of course, on Scott's part, since Lindisfarne had been in ruins centuries before the battle of Flodden. The motto from Horace on the title page of "The Monk" sums up its contents, and indeed the contents of most of its author's writings, prose and verse—

> " Somnia, terrores magicos, miracula, sagas,
> Nocturnos lemures portentaque.

The hero Ambrosio is the abbot of St. Francis' Capuchin monastery in Madrid; a man of rigid austerity, whose spiritual pride makes him an easy prey to the temptations of a female demon, who leads him by degrees through a series of crimes, including incest and parricide, until he finally sells his soul to the devil to escape from the dungeons of the Inquisition and the *auto da fe*, subscribing the agreement, in approved fashion, upon a parchment scroll with an iron pen dipped in blood from his own veins. The fiend, who enters with thunder and lightning, over whose shoulders "waved two enormous sable wings," and whose hair "was supplied by living snakes," then snatches up his victim and soars with him to a peak of the Sierra Morena, where in a Salvator Rosa landscape of torrents, cliffs, caverns, and pine forests, by the light of an opera moon, and to the sound of the night wind sighing hoarsely and "the shrill cry of mountain eagles," he drops him over a precipice and makes an end of him.

A passage from the episode of Agnes de Medina, the incarcerated nun, will illustrate Lewis' wonder-working arts: "A faint glimmering of light which strained through the bars permitted me to distinguish the surrounding horrors. I was oppressed by a noisome, suffocating smell; and perceiving that the grated door was unfastened, I thought that I might possibly effect my escape. As I raised myself with this design, my hand rested upon something soft. I grasped it and advanced it toward the light. Almighty God! what was my disgust! my consternation! In spite of its putridity and the worms which preyed upon it, I perceived a corrupted human head, and recognized the features of a nun who had died some months before. . . A sepulchral lamp was suspended from the roof by an iron chain and shed a gloomy light through the dungeon. Emblems of death were seen on every side; skulls, shoulder-blades, thigh-bones and other relics of mortality were scattered upon the dewy ground. . . As I shrunk from the cutting wind which howled through my subterraneous dwelling, the change seemed so striking, so abrupt, that I doubted its reality. . . Sometimes I felt the bloated toad, hideous and pampered with the poisonous vapors of the dungeon,

dragging his loathsome length along my bosom; sometimes the quick, cold lizard roused me, leaving his
slimy track upon my face, and entangling itself in the
tresses of my wild and matted hair. Often have I, at
waking, found my fingers ringed with the long worms
which bred in the corrupted flesh of my infant."

" The Monk " won for its author an immediate and
wide celebrity, assisted no doubt by the outcry against
its immorality. Lewis tried to defend himself by
pleading that the outline and moral of his story were
borrowed from " The History of Santon Barsisa " in
the *Guardian* (No. 148). But the voluptuous nature
of some of the descriptions induced the Attorney
General to enjoin the sale of the book, and Lewis
bowed to public opinion so far as to suppress the objectionable passages in later editions. Lewis' melodrama "The Castle Specter" was first performed
December 14, 1797, at Drury Lane, ran sixty nights
and "continued popular as an acting play," says the
biographer, "up to a very recent period." * This is
strong testimony to the contemporary appetite for
nightmare, for the play is a trumpery affair. Sheridan,
who had a poor opinion of it, advised the dramatist to
keep the specter out of the last scene. " It had been
said," explains Lewis in his preface, "that if Mr.
Sheridan had not advised me to content myself with a
single specter, I meant to have exhibited a whole
regiment of ghosts." The prologue, spoken by
Mr. Wroughton, invokes " the fair enchantress, Romance ":

" The moonstruck child of genius and of woe,"

* The printed play had reached its eleventh edition in 1803.

who

> "—Loathes the sun or blazing taper's light ;
> The moonbeamed landscape and tempestuous night
> Alone she loves ; and oft with glimmering lamp
> Near graves new opened, or midst dungeons damp,
> Drear forests, ruined aisles and haunted towers,
> Forlorn she roves and raves away the hours."

The scene of the drama is Conway Castle in Wales, where abides Earl Osmond, a feudal tyrant of the "Otranto" type, who is planning an incestuous marriage with his own niece, concerning which he thus soliloquizes: "What though she prefer a basilisk's kiss to mine? Because my short-lived joy may cause her eternal sorrow, shall I reject those pleasures sought so long, desired so earnestly? That will I not, by Heaven! Mine she is, and mine she shall be, though Reginald's bleeding ghost flit before me and thunder in my ear 'Hold! Hold!'—Peace, stormy heart, she comes." Reginald's ghost does not flit, because Reginald is still in the flesh, though not in very much flesh. He is Osmond's brother and Angela's father, and the wicked Earl thought that he had murdered him. It turns out, however, that, though left for dead, he has recovered of his hurts and has been kept unbeknown in solitary confinement, in a dungeon vault under the castle, for the somewhat long period of sixteen years. He is discovered in Act V., "emaciated, in coarse garments, his hair hanging wildly about his face, and a chain bound round his body."

Reginald's ghost does not flit, but Evelina's does. Evelina is Reginald's murdered wife, and her specter in "white and flowing garments, spotted with blood," appears to Angela in the oratory communicating with the cedar room, which is furnished with an antique bedstead and the portrait of a lady on a sliding panel. In truth, the castle is uncommonly well supplied with apparitions. Earl Herbert rides around it every night on a white horse; Lady Bertha haunts the west pinnacle of the chapel tower; and Lord Hildebrand may be seen any midnight in the great hall, playing football with his own head. So says Motley the jester, who affords the comedy element of the play, with the help of a fat friar who guzzles sack and stuffs venison pasties, and a soubrette after the " Otranto " pattern.

A few poems were scattered through the pages of "The Monk," including a ballad from the Danish, and another from the Spanish. But the most famous of these was "Alonzo the Brave and the Fair Imogene," original with Lewis, though evidently suggested by " Lenore." It tells how a lover who had gone to Palestine presented himself at the bridal feast of his faithless fair one, just as the clock struck one and the lights burned blue. At the request of the company, the strange knight raises his visor and discloses a skeleton head:

> " All present then uttered a terrified shout ;
>   All turned with disgust from the scene ;
>   The worms they crept in and the worms they crept out,
>   And sported his eyes and his temples about
>   While the spectre addressed Imogene."

He winds his arms about her and sinks with his prey through the yawning ground; and

> " At midnight four times in each year does her sprite,
>   When mortals in slumber are bound,

> Arrayed in her bridal apparel of white,
> Appear in the hall with a skeleton knight
>   And shriek as he whirls her around.

> " While they drink out of skulls newly torn from the grave,
>   Dancing round them pale spectres are seen.
> Their liquor is blood, and this horrible stave
> They howl : ' To the health of Alonzo the Brave
>   And his consort, the Fair Imogene ! ' "

Lewis' own contributions to his " Tales of Terror " and
" Tales of Wonder," were of this same raw-head and
bloody-bones variety.   His imagination rioted in
physical horrors.   There are demons who gnash with
iron fangs and brandish gore-fed scorpions; maidens
are carried off by the Winter King, the Water King,
the Cloud King, and the Sprite of the Glen; they are
poisoned or otherwise done to death, and their wraiths
revisit their guilty lovers in their shrouds at midnight's
dark hour and imprint clammy kisses upon them with
livid lips; gray friars and black canons abound; requiem
and death knell sound through the gloom of the
cloisters; echo roars through high Gothic arches;
the anchorite mutters in his mossy cell; tapers burn
dim, torches cast a red glare on vaulted roofs; the
night wind blows through dark aisles; the owl hoots
in the turret, and dying groans are heard in the lonely
house upon the heath, where the black and tattered
arras molders on the wall.

The " Tales of Wonder " included translations by
Lewis from Goethe's " Fisher " and " Erl-King," and
from German versions of Runic ballads in Herder's
" Stimmen der Völker."   Scott's " Wild Huntsman,"
from Bürger, was here reprinted, and he contributed,
in addition, " Frederick and Alice," paraphrased from

a romance-fragment in Goethe's opera " Claudina von
Villa Bella "; and three striking ballads of his own,
" The Fire King," a story of the Crusades, and " Glen-
finlas " and " The Eve of St. John," Scottish tales of
" gramarye." There were two or three old English
ballads in the collection, such as " Clerk Colvin" and
" Tam Lin "; a contribution from George Colman,
Jr., the dramatist, and one from Scott's eccentric
friend Leyden; and the volume concluded with Taylor's " Lenora." *

It is comical to read that the Monk gave Scott lectures in the art of versification and corrected the
Scotticisms and false rhymes in his translations from
Bürger; and that Scott respectfully deferred to his
advice. For nothing can be in finer contrast with
Lewis' penny dreadful, than the martial ring of the
verse and the manly vigor of the style in Scott's part
of the book. This is how Lewis writes anapæsts,
e. g.:

> " All shrouded she was in the garb of the tomb,
> Her lips they were livid, her face it was wan ;
> A death the most horrid had rifled her bloom
> And each charm of beauty was faded and gone."

And this is how Scott writes them:

> " He clenched his set teeth and his gauntleted hand,
> He stretched with one buffet that page on the sand. . .
> For down came the Templars like Cedron in flood,
> And dyed their long lances in Saracen blood."

It is no more possible to take Monk Lewis seriously
than to take Horace Walpole seriously. They are

---

* The " Tales of Terror," and " Tales of Wonder " are reprinted in
a single volume of " Morley's Universal Library," 1887.

both like children telling ghost-stories in the dark and trying to make themselves shudder. Lewis was even frivolous enough to compose parodies on his own ballads. A number of these *facetiæ*—"The Mud King," "Giles Jollup the Grave and Brown Sally Green," etc.—diversify his "Tales of Wonder."

Scott soon found better work for his hands to do than translating German ballads and melodramas; but in later years he occasionally went back to these early sources of romantic inspiration. Thus his poem "The Noble Moringer" was taken from a "Sammlung Deutscher Volkslieder" published at Berlin in 1807 by Busching and Von der Hagen. In 1799 he had made a *rifacimento* of a melodrama entitled "Der Heilige Vehme" in Veit Weber's "Sagen der Vorzeit." This he found among his papers thirty years after (1829) and printed in "The Keepsake," under the title of "The House of Aspen." Its most telling feature is the description of the Vehm-Gericht or Secret Tribunal, but it has little importance. In his "Historic Survey," Taylor said that "Götz von Ber-lichingen" was "translated into English in 1799 at Edinburgh, by Wm. Scott, Advocate; no doubt the same person who, under the poetical but assumed name of Walter, has since become the most extensively popular of the British writers"! This amazing state-ment is explained by a blunder on the title-page of Scott's "Götz," where the translator's name is given as *William* Scott. But it led to a slightly acrimonious correspondence between Sir Walter and the Norwich reviewer.*

The tide of German romance had begun to ebb

* See "Memoir of Wm. Taylor," Vol. II. pp. 533-38.

before the close of the century. It rose again a few years later, and left perhaps more lasting tokens this second time; but the ripple-marks of its first invasion are still discernible in English poetry and prose. Southey was clearly in error when he wrote to Taylor, September 5, 1798: "Coleridge's ballad, 'The Ancient Mariner' is, I think, the clumsiest attempt at German sublimity I ever saw.*" The "Mariner" is not in the least German, and when he wrote it, Coleridge had not been in Germany and did not know the language. He had read "Die Räuber," to be sure, some years before in Tytler's translation. He was at Cambridge at the time, and one night in winter, on leaving the room of a college friend, carelessly picked up and took away with him a copy of the tragedy, the very name of which he had never heard before. "A winter midnight, the wind high and 'The Robbers' for the first time. The readers of Schiller will conceive what I felt." He recorded, in the sonnet "To Schiller" (written December, 1794, or January, 1795), the terrific impression left upon his imagination by

> —" The famished father's cry
> From the dark dungeon of the tower time-rent,"

and wished that he might behold the bard himself, wandering at eve—

> " Beneath some vast old tempest-swinging wood."

Coleridge was destined to make the standard translation of "Wallenstein"; and there are motives borrowed from "The Robbers" and "The Ghost-Seer"

* " Memoir of Taylor," Vol. I. p. 223

ın his own very rubbishy dramas, "Zapolya"—of which Scott made some use in "Peveril of the Peak"—and "Osorio" (1797). The latter was rewritten as "Remorse," put on at Drury Lane January 23, 1813, and ran twenty nights. It had been rejected by Sheridan, who expressed a very proper contempt for it as an acting play. The Rev. W. L. Bowles and Byron, who had read it in manuscript and strangely overvalued it, both made interest with the manager to have it tried on the stage. "Remorse" also took some hints from Lewis' "Monk."

But Coleridge came in time to hold in low esteem, if not precisely "The Robbers" itself, yet that school of German melodrama of which it was the grand exemplar. In the twenty-third chapter of the "Biographia Literaria" (1817) he reviewed with severity the Rev. Charles Robert Maturin's tragedy "Bertram, or the Castle of St. Aldobrand," * and incidentally gave the genesis of that whole theatric species "which it has been the fashion, of late years, at once to abuse and to enjoy under the name of the German Drama. Of this latter Schiller's 'Robbers' was the earliest specimen, the first-fruits of his youth. . . Only as *such* did the maturer judgment of the author tolerate the play." Coleridge avows that "The Robbers" and its countless imitations were due to the popularity

---

* This was one of the latest successes of the kind. It was played at Drury Lane in 1816 for twenty-two nights, bringing the author £1000, and the printed play reached the seventh edition within the year. Among Maturin's other works were "The Fatal Revenge" (1807), "Manuel" (Drury Lane, 1817) "Fredolfo" (Covent Garden, 1817), and his once famous romance, "Melmoth the Wanderer" (1820), see *ante*, p. 249.

in Germany of the translations of Young's "Night Thoughts,' Hervey's "Meditations," and Richardson's "Clarissa Harlowe." "Add the ruined castles, the dungeons, the trap-doors, the skeletons, the flesh-and-blood ghosts, and the perpetual moonshine of a modern author * (themselves the literary brood of the 'Castle of Otranto,' the translations of which, with the imitations and improvements aforesaid, were about that time beginning to make as much noise in Germany as their originals were making in England), and, as the compound of these ingredients duly mixed, you will recognize the so-called *German* Drama," which "is English in its origin, English in its materials, and English by readoption; and till we can prove that Kotzebue, or any of the whole breed of Kotzebues, whether dramatists or romantic writers or writers of romantic dramas, were ever admitted to any other shelf in the libraries of well-educated Germans than were occupied by their originals . . . in their mother country, we should submit to carry our own brat on our own shoulders."

Germany, rather than Italy or Spain, became under these influences for a time the favored country of romance. English tale-writers chose its forests and dismantled castles as the scenes of their stories of brigandage and assassination. One of the best of a bad class of fictions, *e. g.*, was Harriet Lee's "The German's Tale: Kruitzner," in the series of "Canterbury Tales" written in conjunction with her sister Sophia (1797–1805). Byron read it when he was fourteen, was profoundly impressed by it, and made it the basis of "Werner," the only drama of his which

* Mrs. Radcliffe.

had any stage success. "Kruitzner" is conceived with some power, but monotonously and ponderously written. The historic period is the close of the Thirty Years' War. It does not depend mainly for its effect upon the time-honored "Gothic" machinery, though it makes a moderate use of the sliding panel and secret passage once again.

We are come to the gate of the new century, to the date of the "Lyrical Ballads" (1798) and within sight of the Waverley novels. Looking back over the years elapsed since Thomson put forth his "Winter," in 1726, we ask ourselves what the romantic movement in England had done for literature; if indeed that deserves to be called a "movement" which had no leader, no programme, no organ, no theory of art, and very little coherence. True, as we have learned from the critical writings of the time, the movement, such as it was, was not all unconscious of its own aims and directions. The phrase "School of Warton" implies a certain solidarity, and there was much interchange of views and some personal contact between men who were in literary sympathy; some skirmishing, too, between opposing camps. Gray, Walpole, and Mason constitute a group, encouraging each other's studies in their correspondence and occasional meetings. Shenstone was interested in Percy's ballad collections, and Gray in Warton's "History of English Poetry." Akenside read Dyer's "Fleece," and Gray read Beattie's "Minstrel" in MS. The Wartons were friends of Collins; Collins a friend and neighbor of Thomson; and Thomson a frequent visitor at Hagley and the Leasowes. Chatterton sought to put Rowley under Walpole's protection, and had his verses examined by Mason and Gray. Still, upon the whole, the English romanticists had little community; they worked individually and were scattered and isolated as to their residence, occupations, and social affiliations. It does not appear that Gray ever met Collins, or the Wartons, or Shenstone or Akenside; nor that MacPherson, Clara Reeve, Mrs. Radcliffe, and Chatterton ever saw each other or any of those first mentioned. There was none of that united purpose and that eager partisanship which distinguished the Parisian *cénacle* whose history has been told by Gautier, or that *Romantische Schule* whose members have been so brilliantly sketched by Heine.

But call it a movement, or simply a drift, a trend; what had it done for literature? In the way of stimulus and preparation, a good deal. It had relaxed the classical bandages, widened the range of sympathy, roused a curiosity as to novel and diverse forms of art, and brought the literary mind into a receptive, expectant attitude favorable to original creative activity. There never was a generation more romantic in temper than that which stepped upon the stage at the close of the eighteenth century: a generation fed upon "Ossian" and Rousseau and "The Sorrows of Werther" and Percy's "Reliques" and Mrs. Radcliffe's romances. Again, in the department of literary and antiquarian scholarship much had been accomplished. Books like Tyrwhitt's "Chaucer" and Warton's "History of English Poetry" had a real importance, while the collection and preservation of old English poetry, before it was too late, by scholars like Percy, Ritson, Ellis, and others was a pious labor.

But if we inquire what positive additions had been

made to the modern literature of England, the reply
is disappointing.   No one will maintain that the
Rowley poems, ' Caractacus," " The Monk," " The
Grave of King Arthur," " The Friar of Orders Gray,"
" The Castle of Otranto," and " The Mysteries of
Udolpho " are things of permanent value: or even
that "The Bard," " The Castle of Indolence," and
the " Poems of Ossian " take rank with the work done
in the same spirit by Coleridge, Scott, Keats, Rossetti,
and William Morris.   The two leading British poets
of the *fin du siècle*, Cowper and Burns, were not among
the romanticists.   It was left for the nineteenth
century to perform the work of which the eighteenth
only prophesied.

BIBLIOGRAPHY.

———

[This bibliography is intended to give practical aid to any reader who may wish to follow up the history of the subject for himself. It by no means includes all the books and authors referred to in the text; still less, all that have been read or consulted in the preparation of the work.]

Addison, Joseph. Works. New York, 1856. 6 vols.

Akenside, Mark. Poetical Works. Gilfillan's ed. Edinburgh, 1857.

Amherst, Alicia. "History of Gardening in England." London, 1896.

Arnold, Matthew. "The Study of Celtic Literature," and "Lectures on Translating Homer." London, 1893.

Austen, Jane. "Northanger Abbey," London, 1857.

Bagehot, Walter. "Literary Studies." London, 1879. 2 vols.

Beattie, James. Poetical Works. Gilfillan's ed. Edinburgh, 1854.

Beckford, William. "History of the Caliph Vathek." New York, 1869.

Bell, John. "Classical Arrangement of Fugitive Poetry." London, 1790–97. 18 vols.

Blair, Robert. Poetical Works. Gilfillan's ed. Edinburgh, 1854.

Boswell, James. "Life of Samuel Johnson." Fitzgerald's ed. London, 1874. 3 vols.

Boswell, James. "Life of Samuel Johnson." Abridged ed. New York, 1878.

Boyesen, H. H. "Essays on German Literature." New York, 1892.

Brandl, Alois. "Lenore in England," in "Characteristiken," by Erich Schmidt. Berlin, 1886.

Brunetière, Ferdinand. "Études Critiques." Troisième Série. Tome III. Paris, 1890.

Bryant, Jacob. "Observations upon the Poems of Thomas Rowley." London, 1781. 2 vols.

Brydges, Samuel Egerton. Poems. 4th ed. London, 1807.

Bürger, Gottfried August. "Sämmtliche Werke." Göttingen, 1844. 4 vols.

Byron, Geo. Gordon Noel. Works. London, 1832–33. 15 vols.

Cambridge, Richard Owen. Works. London, 1803.

Cameron, Ewen. "The Fingal of Ossian, rendered into Heroic Verse." Warrington, 1776.

Campbell, J. F. "Leabhar na Feinne." London, 1872.

Campbell, J. F. "Popular Tales of the West Highlands." Edinburgh, 1862. 4 vols.

Canning, George, **Ellis,** and **Frere.** "The Poetry of the Anti-Jacobin." London, 1890. (Carisbrooke Library, Vol. VI.)

Carlyle, Thomas. Works. London, 1869–72. 31 vols.

Chateaubriand, F. A. R. de. "The Beauties of Christianity." Translation of F. Shoberl. Philadelphia, 1815.

Chatterton, Thomas. Poetical Works. Skeat's ed. London, 1871. 2 vols.

Chatterton, Thomas. "The Rowley Poems." Tyrwhitt's ed. London, 1777.

Chatterton, Thomas. "The Rowley Poems." Mille's ed. London, 1782.

Chatterton. "A Story of the Year 1770." By David Masson. London, 1874.

Chatterton, Thomas. Article in "Dictionary of National Biography."

Chatterton, Thomas. "A Biographical Study." By D. Wilson. London, 1869.

Chaucer, Geoffrey. "The Canterbury Tales." Tyrwhitt's ed. Oxford, 1798. 2 vols. 2d ed.

Child, F. J. "The English and Scottish Popular Ballads." Boston and New York, 1882–98. 5 vols.

Coleridge, S. T. Works. New York, 1884. 7 vols.

Collins, William. Poetical Works. Gilfillan's ed. Edinburgh, 1854.

Colvin, Sidney. "Preface to Selections from Landor." London, 1882.

Croft, Sir Herbert. "Love and Madness." London, 1786. New ed.

Cumberland, Richard. Memoirs. Philadelphia, 1856.

Dennis, John. "Essay on Shakspere." London, 1712.

Dodsley, Robert. "A Collection of Poems by Several Hands." London, 1766–68. 6 vols.

Dodsley, Robert. "A Select Collection of Old Plays." Hazlitt's 4th ed. London, 1874–76. 15 vols.

Dryden, John. Works. Saintsbury-Scott ed. Edinburgh, 1882–93. 18 vols,

Dyer, John. Poetical Works. Gilfillan's ed. Edinburgh, 1858.

Eastlake, Sir Charles L. "A History of the Gothic Revival." London, 1872.

Edwards, Thomas. Sonnets in "Canons of Criticism." London, 1765.

Ellis, George. "Specimens of Early English Metrical Romances." London, 1811. 2d ed. 3 vols.

Ellis, George. "Specimens of the Early English Poets." London, 1803. 3d ed. 3 vols.

Evans, Evan. "Some Specimens of the Poetry of the Ancient Welsh Bards." London, 1764.

Fergusson, James. "History of Architecture." London, 1865–76. 4 vols.

Gates, Lewis E. "Introduction to Selections from Newman." New York, 1895.

Gautier, Théophile. "Histoire du Romantisme." Paris, 1884.

Gildon, Charles. "The Complete Art of Poetry." London, 1718. 2 vols.

Gilpin, William. "The Highlands of Scotland." London, 1808. 3d ed. 2 vols.

Gilpin, William. "The Mountains and Lakes of Cumberland and Westmoreland." London, 1808. 3d ed. 2 vols.

Gilpin, William. "Remarks on Forest Scenery." London, 1808. 3d ed. 2 vols.

Goethe, J. W. von. "Sorrows of Werter." (Trans.) London, 1784. 2 vols.

Goethe, J. W. von. "Götz von Berlichingen" (trans.) in Walter Scott's Poetical Works. Vol. IX. Boston, 1871.

Goldsmith, Oliver. Miscellaneous Works. Globe ed. London, 1869.

Goldsmith, Oliver. Poetical Works. Dobson-Mitford ed. London, 1895.

Gosse, Edmund. "From Shakspere to Pope." London, 1885.

Gosse, Edmund. "History of Eighteenth Century Literature." London, 1889.

Graves, Richard. "Recollections of Shenstone." London, 1788.

Gray, Thomas. Works. Gosse's ed. New York, 1885. 4 vols.

Grundtvig, Svend. "Danmark's Gamle Folkeviser." Kjöbenhavn, 1853–90. 5 vols.

Harvey, George. "Ossian's Fingal Rendered into English Verse." London, 1814.

Hedge, F. H. "Classic and Romantic." *Atlantic Monthly*, Vol. LVII.

Heine, Heinrich. "The Romantic School." (Trans.) New York, 1882.

Herder, J. G. von. "Stimmen der Völker," in Vol. II. Werke. Stuttgart, 1894 ("Deutsche National Litteratur").

Hettner, Hermann J. T. "Litteraturgeschichte." Theil III. Braunschweig, 1872.

Hickes, George. " Thesaurus Linguarum Vett. Septentrio-
nalium." Oxford, 1703–05. 3 vols. Folio.

Highland Society. " Report on the Poems of Ossian." Edinburgh, 1805.

Hole, R. " Fingal Rendered into Verse." London, 1786.

Howitt, William. " Homes of the Poets." New York, 1846.
2 vols.

Hugo, Victor Marie. " Preface to Cromwell " in Vol. I.,
" Œuvres Complètes." Paris, 1863.

Hurd, Richard. Works. London, 1811. 8 vols.

Johnson, Samuel. " Lives of the Poets." Hale's ed. London, 1890. 3 vols.

Johnson, Samuel. " Lives of Milton, Dryden, Swift, Addison, Pope, and Gray." Arnold's ed. New York, 1878.

Jchnson, Samuel. " Preface to Shakspere," in vol. II., Works.
Murphy's ed. London, 1816.

Kavanagh, Julia. " English Women of Letters." London,
1863. 2 vols.

Keats, John. " Life and Letters." By R. Monckton Milnes.
New York, 1848.

Keats, John. " Poetical Works." Rossetti's ed. London,
1876.

Knight, Charles. " Pictorial Shakspere." London, 1867.
2d ed. 8 vols.

Knox, V. " Essays." London, 1803. 15th ed. 3 vols.

Kotzebue, A. F. F. von. " The Stranger," in " Sargent's
Modern Standard Drama." New York, 1847. 2 vols.

Laing, Malcolm. " Dissertation on Ossian's Poems." Appendix to " History of Scotland." London, 1804. 2d
ed. 4 vols.

Langbaine, Gerard. " An Account of the English Dramatic
Poets." Oxford, 1691.

Lee, Harriet. " Canterbury Tales." New York, 1857 2
vols.

Leland, Thomas. "Longsword, Earl of Salisbury." London, 1762. 2 vols.

Lennox, Charlotte. "Shakspere Illustrated." London, 1753–54. 3 vols.

Lessing, G. E. " Sämmtliche Schriften." Berlin, 1838–44. 13 vols.

Lewis, M. G. Poems. London, 1812.

Lewis, M. G. "Tales of Terror and Wonder." Morley's Universal Library. London, 1887.

Lewis, M. G. " The Monk." London, 1796. 3 vols.

Lockhart, J. G. " Life of Scott." Boston and Philadelphia, 1837–38. 7 vols.

Lowell, J. R. "My Study Windows." Boston, 1871.

Lowth, Robert. " De Sacra Poesi Hebræorum." Oxford, 1775. 3d ed.

Lyttelton, George. Works. London, 1776. 3d ed. 3 vols.

McClintock, W. D. " The Romantic and Classic in English Literature." *Chautauquan*, Vol. XIV.

MacPherson, James. "Poems of Ossian." Clerk's ed. Edinburgh, 1870. 2 vols.

Mallet, P. H. " Northern Antiquities." (Percy's trans.) London, 1770. 2 vols.

Mason, William. Works. London, 1811. 4 vols.

Masson, David. "Chatterton." London, 1874.

Maturin, Chas. R. " Bertram," in "Sargent's Standard Drama." New York, 1847.

Mendez, Moses. "A Collection of the Most Esteemed Pieces of Poetry." London, 1767.

Mickle, Wm. J. Poetical Works, in "Chalmers' Poets," Vol. XVII. London, 1810.

Miller, Hugh. " First Impressions of England." Boston, 1851.

Milton, John. "Poems upon Several Occasions." Warton's ed. London, 1785.

Musset, L. C. A. de. " Lettres de Dupuis et Cotonet," in Vol. IX., " Œuvres Complètes." Paris, 1881.

Noel, Roden. " Essays on Poetry and Poets." London, 1886

Ossian in the Original Gaelic. Clerk's ed. (See MacPherson.)

Ossian in the Original Gaelic. Highland Society's ed. London, 1807. 3 vols.

Ossian. Article in *Macmillan's Magazine*, Vol. XXIV.

Pater, Walter. "Romanticism." *Macmillan's Magazine*, Vol. XXXV.

Pearch, George. "A Collection of Poems by Several Hands." London, 1783. New ed. 4 vols.

Peck, Francis. "New Memoirs of the Life and Poetical Works of Milton." London, 1740.

Pellissier, Georges. "The Literary Movement in France." (Brinton's trans.) New York, 1897.

Percy, Thomas. "Reliques of Ancient English Poetry." Gilfillan's ed. Edinburgh, 1858. 3 vols.

Perry, Thos. S. "English Literature in the Eighteenth Century." New York, 1883.

Phelps, W. L. "English Romantic Movement." Boston, 1893.

Philips, Edward. "Theatrum Poetarum." London, 1675. 2 vols.

Philips, John. Poems in "Johnson's Poets."

Phillimore, Robert. "Memoirs and Correspondence of Geo. Lord Lyttelton." London, 1845. 2 vols.

Pope, Alexander. Works. Courthope-Elwin ed. London, 1871–86. 10 vols.

Prior, Matthew. Poetical Works. Gilfillan's ed. Edinburgh, 1858.

Radcliffe, Anne. Novels in Vol. X. of Ballantyne's "Novelists' Library." London, 1824.

Radcliffe, Anne. "Journey through Holland." London, 1795.

Radcliffe, Anne. Poetical Works—"St. Alban's Abbey," etc. London, 1834. 2 vols.

Reeve, Clara. "The Old English Baron." London, 1778.

Reeve, Clara. "The Progress of Romance." London, 1785. 2 vols.

Ritson, Joseph. "Ancient English Metrical Romances." London, 1802. 3 vols.

Ritson, Joseph. "Ancient Songs." London, 1792.

Ritson, Joseph. "English Anthology." London, 1793–94. 3 vols.

Ritson, Joseph. "Pieces of Ancient Popular Poetry." London, 1833. 2d ed.

Ritson, Joseph. "Robin Hood." London, 1832. 2d ed. 2 vols.

Robberds, J. W. "Memoir of Wm. Taylor of Norwich." London, 1843. 2 vols.

Ruskin, John. "Modern Painters." New York, 1857–60. 5 vols.

Rymer, Thomas. "The Tragedies of the Last Age Considered and Examined." London, 1692. 2d ed.

Sainte Palaye, J. B. de la Curne de. "Mémoires sur l'Ancienne Chevalerie." Paris, 1759. 3 vols.

Scherer, Wilhelm. "History of German Literature." (Conybeare's trans.) New York, 1886. 2 vols.

Schiller, Friedrich. "Die Räuber," in Vol. II., Sämmtliche Werke. Stuttgart and Tübingen, 1838.

Schiller, Friedrich. "Uber naive und sentimentale Dichtung," Vol. XII., Sämmtliche Werke.

Schlegel, A. W. von. "Lectures on Dramatic Art and Literature." (Black's trans.) London, 1846.

Scott, Walter. "Critical and Miscellaneous Essays." Philadelphia, 1841. 3 vols.

Scott, Walter. Poetical Works. Dennis' ed. London, 1892. 5 vols.

Shairp, J. C. "Aspects of Poetry." Boston, 1882.

Shelley, Mary. "Frankenstein." Philadelphia, 1833.

Sheridan, R. B. "Pizarro." Works. London, 1873.

Shenstone, William. Poetical Works. Gilfillan's ed. Edinburgh, 1854.

Stendhal, de (Marie Henri Beyle). "Racine et Shakespere." Paris, 1854. New ed.

Stephen, Leslie. "History of English Thought in the Eighteenth Century." New York, 1876. 2 vols.

Stephen, Leslie. " Hours in a Library." 2d Series. London, 1876.

Stillingfleet, Benjamin. "Literary Life and Select Works." London, 1811. 2 vols.

Sullivan, Wm. R. Article on Celtic Literature in " Encyclopedia Britannica."

Taylor, William. " Historical Survey of German Poetry." London, 1830. 3 vols.

Thompson, William. " Poems on Several Occasions." Oxford, 1757.

Thomson, James. Poetical Works. Gilfillan's ed. Edinburgh, 1853.

Vigny, Alfred de. "Stello," Vol. IV. Œuvres. Paris, 1836. 3d ed.

Walpole, Horace. " The Castle of Otranto." Philadelphia, 1840.

Walpole, Horace. Works. London, 1798. 5 vols.

Ward, T. H. " The English Poets." London, 1880–81. 4 vols.

Warton, Joseph. "Essay on Pope." London, 1806. 5th ed. 2 vols.

Warton, Joseph. Poems, in " Chalmers' Poets," Vol. XVIII. 1810.

Warton, Thomas, Sr. " Poems on Several Occasions." London, 1748.

Warton, Thomas, Jr. " History of English Poetry. " Ed. Hazlitt. London, 1871. 4 vols.

Warton, Thomas. " Observations on the Faëry Queene." London, 1807. 2 vols. New ed.

Weber, H. W. " English Metrical Romances." Edinburgh, 1810. 3 vols.

West, Gilbert. Poetical Works in " Chalmers' Poets," Vol. XIII. 1810.

Wilkie, William. Poetical Works in " Chalmers' Poets," Vol. XVI., 1810.

Winstanley, William. " Lives of the English Poets." London, 1687.

Wodrow, John. "Carthon, etc., Attempted in English Verse." Edinburgh, 1769.

Wodrow, John. "Fingal Translated into English Heroic Rhyme." Edinburgh, 1771. 2 vols.

Wood, Robert. "Essay on Homer." Dublin, 1776.

Wordsworth, William. Poetical Works. Centenary ed. London, 1870. 6 vols.

Young, Edward. "The Complaint; or, Night Thoughts." Gilfillan's ed. Edinburgh, 1853.

Young, Edward. Works in Prose. London, 1765.

INDEX.

435

THE END.